Intermediate Accounting

The Robert N. Anthony
Willard J. Graham Series in Accounting

Intermediate
Accounting

Glenn A. Welsch
D. Paul Newman
Charles T. Zlatkovich
all of the College of Business Administration
The University of Texas at Austin

1986   Seventh Edition

Homewood, Illinois   60430

ISBN 0–256–03328–5

Library of Congress Catalog Card No. 85–81406

Printed in the United States of America

3 4 5 6 7 8 9 0 V 3 2 1 0 9 8 7

Preface

This Seventh Edition continues the leadership role of prior editions in establishing the highest standards of comprehensiveness, academic excellence, and topical presentation. This edition represents a *major rewrite* rather than a piecemeal revision. The primary emphasis in preparing this revision was to further enhance the text's clarity and conciseness, while maintaining its reputation for technical quality. Reviews of the revised manuscript have been exceptionally favorable.

This textbook is designed primarily for students who have successfully completed a reasonably adequate course in the fundamentals of financial accounting. It is equally adaptable for use by schools that use the semester or the quarter system. Two semesters or three quarters or their equivalent normally are required for complete coverage of all chapters.

Although accounting and external reporting have become increasingly rule-oriented, the authors provide a solid conceptual foundation. This foundation is referred to specifically throughout all of the chapters to support and explain the application procedures presented. Our primary emphasis is on *why* and our secondary emphasis is on *how*—this emphasis decreases the need for memorization.

Chapter 1 presents an overview of the conceptual foundation of accounting with special emphasis on the *FASB Statements of Financial Accounting Concepts*. It includes an understandable discussion, with illustrations, of the latest statement—*No. 5, "Recognition and Measurement in Financial Statements of Business Enterprises."* Income recognition concepts are discussed and expanded in Chapter 22.

The primary considerations emphasized in rewriting this textbook were: (1) a clear, direct, and concise style of writing; (2) integration of concepts and applications; and (3) maximum flexibility in use. A unique degree of flexibility is attained in the following ways:

— Subdivision of each chapter into clearly differentiated *parts*—this includes textual material and all homework material.
— Numerous end-of-chapter supplements.
— Careful selection of topical sequence within each chapter. Categories of topical material are designed to stand alone.
— Distinctive captions within each chapter (four caption levels).
— Careful design of all homework assignments including an unexcelled inventory of questions, exercises, problems, and cases carefully coordinated with each chapter.

For the instructor, this flexibility has the following advantages: design of a course to accommodate the objectives and time constraints of the curriculum; clearly delineated daily assignments; selective variations in topical sequences; and the option to use expanded, typical, or minimal emphasis of individual topics presented. Given the significantly increasing scope of topics currently included in intermediate accounting courses, maximum flexibility in emphasis is essential.

Chapters are arranged in a teachable and logical sequence and are grouped to facilitate both rearrangement and division of materials over semester or quarter intervals as follows:

Chapters by	
Semester	**Quarter**
1–12	1–8
13–24	9–16
	17–24

Chapter 1 presents an introductory overview of the foundations of accounting concepts based upon the FASB's Conceptual Framework. It sets the stage for chapters that follow. Chapters 2 through 4 comprehensively review financial accounting and reporting fundamentals and extend the usual topical coverage of traditional introductory financial accounting courses. Present and future value concepts and some of their primary accounting applications are introduced in Chapter 5. Chapter 6 discusses cash, short-term investments, and accounts receivable. Chapters 7 through 9 discuss inventory. Chapter 10 discusses liabilities and accounting for income tax. Chapters 11 through 13 deal with operational assets (i.e., property, plant, and equipment). Corporations are discussed in Chapters 14 and 15. Stocks and bonds (both from issuers' and investors' standpoints) are discussed in Chapters 16 and 17. Chapters 18, on pensions, and 19, on leases, provide coverage of two difficult and controversial accounting topics. Chapter 20 is devoted to accounting changes and error corrections, and Chapter 21 combines financial statement analysis and interim and segment reporting. Chapter 22, Part A, comprehensively treats the complex topics of revenue and expense recognition. Chapter 22, Part B, provides a concise but thorough treatment of earnings per share. The statement of changes in financial position is presented in Chapter 23. Chapter 24 concludes the book and deals with reporting the effects of changing prices. Part A considers general inflation, and Part B discusses current cost.

The major changes and new features of this Seventh Edition can be summarized as follows:

— Major rewrite of all the expository materials to enhance understandability and conciseness; special editing to avoid redundancies.

— Redesigned format—one-column for textual material; boldface and color throughout for emphasis; four caption levels to emphasize topical development.

— New chapter introductions—overview and purpose. Includes explanation of the chapter's relationship to prior and following chapters; concise statement of the purpose of the chapter; and a sequential list, by chapter parts, of the major topics discussed.

— Clarity in presenting and illustrating complex and controversial accounting issues. Does not give oversimplified explanations of such topics. Authoritative and conceptually sound analyses and responses are given. The text continues to give the innovative comprehensive exhibits that provide: Panel A—situation; Panel B—analysis; Panel C—accounting entries; and Panel D—reporting.

— Conceptual framework of financial accounting is thoroughly developed and referenced throughout. Emphasis is given to conceptual and practical rationale of the accounting methods and procedures discussed. Preferred terminology is used consistently in the book.

— Text provides approximately 1,500 different units from which to select homework assignments. This textbook clearly discriminates between: **Questions** for discussion (a review objective); **Exercises** (application experience directly related to a specific issue discussed in the chapter); **Problems** (integrates several issues in the chapter and in prior but not subsequent chapters); **Cases** (practical situations requiring decisions that are seldom obvious). This textbook maintains an unusual clear-cut distinction among the questions, exercises, problems, and cases.

— Numerous changes (minor to major) in the textual materials including: addition of *FASB Concepts Statement 5,* expanded discussion of the standards-setting environment; characteristics of liablities; compensated absences, accounting for income taxes; goodwill, stock options; SARs; junior stock; push-down accounting; futures contracts; induced conversions of convertible debt; in-substance defeasance; analysis of accounting errors; income recognition; earnings per share; statement of changes in financial position; and price changes.

— Revised and new exercises, problems, and cases, approximately 60 percent.

— Unique and comprehensive examination bank for instructor-adopters.

Teaching Aids available for adopters include:
For the professor:

1. A comprehensive instructor's manual including several typical assignment schedules and detailed step-by-step computations for each homework item.
2. Transparencies for assorted assignment materials.
3. Examination bank—over 3,000 questions classified by chapter. Categories: true-false; multiple-choice nonquantitative; multiple-choice quantitative; matching and short-answer; problems and cases; and selected CPA examination multiple-choice questions.
4. Periodic supplements covering FASB statements issued subsequent to publication of the text. Designed for distribution to students.

For the student:

5. A student study guide in two volumes that incorporates for each chapter *(a)* study suggestions, *(b)* a summary of important points with illustrations, *(c)* questions for self-evaluation, and *(d)* answers to the questions for self-paced study.
6. Two comprehensive review practice sets. Both sets are designed for review purposes (Chapters 2–4). One set is manual and is published separately. The second set, Kellogg Business Systems, Inc., is designed for use with either the IBM PC or the Apple II$^+$, IIe, or II^c microcomputers.
7. A complete set of working papers in two volumes (forms with selected captions provided) for working each exercise and problem.
8. A list of key solution figures (provided upon request of the professor).

Acknowledgments

We are indebted to numerous colleagues and users whose comments and suggestions have led to the improvements reflected in this latest edition. We appreciate the permissions granted by the FASB, American Accounting Association, and American Institute of CPAs to quote from their pronouncements. The AICPA also permitted us to make liberal uses of selected materials adapted from the

Uniform CPA Examinations. We are indebted to The Quaker Oats Company for permission to reproduce their annual report as an appendix to the text.

We are particularly appreciative of the technical and editorial assistance of graduate students, Kathleen A. Springer, Joanna Ho, and Evelyn Patterson, The University of Texas at Austin, and Ellen Wood, Stanford University. We also express special thanks to Jody Saari Dachtler, May-Lin Melissa Gan, Annick Michele Barton, and Erica Peters, students at the University of Texas at Austin for their competent and dedicated assistance. Our special thanks to Hang Dinh and Tuong Vi Chu for expert clerical assistance.

We especially appreciate the valuable reviews, comments, and suggestions by the following professors: M. H. Granof, K. D. Larson, W. T. Harrison, D. G. Short, R. Thompson, J. C. Olsen, J. R. Dietrich, and J. C. Fellingham, all of the University of Texas at Austin; Robert N. Freeman, University of Florida; Sandra D. Byrd and David Byrd, Southwest Missouri State University; Petrea Sandlin, University of Texas at San Antonio; Benzion Barlev and Sasson Bar-Yosef, Hebrew University of Jerusalem; Gary M. Cunningham, Polytechnic Institute and State University; Randall B. Hayes, Michigan State University; D. Raymond Bainbridge, Lehigh University; Dennis L. Knutson, Marquette University; David Nix, Boise State University; David R. Finley, University of Houston; and James Volkert, Northeastern University.

Glenn A. Welsch
D. Paul Newman
Charles T. Zlatkovich

Contents

11   Operational Assets: Property, Plant, and Equipment— Acquisition and Retirement

15 Corporations—Retained Earnings and Stock Rights and Options

830

22   Income Recognition and Earnings per Share   1328

Intermediate Accounting

Chapter 1

The Environment and Conceptual Foundation of Accounting

OVERVIEW AND PURPOSE

Accounting is a professional service activity that identifies, measures, records, and communicates economic information about an enterprise such as a business, a health-care organization, or a governmental unit. Primarily it serves the manager, owners (or sponsors) and creditors of the enterprise, and the interests of the general public. As an information processing system, accounting communicates economic information by using periodic financial statements. The characteristics of the financial statements depend on the problems, types of decisions, and interests of the users.

This textbook is primarily directed toward business entities—single-owner businesses, partnerships, and corporations. This area of accounting is called **financial accounting**, as opposed to management accounting, which serves the internal needs of the managers of the entity.

Although accounting may seem to be a procedural and clerical activity, it is very challenging. Accounting has an extensive theoretical foundation. It requires a high level of analytical competence and communication skills. Accounting also has significant behavioral implications (i.e., how it influences people and their decisions). Also, accounting is highly subjective because it requires a wide range of professional and technical judgments.

The purpose of this chapter is to describe the dynamics of the environment in which accounting operates and to present the conceptual foundation of accounting. The environment exerts a significant impact on financial accounting. The conceptual foundation provides the framework for making important accounting decisions. Therefore, this chapter is subdivided as follows:

Part A: The Environment of Accounting
1. Expectations of internal and external decision makers.
2. Environmental impact of accounting organizations.
3. Developing accounting standards.

Part B: The Conceptual Framework and Implementation Principles of Accounting
1. Nature of accounting theory and concepts.
2. FASB conceptual framework.
3. Implementation assumptions and principles.

Supplement 1–A: List of Official Accounting Pronouncements
Supplement 1–B: Organizations Actively Involved in Setting Accounting Standards

PART A: THE ENVIRONMENT OF ACCOUNTING

The environment of accounting consists of the influences, constraints, and demands that are imposed on the conceptual foundation and implementation of that foundation as a professional activity. This part of the chapter discusses the primary environmental factors.

EXPECTATIONS OF INTERNAL AND EXTERNAL DECISION MAKERS

The users of financial information can be classified as either internal or external decision makers.

Internal decision makers are the managers of the enterprise. These managers are responsible for planning the future of the entity, implementing those plans, and controlling daily operations. Because of their close and direct relationship with the entity, they can obtain whatever financial data they need at dates of their choice. Much of this information is not intended to be relayed to outsiders. The process of developing and reporting financial information for internal users is called **management accounting.** The reports are called internal management reports. Because of the confidential nature of these reports and their primary focus on internal decision making, there is no requirement (other than that specified by the management) that they conform to generally accepted accounting principles (GAAP).

External decision makers are those groups that do not have direct access to the internal operations of the entity. They make decisions regarding the entity, such as whether to invest or disinvest, whether to extend credit to the entity, and what public policy constraints and advantages should apply to the entity.

The potential external users are owners, lenders, suppliers, potential investors and creditors, employees, customers, financial analysts and advisors, brokers, underwriters, stock exchanges, lawyers, economists, taxing and regulatory authorities, legislators, financial press and reporting agencies, labor unions, trade associations, business researchers, teachers and students, and the public.[1]

The process of developing and reporting financial information to external decision makers is called **financial accounting;** it is the subject of this textbook.[2] External users, because of their detachment from the entity, cannot directly command specific financial information from the entity; therefore, they must rely on **general-purpose financial statements.** To meet their information needs, the accounting profession has developed a network of accounting concepts, standards,

---

[1] Financial Accounting Standards Board, *Statement of Financial Accounting Concepts No. 1,* "Objectives of Financial Reporting by Business Enterprises" (Stamford, Conn., November 1978), p. 11.

[2] The subject matter of this textbook is directly concerned with accounting for the affairs of business enterprises, although many of the concepts apply to not-for-profit entities as well.

principles, practices, and procedures designed to assure that these external financial statements are **relevant** and **reliable.**[3] This network of concepts, principles, and procedures is called **generally accepted accounting principles** (GAAP).

OBJECTIVES OF EXTERNAL FINANCIAL REPORTING

The **objective** of external financial statements is to communicate the economic effects of completed transactions and other events on the financial position and operations of the entity. Although there are other means of communicating financial information, such as a prospectus (for security offerings), news releases, and management "letters," the primary means are the periodic financial statements. General-purpose financial statements report financial information relevant to (1) investment decisions (by investors), (2) credit decisions (by creditors), and (3) public policy decisions. To accomplish these three objectives, two types of financial statements are used:

1. **Statement of financial position** (balance sheet), which reports assets, liabilities, and owners' equity **at a particular time.**
2. **Statements reporting changes** that relate to a **period of time;** the principal change statements are the:
   a. Income statement.
   b. Statement of changes in financial position (SCFP).

These financial statements are supplemented with numerous **disclosure** notes. These notes are an integral part of the statements.

FASB Statement of Financial Accounting Concepts 1 recognizes this environmental expectation that (emphasis supplied):

> Financial reporting should provide information that is useful to present and potential investors and creditors and other users in making rational **investment, credit, and similar decisions.** The information should be comprehensible to those who have a **reasonable understanding** of business and economic activities and are **willing to study** the information with reasonable diligence [par. 34].
>
> Financial reporting should provide information to help present and potential investors and creditors and other users in assessing the **amounts, timing, and uncertainty of prospective cash receipts** from dividends or interest and the proceeds from the sale, redemption, or maturity of securities or loans. The prospects for those cash receipts are affected by an enterprise's ability to generate enough cash to meet its obligations when due and its other cash operating needs, to reinvest in operations, and to pay cash dividends and may also be affected by perceptions of investors and creditors generally about that ability, which affect market prices of the enterprise's securities. Thus, financial reporting should provide information to help investors, creditors, and others assess the amounts, timing, and uncertainty of prospective net cash inflows to the related enterprise [par. 37].
>
> Financial reporting should provide information about the **economic resources**

---

[3] FASB, *Statement of Financial Accounting Concepts No. 2,* "Qualitative Characteristics of Accounting Information" (Stamford, Conn., May 1980), identifies **relevance** and **reliability** as the two primary qualitative characteristics that accounting information is designed to possess. These and other qualitative characteristics are discussed in Part B.

of an enterprise, the **claims** to those resources (obligations of the enterprise to transfer resources to other entities and owners' equity), and the effects of transactions, events, and circumstances that change resources and claims to those resources [par. 40].

PROFESSIONAL ACCOUNTING

The environment in which accounting operates reflects a long history. Also, it reflects unique professional independence that exerts a significant impact on present and future concepts and practices.

Accounting dates back to about 3600 B.C. The first published work describing the double-entry system of accounting was authored by Luca Pacioli in 1494 in Venice. Pacioli's work described double-entry accounting in much the same way as it is used today. Since that time, the industrial revolutions in Europe and the United States, the emergence of the corporation as a major form of business entity, and many other factors have affected accounting. Today, professional accountants have an important and unique role in society. The professional accountant is usually a **certified public accountant (CPA).** As with lawyers, physicians, and engineers, accountants have many functions. The primary functions are:

1. **Public accounting**—An independent CPA offers services such as *(a)* auditing (the attest function), *(b)* tax planning and determination of tax liability, and (c) management consulting services. CPAs in public practice have a unique relationship with their clients. These CPAs are **independent** and impartial reviewers of the financial statements. Although **independent CPAs** are paid by the client, the independence concept extends their responsibilities to third parties as well, such as the users of the financial statements.

The primary service of the independent CPA is the attest function. This is achieved as the result of an **audit** of the financial statements, including an auditor's report. An **auditor's report** *(a)* states the scope of the audit examination and *(b)* expresses the auditor's professional "opinion" as to whether the financial statements are presented in accordance with generally accepted accounting principles (GAAP). The attest function is important to external statement users because it protects them against misrepresentation and bias from the reporting entity. The attest function provides reliability to the financial statements because of the auditor's independence from the client.

2. **Management (or industrial) accounting**—Many CPAs and certified management accountants (CMAs) work in businesses as accountants, internal auditors, tax specialists, systems experts, controllers, financial vice presidents, and chief executives. **As employees of a particular company, they are not independent CPAs.**

3. **Governmental and nonprofit accounting**—CPAs serve at all levels of government and not-for-profit entities: local, state, national, and international. **In these capacities, they are not independent CPAs.**

Because of the importance of financial reports to users, there is widespread interest in **accounting standards** and how they are established. Recently, interest in the response of the accounting profession to its public responsibility to establish relevant and consistent accounting standards has increased. For example, accounting standards for oil and gas companies potentially affect the national energy policy of the United States because they affect the public's awareness of available petroleum reserves. Financial information provided by accountants is important to the effective operation of our economic system. Such information facilitates an efficient allocation of capital among business enterprises. Therefore, it is easy to understand why users of financial statements and the general public are concerned about financial accounting standards. Part B of this chapter discusses accounting concepts, standards, and procedures.

ENVIRONMENTAL IMPACT OF ACCOUNTING ORGANIZATIONS

At the present time there are many accounting-related organizations in the United States. The most influential are the Financial Accounting Standards Board (FASB), the American Institute of Certified Public Accountants (AICPA), the Securities and Exchange Commission (SEC), the American Accounting Association (AAA), and the Financial Executives Institute (FEI).

American Institute of Certified Public Accountants (AICPA). The AICPA is the national professional organization of certified public accountants. It responds primarily to the needs of CPAs in public practice. Therefore, its efforts and publications focus on the practice of public accounting. Its primary publications and standard-setting activities include the following:

1. *Journal of Accountancy*—a monthly magazine containing pronouncements, articles, and special sections of interest to independent CPAs.
2. *Accountants' Index*—an annual classified bibliography of the accounting literature published during the year.
3. *Accounting Trends & Techniques*—an annual publication containing a survey of the characteristics of the annual financial reports of 600 corporations.
4. *Accounting Research Studies*—series of early studies that focused on specific accounting issues that provided background information, alternative solutions, and in many cases recommended practices.
5. *Statement of Auditing Standards*—audit practices promulgated by the Auditing Standards Board.
6. Statements that dealt with specific accounting principles, standards, and procedures:
   a. *Accounting Research Bulletins (ARBs)*—During the period between 1938 and 1959, the AICPA's Committee on Accounting Procedure (CAP) was responsible for "narrowing the areas of differences and inconsistencies" in accounting practice. To this end, the Committee issued 51 *Accounting Research Bulletins* and 4 *Accounting Terminology Bulletins* which are a part of GAAP.
   b. *Opinions of the Accounting Principles Board (APB)*—In 1959, the AICPA

established the Accounting Principles Board (APB) to replace its Committee on Accounting Procedures. The APB designated its pronouncements as *Opinions.* During its existence from 1959 to 1973, the APB issued 31 *Opinions* and 4 *Statements.* In contrast to the *Opinions,* the *Statements* presented recommendations, rather than requirements, for improvement in financial accounting and reporting to external decision makers.[4]

7. Auditing Standards Division, established in 1974, and its Accounting Standards Executive Committee (AcSEC)—Develops *Issue Papers* that identify, consider alternatives, and present recommendations about current financial reporting issues. This activity assists the FASB in setting its topical agenda.

Securities and Exchange Commission (SEC).   A number of government regulatory agencies influence accounting and reporting by businesses. Among these agencies are the Internal Revenue Service, Federal Power Commission, Interstate Commerce Commission, and Securities and Exchange Commission. The SEC has a powerful influence on the development of accounting standards.

Because of conditions in the securities market at the beginning of the depression of the 1930s, Congress passed the Securities Act of 1933, the Securities Exchange Act of 1934, and the Public Utility Holding Company Act of 1935. The 1934 act created the Securities and Exchange Commission. The act gave it broad authority to regulate all aspects of the issuance and sale of securities in interstate commerce. Congress gave the Commission authority to prescribe external financial reporting requirements for companies under its jurisdiction. These are the "listed" companies, which means those companies whose shares are sold in interstate commerce. To obtain permission to sell an issue of securities (interstate), a company must submit a **prospectus** to the SEC.

This prospectus is a public record. The prospectus, which is prepared only for a new security issuance, reports information about the company, its officers, securities, and financial affairs. The financial portion of the prospectus must be audited by an independent CPA. After receiving permission to sell securities, the company must file with the SEC, as a matter of public record, audited financial statements **each subsequent year** (10-K reports) and unaudited quarterly statements (10-Q reports). In most material respects, the annual 10-K reporting requirements are satisfied by the "published financial statements."

The SEC filing and reporting requirements are published as:

1. *Regulation S–X*—This is the original and comprehensive document issued by the Commission, as amended and supplemented. It prescribes the reporting requirements and forms to be filed with the SEC.
2. *Accounting Series Releases (ASRs)*—These releases are amendments, extensions, and additions to *Regulation S–X.*
3. *Special SEC Releases*—These relate to current issues as they arise.

---

[4] The contents of these *Bulletins, Opinions,* and *Statements* are listed in Supplement 1–A to this chapter.

4. *Staff Accounting Bulletins (SABs)*—These serve as interpretations of *Regulation S-X* and the *Accounting Series Releases (ASRs)*.

These publications continue in force as amended and superseded by the SEC.

The SEC has wide statutory authority to prescribe financial accounting and external reporting requirements for "listed" companies. However, the Commission has relied on the accounting profession to set and enforce accounting standards and to regulate the profession. The working relationship between the SEC and the accounting profession has been positive, and accounting regulation has remained in the private sector. However, on occasion the SEC has forced the accounting profession to move forward in tackling critical problems. These situations occurred in areas where the SEC concluded that the public interest was not being fully served on a timely basis. In a few instances, the SEC has imposed certain accounting and reporting practices without waiting for the profession to act, such as requiring companies to disclose specific replacement cost data (Chapter 24).

American Accounting Association (AAA). The American Accounting Association is an organization primarily for accounting educators; however, its membership includes accountants in public practice, industry, and not-for-profit organizations.

Its objectives are to develop accounting theory, encourage and sponsor accounting research, and improve education in accounting. The statements of the AAA do not express GAAP. The Association operates through committees and publishes monographs, committee reports, and a quarterly periodical, *The Accounting Review*. This periodical has articles and sections on a wide range of subjects about research and accounting education.

Since 1936, the AAA, through its committees, has issued a series of statements on accounting theory. Beginning in June 1936 when *A Tentative Statement of Accounting Principles Underlying Corporate Financial Statements* was published, the Association has maintained an active research program on accounting theory. The 1936 statement was revised and supplemented three times; the latest revision was called *Accounting and Reporting Standards for Corporate Financial Statements, 1957 Revision.* Another statement, prepared by a special AAA committee and published in 1966, was entitled *A Statement of Basic Accounting Theory.* Like prior AAA statements, it dealt with accounting theory, as opposed to accounting practice and procedures. The latest publication in this series is *Statement on Accounting Theory and Theory Acceptance,* developed by the Committee on Concepts and Standards for External Financial Reports of the AAA in 1977.

The statements relating to accounting theory and principles issued by the AAA are **normative** rather than descriptive. That is, they tend to express what accounting **should be,** rather than what it is. The AAA continues to have a significant impact on accounting standards through its research program, responses to proposed statements of the FASB, and the teaching, writing, and participating activities of its members.

Financial Executives Institute (FEI). The FEI and its Financial Executives Research Foundation have influenced accounting standards favorably in recent years.

The activities of the FEI include research, progressive position papers on issues being considered by the FASB, and the *Financial Executive* magazine.

Other organizations that have environmental impacts on accounting are the National Association of Accountants (NAA), Cost Accounting Standards Board (CASB), and the Internal Revenue Service (IRS).

DEVELOPING ACCOUNTING STANDARDS

There is widespread interest in the process used to develop accounting standards because of *(a)* concern about misleading and inadequate reporting on financial statements, *(b)* the impact of accounting rules on choices made by decision makers, and *(c)* special interests. Developing accounting standards is a process that involves technical competence, sound judgment, and consideration of economic consequences and effects of social policies, all within the context of a dynamic political environment. Accounting standards are the result of logic, practical experience, and the interaction of interested groups.

The interested groups are the *(a)* **preparers,** that is, the enterprises that apply accounting standards to develop their own financial statements; (2) **auditors,** who give an opinion on the representations in those statements; and (3) **users**—those groups that rely on financial statements in decision making. The interests and motivations of these groups often are in conflict because each standing alone may not adequately satisfy the social policy aspirations of the general public. Therefore, the standard-setting authority for accounting must reconcile and reach a consensus on these conflicting interests and motivations. The resolution of such conflicts involves an enlightened **political process.** The objective is to attain a consensus that serves the public interest rather than the self-interest of one or more of the constituent groups. The term *political* often gives a negative impression of self-interest groups. In contrast, the term *political process* is used in the context of attaining a consensus when preparers, auditors, and users negotiate in good faith to resolve their legitimate differences with the general interest dominating. It provides a public forum for all inputs, logical analysis, sound judgment, and compromises to serve the general interest.

In addition to the preparers, auditors, and users, a very powerful force—the U.S. Congress—has become involved in the area of accounting standards and compliance with those standards.[5]

Concern about generally accepted accounting principles arose around 1913 when the first federal income tax was approved by constitutional amendment. That law posed the question of how net income should be computed. Next, the depression of the 1930s brought into focus the need for generally accepted accounting principles. Therefore, in 1938, the AICPA appointed the **Committee on Accounting Procedures** to provide some definitive accounting principles (see AICPA, page 7). The committee issued a number of *Accounting Research Bulletins (ARBs)* that set forth what the committee believed GAAP should be. However,

---

[5] *The Wall Street Journal,* "Rep. Dingell to take Aim at Accountants, SEC in Hearings on Profession's Role as Watchdog," February 19, 1985, p. 4.

ARBs were **recommendations** only. They were not binding on the profession because there was no requirement for adherence.

The committee made a substantive start in developing accounting standards. However, it was a part-time committee and could not devote sufficient time to formulating accounting standards. By the mid-1950s the committee had become inactive, and the AICPA decided new charges should be specified. Therefore, in 1959, the **Accounting Principles Board** was set up. Its basic charge was to *(a)* develop a statement of accounting concepts (i.e., a theoretical foundation of accounting) and *(b)* issue pronouncements on current accounting issues. The APB designated their pronouncements as *Opinions* and issued 31 such *Opinions.*

At the outset, the force of the *APB Opinions,* as had been the case with the ARBs, depended upon their general acceptance. Acceptance was encouraged by **persuasion;** that is, by convincing independent CPAs that these recommendations were the preferred solution to selected accounting problems. By 1964, many leaders of the profession were convinced that persuasion could not reduce the wide range of existing accounting and reporting differences and inconsistencies. In numerous cases, identical transactions could be accounted for by any of several methods. Net income could be manipulated by selecting a particular accounting approach from among several that were considered to be "generally accepted."

Therefore, a milestone in the development of accounting practice occurred in October 1964. At that time the Council (i.e., the governing body) of the AICPA adopted a requirement that was incorporated into the **rules of ethics** for CPAs as follows:

> *Rule 203—Accounting principles.* A member shall not express an opinion that financial statements are presented in conformity with generally accepted accounting principles if such statements contain any departure from an accounting principle [*] promulgated by the body designated by Council to establish such principles which has a material effect on the statements taken as a whole, unless the member can demonstrate that due to unusual circumstances the financial statements would otherwise have been misleading. In such cases his report must describe the departure, the approximate effects thereof, if practicable, and the reasons why compliance with the principle would result in a misleading statement.
>
> * This requirement applies to the *FASB Statements of Financial Accounting Standards* and those *Accounting Research Bulletins (ARBs)* and *APB Opinions* that have not been superseded by action of the FASB.

This compliance requirement caused an increased interest in, and concern about, the *APB Opinions* and the *ARBs*. The APB continued the *APB Opinions* and *ARBs* in force because preparers and auditors were required to implement the prescribed accounting standards. Criticisms of the APB increased significantly. Starting in the late 1960s and continuing in the early 1970s, there were many complaints about the institutional arrangements by which accounting standards were established. These complaints criticized *(a)* lack of participation by organizations other than the AICPA, *(b)* "quality" of the *APB Opinions, (c)* failure of the APB to develop a "statement of the objectives and principles" underlying external financial reports, and *(d)* insufficient output by the APB.

A major study recommended that another more independent standard-setting organization succeed the Accounting Principles Board; this recommendation was approved by the AICPA, to be effective July 1, 1973.

Financial Accounting Standards Board (FASB)

Since July 1, 1973, the Financial Accounting Standards Board has been responsible for establishing the accounting standards that comprise "generally accepted accounting principles" (GAAP). The FASB is **independent** because it is not affiliated with, nor a part of, any other organization.

The report of the special committee to replace the APB with the FASB, as adopted by the AICPA, recommended the following:

1. **Financial Accounting Foundation**—composed of nine trustees appointed by the Board of Directors of the AICPA. **Responsibilities:** to appoint members of the Financial Accounting Standards Board, to appoint a Financial Accounting Standards Advisory Council, to raise funds to support the new structure, and to periodically review and revise the basic structure.

2. **Financial Accounting Standards Board (FASB)**—composed of seven full-time members. **Responsibilities:** to establish financial accounting standards, and to direct the research program to support the standard-setting process.

3. **Financial Accounting Standards Advisory Council**—approximately 35 members. **Responsibilities:** to work closely with the FASB in an advisory capacity; and to establish priorities, establish task forces, and react to proposed standards.

4. **Research activities**—structured to accomplish specific objectives.[6]

The first official action of the FASB was to continue in force the then-existing body of GAAP. This body consisted of (1) the *Accounting Research Bulletins (ARBs)* of the Committee on Accounting Procedure (CAP) and (2) the *Opinions* of the Accounting Principles Board (APB). Prior to that time the CAP and then the APB had been official subentities of the AICPA. To date, the FASB has issued categories of pronouncements designated as:

1. *Statements of Financial Accounting Concepts*—The purpose of this series is to set fundamental concepts on which financial accounting and reporting standards will be based.

2. *Statements of Financial Accounting Standards*—The FASB calls its major pronouncements *Statements of Standards* rather than *Opinions,* which was used by the APB. These statements give accounting principles and procedures on specific accounting issues.

3. *Interpretations*—These interpret *ARBs, APB Opinions,* and *FASB Statements of Financial Accounting Standards.*

4. *Technical Bulletins*—These are prepared by the FASB staff to provide guidance on specific accounting and reporting problems on a timely basis.

---

[6] *Establishing Financial Accounting Standards, Report of the Study on Establishment of Accounting Principles, American Institute of Certified Public Accountants,* March 1972, p. 105 (chair of the Committee, Francis M. Wheat). For a comprehensive and up-to-date description of the mission and operations of the FASB, see Paul B. W. Miller and Rodney J. Redding, *The FASB: The People, the Process, and the Politics* (Homewood, Ill.: Richard D. Irwin, Inc., 1986).

Currently, the FASB operates under a "due process" system. This system is open and provides an opportunity for all interested parties to express their views. The process used by the FASB involves the following steps:

1. Select and prioritize issues for the Board's agenda.
2. Appoint a representative task force to identify and define the problems and alternatives related to the issue assigned to each task force.
3. Conduct research and analysis of the issue by internal staff and outside experts.
4. Prepare a *Discussion Memorandum* on the issue and distribute to interested parties, with an invitation to comment.
5. Schedule a public hearing (usually within three months following the *Discussion Memorandum*).
6. Prepare analysis by the Board of all comments received about the issue.
7. Decide whether to issue a standard. If the decision is yes, prepare, and distribute to all interested parties an **Exposure Draft** of the standard. An invitation to comment is included.
8. Conduct an analysis by the Board of all comments received about the Exposure Draft. Revise the Exposure Draft as needed.
9. Approve (or disapprove) the Exposure Draft as revised, by a vote of at least four of the seven Board members. If approved, distribute the new standard. With complex and controversial issues, some of these steps may be repeated.

Official Accounting Pronouncements

Supplement 1–A has a list of official pronouncements that are currently in force. For easy reference, for each pronouncement is given the *(a)* designated number, *(b)* date issued, *(c)* title, and *(d)* current status. The pronouncements listed in the supplement are:

1. *Accounting Research Bulletins (ARBs) Nos. 1–51;* issued by the AICPA, 1939–59.
2. *Accounting Terminology Bulletins Nos. 1–4;* issued by the AICPA, 1953–59.
3. *Accounting Principles Board (APB) Opinions Nos. 1–31;* issued by the AICPA, 1962–73.
4. *Statements of Financial Accounting Concepts Nos. 1–5;* issued by the FASB, 1978–84.
5. *Statements of Financial Accounting Standards Nos. 1–85;* issued by the FASB, 1973–April 1, 1985.
6. *Interpretations Nos. 1–38;* issued by the FASB, 1974–April 1, 1985.
7. *Technical Bulletins Nos. 79–1 to 85–2;* issued by the FASB, 1979–April 1, 1985.

Supplement 1–B provides a list of organizations (with addresses) that are actively involved in setting accounting standards.

Attaining a Consensus in Setting Accounting Standards

The preceding discussion shows that the development of generally accepted accounting principles (GAAP) has been pursued from the early 1930s to the current time. Throughout those efforts, the primary objective was to develop a theoretical structure and related implementation guidelines that would represent a **consensus** of the profession. This goal was never wholly attained. The benefits of a conceptual foundation and implementation guidelines were never in doubt. These guidelines would serve the preparers, auditors, and users alike. That is, each of these groups can benefit from financial statements that have the qualitative characteristics of relevance and reliability. The diverse goals, interests, and influence of each of these three groups have created many difficulties and conflicts. A **political process** is involved that must reconcile the general interest, the theoretical and technical characteristics of accounting itself, and the specific interests of the three groups—preparers, auditors, and users.

The cooperative approach of the accounting profession to attain a consensus involved *(a)* establishment of the FASB (1973) as an independent, highly qualified, decision-making group; *(b)* development of a process for resolving accounting issues (see the nine steps summarized on page 13; and *(c)* a requirement that the decisions of the FASB on accounting issues be followed with actual compliance. In the opinion of many people, the success of this process of formulating a **consensus** on accounting standards will depend upon the theoretical soundness, absence of bias, and appropriate cost-benefit trade-offs in application of the decisions of the FASB.

A directly related issue is compliance with the prescribed accounting standards. The FASB has no authority or responsibility to enforce compliance. That responsibility rests with the accounting profession primarily through the AICPA. Many observers believe that compliance is the weak link in the chain. This view is supported to some extent by *(a)* recurring oversight actions of the SEC, *(b)* increasing litigations in the courts, and *(c)* escalating cost of liability insurance premiums paid by auditing firms.

Throughout the evolution of the standard-setting activities and compliance, the issue persists as to whether these activities should continue to be a responsibility of the private sector or should be taken over by the public sector, that is, by legislative action of the Federal Congress and a federal agency. Many people believe that these activities should reside with the private sector exclusively. They argue that governmental regulation would not be effective. They believe that the preparers, auditors, and users can provide adequate "policing" action to protect the public interest. They also believe that legislative action and a federal agency would result in inflexibility in meeting new challenges, slow reaction time to problems, an ineffective public forum, stereotyped reporting, and a rule-bound environment.

Others believe that legislative action and a responsible governmental agency are necessary to effectively "police" the rule making and enforcement.

Still others believe that a cooperative effort by the private and public sectors would be more effective. It should be noted that many interested observers believe that the cooperative joint-effort approach between the public sector (i.e., by the

SEC) and the private sector (i.e., the FASB) is reasonably effective. Of course, both parties should strive to continuously improve the process now in existence.

Given this overview of the environment in which accounting operates, we will now discuss the conceptual framework of accounting developed by the FASB.

PART B: THE CONCEPTUAL FRAMEWORK AND IMPLEMENTATION PRINCIPLES OF ACCOUNTING

The purpose of this part of the chapter is to discuss the conceptual framework of accounting and the related implementation guidelines. An understanding of these guidelines is useful to preparers, auditors, and users of financial statements. An overview of the topics discussed in this part is presented in **Exhibit 1–1.**

This part should be studied carefully; however, it is unrealistic to expect complete understanding and knowledge of its contents at this point. This part of the chapter is a reference for study throughout the remaining chapters. As the

EXHIBIT 1–1

Overview of the Conceptual Framework and Implementation Guidelines

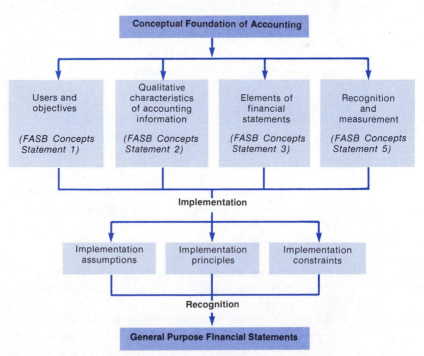

* FASB, *Statement of Financial Accounting Concepts No. 4,* "Objectives of Financial Reporting by Nonbusiness Organizations" (Stamford, Conn., December 1980) is outside the scope of this textbook.

concepts, principles, and procedures are discussed in subsequent chapters, you may need to return to this part to review the relevant concepts.

NATURE OF ACCOUNTING THEORY AND CONCEPTS

A general definition of **theory,** appropriate for accounting, is a "coherent set of hypothetical, conceptual, and pragmatic principles forming a general frame of reference for a field of inquiry."[7] **Concepts** can be viewed as components of theory; they are generalizations about the environment, observable events, and an existing body of knowledge. Accounting concepts are human-made; therefore, they change according to the evolving social and economic environment within which the accounting process is applied. Thus, accounting concepts involve continuous evolution. The organizations and the "political process" discussed in Part A of this chapter have been influential in the evolution of accounting concepts and standards.

Accounting concepts are based upon inductive and deductive reasoning, economic theory, experience, pragmatism, and general acceptability. Because accounting concepts are human-made, they cannot be derived from, or proven by, the laws of nature as can be done in mathematics and the natural sciences.

The **inductive** approach involves moving from empirical observations, experimentation, and general acceptance to the apex—concepts. In contrast, the **deductive** approach first develops concepts and then uses those concepts to guide what is done. Accounting concepts are the result of inductive reasoning. This approach is subject to two basic flaws: *(a)* what is already being done is not necessarily what should be done, and *(b)* observations from practice may lead to more than one explanation (i.e., conflicting concepts). Use of the inductive approach partially explains why numerous alternative accounting methods are currently permitted (e.g., an optional choice from several acceptable depreciation methods regardless of how the asset is used). The conceptual framework of accounting presented in the *FASB Concepts Statements* reflects the inductive approach.

In response to one of its primary responsibilities, the FASB has devoted resources to develop a **conceptual framework of accounting.** The accounting profession believes that a conceptual framework is essential for the following reasons:

1. The accounting standard on each accounting issue should be consistent with a conceptual framework developed by a prior consensus. This process assures consistency among the guidelines and procedures used in accounting.
2. New and unique accounting problems on which there are no current guidelines can be more consistently resolved by statement preparers in conformity with a conceptual framework.
3. Relevance and reliability of financial statements may be enhanced significantly.
4. Users of financial statements can benefit because of a better understanding of what financial statements are designed to accomplish.

---

[7] *Webster's Third New International Dictionary, Unabridged* (Springfield, Mass.: G C. Merriam, 1961), p. 2371.

THE FASB CONCEPTUAL FRAMEWORK

The FASB issued a *Discussion Memorandum* in 1976 entitled "Conceptual Framework for Financial Accounting and Reporting." This *Discussion Memorandum* specified the major components of a conceptual accounting framework. Consistent with the recommendations of that memorandum, the FASB has issued the five *Concepts Statements* outlined in **Exhibit 1–2.** These *Statements* will be discussed below and will be followed by a discussion of the implementation assumptions, principles, and constraints.

EXHIBIT 1–2

FASB Statements of Financial Accounting Concepts

No.	Date	Title	Primary topics
1	Nov. 1978	Objectives of Financial Reporting by Business Enterprises	1. Financial statement users defined. 2. Objectives of financial statements. 3. Qualitative characteristics of financial statements. Elaboration: Exhibit 1–3.

2	May 1980	Qualitative Characteristics of Accounting Information	1. Primary qualities:
			  a. Relevance.
			  b. Reliability.
			2. Secondary quality: comparability.
			3. Threshold of recognition; materiality.
			4. Quality constraint: cost-benefit.
			
			Elaboration: Exhibit 1–3.

3	Dec. 1980	Elements of Financial Statements of Business Enterprises	1. Assets, liabilities, owners' equity, investments and distributions by owners, and comprehensive income. 2. Revenues, expenses, and gains and losses. 3. Accrual accounting. Elaboration: Exhibit 1–4.
4	Dec. 1980	Objectives of Financial Reporting by Nonbusiness Organizations	Outside the scope of this textbook.
5	Dec. 1984	Recognition and Measurement in Financial Statements of Business Enterprises	1. Financial statements. 2. Recognition criteria. 3. Guidance in applying criteria to components of earnings. 4. Recognition of changes in assets and liabilities. Elaboration: Exhibit 1–5.

OBJECTIVES OF FINANCIAL REPORTING BY BUSINESS ENTERPRISES *(FASB Concepts Statement 1)*

This objectives statement defines the *(a)* users of financial statements, *(b)* objectives of financial statements, and *(c)* perspective of the conceptual framework. These three topics provide the fundamentals on which financial accounting and reporting is to be based.

Users of Financial Statements

External decision makers use accounting information. At one end of the spectrum is the casual investor who seldom looks at even the pictures in the annual financial report and never analyzes the financial statements. At the opposite extreme is the chartered financial analyst (CFA), who, like a CPA, has shown competence in a professional discipline. Because of this diversity, accounting information realistically cannot be directed at users at either end of the spectrum, nor can it be directed at any **one** group. Rather, *FASB Concepts Statement 1* establishes accounting standards to meet the information needs of the large group of external users. These users "lack the authority to prescribe the information they want and must rely on information management communicates to them." Also, they "have a reasonable understanding of business and economic activities and are willing to study the information with reasonable diligence." *FASB Concepts Statement 1* identifies these users as "investors and creditors" . . . and "also those who advise or represent them." Thus, by selecting these users as the focus for the objectives of financial reporting, the FASB defined their conception of the "average prudent investor" to be a reasonably sophisticated decision maker.

Financial Reporting Objectives

FASB Concepts Statement 1 states the objectives of financial reporting by business enterprises. The objectives focus on the decision makers (financial statement users) identified in the immediately preceding paragraphs. The objectives state that financial reporting should provide information—

1. That is useful to present and potential investors and creditors and other users in making **rational investment, credit, and similar decisions.**
2. To help current and potential investors and creditors and other users in **assessing** the amounts, timing, and uncertainty of prospective cash receipts from dividends or interest and the proceeds from the sale, redemption, or maturity of securities or loans. Investors' and creditors' cash flows are related to enterprise cash flows; therefore, financial reporting should provide information to help investors, creditors, and others assess the amounts, timing, and uncertainty of **prospective net cash flows** of the related enterprise.

3. About the economic resources of an enterprise, the claims to those resources (obligations of the enterprise to transfer resources to other entities) and the effects of transactions, events, and circumstances that change its resources and claims to those resources.

FASB Concepts Statement 1 implicitly recognizes an investment decision model that investors and creditors often use to value an investment by predicting the future net cash receipts they can expect from an investment in or loan to a particular business enterprise. It may be useful for you to think in terms of a discounted cash flow analysis in which the investor or creditor will pay for an investment a price that is equal to the present value (at the expected rate of return) of the future net cash receipts expected from the investment or loan. To project the net cash flows, investors usually need information about (1) the timing and amounts of expected net cash flows of the enterprise and (2) the risk that the business may not realize these cash flows.

Summary—A Perspective of the Conceptual Framework

The discussions above focused on the users and objectives of general-purpose financial statements. A conceptual framework must also include an identification of the qualities of accounting information that are needed to attain the objectives. Also, the elements of financial statements, recognition and measurement of those elements, and their display (i.e., how reported) on financial statements must be specified. These matters are the subject of subsequent *FASB Concepts Statements.*

QUALITATIVE CHARACTERISTICS OF ACCOUNTING INFORMATION *(FASB Concepts Statement 2)*

FASB Concepts Statement 2 continues the emphasis of *Concepts Statement 1.* The purpose of *Concepts Statement 2* is to identify and define a "hierarchy" of characteristics of accounting information to enhance its usefulness for decision making. An adaptation of the hierarchy of the **qualitative characteristics** is given in **Exhibit 1–3.**

Primary Qualities—Relevance and Reliability

FASB Concepts Statement 2 identifies **relevance and reliability as the two primary qualities** that make accounting information useful for decision making.

Relevance.   The dictionary defines relevance as bearing upon the matter at hand. Relevance then is the capacity of accounting information to make a difference in a decision by helping users to form predictions about the outcomes of past, present, and future events (i.e., has predictive value) or to confirm or correct prior expectations (i.e., has feedback value).

EXHIBIT 1–3:

FASB Hierarchy of Qualitative Characteristics of Accounting Information

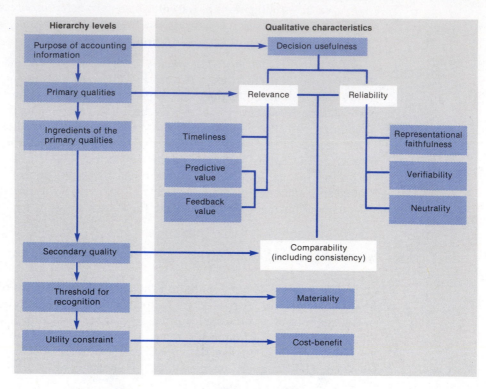

Source: Adapted from FASB, *Statement of Financial Accounting Concepts No. 2,* "Qualitative Characteristics of Accounting Information" (Stamford, Conn., May 1980), p. 15.

Relevance depends upon three ingredients as follows:

1. **Timeliness**—having information available to a decision maker before it loses its capacity to influence decisions. Lack of timeliness can reduce the level of relevance.
2. **Predictive value**—the quality of information that helps users to increase the likelihood of correctly forecasting the outcome of past or present events. Users prefer information that has the highest predictive value in attaining their objectives.
3. **Feedback value**—the quality of information that enables users to confirm or correct prior expectations.

Reliability.   Reliability is the quality of accounting information that assures that it is reasonably free from error and bias and faithfully represents what it purports to represent. Users must be confident that they can depend on the information contained in financial statements (that it is believable).

Reliability depends upon three ingredients as follows:

1. **Representational faithfulness**—correspondence or agreement between a measure or description and the phenomenon that it purports to represent (sometimes called validity). Accounting information must report in words and numbers the economic substance of a transaction rather than its form or a misleading description.
2. **Verifiability**—the dictionary defines verify as to confirm or substantiate. It involves the ability through consensus (i.e., confirmation) among measurers to ensure that accounting information is, and can be verified as, what it purports to represent.
3. **Neutrality**—absence of bias in reported information with no intention to attain a predetermined result or to induce a particular mode of behavior. Accounting information should not be biased toward or against a particular viewpoint, predetermined result, particular party, nor should it be consistently too high or too low.[8]

Secondary Quality—Comparability

FASB Concepts Statement 2 summarizes this quality as follows:

Information about a particular enterprise gains greatly in usefulness if it can be compared with similar information about other enterprises and with similar information about the same enterprise for some other period or some other point in time. Comparability between enterprises and consistency in the application of methods over time increases the informational value of comparisons of relative economic opportunities or performance.

Comparability involves the comparison of accounting information of an enterprise with similar information about other enterprises and with similar information about the same enterprise for some other period.

Consistency is the application of accounting standards, or principles, from period to period in the same manner. *APB Opinion 20,* "Accounting Changes," states that "there is a presumption that an accounting principle once adopted should not be changed." However, if consistency is carried too far, relevance may be adversely affected. A change to a preferred accounting principle is per-

---

[8] **Bias** is used in the definitions of reliability, verifiability, and neutrality. In measurement, bias is the tendency of a measure to fall more often on one side than the other of what it represents instead of being equally likely to fall on either side. Bias in accounting measures means a tendency to be consistently too high or too low.

   Error is used in the definitions of reliability and verifiability. Error in accounting usually is defined as deviation from truth or accuracy, as in a mistake, either intentional or unintentional. Another kind of error of concern to decision makers is called statistical measurement error, which is a difference between estimated and actual values.

mitted, although this would impair consistency. This conflict is resolved by supplemental disclosures to retain consistency (and comparability) between the financial statements before and after the change.

Threshold for Recognition—Materiality

Materiality is defined in *FASB Concepts Statement 2* as: "The magnitude of an omission or misstatement of accounting information that, in the light of surrounding circumstances, makes it probable that the judgment of a reasonable person relying on the information would have been changed or influenced by the omission or misstatement."

This quotation means that the omission or inclusion of an **immaterial** item or amount would not change or influence the decision of a rational decision maker. The materiality threshold does not mean that immaterial items and amounts do not have to be accounted for nor reported. Rather it means that strict adherence to the related accounting standard is not required. To illustrate, in conformity with GAAP, discount and premium on bonds payable should be amortized using the interest method (based on the effective interest rate). However, straight-line amortization can be used providing the results are not materially different. Similarly, a low-cost asset, such as a $9.95 pencil sharpener, can be recorded as expense in full when purchased because the amount is not material.

Materiality judgments are situation specific. This means that an amount that is material in one situation may be immaterial in another situation due to the magnitude of related amounts such as income, total assets, and total liabilities. Because of the uniqueness of specific materiality judgments, the FASB has not been able to specify **general** materiality guidelines that apply to a wide variety of situations. In practice, materiality guidelines such as "5% of net income" or "5% of total assets" are used.

Utility Constraint—Cost-Benefit

FASB Concepts Statement 2 discusses a utility constraint that often affects accounting information. The underlying concept is that the **benefits** to be derived by **users** from specific information must exceed the cost of providing it. Although the concept is important, it is difficult to quantify either the benefits or the costs. The FASB viewed this concept at two levels: *(a)* a standard-setting body must "do its best" to implement the conceptual framework in the standard-setting process and *(b)* individual businesses should implement the framework in the accounting and reporting of information (for external users).

In summary, *FASB Concepts Statement 2* does not establish accounting standards that prescribe specific accounting procedures and reporting requirements. Rather, it sets forth qualitative characteristics of accounting information that should be used for **developing** and **evaluating** accounting standards and implementation guidelines.

ELEMENTS OF FINANCIAL STATEMENTS OF BUSINESS ENTERPRISES *(FASB Concepts Statement 3)*

Elements of Financial Statements Defined

The primary medium used to communicate accounting information about a business enterprise is its periodic financial statements. The building blocks of financial statements are called **elements.** *FASB Concepts Statement 3* defines 10 elements as shown in **Exhibit 1–4** (also refer to Exhibit 1–1). The first four elements (revenues, expenses, gains, and losses) relate directly to the income statement; and the next three elements (assets, liabilities, and equity) relate directly to the balance sheet. Thus, these seven elements are relevant because they provide **authoritative definitions** of the major classifications used in current financial statements.

The next two elements, **investments by owners and distributions to owners,** are related to the balance sheet, although they encompass a **period of time** (as does the income statement). In contrast, the last element listed in Exhibit 1–4, **comprehensive income,** is new and unique because *(a)* it does not appear in the current income statement and *(b)* it changes the traditional income statement now in use.

FASB Concepts Statement 3 uses the term *elements* to mean the classes of items that financial statements should contain. The definitions of elements, given in Exhibit 1–4, will be useful throughout this textbook.

RECOGNITION AND MEASUREMENT IN FINANCIAL STATEMENTS OF BUSINESS ENTERPRISES *(FASB Concepts Statement 5)*

This *Concepts Statement* sets forth a full **articulated** set of financial statements, recognition criteria, and guidance on what items should be reported in the financial statements. It builds on the foundation of *FASB Concepts Statements 1–3.*[9] **Exhibit 1–5** gives an **overview** of *FASB Concepts Statement 5.*

---

[9] *FASB Concepts Statement 4* relates to the objectives of **nonbusiness** organizations; therefore, it is outside the scope of this textbook.

EXHIBIT 1–4
Elements of Finan-
cial Statements

Income statement (discussed in Chapter 3):

1. **Revenues** are inflows or other enhancements of assets of an entity or settlements of its liabilities (or a combination of both) during a period from delivering or producing goods, rendering services, or other activities that constitute the entity's ongoing major or central operations.

2. **Expenses** are outflows or other using up of assets or incurrences of liabilities (or a combination of both) during a period from delivering or producing goods, rendering services, or carrying out other activities that constitute the entity's ongoing major or central operations.

3. **Gains** are increases in equity (net assets) from peripheral or incidental transactions of an entity and from all other transactions and other events and circumstances affecting the entity during a period except those that result from revenues or investments by owners.

4. **Losses** are decreases in equity (net assets) from peripheral or incidental transactions of an entity and from all other transactions and other events and circumstances affecting the entity during a period except those that result from expenses or distributions to owners.

Balance sheet (discussed in Chapter 4):

5. **Assets** are probable future economic benefits obtained or controlled by a particular entity as a result of past transactions or events.

6. **Liabilities** are probable future sacrifices of economic benefits arising from present obligations of a particular entity to transfer assets or provide services to other entities in the future as a result of past transactions or events.

7. **Equity** (i.e., owners' equity) is the residual interest in the assets of an entity that remains after deducting its liabilities. In a business enterprise, the equity is the ownership interest.

Other elements:

8. **Investments by owners** are increases in net assets of a particular enterprise resulting from transfers to it from other entities of something of value to obtain or increase ownership interests (or equity) in it. Assets are most commonly received as investments by owners, but that which is received may also include services or satisfaction or conversion of liabilities of the enterprise.

9. **Distributions to owners** are decreases in net assets of a particular enterprise resulting from transfering assets, rendering services, or incurring liabilities by the enterprise to owners. Distributions to owners decrease ownership interests (or equity) in an enterprise (discussed in Chapter 15).

10. **Comprehensive income** is the change in equity (net assets) of an entity during a period from transactions and other events and circumstances from **nonowner sources.** It includes all changes in equity during a period except those resulting from investments by owners and distributions to owners.

Source: FASB, *Statement of Financial Accounting Concepts No. 3,* "Elements of Financial Statements of Business Enterprises," (Stamford, Conn., December 1980), pp. xi and xii.

EXHIBIT 1–5

Recognition and Measurement in Financial Statements of Business Enterprises (overview of *FASB Concepts Statement 5*)

Financial statements of a business

1. Overview and nature of financial statements.
2. A full, articulated, set of financial statements:
   Financial statements as of the end of the reporting period:
      a. Statement of financial position (balance sheet).
   Changes in financial position during the reporting period:
      b. Statement of earnings (income).
      c. Statement of comprehensive income and nonowner changes in equity.
      d. Statement of cash flows.
      e. Statement of investments by and distributions to owners.

Recognition and measurement of items incorporated into financial statements

1. Recognition defined.
2. Recognition criteria:
      a. Definitions.
      b. Measurability.
      c. Relevance.
      d. Reliability.
3. Guidance in applying recognition criteria:
      a. Revenues and gains.
      b. Expenses and losses.
      d. Changes in assets and liabilities.

Source: Adapted from FASB, *Statement of Financial Accounting Concepts No. 5,* "Recognition and Measurement in Financial Statements of Business Enterprises" (Stamford, Conn., December 31, 1984).

OVERVIEW AND NATURE OF FINANCIAL STATEMENTS

FASB Concepts Statement 5 envisions a restructure of the tradition of financial statements used today. It emphasizes that a **full set of financial statements** should include two types of statements:

1. An individual statement **of financial position** dated "as of" the **end** of the reporting period.
2. Four individual statements that report **changes** in financial position **during** the reporting period.

A full set of financial statements should be supported with disclosure notes and other supplementary information. The five individual financial statements of a business for any reporting period **articulate;** that is, each statement is interrelated with (and ties into) the other statements because they are derived from the same data base (i.e., the accounting records).

A FULL AND ARTICULATED SET OF FINANCIAL STATEMENTS

Exhibit 1–5 lists the five restructured financial statements that comprise the full set of articulated statements envisioned in *FASB Concepts Statement 5*. This *Concepts Statement* does not illustrate the five individual statements; nor does it indicate an expected implementation time. The next few sections will discuss and illustrate (in summary fashion) some ideas regarding how the **restructured** statements may evolve.

Statement of Financial Position

This statement reports assets, liabilities, and owner's equity. Owners' equity will reflect a major restructuring because of the importance that will be accorded the four **change** statements. For example, the restructured statement of financial position (old title, balance sheet) may evolve to look like this:

Statement of Financial Position (summarized)
At December 31, 19X
(in thousands)

Assets:
   (by new unspecified classifications) $611

Liabilities:
   (by new unspecified classifications) $150

Owners' equity:
   Accumulated equity contributed by owners $387*
   Accumulated comprehensive income . . . .   74†

     Total owners' equity   461
Total liabilities and owner's equity $611

* From the statement of investments by and distributions to owners (page 28).
† From the statement of comprehensive income (page 27).

Statement of Earnings

The statement of earnings described in *FASB Concepts Statement 5* corresponds to the traditional income statement now used **except** that it is limited to continuing operations, unusual and/or infrequent items, and extraordinary items. It **excludes** items that are extraneous to the current reporting period such as the cumulative effect of a change in accounting principle (discussed in Chapter 20). Thus, the statement of earnings (or income) would look like this:

Statement of Earnings (summarized)
For the Year Ended December 31, 19X
(in thousands)

Revenues		$ 100
Expenses		(80)
Gain from unusual source		3
Income from continuing operations		23
Loss on discontinued operations:		
Income from operating discontinued segment	$ 10	
Loss on disposal of discontinued segment	(12)	(2)
Income before extraordinary items		21
Extraordinary loss		(6)
Earnings		$ 15*

Earnings per share (to be specified):

* Carried to the statement of comprehensive income, shown below.

Statement of Comprehensive Income

This is a new financial statement that will replace the traditional statement of retained earnings. Comprehensive income is defined in *FASB Concepts Statement 5* (par. 39) as comprising **all recognized changes in equity (net assets) of the entity during the period from transactions and other events except those resulting from investments by owners and distributions to owners.** This new statement may evolve into something like this:

Statement of Comprehensive Income
For the Year Ended December 31, 19X
(in thousands)

Balance from prior period		$60
Earnings (from statement of earnings, given above)	$ 15	
Cumulative accounting adjustments:		
Cumulative effect of a change in accounting principle	(2)	
Other nonowner changes in owners' equity:		
Donated assets	1	
Comprehensive income		14
Ending balance, cumulative comprehensive income		$74*

* Carried to statement of financial position (page 26).

Statement of Investments by and Distributions to Owners

This statement is briefly described in *FASB Concepts Statement 5,* pars. 55–57. It reports the "ways the equity increased or decreased from transactions with owners as owners during a period." **Investments by owners** establish or increase owners' equity and "may be received in the form of cash, goods or services, or satisfaction or conversion of the entity's liabilities." **Distributions to owners** decrease owners' equity by means of cash and property dividends when declared and "transactions such as reacquisitions of the entity's equity securities." This statement summarizes all capital changes. It starts with the beginning balance of each category of the capital stock accounts and ends with the balances at the end of the reporting period. The following statement continues the preceding examples:

Statement of Investments by and Distributions to Owners (summarized)
For the Year Ended December 31, 19X
(in thousands)

Items	Common stock (par $)	Contributed capital	Treasury stock	Dividends	Total equity contributed by owners
Balance from prior period	$100	$200	$(10)		$290
Investments by owners:					
Stock issued	50	60			110
Treasury stock sold		2	5		7
Total investments	150	262	(5)		407
Distributions to owners:					
Cash dividend				$(20)	(20)
Stock dividend	30	36		(66)	–0–
Total distributions	30	36		(86)	(20)
Balance, December 31, 19X	$180	$298	$ (5)	$(86)	$387*

* Carried to statement of financial position (page 26).

Statement of Cash Flows

This statement reports an entity's cash receipts classified by major sources. It also reports cash payments classified by major uses during the reporting period. *FASB Concepts Statement 5* does not provide guidance for the format of this statement. Therefore, the traditional cash flow statements are likely to continue. *FASB Concepts Statement 5* does not advocate continuation of a statement of working capital flows (see Chapter 23). A statement of cash flows may be helpful to decision makers in assessing the entity's liquidity, financial flexibility, and risks.

RECOGNITION AND MEASUREMENT OF ITEMS INCORPORATED INTO FINANCIAL STATEMENTS

Recognition is the process of recording and reporting an item as an asset, liability, revenue, gain, expense, loss, and changes in owners' equity. A recognized item is expressed in both words and numbers. Thus, recognition applies to all financial statement elements.

FASB Concepts Statement 5 (pars. 58–63) states that **recognition** of an item is **required when all four** of the following criteria are met:

1. **Definitions**—the item must meet the definition of an element of financial statements as defined in *FASB Concepts Statement 3* (see page 24).
2. **Measurability**—the item has a relevant attribute (i.e., characteristic) that is reliably measurable.
3. **Relevance**—the information about the item is capable of making a difference in user decisions.
4. **Reliability**—the information about the item is representationally faithful, verifiable, and neutral.

Recognition criteria and guidance in applying the criteria to the components of earnings are discussed in Chapter 22.

IMPLEMENTATION ASSUMPTIONS AND PRINCIPLES

The *FASB Concepts Statements* discussed above present and explain the conceptual framework of accounting. To implement that framework, the accounting profession has identified and defined guidelines that involve *(a)* environmental assumptions, *(b)* implementation principles, and *(c)* implementation constraints.

BASIC ENVIRONMENTAL ASSUMPTIONS

Four basic environmental assumptions significantly affect the recording, measuring, and reporting of accounting information. These assumptions relate to the *(a)* boundaries of an accountable entity, *(b)* continuity of the entity, *(c)* monetary units used by the entity, and *(d)* timing of the reporting period used by the entity.

Separate Entity Assumption

Accounting is concerned with specific and separate entities. Thus, each enterprise is considered as an **accounting unit separate and apart from its owners and from other entities.** A corporation and its shareholders are separate entities for accounting purposes. Also, partnerships and sole proprietorships are treated as separate and apart from their owners despite the fact that this distinction is not made in the legal sense.

Under the separate entity assumption, all records and reports are developed from the viewpoint of the particular entity. This assumption provides a basis for clear-cut distinction in analyzing transactions between the enterprise and its owners. For example, the personal residence of an individual owner is not considered an asset for the business to report, although the residence and the business have a common owner.

Continuity Assumption

The continuity assumption frequently is called the "going-concern" assumption. It assumes the business is not expected to liquidate in the foreseeable future. The assumption does not imply that accounting assumes permanent continuance; rather there is a presumption of continuity for a period of time **sufficient to carry out contemplated operations, contracts, and commitments.** This concept establishes the rationale of accounting on a **nonliquidation basis.** Also it provides the theoretical foundation for many of the classifications common in accounting. For example, the classification of assets and liabilities as current or long-term relies upon this assumption. If continuity were not assumed, all assets and liabilities would become current, and the current/long-term distinction would lose its significance.

If an entity expects probable liquidation, conventional accounting based on the continuity assumption would not be appropriate for reporting the enterprise's elements. Such cases call for **liquidation** accounting, wherein all elements are accounted for at estimated net realizable amounts.

Unit-of-Measure Assumption

The unit-of-measure assumption is that accounting will measure and report the results of the economic activities of the entity in terms of a monetary unit (e.g., dollars). It recognizes that the monetary unit is an effective means of communicating financial information. Thus, money is the common denominator—the meterstick—used in accounting.

Unfortunately, use of a monetary unit for measurement purposes poses an accounting dilemma. Unlike the meterstick, which is always the same length, the monetary unit (i.e., the dollar) changes in real value (or purchasing power). Therefore, during inflation or deflation, dollars of different size (i.e., of different purchasing power) are entered in the accounts and intermingled as if they were of equal purchasing power. Because of the practice of ignoring changes in the purchasing power of a dollar, accounting assumes that the value of the monetary unit is stable over time. Chapter 24 discusses techniques that the accounting profession uses to report the effects of changes in prices.

Time Period Assumption

Although the results of operations of a specific business enterprise cannot be known with certainty until the business has completed its life span and gone through final liquidation, short-term financial reports are necessary because financial statement users need relevant (i.e., timely) financial information. Thus the environment—the business community and government—has imposed upon accounting a **calendar constraint,** that is, the necessity to assign changes in the economic elements of an enterprise to a series of short time periods. These **reporting periods** vary; however, a year is the most common. Some companies adhere to the calendar year, whereas other companies use a business year that ends near the lowest point of business activity in each 12-month period—regardless of its relation to the calendar year.

In addition to annual reports, companies also report summarized financial information on an **interim** basis, usually quarterly (discussed in Chapter 21).

The time period assumption recognizes the need of decision makers for short-term financial information. This assumption underlies the use of **accruals** and **deferrals** that distinguish accrual basis accounting from cash basis accounting. If a demand for periodic reports did not exist during the life span of a business, accruals and deferrals of revenues and expenses would not be necessary.

IMPLEMENTATION PRINCIPLES

At the operational level, preparers use implementation principles for recognizing (i.e., recording) and reporting revenues, expenses, gains, and losses. The implementation principles are the cost, revenue, matching, and full-disclosure principles.

These principles focus on the accounting term *recognition.* **Recognition** is the formal process of recording in the accounts and reporting in the financial statements the **elements** of financial statements. These elements are assets, liabilities, investments by owners, withdrawals by owners, revenues, expenses, and gains and losses. A recognized item is depicted in both words and numbers, with the amount included in financial statement totals *(FASB Concepts Statement 5).*

FASB Concepts Statement 5 states that "an item and information about it should meet four fundamental recognition criteria and must be recognized when all of the criteria are met, subject to a cost-benefit constraint and a materiality threshold." The four recognition criteria—definitions, measurability, relevance, and reliability—have already been discussed on page 29.

Cost Principle

The cost principle specifies that cash-equivalent cost is the most useful basis for **initial** accounting recognition of the elements recorded in the accounts and reported on the financial statements. It is important to note that the cost principle applies to the **initial** recording of transactions and events. *FASB Concepts Statement 5,* paragraph 67, explains that cost is "commonly adjusted after acquisition for amortization or other allocations." It lists five different attributes of assets and liabilities used in accounting. These are historical cost, current cost, current market value, net realizable value, and present value of future cash flows. These attributes generally refer to valuations assigned to assets and liabilities **subsequent** to their initial recognition.

The cost principle is supported by the fact that at the time of a completed arm's-length business transaction, the market value of the resources given up in the transaction provides reliable evidence of the valuation of the item acquired in the transaction. The cost principle requires that all of the four recognition criteria listed above be met.

When a noncash consideration is involved, cost is measured as the market value of the resources given, or the market value of the item received, whichever is more **reliably** determinable. For example, an asset may be acquired with a debt given as settlement. Cost in this instance is the **present value** of the amount of cash to be paid in the future, as specified by the terms of the debt. The cost principle applies to all of the elements of financial statements, including liabilities.

The cost principle provides guidance at the original recognition date. However, the original cost of some items acquired is subject to depreciation, depletion, amortization, and write-down in conformity with the matching principle and the conservatism constraint (discussed in the sections that follow).

Revenue Principle

The revenue principle specifies when revenue should be recognized in the accounts and reported in the financial statements. It requires that all four of the **recognition criteria**—definition, measurability, relevance, and reliability—must be met. Also, there must be *(a)* a completed transaction and *(b)* an earnings process must be essentially completed.

Revenue Defined.   Revenue is defined in *FASB Concepts Statement 3* as "inflows or other enhancements of assets of an entity or settlements of its liabilities (or a combination of both) during a period from delivering or producing goods, rendering service, or other activities that constitute the entity's ongoing major or central operations." Revenues "represent actual or expected cash inflows (or the equivalent) that have occurred or will eventually occur as a result of the enterprise's **ongoing major or central operations** during the period."

Measurement of Revenue.   Revenue is measured as the market value of the resources received or the product or service given, whichever is the more reliably determinable. The revenue principle requires that all discounts be viewed as adjustments of the amount of revenue earned. For example, in determining the net cash exchange value of sales subject to a discount, sales discounts should be subtracted from gross sales revenue in measuring the net amount of sales revenue.

Under the revenue principle, revenue from the sale of **goods** is recognized according to the **sales method** (i.e., at the time of sale) because the earning process usually is complete at the time of sale. At that time, the **relevant** information about the asset inflows to the seller would be known with **reliability.**

The conditions for **completion of the earning process** are *(a)* collection from the buyer is reasonably assured and *(b)* the expenses of making the sale can be determined reliably. Condition *(a)*—reasonable assurance of collection—provides the basis for the conclusion that the transaction provided a "probable future economic benefit" (i.e., an asset) to the seller. Without this condition, the concept of revenue recognition would be altogether lacking in substantive economic content. Condition *(b)*—reliable determination of related expenses—provides the basis for measurement of the net economic benefit of the transaction. Without this condition, measurement of the effect of the revenue would ignore the related expenses. It would therefore be partial at best. Condition *(b)* is closely related to the **matching principle,** which is discussed below.

Under the revenue principle, revenue from the sale of **services** is recognized on the basis of performance because performance determines the extent to which the earning process is complete.

The revenue principle requires **accrual basis** accounting rather than cash basis accounting for revenues. For example, completed transactions for the sale of goods or services on credit usually are recognized as revenue in the period in which the sale or service occurred rather than in the period in which the cash is eventually collected.

Other types of revenue transactions posing problems of revenue recognition are installment sales, long-term construction contracts, sales of land with minimal down payments, and sales of franchises that require a certain level of performance on the part of the purchaser. In these and many other cases, both determination of when the earning process is complete and measurement of the amount of revenue are difficult tasks. A discussion of revenue recognition is provided in Chapter 22.

Matching Principle

The matching principle states that for a reporting period revenues should be recognized in conformity with the revenue principle; then the expenses incurred in earning that revenue should be recognized during the same period. If revenue is carried over from a prior period or deferred to a future period in conformity with the revenue principle, all identifiable elements of expense related to that revenue likewise should be carried over from the prior period or deferred to a future period. Many expenditures are recognized as assets because they aid in the earning of **future** revenues. In this case, the matching principle requires that as the revenues are earned, those assets sold or consumed must be recognized and reported as **expenses** of the period in which the related revenue is recognized.

The pattern of expense recognition varies. Some expenses reflect a **direct cause-and-effect** relationship with revenues. That is, the revenue and expense occur simultaneously. Examples are cost of goods sold, sales commission expense, and delivery expense. Other expenses are recognized on a **time basis** because their asset counterparts expire over time rather than reflecting direct cause-and-effect relationships with revenues. Examples are depreciation expense of the home office, interest expense, and property tax expense. For other expenses, there is no direct relationship with **either revenue or time.** Therefore, these expenses must be allocated to reporting periods on some subjective basis. Examples are expenditures for advertising, research and development, and charitable contributions. A common system of allocation is to recognize such costs as expense in full in the period in which they are incurred.

To illustrate the matching principle, assume a home appliance was sold for cash during 19B (the annual accounting period). It was guaranteed for 12 months from date of sale. The sales revenue will be recognized as earned during 19B. The expense of honoring the warranty also should be recognized in 19B, although the actual warranty cost may not be known until the next year. Therefore, at the end of 19B, the warranty expense must be estimated, recorded, and reported. In this way, the warranty expense is **matched** with the 19B revenue to which it is related.

These relationships can be summarized as follows:

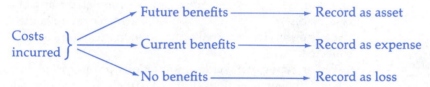

The matching principle is the expense analog to the revenue principle. Because of the wide diversity and large number of types of expenses, it is one of the most pervasive principles of accounting in terms of the number of accounting judgments that it affects.

The matching principle requires the use of **accrual basis** accounting (as opposed to cash basis accounting) to record and report expenses. Thus, **adjusting entries** (discussed in Chapter 2) must be recorded at the end of each period to update certain expenses for the period. Examples are depreciation expense, wage expense, and estimated warranty expense. A discussion of expense recognition under the matching principle is provided in Chapter 22.

Full-Disclosure Principle

The full-disclosure principle requires that the financial statements of a business clearly report all of the relevant information about the economic affairs of the enterprise. This principle rests upon the primary characteristic of relevance (refer to Exhibit 1–2). Full disclosure requires *(a)* reporting of all information that can make a difference in a decision and *(b)* that the accounting information reported must be understandable (i.e., not susceptible to misleading inferences). Full disclosure also requires that the major accounting policies and any special accounting policies used by the company be explained in the notes to the financial statements.

Accounting information may be reported in the *(a)* financial statements themselves, *(b)* disclosure notes to those statements, or *(c)* supplementary schedules and other presentations.

The full-disclosure principle requires the financial report to place **substance over form;** the primary objective is to report the substance of a transaction, rather than the form. This means that the substance should not be made vague or hidden by using the mechanics, rules, and jargon of bookkeeping.

IMPLEMENTATION CONSTRAINTS

The conceptual framework, implementation assumptions, and principles have been discussed. Throughout these discussions, the **implementation constraints** identified were: *(a)* cost-benefit, *(b)* materiality, *(c)* industry peculiarities, and *(d)* conservatism. These constraints exert a modifying influence on financial accounting and reporting.

Cost-Benefit Constraint

The cost of preparing and reporting accounting information should not exceed the value of the benefits that can be derived from using the information (see "Utility Constraint" page 22).

Materiality

The amount of an item is material if its omission, in the light of the surrounding circumstances, makes it probable that the judgment of a reasonable person would have been changed or influenced. Amounts that are not material need not be accounted for in strict conformity with GAAP. However, amounts that are not material must be accounted for; therefore, they usually are aggregated with other amounts to attain a favorable cost-benefit relationship (also see "Threshold for Recognition," page 22).

Industry Peculiarities

Because accounting focuses on usefulness and substance over form, the peculiarities and practices of an industry (such as the utility, railroad, banking, mutual funds, insurance, and extractive industries) may warrant selective exceptions to accounting principles and practices. This modifying exception permits special accounting for specific items where there is a clear precedent in the industry based on uniqueness, usefulness, and substance over form.

Some differences in accounting also occur in response to legal requirements. This is especially true with respect to companies subject to significant and pervasive regulatory controls. Another exception permits the use of a principle or procedure that is at variance with an official pronouncement if it can be clearly shown that it is more useful and is necessary to avoid misleading inferences. In such cases, the departure must be fully disclosed and the reasons therefor given.

Conservatism

The conservatism constraint holds that where two alternatives equally satisfy conceptual and implementation principles for a transaction, the alternative having the **least favorable** effect on net income and/or total assets should be used. In recognizing **assets** where two alternative valuations are acceptable, the lower valuation should be selected. In recognizing **liabilities,** the higher of two alternative liability amounts should be recorded. In recording revenues, expenses, gains, and losses where there is reasonable doubt as to the appropriateness of alternative amounts, the one having the least favorable effect on net income should be chosen.

The constraint implies that when the "correct" treatment or amount is not determinable, the users of financial statements usually are better served by understatement rather than overstatement of net income and assets. Accountants must make many accounting decisions based on judgment in selecting alternatives, making estimates, and applying accounting principles. These choices often affect net income, assets, and owners' equity, and they do not always have a single "correct" answer.

The concept of conservatism provides a time-tested guideline for making these choices. Examples of the use of conservatism are the use of lower of cost or market in valuing inventories and equity investments, minimizing the estimated life and residual value of depreciable assets, and the classification of gains as extraordinary and losses as ordinary in the same situation (e.g., debt restructuring).

SUMMARY

This chapter discussed the environmental influences affecting accounting, how accounting standards are set, and the conceptual framework and standards of accounting. The concepts and standards were discussed in the following order:

Conceptual framework of accounting:
    Users and objectives of financial statements.
    Qualitative characteristics of accounting information.
      Primary characteristics:
        Relevance
        Reliability
      Secondary characteristics:
        Comparability (includes consistency)
    Elements of financial statements.
    Recognition and measurement in financial statements.

Implementation assumptions.

Implementation principles.

Implementation constraints.

The discussion of the theoretical foundation of financial accounting and reporting and the implementation guidelines in this chapter are intended to provide a **frame of reference for your study of subsequent chapters.** Rather than presenting these concepts piecemeal throughout the textbook, the authors have chosen to discuss them in this first chapter. Of particular importance are the relationships portrayed in Exhibits 1–1 and 1–2, which summarize the **conceptual and implementation foundation.** The remaining chapters discuss and illustrate numerous examples of the implementation of this foundation. As a result, those chapters continue the emphasis upon the qualitative characteristics, elements, assumptions, principles, and financial statements.

SUPPLEMENT 1–A: LIST OF OFFICIAL ACCOUNTING PRONOUNCEMENTS

This supplement is included to help students *(a)* gain an overview of the official pronouncements that provide the basis for a large part of GAAP and *(b)* identify appropriate source documents for numerous accounting issues discussed in this book. Further study of these issues in the source documents often is desirable.

Accounting Research Bulletins (ARBs), Accounting Procedures Committee, AICPA (1939–59)

ARB No.	Date issued	Title	Status to April 1, 1985
43	June 1953	Restatement and Revisions of *Accounting Research Bulletins Nos. 1–42* (issued individually 1939–53)	Generally continued in force by *APB Opinion 6* (as amended)
		Chap. 1. Prior Opinions	Amended
		Chap. 2. Form of Statements	Amended and partially superseded
		Chap. 3. Working Capital	Amended and partially superseded
		Chap. 4. Inventory Pricing	Amended
		Chap. 5. Intangible Assets	Superseded by *APB Opinions 16 and 17*
		Chap. 6. Contingency Reserves	Superseded by *FASB Statement 5*
		Chap. 7. Capital Accounts	Amended and partially superseded
		Chap. 8. Income and Earned Surplus	Superseded by *APB Opinion 9*
		Chap. 9. Depreciation	Amended and partially superseded
		Chap. 10. Taxes	Amended and partially superseded
		Chap. 11. Government Contracts	Amended
		Chap. 12. Foreign Operations and Foreign Exchange	Amended by *FASB Statement 8*
		Chap. 13. Compensation (Pension Plans)	Amended and partially superseded

Accounting Research Bulletins (ARBs), Accounting Procedures Committee, AICPA (1939–59) *(continued)*

ARB No.	Date issued	Title	Status to April 1, 1985
		Chap. 14. Disclosure of Long-Term Leases in Financial Statements	Superseded by *APB Opinion 5*
		Chap. 15. Unamortized Discount, Issue Cost, and Redemption Premium on Bonds Refunded	Superseded by *APB Opinion 26*
44	Oct. 1954	Declining-Balance Depreciation; Revised July 1958	Amended
45	Oct. 1955	Long-Term Construction-Type Contracts	Unchanged
46	Feb. 1956	Discontinuance of Dating Earned Surplus	Unchanged
47	Sept. 1956	Accounting for Costs of Pension Plans	Superseded by *APB Opinion 8*
48	Jan. 1957	Business Combinations	Superseded by *APB Opinion 16*
49	Apr. 1958	Earnings per Share	Superseded by *APB Opinion 9*
50	Oct. 1958	Contingencies	Superseded by *FASB Statement 5*
51	Aug. 1959	Consolidated Financial Statements	Amended and partially superseded

Accounting Terminology Bulletins, Committee on Terminology, AICPA (discontinued in 1959)

ATB No.	Date issued	Title	Status to April 1, 1985
1	Aug. 1953	Review and Resume (of eight original terminology bulletins)	Partially superseded
2	Mar. 1955	Proceeds, Revenue, Income, Profit, and Earnings	Amended
3	Aug. 1956	Book Value	Unchanged
4	July, 1957	Cost, Expense, and Loss	Amended

Accounting Principles Board (APB) Opinions, AICPA (1962–73)

APB No.	Date issued	Title	Status to April 1, 1985
1	Nov. 1962	New Depreciation Guidelines and Rules	Unchanged
2	Dec. 1962	Accounting for the "Investment Credit"	Amended and interpreted
		Addendum to *Opinion 2*—Accounting Principles for Regulated Industries	Unchanged
3	Oct. 1963	The Statement of Source and Application of Funds	Superseded
4	Mar. 1964	Accounting for the "Investment Credit" (Amending *Opinion 2*)	Unchanged, but interpreted
5	Sept. 1964	Reporting of Leases in Financial Statements of Lessee	Superseded
6	Oct. 1965	Status of *Accounting Research Bulletins*	Amended and partially superseded
7	May 1966	Accounting for Leases in Financial Statements of Lessors	Superseded

Accounting Principles Board (APB) Opinions, AICPA (1962–73) *(continued)*

APB No.	Date issued	Title	Status to April 1, 1985
8	Nov. 1966	Accounting for the Cost of Pension Plans	Amended and interpreted
9	Dec. 1966	Reporting the Results of Operations	Amended and partially superseded
10	Dec. 1966	Omnibus Opinion—1966	Amended and partially superseded
11	Dec. 1967	Accounting for Income Taxes	Amended, partially superseded, and interpreted
12	Dec. 1967	Omnibus Opinion—1967	Amended and partially superseded
13	Mar. 1969	Amending Paragraph 6 of *APB Opinion No. 9,* Application to Commercial Banks	Unchanged
14	Mar. 1969	Accounting for Convertible Debt and Debt Issued with Stock Purchase Warrants	Unchanged
15	May 1969	Earnings per Share	Amended and interpreted
16	Aug. 1970	Business Combinations	Amended and interpreted
17	Aug. 1970	Intangible Assets	Amended and interpreted
18	Mar. 1971	The Equity Method of Accounting for Investments in Common Stock	Amended, partially superseded, and interpreted
19	Mar. 1971	Reporting Changes in Financial Position	Unchanged
20	July 1971	Accounting Changes	Amended and interpreted
21	Aug. 1971	Interest on Receivables and Payables	Unchanged, but interpreted
22	Apr. 1972	Disclosure of Accounting Policies	Unchanged
23	Apr. 1972	Accounting for Income Taxes—Special Areas	Amended and interpreted
24	Apr. 1972	Accounting for Income Taxes—Equity Method Investments	Unchanged, but interpreted
25	Oct. 1972	Accounting for Stock Issued to Employees	Unchanged
26	Oct. 1972	Early Extinguishment of Debt	Amended and interpreted
27	Nov. 1972	Accounting for Lease Transactions by Manufacturer or Dealer Lessors	Superseded
28	May 1973	Interim Financial Reporting	Partially superseded and interpreted
29	May 1973	Accounting for Nonmonetary Transactions	Unchanged, but interpreted
30	June 1973	Reporting the Results of Operations	Amended and partially superseded
31	June 1973	Disclosure of Lease Commitments by Lessees	Superseded

Financial Accounting Standards Board (FASB), *Statement of Financial Accounting Concepts* **(1978–85)**

FASB No.	Date issued	Title	Status to April 1, 1985
1	Nov. 1978	Objectives of Financial Reporting by Business Enterprises	Unchanged
2	May 1980	Qualitative Characteristics of Accounting Information	Unchanged
3	Dec. 1980	Elements of Financial Statements of Business Enterprises	Unchanged
4	Dec. 1980	Objectives of Financial Reporting by Nonbusiness Organizations	Unchanged
5	Dec. 1984	Recognition and Measurement in Financial Statements of Business Enterprises	Unchanged
6	Dec. 1985	Elements of Financial Statements (a replacement of *FASB Concepts Statement No. 3,* incorporating an amendment of *FASB Concepts Statement No. 2*)	Unchanged

Financial Accounting Standards Board (FASB), *Statements of Financial Accounting Standards* **(1973–85)**

FASB No.	Date issued	Title	Status to April 1, 1985
1	Dec. 1973	Disclosure of Foreign Currency	Amended by *FASB Statement 8*
2	Oct. 1974	Accounting for Research and Development Costs	Unchanged, but interpreted
3	Dec. 1974	Reporting Accounting Changes in Interim Financial Statements (amending *APB Opinion 23*)	Unchanged
4	Mar. 1975	Reporting Gains and Losses from Extinguishment of Debt	Unchanged
5	Mar. 1975	Accounting for Contingencies	Amended and interpreted
6	May 1975	Classification of Short-Term Obligations Expected to Be Refinanced	Unchanged, but interpreted
7	June 1975	Accounting and Reporting by Development Stage Enterprises	Unchanged, but interpreted
8	Oct. 1975	Accounting for the Translation of Foreign Currency Transactions and Foreign Currency Financial Statements	Superseded
9	Oct. 1975	Accounting for Income Taxes—Oil and Gas Producing Companies (an Amendment of *APB Opinions 11* and *23*) ...	Superseded
10	Oct. 1975	Extension of "Grandfather" Provisions for Business Combinations (an Amendment of *APB Opinion 16*)	Unchanged
11	Dec. 1975	Accounting for Contingencies—Transition Method (an Amendment of *FASB Statement 5*)	Unchanged
12	Dec. 1975	Accounting for Certain Marketable Securities	Unchanged, but interpreted
13	Nov. 1976	Accounting for Leases	Amended, partially superseded, and interpreted
14	Dec. 1976	Financial Reporting for Segments of a Business Enterprise	Amended and partially superseded
15	June 1977	Accounting by Debtors and Creditors for Troubled Debt Restructurings	Unchanged
16	June 1977	Prior Period Adjustments	Unchanged

Financial Accounting Standards Board (FASB), *Statements of Financial Accounting Standards* **(1973–85)** *(continued)*

FASB No.	Date issued	Title	Status to April 1, 1985
17	Nov. 1977	Accounting for Leases—Initial Direct Costs	Unchanged
18	Nov. 1977	Financial Reporting for Segments of a Business Enterprise—Interim Financial Statements	Unchanged
19	Dec. 1977	Financial Accounting and Reporting by Oil and Gas Producing Companies	Amended, partially suspended (see *FASB Statement 25* below), and interpreted
20	Dec. 1977	Accounting for Forward Exchange Contracts	Unchanged
21	Apr. 1978	Suspension of the Reporting of Earnings per Share and Segment Information by Nonpublic Enterprises	Unchanged
22	June 1978	Changes in the Provisions of Lease Agreements Resulting from Refundings of Tax-Exempt Debt	Unchanged
23	Aug. 1978	Inception of the Lease	Unchanged
24	Dec. 1978	Reporting Segment Information in Financial Statements that Are Presented in Another Enterprise's Financial Report	Unchanged
25	Feb. 1979	Suspension of Certain Accounting Requirements for Oil and Gas Companies (an amendment of *FASB Statement 19*)	Unchanged
26	Apr. 1979	Profit Recognition on Sales-Type Leases of Real Estate (an amendment of *FASB Statement 13*)	Unchanged
27	May 1979	Classification of Renewals or Extension of Existing Sales-Type or Direct Financing Leases (an amendment of *FASB Statement 13*)	Unchanged
28	May 1979	Accounting for Sales with Leasebacks (an amendment of *FASB Statement 13*)	Unchanged, but interpreted
29	June 1979	Determining Contingent Rentals (an amendment of *FASB Statement 13*)	Unchanged
30	Aug. 1979	Disclosure of Information about Major Customers (an amendment of *FASB Statement 14*)	Unchanged
31	Sept. 1979	Accounting for Tax Benefits Related to U.K. Tax Legislation concerning Stock Relief	Unchanged
32	Sept. 1979	Specialized Accounting and Reporting Principles and Practices in AICPA Statements of Position and Guides on Accounting and Auditing Matters (an amendment of *APB Opinion 20*)	Unchanged
33	Sept. 1979	Financial Reporting and Changing Prices	Amended
		Illustrations of Financial Reporting and Changing Prices, *Statement of Financial Accounting Standards 33*	Amended
34	Oct. 1979	Capitalization of Interest Cost	Amended and interpreted
35	Mar. 1980	Accounting and Reporting by Defined Benefit Pension Plans ...	Unchanged
36	May 1980	Disclosure of Pension Information (an amendment of *APB Opinion 8*)	Unchanged

Financial Accounting Standards Board (FASB), *Statements of Financial Accounting Standards* (1973–85) *(continued)*

FASB No.	Date issued	Title	Status to April 1, 1985
37	July 1980	Balance Sheet Classification of Deferred Income Taxes (an amendment of *APB Opinion 11*)	Unchanged
38	Sept. 1980	Accounting for Preacquisition Contingencies of Purchased Enterprises (an amendment of *APB Opinion 16*)	Unchanged
39	Oct. 1980	Financial Reporting and Changing Prices: Specialized Assets—Mining and Oil and Gas (a supplement to *FASB Statement 33*)	Unchanged
40	Nov. 1980	Financial Reporting and Changing Prices: Specialized Assets—Timberlands and Growing Timber (a supplement to *FASB Statement 33*)	Unchanged
41	Nov. 1980	Financial Reporting and Changing Prices: Specialized Assets—Income-Producing Real Estate (a supplement to *FASB Statement 33*)	Unchanged
42	Nov. 1980	Determining Materiality for Capitalization of Interest Cost (an amendment for *FASB Statement 34*)	Unchanged
43	Nov. 1980	Accounting for Compensated Absences	Unchanged
44	Dec. 1980	Accounting for Intangible Assets of Motor Carriers (an amendment of Chapter 5 of *ARB 43* and an interpretation of *APB Opinions 17* and *30*)	Unchanged
45	Mar. 1981	Accounting for Franchise Fee Revenue	Unchanged
46	Mar. 1981	Financial Reporting and Changing Prices: Motion Picture Films	Unchanged
47	Mar. 1981	Disclosure of Long-Term Obligations	Unchanged
48	June 1981	Revenue Recognition When Right of Return Exists	Unchanged
49	June 1981	Accounting for Product Financing Arrangements	Unchanged
50	Nov. 1981	Financial Reporting in the Record and Music Industry	Unchanged
51	Nov. 1981	Financial Reporting by Cable Television Companies	Unchanged
52	Dec. 1981	Foreign Currency Translation	Interpreted
53	Dec. 1981	Financial Reporting by Producers and Distributors of Motion Picture Films	Unchanged
54	Jan. 1982	Financial Reporting and Changing Prices; Investment Companies	Unchanged
55	Feb. 1982	Determining Whether a Convertible Security Is a Common Stock Equivalent	Unchanged
56	Feb. 1982	Designation of AICPA Guide and SOP 81–1 on Contractor Accounting and SOP 81–2 on Hospital-Related Organizations as Preferable for applying *APB Opinion 20*	Unchanged
57	Mar. 1982	Related Party Disclosures	Unchanged
58	April 1982	Capitalization of Interest Cost in Financial Statements that Include Investments Accounted for by the Equity Method ...	Unchanged
59	April 1982	Deferral of the Effective Date of Certain Accounting Requirements for Revision Plans of State and Local Government Units	Unchanged
60	June 1982	Accounting and Reporting by Insurance Enterprises	Unchanged
61	June 1982	Accounting for Title Plant	Unchanged

Financial Accounting Standards Board (FASB), *Statements of Financial Accounting Standards* (1973–85) *(continued)*

FASB No.	Date issued	Title	Status to April 1, 1985
62	June 1982	Capitalization of Interest in Situations Involving Certain Tax-Exempt Borrowings and Certain Gifts and Grants	Unchanged
63	June 1982	Financial Reporting by Broadcasters	Unchanged
64	Sept. 1982	Extinguishment of Debt Made to Satisfy Sinking Fund Requirements	Unchanged
65	Sept. 1982	Accounting for Certain Mortgage Bank Activities	Unchanged
66	Oct. 1982	Accounting for Sales on Real Estate	Unchanged
67	Oct. 1982	Accounting for Costs and Initial Rental Operations of Real Estate Projects	Unchanged
68	Oct. 1982	Research and Development Arrangements	Unchanged
69	Nov. 1982	Disclosures about Oil and Gas Producing Activities (an amendment of *FASB Statements 19, 25, 33,* and *39*)	Unchanged
70	Dec. 1982	Financial Reporting and Changing Prices: Foreign Currency Translation (an amendment of *FASB Statement 33*)	Unchanged
71	Dec. 1982	Accounting for the Effects of Certain Types of Regulation . . .	Unchanged
72	Feb. 1983	Accounting for Certain Acquisitions of Banking or Thrift Institutions (an amendment of *APB Opinion 17,* an interpretation of *APB Opinions 16* and *17,* and an amendment of *FASB Interpretation 9*)	Unchanged
73	Aug. 1983	Reporting a Change in Accounting for Railroad Track Structures (an amendment of *APB Opinion 20*)	Unchanged
74	Aug. 1983	Accounting for Special Termination Benefits Paid to Employees	Unchanged
75	Nov. 1983	Deferral of the Effective Date of Certain Accounting Requirements for Pension Plans of State and Local Governmental Units (an amendment of *FASB Statement 35*)	Unchanged
76	Nov. 1983	Extinguishment of Debt (an amendment of *APB Opinion 26*)	Unchanged
77	Dec. 1983	Reporting by Transferors for Transfers of Receivables with Recourse	Unchanged
78	Dec. 1983	Classification of Obligations that Are Callable by the Creditor (an amendment of *ARB 43,* Chapter 3A)	Unchanged
79	Feb. 1984	Elimination of Certain Disclosures for Business Combinations by Nonpublic Enterprises (an amendment of *APB Opinion 16*)	Unchanged
80	Aug. 1984	Accounting for Futures Contracts	Unchanged
81	Nov. 1984	Disclosure of Postretirement Health Care and Life Insurance Benefits	Unchanged
82	Nov. 1984	Financial Reporting and Changing Prices: Elimination of Certain Disclosures (an amendment of *FASB Statement 33*)	Unchanged
83	Mar. 1985	Designation of AICPA Guides and Statement of Position on Accounting by Brokers and Dealers in Securities, by Employee Benefit Plans, and by Banks as Preferable for Purposes of Applying *APB Opinion 20* (an amendment of *FASB Statement 32* and *APB Opinion 30* and a recission of *FASB Interpretation 10*)	Unchanged

Financial Accounting Standards Board (FASB), *Statements of Financial Accounting Standards* **(1973–85) (continued)**

FASB No.	Date issued	Title	Status to April 1, 1985
84	Mar. 1985	Induced Conversions of Convertible Debt (an amendment of *APB Opinion 26*)	Unchanged
85	Mar. 1985	Yield Test for Determining whether a Convertible Security is a Common Stock Equivalent (an amendment of *APB Opinion 15*)	Unchanged
86	Aug. 1985	Accounting for the Costs of Computer Software to be Sold, Leased, or Otherwise Marketed	Unchanged
87	Dec. 1985	Employers' Accounting for Pensions	Unchanged
88	Dec. 1985	Employers' Accounting for Settlements and Curtailments of Defined Benefit Pension Plans and for Termination Benefits	Unchanged

Financial Accounting Standards Board (FASB) *Interpretations* **(1974–85)**

FASB No.	Date issued	Title	With reference to
1	June 1974	Accounting Changes Related to the Cost of Inventory	*APB Opinion 20*
2	June 1974	Imputing Interest on Debt Arrangements Made under the Federal Bankruptcy Act	Superseded
3	Dec. 1974	Accounting for the Cost of Pension Plans Subject to the Employment Retirement Income Security Act of 1974	*APB Opinion 8*
4	Feb. 1975	Applicability of *FASB Statement 2* to Business Combinations Accounted for by the Purchase Method	*FASB Statement 2*
5	Feb. 1975	Applicability of *FASB Statement 2* to Development Stage Enterprises	*FASB Statement 2*
6	Feb. 1975	Applicability of *FASB Statement 2* to Computer Software	*FASB Statement 2*
7	Oct. 1975	Applying *FASB Statement 7* in Financial Statements of Established Operating Enterprises	*FASB Statement 7*
8	Jan. 1976	Classification of a Short-Term Obligation Repaid Prior to Being Replaced by a Long-Term Security	*FASB Statement 6*
9	Feb. 1976	Applying *APB Opinions 16* and *17* When a Savings and Loan Association or a Similar Institution Is Acquired in a Business Combination Accounted for by the Purchase Method	*APB Opinions 16* and *17*
10	Sept. 1976	Application of *FASB Statement 12* to Personal Financial Statements	*FASB Statement 12*
11	Sept. 1976	Changes in Market Value after the Balance Sheet Date	*FASB Statement 12*
12	Sept. 1976	Accounting for Previously Established Allowance Accounts	*FASB Statement 12*
13	Sept. 1976	Consolidation of a Parent and its Subsidiaries having Different Balance Sheet Dates	*FASB Statement 12*
14	Sept. 1976	Reasonable Estimation of the Amount of a Loss	*FASB Statement 5*
15	Sept. 1976	Translation of Unamortized Policy Acquisition Costs by a Stock Life Insurance Company	*FASB Statement 8*
16	Feb. 1977	Clarification of Definitions and Accounting for Marketable Equity Securities That Become Nonmarketable	*FASB Statement 12*

Financial Accounting Standards Board (FASB) *Interpretations* **(1974–85)** *(continued)*

FASB No.	Date issued	Title	With reference to
17	Feb. 1977	Applying the Lower of Cost or Market Rule in Translated Financial Statements	*FASB Statement 8*
18	Mar. 1977	Accounting for Income Taxes in Interim Periods	*APB Opinion 28*
19	Oct. 1977	Lessee Guarantee of the Residual Value of Leased Property	*FASB Statement 13*
20	Nov. 1977	Reporting Accounting Changes under AICPA Statements of Position	*APB Opinion 20*
21	Apr. 1978	Accounting for Leases in a Business Combination	*FASB Statement 13*
22	Apr. 1978	Applicability of Indefinite Reversal Criteria to Timing Differences	*APB Opinions 11 and 23*
23	Aug. 1978	Leases of Certain Property Owned by a Governmental Unit or Authority	*FASB Statement 13*
24	Sept. 1978	Leases Involving Only Part of a Building	*FASB Statement 13*
25	Sept. 1978	Accounting for an Unused Investment Tax Credit	*APB Opinions 2, 4, 11, and 16*
26	Sept. 1978	Accounting for Purchase of a Leased Asset by the Lessee during the Term of the Lease	*FASB Statement 13*
27	Nov. 1978	Accounting for Loss on a Sublease	*FASB Statement 13 and APB Opinion 30*
28	Dec. 1978	Accounting for Stock Appreciation Rights and Other Variable Stock Option or Award Plans	*APB Opinions 15 and 25*
29	Feb. 1979	Reporting Tax Benefits Realized on Disposition of Investments in Certain Subsidiaries and Other Investees	*APB Opinions 23 and 24*
30	Sept. 1979	Accounting for Involuntary Conversions of Nonmonetary Assets to Monetary Assets	*APB Opinion 29*
31	Feb. 1980	Treatment of Stock Compensation Plans in EPS Computations	*APB Opinion 15 and FASB Interpretation 28*
32	Mar. 1980	Application of Percentage Limitations in Recognizing Investment Tax Credit	*APB Opinions 2, 4, and 11*
33	Aug. 1980	Applying *FASB Statement 34* to Oil and Gas Producing Operations Accounted for by the Full Cost Method	*FASB Statement 34*
34	Mar. 1981	Disclosure of Indirect Guarantees of Indebtedness of Others . . .	*FASB Statement 5*
35	May 1981	Criteria for Applying the Equity Method of Accounting for Investments in Common Stock	*APB Opinion 18*
36	Oct. 1981	Accounting for Exploration Wells in Progress at the End of a Period	*FASB Statement 19*
37	July 1983	Accounting for Translation Adjustments upon Sale of Part of an Investment in a Foreign Entity	*FASB Statement 52*
38	Aug. 1984	Determining the Measurement Date for Stock Options, Purchase, and Award Plans Involving Junior Stock	*APB Opinion 25*

Financial Accounting Standards Board (FASB) *Technical Bulletins* (1979–85)

FASB No.	Date issued	Title	With reference to
79–1	Dec. 1979	Purpose and Scope of FASB Technical Bulletins and Procedures for Issuance—To provide guidance concerning the application of official pronouncements of the FASB, APB, and ARBs	Revised June 1984
79–2	Dec. 1979	Computer Software Costs	*FASB Statement 2* and *FASB Interpretation 6*
79–3	Dec. 1979	Subjective Acceleration Clauses in Long-Term Debt Agreements	*FASB Statement 6*
79–4	Dec. 1979	Segment Reporting of Puerto Rican Operations	*FASB Statement 14*
79–5	Dec. 1979	Meaning of the Term "Customer" as It Applies to Health Care Facilities	*FASB Statement 14*
79–6	Dec. 1979	Valuation Allowances Following Debt Restructure	*FASB Statement 15*
79–7	Dec. 1979	Recoveries of a Previous Writedown under a Troubled Debt Restructuring Involving a Modification of Terms	*FASB Statement 15*
79–8	Dec. 1979	Applicability of *FASB Statements 21* and *33* to Certain Brokers and Dealers in Securities	*FASB Statement 21*
79–9	Dec. 1979	Accounting in Interim Periods for Changes in Income Tax Rates	*FASB Interpretation 18*
79–10	Dec. 1979	Fiscal Funding Clauses in Lease Agreements	*FASB Statement 13*
79–11	Dec. 1979	Effect of a Penalty on the Term of a Lease	*FASB Statement 13*
79–12	Dec. 1979	Interest Rate Used in Calculating the Present Value of Minimum Lease Payments	*FASB Statement 13*
79–13	Dec. 1979	Applicability of *FASB Statement 13* to Current Value Financial Statements	*FASB Statement 13*
79–14	Dec. 1979	Upward Adjustment of Guaranteed Residual Values	*FASB Statement 13*
79–15	Dec. 1979	Accounting for Loss on a Sublease Not Involving the Disposal of a Segment	*FASB Statement 13* and *FASB Interpretation 27*
79–16	Dec. 1979	Effect of a Change in Income Tax Rate on the Accounting for Leveraged Leases	*FASB Statement 13*
79–17	Dec. 1979	Reporting Cumulative Effect Adjustment from Retroactive Application of *FASB Statement 13*	*FASB Statement 13*
79–18	Dec. 1979	Transition Requirement of Certain FASB Amendments and Interpretations of *FASB Statement 13*	*FASB Statements 17, 22, 23, 26, 27, 28,* and *29;* and *FASB Interpretations 19, 21, 23, 24, 26* and *27,* (all related to *FASB Statement 13*)
79–19	Dec. 1979	Investor's Accounting for Unrealized Losses on Marketable Securities Owned by an Equity Method Investee	*FASB Statement 12* and *APB Opinion 18*

Financial Accounting Standards Board (FASB) *Technical Bulletins* **(1979–85)** *(continued)*

FASB No.	Date issued	Title	With reference to
80–1	Dec. 1980	Early Extinguishment of Debt through Exchange for Common or Preferred Stock	*APB Opinion 26, FASB Statement 4,* and *FASB Statement 15*
81–1	Feb. 1981	Disclosure of Interest Rate Futures Contracts and Forward and Standby Contracts	*APB Opinion 22*
81–2	Feb. 1981	Accounting for Unused Investment Tax Credits Acquired in a Business Combination Accounted for by the Purchase Method	*FASB Statement 38* and *FASB Interpretation 25*
81–3	Feb. 1981	Multiemployer Pension Plan Amendments Act of 1980	*APB Opinion 8, FASB Interpretation 3,* and *FASB Statement 36*
81–4	Feb. 1981	Classification as Monetary or Nonmonetary Items	*FASB Statement 33*
81–5	Feb. 1981	Offsetting Interest Cost to Be Capitalized with Interest Income	*FASB Statement 34*
81–6	Nov. 1981	Applicability of *FASB Statement 15* to Debtors in Bankruptcy Situations	*FASB Statement 35*
82–1	Jan. 1982	Disclosure of the Sale or Purchase of Tax Benefits through Tax Leases	*ARB 43,* Ch. 2A par. 36; *APB Opinion 11,* par. 63; *APB Opinion 22; APB Opinion 30;* and *FASB Statement 5*
82–2	Mar. 1982	Accounting for the Conversion of Stock Options into Stock Incentive Plans as a Result of the Economic Recovery Tax Act of 1981	*ARB 43,* Ch. 13B; *APB Opinion 25;* and *FASB Interpretation 2*
83–1	July 1983	Accounting for the Reduction in the Tax Basis of an Asset Caused by the Investment Tax Credit	*APB Opinion 11; AICPA Accounting Interpretation 8, Permanent Differences of APB Opinion 11*
84–1	Mar. 1984	Accounting for Stock Issued to Acquire the Results of a Research and Development Arrangement	*FASB Statement 68* (pars. 11, 13, and 20); *APB Opinion 16* (par. 67)

Financial Accounting Standards Board (FASB) *Technical Bulletins* (1979–85) *(continued)*

FASB No.	Date issued	Title	With reference to
84–2	Sept. 1984	Accounting for the Effects of the Tax Reform Act of 1984 on Deferred Income Taxes Relating to Domestic International Sales Corporations	*APB Opinions 11, 23, and 30; FASB Statement 16*
84–3	Sept. 1984	Accounting for the Effects of the Tax Reform Act of 1984 on Deferred Income Taxes for Life Insurance Enterprises	*APB Opinions 11 and 30; FASB Statements 16 and 60*
84–4	Oct. 1984	In-Substance Defeasance of Debt	*FASB Statement 76*
85–1	Mar. 1985	Accounting for the Receipt of Federal Home Loan Mortgage Participating Preferred Stock	*ARB 43, chap. 7; APB Opinion 29; APB Opinion 30; FASB Statement 12; FASB Concepts 3*
85–2	Mar. 1985	Accounting for Collateralized Mortgage Obligations (CMOs)	*ARB 51; APB Opinion 10; FASB Statements 57, 65, 76, and 77; FASB Technical Bulletin 84–4*
85–3	Nov. 1985	Accounting for Operating Leases with Scheduled Rent Increases	*FASB Statements 13 and 29*
85–4	Nov. 1985	Accounting for Purchases of Life Insurance	*FASB Concepts No. 3*
85–5	Dec. 1985	Issues Relating to Business Combinations	*APB Opinion 6*
85–6	Dec. 1985	Accounting for Purchases of Treasury Stock	*FASB Concepts No. 6; APB Opinions 6, 16, 21, 25, 26, and 30; ARB 43, Chap. 1B*

SUPPLEMENT 1–B: ORGANIZATIONS ACTIVELY INVOLVED IN SETTING ACCOUNTING STANDARDS

American Accounting Association (AAA)
5717 Bessie Drive
Sarasota, Florida 33583

American Institute of Certified Public Accountants (AICPA)
1211 Avenue of the Americas
New York, New York 10036

Association of Government Accountants (AGA)
727 23rd Street
Arlington, Virginia 22202

Financial Accounting Standards Board (FASB)
High Ridge Park
Stamford, Connecticut 06905

Financial Executives Institute (FEI)
10 Madison Avenue
Box 1938
Morristown, New Jersey 07960

Governmental Accounting Standards Board (GASB)
High Ridge Park
Stamford, Connecticut 06905

Institute of Internal Auditors (IIA)
Altamonte Centre
249 Maitland Avenue
Altamonte Springs, Florida 32701

International Accounting Standards Committee
American Institute of Certified Public Accountants
1211 Avenue of the Americas
New York, New York 10036

Institute of Management Accounting (IMA)
570 City Center Building
Ann Arbor, Michigan 48104

National Association of Accountants (NAA)
919 Third Avenue
New York, New York 10022

Securities and Exchange Commission (SEC)
Office of the Chief Accountant
Washington, D.C. 20549

QUESTIONS

PART A

1. Define accounting.
2. Explain the distinction between financial and management accounting. Does this distinction mean that a company should have two accounting systems? Explain.
3. What is meant by general-purpose financial statements? What are their basic components?

4. What is the basic objective of external financial statements?

5. Explain why the emphasis in financial accounting is on measurement and communication.

6. What are the primary areas of service provided by certified public accountants (CPAs)?

7. The independent CPA fulfills a unique professional role that involves the concept of independence. Why is that concept important to society in general?

8. The following statements relate to accounting principles, standards, and procedures. For each, you are to briefly explain its primary purpose and current status.

   a. *Accounting Research Bulletins.*
   b. *Opinions* of the APB.
   c. *FASB Statements of Financial Accounting Standards.*
   d. *FASB Interpretations.*
   e. *FASB Statements of Financial Accounting Concepts.*

9. Explain the developments that led to the establishment of the FASB.

10. Briefly explain the role that the SEC has fulfilled in the establishment of accounting standards. What has been its relationship to the accounting profession in this role?

11. What is the AAA? What role has it fulfilled in the development of accounting theory and standards?

12. Is an approach that is permitted for income tax purposes necessarily "generally accepted" for financial accounting purposes? Explain.

13. Explain why there is widespread interest in the development of accounting standards.

14. Briefly explain the "due process" system that is used by the FASB to develop an accounting standard.

15. Why is a consensus important with respect to accounting standards? How is a consensus attained at the present time?

PART B

16. What are the basic objectives of external financial reporting?

17. Identify and briefly explain the primary qualities of accounting information.

18. What is the secondary quality of accounting information? Briefly explain what it means.

19. Explain the difference between a revenue and a gain.

20. Explain the difference between an expense and a loss.

21. Explain the four basic assumptions that underlie implementation of accounting.

22. What is the basic accounting problem created by the unit-of-measure assumption when there is significant inflation?

23. Explain why the time period assumption causes accruals and deferrals in accounting.

24. Relate the continuity assumption to periodicity of financial statements.

25. Which assumption or principle discussed in this chapter is most affected by the phenomenon of inflation? Give reasons for your choice.

26. Relate the continuity assumption to use of the accrual basis of accounting.

27. Explain the cost principle. Why is it used in the basic financial statements in preference to a current value model?

28. How is cost measured in noncash transactions?

29. Define the revenue principle and explain each of its three aspects: *(a)* definition, *(b)* measurement, and *(c)* realization.

30. How is revenue measured in transactions involving noncash items (exclude credit situations)?

31. Explain the matching principle. What is meant by "the expense should follow the revenue"?
32. Explain why the matching principle usually necessitates the use of adjusting entries. Use depreciation expense and unpaid wages as examples.
33. Relate the matching principle to the revenue and cost principles.
34. Briefly explain the continuity assumption.
35. Briefly explain the technical term *generally accepted accounting principles* (GAAP) as used by the accounting profession.
36. What accounting principle or assumption is manifested in each situation below?

   a. Prepayment for an annual license is ratably debited to expense over the next 12 months.
   b. Jerry Jenkins owns a shoe repair shop, a restaurant, and a service station. Different and independent statements are prepared for each business.
   c. Inventories at King Store are valued at lower of cost or market (LCM).
   d. Although the inflation rate for the most recent fiscal year of Clyde's Auto Dealership was 9%, no cognizance was taken of it in the year-end statements.
   e. While making a delivery, the driver for Cross Appliance Store collided with another vehicle causing both property damage and personal injury. The party sued Cross for damages that could exceed Cross's insurance coverage. Existence of the suit was disclosed on Cross's most recent financial statements.

EXERCISES

PART A: EXERCISES 1–1 TO 1–3

Exercise 1–1

The two basic types of accounting and reporting are called: A—Financial accounting and B—Management accounting. Below are listed 10 characteristics of accounting and reporting. Match the types with the characteristics by entering an A or B in each blank shown to the left. If not applicable enter N.

Type	Characteristics of accounting and reporting
F	1. GAAP must be followed in all respects.
A	2. External users are of primary concern.
M	3. Relates to planning and controlling the operations of an entity.
N	4. Uses cash basis accounting exclusively.
	5. Information for both internal and external use.
F	6. Of particular interest to investors and creditors.
M	7. Does not have to conform to GAAP.
F	8. Provides information that is useful in predicting future cash flows.
M	9. Internal users are of primary concern.
	10. Seldom, if ever, subject to independent audit.
F	11. Must use accrual basis accounting in all respects.
M	12. Information primarily for internal use.
M	13. Usually not available to external users.
F	14. General-purpose financial statements.
M	15. Users have direct access to the internal operations.

Exercise 1–2

Indicate whether each statement is true or false.

T (F) 1. GAAP must be followed for all items in management accounting and financial accounting reports.

(T) F 2. Financial accounting focuses primarily on external users of financial statements.

T (F) 3. General-purpose financial statements are prepared primarily for internal users.

T (F) 4. Management accounting is directly concerned with stockholders and creditors.

T (F) 5. Management accounting reports usually are not subject to an independent audit.

T (F) 6. A CPA always serves in an independent role.

T F 7. CPAs in public accounting practice are not permitted to become involved in management services.

T F 8. The attest and audit functions are the same.

T F 9. Disclosure notes are considered to be an integral part of external financial statements.

T F 10. Management accounting reporting requires a balance sheet, income statement, and a statement of changes in financial position.

T F 11. Internal reporting (i.e., management accounting) must use the accrual basis in all respects.

T F 12. External financial reports (i.e., financial accounting) are directed primarily to stockholders, creditors, and other similarly situated groups.

Exercise 1–3

Listed below are the organizations that are active in setting accounting standards and the designation of some of those standards. To the right are commonly used abbreviations. You are to match the designations with the abbreviations by entering the appropriate letters to the left.

Designation	Abbreviation
_A_ Sample: Certified Public Accountant.	A. CPA.
_H_ 1. Accounting Research Bulletin.	B. FASB.
_G_ 2. Accounting Principles Board.	C. GAAP.
_E_ 3. Committee on Accounting Procedures.	D. AICPA.
_J_ 4. Securities and Exchange Commission.	E. CAP.
_B_ 5. Financial Accounting Standards Board.	F. 10-Q report.
_K_ 6. SEC annual reports (required).	G. APB.
_N_ 7. Cost Accounting Standards Board.	H. ARB.
_D_ 8. American Institute of CPAs.	I. AcSEC.
_F_ 9. SEC quarterly report (required).	J. SEC.
_L_ 10. Financial Executives Institute.	K. 10-K report.
_C_ 11. Generally accepted accounting principles.	L. FEI.
_I_ 12. Accounting Standards Executive Committee.	M. IRS.
_M_ 13. Internal Revenue Service.	N. CASB.
_P_ 14. National Association of Accountants.	O. SCFP.
_O_ 15. Statement of changes in financial position.	P. NAA.

PART B: EXERCISES 1–4 TO 1–11

Exercise 1–4

The *FASB Statements of Accounting Concepts* are as follows:

No.	Title
1.	Objectives of Financial Reporting by Business Enterprises
2.	Qualitative Characteristics of Accounting Information
3.	Elements of Financial Statements of Business Enterprises
5.	Recognition and Measurement in Financial Statements of Business Enterprises

Listed below are primary topics of the above *Statements*. You are to match the topics with the *Statements* by entering the appropriate *Statement* numbers in the blanks to the left.

No.	Primary topics
1	Example: Defines statement users.
_____	*a.* Recognition criteria.
_____	*b.* Defines assets, liabilities, and owners' equity.
_____	*c.* Theshold recognition.
_____	*d.* Quality constraint.
_____	*e.* Reliability.
_____	*f.* Objectives of financial reporting.
_____	*g.* Consistency.
_____	*h.* Comparability.
_____	*i.* Financial statements (described).
_____	*j.* Revenues and expenses (defined).
_____	*k.* Relevance.
_____	*l.* Comprehensive income (defined).
_____	*m.* Cost-benefit.
_____	*n.* Primary qualities of accounting information.
_____	*o.* Guidance in applying recognition criteria.
_____	*p.* Accrual accounting.
_____	*q.* Materiality.
_____	*r.* Gains and losses (defined).
_____	*s.* Investments and distributions by owners (defined).
_____	*t.* Secondary quality of accounting information.

Exercise 1–5

The *FASB Concepts Statement 2* identifies the following "Hierarchy levels of qualitative characteristics of accounting" (lettered for response purposes):

Hierarchy levels

A. Purpose of accounting information.
B. Primary qualities.
C. Ingredients of the primary qualities.
D. Secondary quality.
E. Threshold for recognition.
F. Utility constraint.
G. None of the above is correct.

Listed below are the individual qualitative characteristics that relate to the hierarchy levels. You are to match these characteristics with the hierarchy levels by entering the appropriate letters in the blanks to the left.

Qualitative characteristics

_D_ 1. Comparability. *Secondary*
_B_ 2. Relevance. *Primary*
_C_ 3. Feedback value.
_G_ 4. Accrual basis accounting. *N o A*
_C_ 5. Timeliness.
_E_ 6. Cost-benefit. *+ utility*
_D_ 7. Includes consistency.
_C_ 8. Verifiability.
_E_ 9. Materiality.
_C_ 10. Representational faithfulness.
_B_ 11. Reliability.
_C_ 12. Predictive value.
_G_ 13. Cost principle.
_C_ 14. Neutrality.
_A_ 15. Decision usefulness.

Exercise 1–6

FASB Concepts Statement 1 sets forth relevance and reliability as the primary qualitative characteristics of accounting information. Each primary quality has three "ingredients." This conceptual framework is listed below. You are to provide a brief definition of each hierarchy level listed by using the following format.

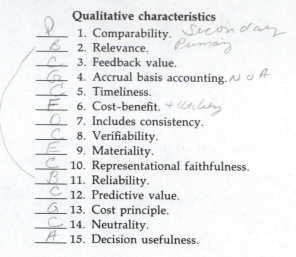

Hierarchy level	Brief definition
A. Relevance.	*Capacity to influence decisions*
1. Timeliness.	*in time to influence decisions*
2. Predictive value.	*has high value to influence decision*
3. Feedback value.	*compare with prior expectations*
B. Reliability.	*free from errors, bias, believable*
1. Representational faithfulness.	*reports what it purports to report*
2. Verifiability.	*can be verified (by audits)*
3. Neutrality.	*free from bias*

Exercise 1–7

FASB Concepts Statement 3 defines the elements of financial statements listed to the left below. To the right, some primary distinctions in the definitions are listed. You are to match the distinctions with the elements by entering appropriate letters in the blanks. More than one letter can be placed in a blank.

Elements of financial statements		Primary distinctions in the definition
A. Revenues.	_G_	1. Residual interest in the assets after deducting liabilities.
B. Expenses.	___	2. Decreases ownership interests.
C. Gains.	_A/B_	3. Constitute the entity's ongoing major or central operations.

**Elements of
financial statements**

D. Losses.
E. Assets.
F. Liabilities.
G. Owners' equity. ✓
H. Investments by owners.
I. Distributions to owners.
J. Comprehensive income.
K. None of the above.

**Primary distinctions
in the definition**

___J___ 4. All changes in equity except investments by, and distributions to, owners.
___E___ 5. Probable future economic benefits obtained by an entity.
___B___ 6. Using up of assets or incurrence of liabilities.
_____ 7. Cash dividends declared and paid.
___A___ 8. Enhancement of assets or settlements of liabilities.
__C&D__ 9. From peripheral or incidental transactions of the entity.
___F___ 10. Probable future sacrifices arising from present obligations.
___K___ 11. Issuance of a stock dividend.
___C___ 12. Increases in equity from peripheral or incidental activities.
___H___ 13. Increases in net assets for an ownership interest.
___I___ 14. Decreases in net assets by transferring assets to entity owners.
___I___ 15. Purchase of treasury stock.
___C___ 16. Sold operational assets above book value.
___H___ 17. Sold treasury stock.

Exercise 1–8

Listed below are the implementation assumptions, principles, and constraints, lettered for response purposes.

Assumptions, principles, and constraints

A. Separate entity assumption.
B. Continuity assumption.
C. Unit-of-measure assumption.
D. Time period assumption.
E. Cost principle.
F. Revenue principle.
G. Matching principle.
H. Full-disclosure principle.
I. Cost-benefit constraint.
J. Materiality (recognition threshold).
K. Industry peculiarities.
L. Conservatism.

Below is a list of key phrases directly related to the above list. You are to match these phrases with the above list by entering the appropriate letters to the left.

Key phrase

___F___ 1. Criteria—definition, measurability, relevance, and reliability.
___L___ 2. Least favorable effect on income and/or total assets.
___C___ 3. Common denominator—the meterstick.
___G___ 4. Expenses incurred in earning the period's revenues.
___I___ 5. Preparation cost versus value of benefit to the user.
___A___ 6. Separate and apart from its owners and other entities.
___H___ 7. Report all relevant information.
___D___ 8. Reporting periods—usually one year.
___E___ 9. Cash-equivalent expenditures to acquire.
___B___ 10. Going-concern basis.

Key phrase

___)___ 11. Relative amount of an item that would not have changed or influenced the judgment of a reasonable person.

___K___ 12. Exception to accounting principles and practices because of uniqueness of the entity.

Exercise 1–9

Indicate whether each statement is true or false.

_____ 1. The users of financial statements that are recognized in the *FASB Concepts Statements* are limited to owners and creditors.

_____ 2. Materiality is identified as the threshold for recognition.

_____ 3. Comparability (including consistency) is a primary quality of accounting information.

_____ 4. Neutrality in accounting information means that it is not biased either in favor of a particular party nor is it consistently too high or too low.

_____ 5. Comparability and consistency are defined in the same way (as qualitative characteristics of accounting information).

_____ 6. The declaration and issuance of a stock dividend is an element on the financial statements called distributions to owners.

_____ 7. Both gains and losses relate to peripheral or incidental transactions of the entity.

_____ 8. Comprehensive income includes investments by and distributions to owners.

_____ 9. All items (resulting from a transaction) must be recognized if they meet the definition of a financial statement item.

_____ 10. The matching principle is completely independent of the cost principle.

Exercise 1–10

The following summarized data were taken from the records of Moby Company at December 31, 19B, end of the accounting year:

a. Sales: 19B cash sales, $150,000; and 19B credit sales, $110,000.

b. Cash collections during 19B: on 19A credit sales, $30,000; on 19B credit sales, $80,000; and on 19C sales (collected in advance), $20,000.

c. Expenses: 19B cash expenses, $180,000; and 19B credit expenses, $70,000.

d. Cash payments during 19B: for 19A credit expenses, $10,000; for 19B credit expenses, $40,000; and for 19C expenses (paid in advance), $7,000.

Required:

1. Complete the following statements for 19B as a basis for evaluating the difference between cash and accrual accounting.

	Cash basis	Accrual basis
Sales revenue	$_____	$_____
Expenses	_____	_____
Net income	_____	_____

2. Which basis is in conformity with GAAP? Explain the basis for your answer.

Exercise 1–11

XV Corporation was organized on January 1, 1945, at which time it acquired an office building that cost $320,000. The building is being depreciated straight line over a 50-year estimated useful life (no residual value). It is 1985, and the company's sales revenue amounted to $980,000. The general price level at the beginning of 1945 was 100, and at the end of 1985 it is 300.

Required:
1. Complete the following for 1985:

Sales revenue .... $_____
Depreciation expense .... $_____

2. Considering the implementation assumptions, principles, and constraints, list the four most directly involved with the amounts in Requirement 1, and explain why each is important.
3. Identify and explain any measurement problem in this situation related to the change in the general price level.

PROBLEMS

PART A: PROBLEMS 1–1 TO 1–2

Problem 1–1

The accounting profession has a long history of developing accounting concepts and their application that constitute generally accepted accounting principles (GAAP). Listed below are some representative documents. You are to identify each document with its source by entering appropriate letters to the left.

	Document	**Source**
B	1. Accounting Research Bulletins (ARBs).	A. Accounting Principles Board.
D	2. Interpretations (of Financial Accounting Standards).	B. AICPA Committee on Accounting Procedures.
D	3. Discussion Memoranda.	C. Securities and Exchange Commission.
E	4. Statement of Basic Accounting Theory.	
D	5. Technical Bulletins.	D. Financial Accounting Standards Board.
G	6. Accounting Terminology Bulletins.	E. American Accounting Association.
D	7. Statements of Financial Accounting Standards.	F. American Institute of Certified Public Accountants.
C	8. Regulation SX.	G. AICPA Committee on Terminology.
D	9. Statements of Financial Accounting Concepts.	
B	10. Accounting Research Studies.	

Document   **Source**

_C_ 11. Accounting Series Releases (ASRs).

_A_ 12. Opinions.

_E_ 13. Accounting and Reporting
        Standards for Corporate Fi-
        nancial Statements.

_F_ 14. Rules of Ethics; 203, Ac-
        counting Principles.

_E_ 15. Statement on Accounting
        Theory and Theory Acceptance.

Problem 1–2

The process of attaining a consensus in developing accounting standards involves three major groups, each of which is directly concerned about general-purpose financial statements. Each major group is composed of various subgroups (i.e., organizations, interest groups, and individuals).

The three major groups and some subgroups are listed below. You are to identify the subgroups with the major groups by entering appropriate letters to the left; provide comments when needed to clarify your response.

Subgroups	**Major groups**
_____ 1. American Institute of CPAs.	A. Preparers.
_____ 2. Current stockholder.	B. Auditors.
_____ 3. General Motors.	C. Users.
_____ 4. WTK Labor Union.	D. None of the above
_____ 5. Financial Executives Institute.	(explain).
_____ 6. X, Y, Z, Big-8 accounting firm.	
_____ 7. Lending institutions.	
_____ 8. Securities and Exchange Commission.	
_____ 9. OK Bookkeeping Service.	
_____ 10. Financial analysts.	
_____ 11. Sole owner of a small business.	
_____ 12. American Accounting Association.	
_____ 13. State Board of Public Accountancy.	
_____ 14. Potential investors.	
_____ 15. Financial Analysts Federation.	
_____ 16. Employees of companies.	
_____ 17. Teachers and students.	
_____ 18. Taxing and regulatory authorities.	
_____ 19. Legislators.	
_____ 20. Two-member local CPA firm.	

PART B: PROBLEMS 1–3 TO 1–8

Problem 1–3

During an audit of Carlin Company, the situations given below were found to exist. For each situation you are to (a) identify and briefly explain the qualitative characteristic of accounting information that is directly involved in each situation, and (b) indicate what the company should do in the future by way of any change in policy.

Situation A:

The company recorded a $19.98 pencil sharpener as expense when purchased, although it had a three-year estimated life and no residual value.

Situation B:

For inventory purposes, the company switched from FIFO to LIFO to FIFO during a five-year period.

Situation C:

The company recognizes earnings on long-term construction contracts at the end of each year of the construction period (based on estimates), while major competitors recognize earnings only at the date the contract is completed (based on actual results).

Situation D:

The company follows a policy of depreciating plant and equipment on the straight-line basis over a period of time that is 50% longer than the reliably estimated useful life.

Situation E:

As an accounting policy, interest expense is reported at the end of each reporting period as the amount of interest expense less interest revenue.

Problem 1–4

A list of statements given below poses conceptual issues. For each statement (a) indicate whether it is correct or incorrect; (b) identify the implementation assumption, principle, or constraint that is controlling; and (c) provide a brief discussion of its implications.

1. The accounting entity is considered to be separate and apart from the owners.
2. A transaction involving a very small amount does not need to be recorded because of materiality.
3. The monetary unit is not stable over time.
4. GAAP always requires supplementary notes to the financial statements.
5. GAAP requires that LCM often be used in valuing inventories.
6. The cost principle relates only to the income statement.
7. Revenue should be recognized only when the cash is received.
8. Accruals and deferrals are necessary because of the separate entity assumption.
9. Revenue should be recognized as early as possible and expenses as late as possible.
10. Relevance and reliability dominate all of the qualitative characteristics of accounting information.

Problem 1–5

Bad Luck Corporation was experiencing a bad year because it was operating at a loss. To minimize the loss, the company recorded certain transactions as indicated below. Determine for each transaction what accounting principle was violated (if any) and explain the nature of the violation.

a. At the beginning of the year, a new machine was purchased for $80,000 cash for use in the business. The estimated useful life was 10 years, and the estimated residual value was $10,000. The following depreciation entry was made at the end of the reporting period:

Depreciation expense 3,500
    Accumulated depreciation 3,500

b. A patent was being amortized over a 17-year useful life. The amortization entry at the end of the current year was:

Retained earnings	500	
Patent		500

c. Two delivery trucks were repaired (engine tuneup, new tires, brakes relined, front end realigned) at a cost of $2,300. The follow entry was made:

Operational asset—trucks	2,300	
Cash		2,300

d. Although the bad debt loss rate did not change, an adjusting entry was not made for the estimate of $2,000.

e. Goods for resale (inventory) were being purchased at $1 per unit. However, the company located a good deal and acquired 10,000 units for $7,500 cash. They recorded the purchase as follows:

Inventory	10,000	
Cash		7,500
Revenue		2,500

f. The company sold its long-term investment in the capital stock of another company for $32,000 cash. The book value of the investment when sold was $20,000. The company made the following entry:

Cash	32,000	
Sales revenue		32,000

Problem 1–6

An inspection of the annual financial statements and the accounting records revealed that the company had violated some implementation assumptions, principles, and constraints. The following transactions were involved:

a. Merchandise purchased for resale was recorded as a debit to Inventory for the invoice price of $10,000 (Accounts Payable was credited for the same amount), terms were 2/10, n/30. Ten days later the account was paid (Cash was credited for $9,800).

b. Accounts receivable of $60,000 was reported on the balance sheet; this amount included a $20,000 loan to the company president that was indefinite about the maturity date.

c. Usual and ordinary repairs on operational assets were recorded as follows: debit Operational Assets, $12,000; credit Cash, $12,000.

d. The company sustained a $20,000 storm damage loss during the current year (no insurance). The loss was recorded and reported as follows:

Income statement: Extraordinary item—storm loss, $2,000.
Balance sheet (assets): Deferred charge, storm loss, $18,000.

e. Treasury stock (i.e., stock of the company that was sold and subsequently bought back from the shareholders) was properly debited to Treasury Stock and was reported on the balance sheet as an asset at the purchase cost, $18,000.

f. Depreciation expense of $41,000 was recorded as a debit to Retained Earnings and was deducted directly from retained earnings on the balance sheet.

g. Income tax expense of $48,000 was recorded as a debit to Retained Earnings and was deducted directly from retained earnings on the balance sheet.

Required:

For each transaction identify *(a)* the inappropriate treatment and *(b)* the assumptions, principles, and constraints violated. Also, give the entry that should have been made and the appropriate reporting.

Problem 1–7

The transactions summarized below were recorded as indicated during the current year. Determine for each transaction what implementation accounting principle was violated (if any) and explain the nature of the violation. Also in each instance indicate how the transaction should have been recorded.

a. The company needed a small structure for temporary storage. A contractor quoted a price of $650,000. The company decided to build it themselves. The cost was $550,000, and construction required three months. The following entry was made:

Operational assets—warehouse	650,000	
Cash		550,000
Revenue		100,000

b. The company owns a plant that is located on a river that floods every few years. As a result, the company suffers a flood loss regularly. During the current year, the flood was severe causing an uninsured loss of $12,000, which was the amount spent to repair the flood damage. The following entry was made:

Retained earnings, flood loss	12,000	
Cash		12,000

c. The company originally sold and issued 50,000 shares of $10 par value common stock. During the current year, 45,000 of these shares were outstanding and 5,000 were held by the company as treasury stock (they had been repurchased from the shareholders in prior years). Near the end of the current year, the board of directors declared and paid a cash dividend of $2 per share. The dividend was recorded as follows:

Retained earnings	100,000	
Cash		90,000
Investment income		10,000

d. The company purchased a machine that had a quoted price of $20,000. The company paid for the machine in full by issuing 1,000 shares of its common stock, par $10 (market price $18). The purchase was recorded as follows:

Machine	10,000	
Capital stock		10,000

e. On December 28, the company collected $11,000 cash in advance for merchandise to be available and shipped during February of the next accounting year (the accounting period ends December 31). This transaction was recorded on December 28 as follows:

Cash	11,000	
Sales revenue		11,000

Problem 1–8

The following summarized data were taken from the records of Trippett Corporation at the end of the annual accounting period, December 31, 19B:

Sales for cash	$261,000
Sales on account	84,000
Cash purchases of merchandise for resale	170,000
Credit purchases of merchandise for resale	40,000
Expenses paid in cash (includes any prepayments)	71,000
Accounts receivable:	
Balance in account on 1/1/19B	23,000
Balance in account on 12/31/19B	30,000
Accounts payable:	
Balance in account on 1/1/19B	14,000
Balance in account on 12/31/19B	16,000
Merchandise inventory:	
Beginning inventory, 1/1/19B	50,000
Ending inventory, 12/31/19B	60,000
Accrued (unpaid) wages at 12/31/19B (none at 1/1/19B)	2,000
Prepaid expenses at 12/31/19B (none at 1/1/19B)	3,000
Operational assets—equipment:	
Cost when acquired	100,000
Annual depreciation	10,000

Required:

1. Based on the above data, complete the following income statements for 19B in order to evaluate the difference between cash and accrual basis (show computations):

	Accrual basis	Cash basis
Sales revenue	$_____	$_____
Less expenses:		
Cost of goods sold	$____	$____
Depreciation expense	____	____
Remaining expenses	____	____
Total expenses	____	____
Pretax income	$65,000	$59,000

2. Which basis is in conformity with GAAP? Give support for your answer.

CASES

Case 1–1

At the completion of the annual audit of the financial statements of AB Corporation, the president of the company asked about the meaning of the phrase "generally accepted accounting principles" that appears in the audit report on the management's financial statements. He observes that the meaning of the phrase must include more than what he considers to be "principles."

You have been asked to respond to the president's question. You have decided to respond in terms of the following:

1. The meaning of the term *accounting principles* as used in audit reports (excluding what "generally accepted" means).
2. How the determination is made as to whether or not an "accounting principle" is generally accepted. Consider sources of evidence to determine whether or not there is substantial authoritative support (do not merely list titles of documents).
3. Diversity in accounting practice will, and should, always exist among companies despite efforts to improve comparability. Discuss arguments that support this statement.

(AICPA adapted)

Case 1–2

The four primary "sources" of specified accounting standards (GAAP) include the Committee on Accounting Procedures, Accounting Principles Board, Financial Accounting Standards Board, and the Securities and Exchange Commission. This case involves consideration of these sources, their current status, their characteristics, and some assessments of the related successes and shortcomings.

Required:
1. Background—For each of the four sources of specified GAAP, identify the sponsoring, or appointing, organization and give the time period of activity.
2. Background continued—Give the designations of the pronouncements (or publications) issued; the numbers issued; and, in general, their current status.
3. Characterize each of the four sources of accounting standards as either a public or private sector organization. Assess the successes and weaknesses of each source.
4. Explain and assess the following approaches to setting accounting standards: *(a)* private sector exclusively, *(b)* public sector exclusively, and *(c)* jointly. Include a consideration of the "politics" of a standard-setting approach.

PART B: CASES 1–3 TO 1–7

Case 1–3

Two independent cases given below violate some parts of the conceptual framework of accounting. For each case, explain *(a)* the nature of the incorrect accounting and reporting, and *(b)* what parts of the conceptual framework were directly violated.

Case A:
    The financial statements of Phillips Corporation included the following note: "During the current year, plant assets were written down by $6,000,000 to make possible substantial savings to the company in the future. Depreciation and other expenses in future years will be lower as a result; this will benefit profits of future years."

Case B:
    During an audit of Bliss Company, you find certain liabilities, such as taxes, which appear to be overstated. Also some semiobsolete inventory items seem to be undervalued, and the tendency is to expense rather than to capitalize as many items as possible.
    In talking with the management about the policies, you are told that "the company has always taken a very conservative view of the business and its future prospects." Management suggests that they do not wish to weaken the company by reporting any more earnings or paying any more dividends than are absolutely necessary,

because they do not expect business to continue to be good. They point out that the undervaluation of assets, and so on, does not lose anything for the company and creates reserves for "hard times."

Case 1–4

At the end of 19X, Bronson Corporation reported the following (summarized):

Balance Sheet

Total assets	$100,000
Total liabilities	30,000
Total equity	70,000

Income Statement

Sales revenue	$180,000
Expenses	150,000
Net income	30,000

Required:
1. This problem focuses on the concept of materiality. Define materiality.
2. On the basis of your definition, use your best judgment to respond to each of the following examples. For each example make a choice as to materiality and give your reason.

 (a) At the beginning of the accounting year, an operational asset, with an estimated useful life of five years and no residual value, was purchased. If the cost is not capitalized, it will be expensed as incurred. The cost of the asset is material if the amount is (check for "yes" response):

_____	$ 100	_____	$ 10,000
_____	500	_____	20,000
_____	1,000	_____	50,000
_____	5,000	_____	100,000

 (b) At the end of the accounting year, the amount of accrued wages payable is material if the amount is (check for "yes" response):

_____	$ 100	_____	$ 10,000
_____	500	_____	20,000
_____	1,000	_____	50,000
_____	5,000	_____	100,000

 (c) At the end of the accounting year, unearned revenue (cash collected in advance) is material if the amount is (check for "yes" response):

_____	$ 100	_____	$ 10,000
_____	500	_____	20,000
_____	1,000	_____	50,000
_____	5,000	_____	100,000

Case 1–5

Explain how each of the following items, as reported on Cate Corporation's balance sheet, violated (if it did) the full-disclosure principle.

a. There was no comment or explanation of the fact that the company changed its inventory method from FIFO to LIFO at the beginning of the current reporting period. A large change-over difference was involved.

b. Owners' equity reported only two amounts: capital stock, $100,000; and retained earnings, $80,000. The capital stock has a par value of $100,000 and originally sold for $150,000 cash.

c. Sales revenue was $900,000 and cost of goods sold, $500,000; the first line reported on the income statement was revenues, $400,000.

d. No earnings per share (EPS) amounts were reported.

e. Current assets amounted to $200,000 and current liabilities, $180,000; the balance sheet reported as a single amount, working capital, $20,000.

f. The income statement showed only the following classifications:
Gross revenues
Costs
Net profit   (AICPA adapted)

Case 1–6

This case relates to the 1984 financial statements of Quaker Oats Company (given in the Appendix immediately following Chapter 24).

Required:

1. To become familiar with the 1984 financial statements respond to the following:
   a. Date the annual reporting period ends is: _____ .
   b. Net sales for 1984 were: $_____ .
   c. Net increase (decrease) in cash and marketable securities for 1984 was: $_____ .
   d. Total assets at the end of the 1984 reporting period was: $_____ .
   e. Note No. 1 to the consolidated financial statements was titled as follows: _____ .
   f. What is the name of the auditing firm?
2. Examine the Notes to the financial statements relating to *(a)* inventories and *(b)* intangibles. Explain how these notes reflect the matching principle and the implementation constraint of conservatism.
3. Examine the auditor's report. Explain the reference, if any, to the secondary qualitative characteristic of comparability.

Case 1–7

The following quotation is from *Forbes* magazine, November 7, 1983, p. 106:

Last summer followers of Rockwell International, the $7.4 billion conglomerate, probably noticed a *Wall Street Journal* article giving painful details of the company's computer-leasing fiasco with OPM Leasing Service. The story said that Rockwell has not revealed the amount of the losses, calling them "immaterial." But tucked away was the *Journal*'s assertion that a member of the company's outside accounting firm, Deloitte, Haskins & Sells, told the paper that fraud-related losses that are less than 10% of the company's $2.2 billion in shareholder equity might properly be considered not material. Both Rockwell and Deloitte insist that the comment in question was taken out of context.

Required:

1. Explain the qualitative characteristic of accounting information that is at issue in this quotation.
2. Assess the situation as described in the quotation.

Chapter 2

Review—The Accounting Model and Information Processing

OVERVIEW AND PURPOSE

The broad objective of accounting is to provide relevant financial information to internal and external decision makers. An entity should have an efficient **accounting system** to *(a)* implement the theoretical concepts, principles, and procedures of accounting (see Chapter 1, Part B); and *(b)* facilitate management decisions.

An accounting system must be designed to (1) collect and measure economic data relating to the entity, (2) classify and process the data, and (3) summarize economic effects in financial reports for decision makers. An accounting system must be tailored to such characteristics of the entity as size, nature of operations, volume of data to be processed, organizational structure, information needs of the internal and external decision makers, and extent of governmental regulation.

The purpose of this chapter is to **review** and illustrate the primary features of the accounting model, the processing of financial data during and at the end of an accounting period, and the reporting of the resulting information in the periodic financial statements. To accomplish this aim, the chapter is subdivided:

Part A: The Accounting Model and Information Processing during the Accounting Period

1. Basic accounting model.
2. Nature of transactions.
3. Accounting information processing cycle.

Part B: Information Processing at the End of the Accounting Period

1. Accounting information processing cycle continued.
2. Adjusting entries.
3. Worksheet to facilitate end-of-period processing.
4. Closing entries.

Supplement 2–A: Control Accounts, Subsidiary Ledgers, and Special Journals

PART A: THE ACCOUNTING MODEL AND INFORMATION PROCESSING DURING THE ACCOUNTING PERIOD

THE BASIC ACCOUNTING MODEL

The three required financial statements—balance sheet, income statement, and statement of changes in financial position (SCFP)—report the **financial statement**

elements identified in *FASB Concepts Statement 3*, "Elements of Financial Statements of Business Enterprises" (see Exhibit 1–4). An accounting system should be designed to accumulate and report the detailed data about each element. These data are recorded in an accounting format that may be called the **basic accounting model.** The primary components of this model are outlined as follows:[1]

5 components of Basic Accounting model

1. **Financial Position** (the balance sheet equation):

$$\text{Assets} = \text{Liabilities} + \text{Owners' Equity}$$

2. **Results of Operations** (the income statement equation):

$$\text{Revenues} + \text{Gains} - \text{Expenses} - \text{Losses} = \text{Income}$$

3. **Funds Flow** (the statement of changes in financial position equation):

$$\text{Funds Inflow} - \text{Funds Outflow} = \text{Change in Funds}$$

4. Recording increases and decreases in the accounts (algebraic balancing):

$$\text{Debits} = \text{Credits}$$

5. **Application of the theoretical concepts, principles, and procedures of accounting** (analysis, recording, and reporting the economic effects of each transaction; see Chapter 1, Part B).

All transactions and events are recorded in an accounting system in terms of the financial position equation: $A = L + OE$, and the debit-credit concept. These two features of the basic accounting model may be summarized in the "T-account" format that follows:

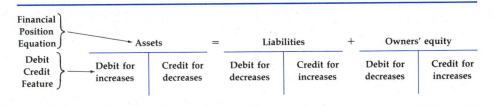

Because (1) investments by owners, revenues, and gains **increase** owners' equity and (2) distributions to owners, expenses, and losses **decrease** owners' equity, the model can be expanded as follows:

Assets		=	Liabilities	+	Owners' equity	
Debit for increases	Credit for decreases		Debit for decreases	Credit for increases	Debit for decreases: a. Distributions to owners. b. Expenses. c. Losses.	Credit for increases: a. Investments by owners. b. Revenues. c. Gains.

---

[1] According to *Webster's Dictionary*, the definition of a model is: "a system of postulates, data, and inferences, presented as a mathematical model of an entity or state of affairs."

In the preceding diagram, the debits are **always** on the left and the credits are **always** on the right. Therefore, **the increases and decreases are in opposite positions on each side of the equation.** That is, debits represent increases to assets and decreases to liabilities and owners' equity, whereas credits represent decreases to assets and increases to liabilities and owners' equity. Expenses and losses are recorded as debits, and revenues and gains as credits. This algebraic arrangement forces debits to always equal credits. Thus, the fundamental accounting model always has a **dual balancing feature:**

1. Assets = Liabilities + Owners' equity.
2. Debits = Credits.

Because of this dual feature, the accounting model often is referred to as a **double-entry accounting system.** The balancing features add reliability to the output of an accounting system by calling attention to those errors which cause an imbalance in the model.

Whether an accounting system is maintained manually, mechanically, or electronically, each entry is recorded in the format of the basic accounting model. Thus, each entry recorded in an accounting system retains the dual-balancing feature standing alone and also on a cumulative basis.

Application of the basic accounting model for seven typical transactions is reviewed in **Exhibit 2–1.** Notice the following aspects of that exhibit:

a. Column B, the accounting analysis of each transaction to determine its effects on assets, liabilities, and owners' equity.

b. Column C, the effects of each transaction, which balance both individually and cumulatively.

c. Column D, the journal entry that records each transaction (discussed below).

We suggest that you study this exhibit to review the methods learned in your fundamentals course.[2]

NATURE OF TRANSACTIONS

Two kinds of transactions are **recorded** in the accounting system of an entity:

1. External transactions between the entity and one or more external parties that change some combinations of the entity's assets, liabilities, and owners' equity. These transactions may be either (a) **reciprocal,** when the entity **both** transfers and receives resources or services (e.g., payment for services received), or (b) **nonreciprocal,** when the entity **either** transfers or receives resources (e.g., payment of a cash dividend or receipt of a gift) or nonresources (e.g., a stock dividend).

2. Internal events (within the entity) and external transactions that are **not**

---

[2] See Welsch, Anthony, and Short, *Fundamentals of Financial Accounting,* 4th ed. (Homewood, Ill.: Richard D. Irwin, 1984).

EXHIBIT 2–1: Application of the Basic Accounting Model

Column A	Column B	Column C Effect on the balance sheet equation			Column D Journal entry into the accounting system		
Typical transaction	Transaction analysis	A	= L	+ OE	Accounts	Debit	Credit
1. Service Corporation was organized; owners invested $100,000 cash and received nopar common stock.	Asset increased—cash, $100,000 .... Owners' equity increased—common stock, $100,000 ... Liabilities—no effect.	+100,000		+100,000	Cash .... Common stock	100,000	100,000
Cumulative balance		100,000	–0–	100,000		100,000	100,000
2. Borrowed $50,000 on a note payable.	Asset increased—cash, $50,000 ..... Liabilities increased—notes payable, $50,000 .. Owners' equity—no effect.	+50,000	+50,000		Cash .... Notes payable	50,000	50,000
Cumulative balance		150,000	50,000	100,000		150,000	150,000
3. Purchased equipment for use in the business, $40,000; paid cash.	Asset increased—equipment, $40,000 Asset decreased—cash, $40,000 ..... Liabilities—no effect. Owners' equity—no effect.	+ 40,000 − 40,000			Equipment .... Cash	40,000	40,000
Cumulative balance		150,000	50,000	100,000		190,000	190,000
4. Services rendered to clients, $20,000, of which $15,000 was collected in cash.	Assets increased—cash, $15,000 ..... accounts receivable, $5,000 .... Owners' equity increased—revenue, $20,000 .... Liabilities—no effect.	+ 15,000 + 5,000		+ 20,000	Cash .... Accounts receivable .... Service revenue	15,000 5,000	20,000
Cumulative balance		170,000	50,000	120,000		210,000	210,000
5. Incurred operating expenses, $11,000, of which $8,000 was paid in cash.	Asset decreased—cash, $8,000 ...... Liability increased—accounts payable, $3,000 .... Owners' equity decreased—expense, $11,000	− 8,000	+ 3,000	− 11,000	Expenses .... Cash .... Accounts payable ..	11,000	8,000 3,000
Cumulative balance		162,000	53,000	109,000		221,000	221,000
6. Paid $2,000 on accounts payable (5 above).	Asset decreased—cash, $2,000 ...... Liability decreased—accounts payable, $2,000 .... Owners' equity—no effect.	− 2,000	− 2,000		Accounts payable ...... Cash	2,000	2,000
Cumulative balance		160,000	51,000	109,000		223,000	223,000
7. Depreciation for 1 year on equipment; estimated life, 10 years, no residual value (3 above).	Asset decreased—accumulated depreciation, $4,000 ..... Owners' equity decreased—depreciation expense, $4,000 .... Liabilities—no effect.	− 4,000		− 4,000	Depreciation expense ... Accumulated depreciation, equipment	4,000	4,000
Cumulative balance		156,000	51,000	105,000		227,000	227,000

exchange transactions but nevertheless change some combination of the entity's assets, liabilities, or owners' equity (e.g., depreciation of equipment, use of inventory in the production of other goods, and casualty losses and gains).[3]

THE ACCOUNTING INFORMATION PROCESSING CYCLE

An accounting system should provide a systematic and efficient process that records all transactions, classifies the data, and produces the periodic financial statements. Transactions occur and must be recorded each business day. Because the financial statements are produced at the end of the **reporting period,** the accounting process involves a series of sequential phases (or steps) that are repeated for each accounting period. These sequential phases are usually referred to as the **information processing (or accounting) cycle.**

Exhibit 2–2 diagrams a typical information processing cycle; it shows the sequence in which the various phases usually are completed. Notice that *(a)* Phases 1–4 occur continuously **during** the accounting period, *(b)* Phases 5–10 occur **only** at the end of the accounting period, and *(c)* Phase 11 occurs **only** at the **start** of the **next** accounting period. Phases 1–5 will be discussed in this section, and the remaining phases are discussed in Part B of this chapter.

Collection of Economic Data on Each Transaction (Phase 1)

An accounting system must collect data about each transaction and event that should be recorded by the entity during the reporting year. Economic data are collected from all parts of the entity's operations by means of source documents. Because exchange transactions involve external parties, they generate their own source documents—sale invoices, freight bills, notes signed by debtors, purchase invoices, deposit slips, checks, and so on. For nontransaction events, the entity itself creates the source documents. The source documents are important because *(a)* they provide data necessary for transaction analysis (and the resulting journal entry), and *(b)* they constitute a tangible record so that each transaction and event, and the measurement of its effects on the entity, can be subsequently verified.

Analysis of Each Transaction (Phase 2)

The analysis of each transaction during the **reporting period,** based upon the data provided by source documents, involves an assessment of the transaction's

---

[3] The term **transactions** will be used to include both transactions and the other events to be recognized.

EXHIBIT 2–2: Diagram of a Typical Accounting Information Processing Cycle[a]

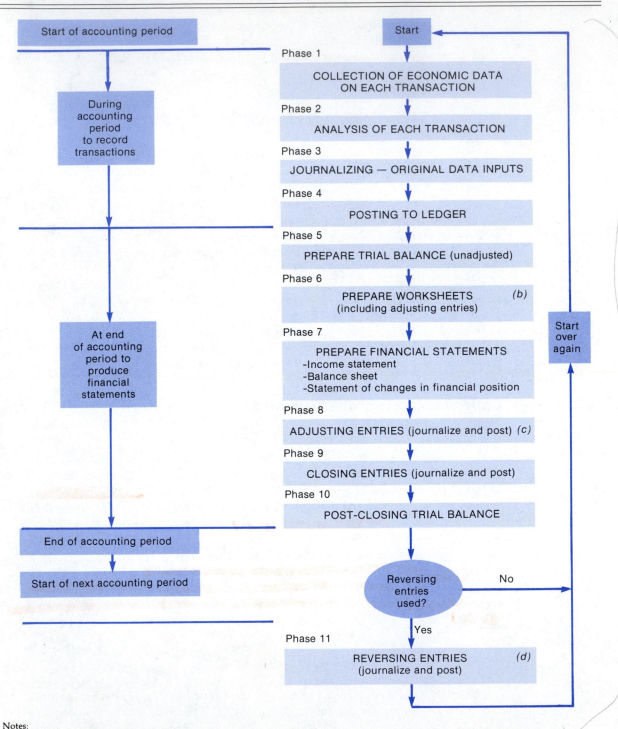

Notes:
(a) See Exhibit 2–10 for a complete summary.
(b) A worksheet is optional. If not used, prepare an **adjusted** trial balance after Phase 8 as a basis for preparing the financial statements.
(c) Usually completed after the financial statements in order to allow **distribution** of the financial statements at the earliest possible date.
(d) Reversing entries are optional.

economic impact on the entity in terms of the assets, liabilities, owners' equity, revenues, expenses, gains, and losses of the entity. This analysis is needed to develop the **accounting entry,** or entries, that must be recorded in the accounting system. Transaction analysis often requires a high degree of accounting sophistication to ensure that the periodic financial statements are reliable. Effective transaction analysis depends upon a sound knowledge of the theoretical concepts, principles, and procedures of accounting discussed in Chapter 1, Part B.

Journalizing—The Original Data Input (Phase 3)

This phase inputs the **original recording** of each transaction during the reporting year into an accounting system. Each transaction is first recorded in a **journal,** which is a chronological record (i.e., by order of transaction date). **Journalizing is the process of recording the effects of transactions in the journal.** A journal entry lists the date of the transaction, the account(s) debited and credited, and their respective amounts. Each entry is recorded so that the duality of the system is maintained: $A = L + OE$ and Debits = Credits. Although the journal is not essential (one could input directly to the ledger), it is important because it (a) maintains a chronological record of the transactions recognized in the system, which is useful for tracing, and (b) shows all aspects of each transaction (i.e., all accounts affected and the amounts). Accounting systems usually have two types of journals: (1) the general journal and (2) several special journals. Special journals are useful for transactions that are highly repetitive. Commonly used special journals are credit sales, credit purchases, cash receipts, cash payments, and the voucher journal. Special journals are discussed and illustrated in Supplement 2–A of this chapter. A general journal is used in subsequent chapters because it is especially useful for instructional purposes. The general journal format, with a typical entry, is illustrated in **Exhibit 2–3.**

Many companies use computerized accounting systems that bypass the traditional journal at various stages. For example, the systems used by many retailers record simultaneously at the cash register, the increase in cash or account receivable for each sale and the decrease in the inventory of the item sold. Thus, they effectively bypass the journal and record directly in the ledger.

Posting to the Ledger (Phase 4)

After the initial recording in the journal, the next phase that occurs during the reporting period is the **transfer** of the information to the ledger. This transfer process, called **posting,** reclassifies the information from the chronological format in the journal to an account classification format in the **ledger.**

The **ledger** (usually called the general ledger) consists of a large number of separate accounts. There are accounts for each kind of asset (such as cash, accounts receivable, investments, land, buildings, and equipment), liability (such as accounts payable and bonds payable), owners' equity (such as capital stock and retained

EXHIBIT 2–3

**General Journal
and General Ledger
Illustrated**

Date	Accounts and Explanation	Ledger Folio*	Amount	
	General Journal Page ___J-16___			
19J			Debit	Credit
Jan.2	Equipment	150	15,000	
	Cash	101		5,000
	Notes payable	215		10,000
	Purchased equipment for use			
	in the business. Paid $5,000			
	cash and gave a $10,000, one-			
	year note payable with 15%			
	interest payable at maturity.			

* The figures in this column indicate (1) that the amount has been posted to the ledger and (2) the account number in the ledger to which posted.

General Ledger

CASH   Acct. 101

19J			19J		
Jan.1	balance	18,700	Jan.2	J-16†	5,000

EQUIPMENT   Acct. 150

19J					
Jan.1	balance	62,000			
2	J-16†	15,000			

NOTES PAYABLE   Acct. 215

			19J		
			Jan.2	J-16†	10,000

† This is the journal page from which the amount was posted.

EXHIBIT 2–4
Unadjusted Trial
Balance

ACE RETAILERS
Unadjusted Trial Balance
December 31, 19J

Account	Debit	Credit
Cash	$ 67,300	
Short-term notes receivable	8,000	
Accounts receivable	45,000	
Allowance for doubtful accounts		$ 1,000
Interest receivable		
Inventory (periodic system)	75,000	
Prepaid insurance	600	
Land	8,000	
Building	160,000	
Accumulated depreciation, building		90,000
Equipment	91,000	
Accumulated depreciation, equipment		27,000
Accounts payable		29,000
Income tax payable		
Interest payable		
Rent revenue collected in advance		
Bonds payable, 6%		50,000
Common stock, par $10		150,000
Contributed capital in excess of par		20,000
Retained earnings		31,500
Sales revenue		325,200
Interest revenue		500
Rent revenue		1,800
Purchases	130,000	
Freight on purchases	4,000	
Purchase returns		2,000
Selling expenses*	104,000	
General and administrative expenses*	23,600	
Interest expense	2,500	
Extraordinary loss	9,000	
Income tax expense		
Totals	$728,000	$728,000

* These broad categories of **expenses** are used to conserve space. They might represent control accounts.

earnings), revenue, expense, gain, and loss. Posting amounts from the journal to the ledger results in reclassification of the data by accounts, which is compatible with the classifications of information in the financial statements.

Posting from the general journal to the general ledger is illustrated in Exhibit 2–3. Notice the use of **folio numbers** in both the journal and ledger to enhance reliability in the posting process.

Prepare a Trial Balance—Unadjusted (Phase 5)

At the end of each accounting (i.e., reporting) period, after all of the regular entries for completed transactions have been journalized and posted to the ledger, a trial balance should be prepared. This trial balance is prepared **before** the adjusting entries are made; therefore, it is often called the **unadjusted trial balance.** A trial balance is a list of all of the accounts in the general ledger and their respective debit or credit balances. A trial balance, prepared after all of the regular entries but before the adjusting entries, serves the following purposes:

1. It verifies that debits equal credits.
2. It provides important information for development of the:
   a. Worksheet, and
   b. End-of-period adjusting entries.

An unadjusted trial balance for Ace Retailers, Inc., is shown in **Exhibit 2–4.** After the unadjusted trial balance is completed, the **information processing at the end of the period** continues. These phases, 6–10 (see Exhibit 2–2), are discussed in Part B of this chapter.

PERMANENT AND TEMPORARY ACCOUNTS

The accounts in the ledger may be classified as follows:

1. **Permanent accounts**—These are the balance sheet accounts. They are called **permanent** or real accounts because they are not closed at the end of each accounting period. They are the asset, liability, and owners' equity accounts. The related contra accounts (e.g., Allowance for Doubtful Accounts and Accumulated Depreciation) also are permanent accounts.
2. **Temporary accounts**—These are the income statement accounts. Called **temporary** or nominal accounts because they are closed at the end of each accounting period. They are the revenue, expense, gain, and loss accounts.[4]

A permanent or temporary account may be "mixed" at any specific time because its **balance** may contain **both** a permanent (i.e., balance sheet) component and a temporary (i.e., income statement) component. To illustrate, assume that on Jan. 1 of the current year, a three-year insurance premium of $600 was paid and

---

[4] Revenue, expense, gain, and loss accounts are subaccounts of owners' equity.

debited in full to a permanent account, Prepaid Insurance. On December 31 of the current year, of the $600, the temporary component, Insurance Expense, is $200 and the permanent component, Prepaid Insurance, is $400 (an asset). An adjusting entry on Dec. 31, debiting Insurance Expense and crediting Prepaid Insurance for $200, is necessary to transfer from the Prepaid Insurance asset account the temporary component of $200 to a temporary account, Insurance Expense.

SUBSIDIARY LEDGERS AND CONTROL ACCOUNTS

Most companies use both a **general ledger** and one or more **subsidiary ledgers.** Each subsidiary ledger has a related **control account** in the general ledger. The control account has summary information, whereas the subsidiary ledger has the details that support the control account. The general ledger contains control accounts for all, or some, of the assets, liabilities, and owners' equity accounts, including revenues, expenses, gains, and losses, depending upon the size and complexity of the company.

The subsidiary ledgers provide the details of a particular control account in the general ledger. To illustrate, a department store may have approximately 10,000 credit customers. A separate account receivable must be kept for each customer. Rather than keeping 10,000 different receivable accounts in the general ledger, one controlling account, Accounts Receivable Control, usually is used. An accounts receivable **subsidiary ledger** composed of a separate account for each customer would also be kept. **Each credit sale** would be posted daily to the customer's account in the subsidiary ledger, and the **total of all credit sales** would be posted periodically (e.g., daily or weekly) to the Accounts Receivable Control account in the general ledger. Thus, when posting is complete, the sum of the balances in all of the customer accounts in the subsidiary ledger would agree with the single balance in the Accounts Receivable Control account.

Subsidiary ledgers often are used for cash (when there are numerous cash and bank accounts), accounts receivable, accounts payable, operational assets, revenues, gains, expenses, losses, and capital stock. Subsidiary ledgers and control accounts are discussed in Supplement 2–A.

PART B: INFORMATION PROCESSING AT THE END OF THE ACCOUNTING PERIOD

CONTINUATION OF THE ACCOUNTING INFORMATION PROCESSING CYCLE

When the **unadjusted trial balance** is completed, the remaining phases of the cycle (see Exhibit 2–2) can be completed in the following order:

Phase	Activity
6 . . .	Worksheet
7 . . .	Financial statements
8 . . .	Adjusting entries journalized and posted
9 . . .	Closing entries journalized and posted
10 . . .	Post-closing trial balance
11 . . .	Reversing entries journalized and posted (at the start of the next period)

Although these phases occur at the end of the accounting (i.e., reporting) period, the actual work is done early during the next period.

We will now discuss and illustrate each of these remaining phases.

Preparation of a Worksheet (Phase 6)

The financial statements cannot be prepared until all of the necessary **adjusting entries** have been formulated. The **unadjusted** trial balance must be adjusted to incorporate the effects of all of the adjusting entries. This adjustment may be accomplished by either *(a)* recording all of the adjusting entries in the journal followed by immediate posting to the general ledger and then taking an **adjusted** trial balance from the ledger to use in preparing the financial statement, or *(b)* entering the unadjusted trial balance in worksheet format (in computer terminology, a spreadsheet), then entering all of the adjusting entries directly on that worksheet; this worksheet can be designed to include the **adjusted** trial balance and the unclassified income statement, statement of retained earnings, and balance sheet. A separate worksheet is needed to develop the SCFP (see Chapter 23).

The worksheet technique is widely used because it *(a)* is an organized approach that facilitates a timely distribution of the financial statements, *(b)* provides an opportunity to develop all of the adjusting entries and "clean up" errors that may exist prior to journalizing and posting both the adjusting and closing entries, and *(c)* provides the accounts and amounts for the financial statements. A worksheet or spreadsheet is not a part of the basic accounting records of the entity; it is a separate **facilitating** technique that usually increases efficiency and minimizes processing errors. It does not replace the financial statements or any entries in the accounts.

Exhibit 2–5 illustrates a typical worksheet prepared as follows:[5]

---

[5] If you are not interested in the worksheet technique presented in this chapter, omit the material under the caption "Completion of the Worksheet." However, mastery of techniques for organizing and analyzing large amounts of data is essential in any accounting or financial capacity. Experience with traditional accounting worksheet techniques is helpful in acquiring this skill.

1. Enter the ledger account titles and their balances (Exhibit 2–4) on the worksheet (this will be the unadjusted trial balance; see Exhibit 2–4). Use the **accounts column** and the first pair of **amount columns** as shown in Exhibit 2–5.
2. Formulate the adjusting entries and enter them in the second pair of columns in the worksheet.
3. Extend the unadjusted balances, plus or minus the adjusting amounts, to the **Adjusted** Trial Balance columns and check for balance (i.e., $746,800 = $746,800).
4. Extend each adjusted amount shown in the Adjusted Trial Balance columns to the right, line by line, to the pair of columns under the financial statement on which each should be reported: Income Statement, Retained Earnings, or Balance Sheet.
5. Check each pair of columns to ensure that debits and credits are equal.

Formulating adjusting entries is a major task in completing a worksheet. Therefore, we will discuss adjusting entries first and then discuss completion of the worksheet.

Adjusting Entries

An adjusting entry is a "catchup" entry made at the end of the accounting period. **Accrual** basis accounting requires adjustments to some of the unadjusted account balances because they are not up-to-date at the end of the accounting period. **Adjusting entries** are necessary to adjust certain balance sheet and income statement accounts so their balances will conform with the **time period assumption** and the **revenue, cost, and matching principles.**

There are two possible situations that create the need for adjusting entries. First, some account balances include both permanent and temporary components, which must be separated. Second, some external and internal transactions and events have not yet been recorded in the accounts. Adjusting entries are needed for both of these situations.

The primary characteristics of **adjusting** entries are as follows:

1. They are end-of-period entries only. They are **dated** as of the end of the accounting period; however, the actual work is done early in the next period.
2. They separate permanent (i.e., balance sheet) amounts from temporary (i.e., income statement) amounts.
3. They relate to originating transactions that occur in one accounting period with economic effects that extend over more than one accounting period.
4. They are recorded in the journal and posted to the ledger.

Adjusting entries may be classified into three major types: deferred items, accrued items, and cost allocations.

EXHIBIT 2–5:   Worksheet

Worksheet for the Year Ended December 31, 19]

Accounts	Unadjusted Trial Balance Debit	Unadjusted Trial Balance Credit	Adjusting Entries Debit	Adjusting Entries Credit	Adjusted Trial Balance Debit	Adjusted Trial Balance Credit	Income Statement Debit	Income Statement Credit	Retained Earnings Debit	Retained Earnings Credit	Balance Sheet Debit	Balance Sheet Credit
Cash	67,300				67,300						67,300	
Short-term notes receivable	8,000				8,000						8,000	
Accounts receivable	45,000				45,000						45,000	
Allowance for doubtful accounts		1,000		(f) 1,200		2,200						2,200
Interest receivable			(d) 100		100						100	
Inventory (periodic system)	75,000		(g) 90,000	(g) 75,000	90,000*						90,000	
Prepaid insurance	600			(a) 200	400						400	
Land	8,000				8,000						8,000	
Building	160,000				160,000						160,000	
Accumulated depreciation, building		90,000		(e) 10,000		100,000						100,000
Equipment	91,000				91,000						91,000	
Accumulated depreciation, equipment		27,000		(e) 9,000		36,000						36,000
Accounts payable		29,000				29,000						29,000
Interest payable				(c) 500		500						500
Rent revenue collected in advance				(b) 600		600						600

Account	TB Dr	TB Cr	Adj. Dr	Adj. Cr	Adj. TB Dr	Adj. TB Cr	Inc. Stmt. Dr	Inc. Stmt. Cr	Ret. Earn. Dr	Ret. Earn. Cr	Bal. Sheet Dr	Bal. Sheet Cr
Bonds payable, 6%		50,000				50,000						50,000
Common stock, par $10		150,000				150,000						150,000
Contributed capital in excess of par		20,000				20,000						20,000
Retained earnings		31,500				31,500				31,500		
Sales revenue		325,200				325,200		325,200				
Interest revenue		500		(d) 100		600		600				
Rent revenue		1,800	(b) 600			1,200		1,200				
Purchases	130,000			(g) 130,000								
Freight on purchases	4,000			(g) 4,000								
Purchase returns		2,000	(g) 2,000									
Cost of goods sold			(g) 117,000		117,000		117,000					
Selling expenses	104,000		(e) 8,200 (f) 1,200		113,400		113,400					
General and administrative expenses	23,600		(a) 200 (e) 10,800		34,600		34,600					
Interest expense	2,500		(c) 500		3,000		3,000					
Extraordinary loss	9,000				9,000		9,000					
Totals	728,000	728,000	230,600	230,600	746,800	746,800	277,000	327,000				
Income tax expense			(h) 20,000†				20,000					
Income tax payable				(h) 20,000								20,000
							297,000	327,000				
Net income to retained earnings							30,000			30,000		
Retained earnings to balance sheet									61,500			61,500
Totals							327,000	327,000	61,500	61,500	469,800	469,800

* Periodic inventory system. This is one way to handle inventory on a worksheet.

† ($327,000 − $277,000) × 40% = $20,000. There are other ways to reflect income tax on a worksheet.

A. **Deferred items**—result from transactions where cash flow **precedes** recognition of the related expense or revenue. The two general situations are:
   1. **Deferred expense**—cash is **paid before** the related expense should be recognized; for example, insurance premium paid in advance.
   2. **Deferred revenue**—cash is **collected before** the related revenue should be recognized; for example, rent revenue collected in advance of occupancy.

B. **Accrued items**—result from transactions where cash flow **lags** (i.e., follows) recognition of the related expense or revenue. The two general situations are:
   1. **Accrued expense**—cash is **paid after** the related expense is incurred; for example, wages earned by an employee but not yet paid.
   2. **Accrued revenue**—cash is **collected after** the related revenue is earned; for example, interest revenue earned but not yet collected.

C. **Other**—**internal cost allocations not yet recorded;** for example, estimated bad debt expense and depreciation expense, and cost of goods sold (with a periodic inventory system).

Each kind of adjusting entry will be discussed and illustrated. You should study each adjusting entry illustrated in the worksheet in Exhibit 2–5. If used, the worksheet would be followed by preparation of the financial statements (Phase 7), then the journalizing and posting of the adjusting entries (Phase 8). If the worksheet technique is **not used,** these adjusting entries would be directly journalized and posted (Phase 8), followed by preparation of the financial statements (Phase 7).

Deferred Expense.   A deferred expense, usually called a **prepaid expense,** occurs when services or supplies are paid for in one accounting period but are not **fully** used or consumed in that period.

To illustrate, on January 1, 19J, Ace Retailers paid a three-year insurance premium of $600 in advance. At that date, the $600 payment was recorded as a debit to Prepaid Insurance and a credit to Cash. On the unadjusted trial balance, the $600 is reflected as the debit balance of an asset account, Prepaid Insurance. Because $200 of this service was **used** (in this instance, expired) in 19J, a $400 balance should remain in the **prepaid** expense account. Therefore, on December 31, 19J, an adjusting entry must be made as follows (the letter code to the left is used for reference):

a. December 31, 19J:

    Insurance expense (general and administrative expense)   200
            Prepaid insurance   200

The effects of this entry are (1) to adjust the asset account to $400, which is then reported on the balance sheet; and (2) to record the $200 expense component, which is reported on the income statement.

In the originating entry, a deferred expense can be debited to a permanent (real) account (Prepaid Insurance as above), or to a temporary (nominal) account. In either case, an adjusting entry is required. To illustrate, assume the $600 was initially debited to **Insurance Expense.** The adjusting entry would be: debit Prepaid Insurance, $400; credit Insurance Expense, $400. In either case the net effect on the financial statements is exactly the same.[6]

Deferred Revenue.   A deferred revenue, usually called **revenue collected in advance,** occurs when payment for goods or services are collected in one accounting period but are not **fully** earned in that period.

To illustrate, on January 1, 19J, Ace Retailers leased a small office in its building to Tom Jones. At that time, Ace collected $1,800 cash in advance for 18 months rent. The collection was recorded as a debit to Cash and a credit to Rent Revenue. On December 31, 19J, the $1,800 balance in the Rent Revenue account included $600 **unearned** rent revenue. Therefore, the adjusting entry was:

b. December 31, 19J:

Rent revenue 600
    Rent revenue collected in advance*   600

* Sometimes called Unearned Rent Revenue.

This entry leaves $1,200 in the Rent Revenue account for 19J and records a liability of $600 for the unearned rent revenue. The $600 is a liability on December 31, 19J, because Ace owes that amount of future "occupancy" to Jones. In 19K, the $600 will be transferred from the liability account to the Rent Revenue account.

In the originating entry, a deferred revenue can be credited to a temporary (nominal) account (rent revenue as above) or to a permanent (real) account. In either case, an adjusting entry is required. To illustrate, assume the $1,800 was initially credited to **Rent Revenue Collected in Advance.** The adjusting entry would be: debit Rent Revenue Collected in Advance and credit Rent Revenue for $1,200 each.[7]

Accrued Expense.   Accrued expense, usually called an **accrued liability,** occurs when an expense has been incurred but is not yet recorded or paid. Incurred means that it should be recorded as an expense. Therefore, the adjusting entry should recognize both the **expense** and the related **liability.**

To illustrate, Ace Retailers has a liability for bonds payable of $50,000. These bonds require payments of 6% annual interest on each October 31. Therefore, on December 31, 19J, accrued (unpaid) interest expense was $50,000 $\times$ 6% $\times$ $\frac{2}{12}$ = $500. This accrued interest must be recognized by the following adjusting entry:

c. December 31, 19J:

Interest expense 500
    Interest payable   500

---

[6] The first approach usually is used because the asset account typically continues to exist for a long period of time due to successive renewals.

[7] The first approach usually is used because rent revenue typically is credited when rent is collected.

This adjusting entry records (1) 19J expense (interest expense) for income statement purposes and (2) the liability (interest payable) for the 19J balance sheet.

Accrued Revenue. Accrued revenue, usually called **uncollected revenue** or revenue earned but not yet collected, occurs when a revenue has been earned and should be recognized but has not yet been collected or recorded. Therefore, the adjusting entry should recognize both **revenue** and the related **receivable.**

To illustrate, Ace Retailers held short-term notes receivable amounting to $8,000. These notes earn 15% annual interest which is collected each November 30. Because interest revenue was earned but not yet collected for the month of December, an adjusting entry must be made as follows:

d. December 31, 19J:

> Interest receivable 100
> Interest revenue ($8,000 × 15% × $\frac{1}{12}$) 100

This adjusting entry records (1) the asset (interest receivable) for the 19J balance sheet and (2) 19J revenue (interest revenue) for income statement purposes.

Internal Cost Allocations Not Yet Recorded. In addition to the adjusting entries for deferrals and accruals, adjusting entries must be made for certain allocations of cost to periodic expense. Usually these adjusting entries are based on **estimated amounts.** Examples of such internal cost allocations are: depreciation expense, bad debt expense, and cost of goods sold.

Depreciation Expense. When certain assets, such as a building or equipment, are acquired for use in operating a business (i.e., not for sale), they are "used up" over time through wear and obsolescence. The amount of the **use cost** of such assets is measured each accounting period and recorded as **depreciation expense.** Depreciation expense always is an estimate because the amount recognized depends upon a known amount, the cost of the asset, and two estimates, useful life and residual value (RV).

To illustrate, at the end of 19J, Ace Retailers had the following assets subject to depreciation:

Asset	Cost	RV	Useful life—years	Proportionate use by function	
				Selling function	G & A* function
Building	$160,000	$10,000	15	46%	54%
Equipment	91,000	1,000	10	40	60
* General and administrative.					

The adjusting entry for these two assets is:

e. December 31, 19J:

Selling expense (depreciation)	8,200	
General and administrative expense (depreciation)	10,800	
Accumulated depreciation, building		10,000
Accumulated depreciation, equipment		9,000

Computation:

			Total	Selling	General and administrative
Building: [($160,000 − $10,000) ÷ 15 yrs.]	=	$10,000	× 46% = $4,600	× 54% = $ 5,400
Equipment: [($91,000 − $1,000) ÷ 10 yrs.]	=	9,000	× 40% = 3,600	× 60% = 5,400
Totals		$19,000	$8,200	$10,800

Depreciation expense was debited to **two** expense accounts because the company follows the typical policy of **allocating** it to expense based upon the proportionate use of the assets in each function. This entry (1) records the 19J **expense** for the income statement and (2) reduces the book values of the building and equipment for the 19J balance sheet. Recall that accumulated depreciation is a contra (i.e., offset) to the related asset account.

Bad Debt Expense.   Sales and services billed on **credit** usually result in some losses due to uncollectible accounts receivable (i.e., bad debts). The fact that a specific account will be uncollectible usually is not known for one or more periods subsequent to the period in which the credit was extended. The sale or service is recognized as revenue in conformity with the **revenue principle.** The **matching principle** requires that all **expenses** associated with sales and service revenue be recognized in the period in which the revenue is reported. Therefore, bad debt expense must be recognized in the revenue-recognition period. This matching can be accomplished only by **estimating** the bad debt expense based on past experience.

To illustrate, Ace Retailers extended credit on sales during 19J amounting to $120,000. Prior experience indicated an expected average bad debt loss rate of 1% of credit sales. Therefore, the following adjusting entry is required:

f. December 31, 19J:

Bad debt expense (selling)	1,200	
Allowance for doubtful accounts		1,200

Computation: $120,000 × 1% = $1,200.

The credit is made to an "allowance" account rather than directly to Accounts Receivable because the identities of the specific customers that will not eventually pay are not known. Bad debt expense is reported on the income statement, and the allowance account is reported on the balance sheet as a deduction from accounts receivable (i.e., it is a contra account). When a customer's account is determined to be uncollectible, it is written off by a debit to the allowance account and a credit to Accounts Receivable; this write-off will not change the net book (i.e., carrying) value of accounts receivable.

Inventory Systems

Perpetual
Periodic

Cost of Goods Sold.   Prior to discussing this adjusting entry, let's review the difference between the perpetual and periodic inventory systems.[8]

Perpetual inventory system.   This system requires the keeping of a **detailed inventory record** for each kind of item stocked. This record contains data on each purchase and each issue (i.e., cost of goods sold), and an up-to-date inventory balance. The cost of each item purchased is debited directly to the Inventory account (i.e., no Purchases account is used). Under this inventory system, a sale requires two entries: At sales price—debit Cash or Accounts Receivable and credit Sales Revenue; at cost—debit Cost of Goods Sold and credit Inventory. The **unadjusted** trial balance reflects only the **ending inventory** and the amount of **cost of goods sold;** therefore, **no adjusting entry is required.**

Periodic inventory system.   This system does not maintain a detailed inventory record. Instead, a physical inventory count is taken and valued at cost at the end of each accounting period. This means that cost of goods sold is determined at the end of each accounting period **after** the inventory is counted and valued. The cost of items purchased is debited to Purchases (not inventory), and a sale is recorded **only** at sales price—debit Cash or Accounts Receivable and credit Sales Revenue.

The **unadjusted** trial balance at the end of the accounting period reflects the **beginning** (not ending) inventory amount and **does not** reflect cost of goods sold. Therefore, an **adjusting entry is required** to *(a)* remove the beginning inventory amount and replace it with the **ending** inventory amount, and *(b)* record **cost of goods sold.**[9] To illustrate, after the ending inventory was counted and valued, Ace Retailers cost of goods sold is computed as follows:

ACE RETAILERS December 31, 19J		
Beginning inventory (carried over from the prior period)		$ 75,000
Add (from the current-year accounts):		
Purchases	$130,000	
Freight on purchases	4,000	
Purchase returns	(2,000)	
Purchase discounts and allowances	(–0–)	
Net purchases		132,000
Total goods available for sale		207,000
Less: Ending inventory (per physical count)		90,000
Cost of goods sold (as computed)		$117,000

[8] These inventory systems are discussed and illustrated in Chapters 7 and 8.

[9] Because this entry has both adjusting and closing characteristics, some accountants consider it to be an adjusting entry, whereas others consider it to be a closing entry; however, the end results are the same.

When the periodic inventory system is used, the inventory and cost of goods sold adjusting entry is as follows:[10]

g. December 31, 19J:

Inventory (ending)	90,000	
Purchase returns	2,000	
Purchase discounts and allowances	–0–	
Cost of goods sold (balancing amount)	117,000	
Inventory (beginning)		75,000
Purchases		130,000
Freight on purchases		4,000

Completion of the Worksheet (Phase 6 Continued)

After the adjusting entries are entered on the worksheet, it is completed by extending each account balance (i.e., the trial balance amount plus or minus any adjusting amounts) to the next columns as illustrated in Exhibit 2–5. Observe that debits are extended as debits and credits as credits. When all of the amounts have been extended, the difference between the debits and credits under the Income Statement column represents **pretax income.** This amount is needed to compute income tax expense, for which an adjusting entry must be made. To illustrate, for Ace Retailers, Inc., the computation would be as follows, assuming an average 40% income tax rate:

Income Statement column totals (pretax):	
Credit total	$327,000
Debit total	277,000
Pretax income	50,000
Income tax expense ($50,000 × 40%)	20,000
Net income	$ 30,000

The adjusting entry for income tax would be as follows:

h. December 31, 19J:

Income tax expense	20,000	
Income tax payable		20,000

After this adjusting entry is made, the extensions can be completed. The amount of net income, $30,000, is entered on the worksheet as a debit to Income Statement and a credit to Retained Earnings. The ending balance of Retained Earnings is then extended to the balance sheet and the last two pairs of columns are summed; in the absence of errors, each pair of columns on the worksheet will balance.

---

[10] This compound entry also could be made as a series of individual entries, or groupings, with the same effect.

The worksheet can be used as a framework for completing the remaining phases in the cycle.

Prepare Financial Statements (Phase 7)

The income statement, statement of retained earnings, and balance sheet can be prepared directly from the completed worksheet. An income statement and balance sheet, taken directly from the worksheet (Exhibit 2–5), are presented in **Exhibits 2–6 and 2–7,** respectively. Phase 7 usually precedes Phase 8 because of the need to distribute the financial statements at the earliest possible date. The **issuance date** of the financial statements is critical because the longer they are delayed the less relevant they are to decision makers. Financial statements are discussed in more detail in Chapters 3 and 4.

Journalizing and Posting Adjusting Entries (Phase 8)

The adjusting entries should be entered in the general journal and then posted to the general ledger, dated the last day of the accounting period. The adjusting entries **update** the ledger accounts by separating the account balances into their permanent (i.e., balance sheet) and temporary (i.e., income statement) components. The adjusted temporary accounts are then ready to close. Also, the adjusting entries bring the general ledger accounts into agreement with the financial statements.

If a worksheet, such as Exhibit 2–5, is developed, the adjusting entries can be taken directly from it. Note that after the adjusting entries are posted to the general ledger, each account will reflect the account balances shown in Exhibit 2–5 in the column labeled Adjusted Trial Balance.

Closing Entries (Phase 9)

After the financial statements are prepared and the adjusting entries have been journalized and posted, the **closing process,** Phase 9, must be completed. The purpose of the closing process is to transfer the balances of all of the **temporary** (i.e., income statement) accounts to the Retained Earnings account. The result is that (a) retained earnings will be increased by the amount of net income, or decreased by net loss, and (b) each temporary account will start the next year with a zero balance. The permanent (i.e., balance sheet) accounts are not affected by the closing process except for the change in retained earnings.

The temporary accounts are used each accounting period to accumulate and classify the revenues, expenses, gains, and losses. At the end of the accounting period, when they have served this temporary information processing purpose,

EXHIBIT 2–6
Income Statement

ACE RETAILERS
Income Statement*
For the Year Ended December 31, 19J

Revenues:

Sales		$325,200
Interest		600
Rent		1,200
Total revenues		327,000

Expenses:

Cost of goods sold†	$117,000	
Selling	113,400	
General and administrative	34,600	
Interest	3,000	
Total expenses (excluding income taxes)		268,000
Pretax operating income		59,000
Income taxes ($59,000 × 40%)		23,600
Income before extraordinary items		35,400
Extraordinary loss	9,000	
Less tax saving ($9,000 × 40%)	3,600	5,400
Net income		$ 30,000

EPS:

Income before extraordinary items ($35,400 ÷ 15,000 shares) ...	$2.36
Extraordinary loss ($5,400 ÷ 15,000 shares)	(.36)
Net income ($30,000 ÷ 15,000 shares)	$2.00

* This is a single-step income statement; various formats are discussed in Chapter 3.
† Computation of cost of goods sold:

Beginning inventory	$ 75,000
Purchases	130,000
Freight on purchases	4,000
Purchase returns	(2,000)
Total goods available for sale	207,000
Less ending inventory	90,000
Cost of goods sold	$117,000

they are closed (i.e., to zero balances) in order to be ready for **reuse** in the next accounting period. A closing entry transfers a debit balance in one account to another account as a debit, or it transfers a credit balance to another account as a credit.

For closing purposes, a temporary **clearing account,** called **Income Summary,** may be used to aggregate the debits and credits that make up net income or loss. This clearing account is then immediately closed to Retained Earnings as one amount. Cost of goods sold also is used (with a periodic inventory system) in the closing process for a similar reason. These two clearing accounts are used herein primarily for instructional convenience.

EXHIBIT 2–7

Balance Sheet

ACE RETAILERS
Balance Sheet*
At December 31, 19J

Assets			Liabilities		
Current assets:			**Current liabilities:**		
Cash		$ 67,300	Accounts payable		$ 29,000
Notes receivable		8,000	Income taxes payable		20,000
Interest receivable		100	Interest payable		500
Accounts receivable	$ 45,000		Rent revenue collected in		
Allowance for doubtful			advance		600
accounts	2,200	42,800	Total current liabilities		50,100
Inventory		90,000	**Long-term liabilities:**		
Prepaid insurance†		400	Bonds payable, 6%		50,000
Total current assets		208,600	Total liabilities		100,100
Operational assets:			**Stockholders' Equity**		
Land		8,000	**Contributed capital:**		
Building	160,000		Common stock, par $10,		
Accumulated depreciation,			15,000 shares issued		
building	100,000	60,000	and outstanding	$150,000	
Equipment	91,000		Contributed capital in		
Accumulated depreciation,			excess of par	20,000	
equipment	36,000	55,000	Retained earnings	61,500	
Total operational assets		123,000	Total stockholders'		
			equity		231,500
			Total liabilities and stock-		
Total assets		$331,600	holders' equity		$331,600

* Balance sheets and appropriate supplementary information are discussed in Chapter 4.

† Conceptually, $200 of this amount should not be reported as a current asset because it will extend two years into the future. In practice such differences may not be material in amount, as in this situation; the conceptual distinction is not necessary (refer to the discussion of materiality in Chapter 1).

Closing entries are made, and dated, **only** at the end of each accounting period. The closing entries can be *(a)* taken directly from the **worksheet,** or *(b)* developed from the **adjusted** trial balance, if a worksheet is not prepared.

To illustrate, the **closing entries** for Ace Retailers, assuming the Cost of Goods Sold and Income Summary clearance accounts are used, would be taken directly from the Income Statement columns of the worksheet (see Exhibit 2–5):[11]

[11] The closing entries can be grouped in various ways, one of which is illustrated here. Alternatively, a separate closing entry can be made for each temporary account. The net effect of all the closing entries would be the same.

December 31, 19J:

1. To close the revenue and gain accounts to Income Summary:

Sales revenue	325,200	
Interest revenue	600	
Rent revenue	1,200	
Income summary		327,000

2. To close the expense and loss accounts to Income Summary:

Income summary	297,000	
Cost of goods sold		117,000
Selling expenses		113,400
General and administrative expenses		34,600
Interest expense		3,000
Extraordinary loss		9,000
Income tax expense		20,000

3. To close Income Summary (i.e., net income to Retained Earnings):

Income summary	30,000	
Retained earnings		30,000

The closing process is diagrammed in T-account form in **Exhibit 2–8.** Observe that **after the closing process** each income statement (i.e., temporary) account reflects a zero balance. Therefore, each account is ready to be reused during the next accounting period.

Post-Closing Trial Balance (Phase 10)

The purposes of a trial balance are to (a) to verify the equality of the debits and credits and (b) to have the account balances ready for other uses. Two different trial balances have already been discussed: the **unadjusted** trial balance, taken immediately after all of the current entries are journalized and posted for the accounting period but before the adjusting entries; and the **adjusted** trial balance, which reflects the account balances after the adjusting entries. A third trial balance usually is taken after the closing entries have been posted. It is called the **post-closing trial balance.** It is used to verify that the debits and credits are equal at the start of the next accounting period. The post-closing trial balance usually is prepared with a computer, rather than by preparing a formal listing.

Reversing Entries (Phase 11)

After the adjusting and closing entries are journalized and posted to the general ledger, the accounts are ready for information inputs of the next period. Prior to entering the new information inputs, many companies journalize and post **reversing entries.** A reversing entry is dated the first day of the next period

EXHIBIT 2–8

Closing Process Diagrammed

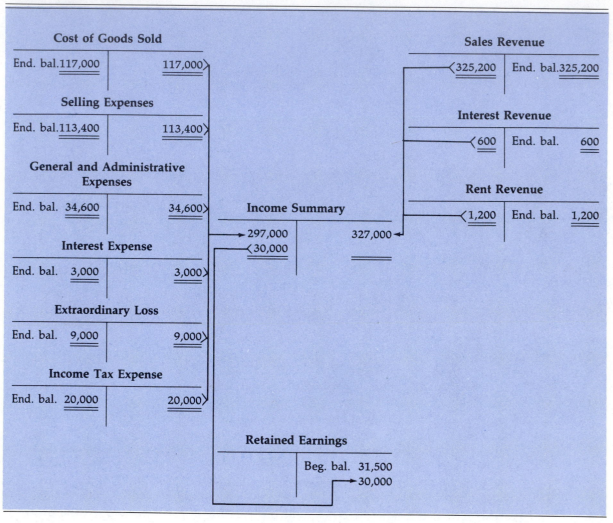

and simply reverses, or "backs out" of the accounts, the amounts of an adjusting entry that was made at the end of the prior period. Thus, a reversing entry uses exactly the same accounts and amounts as in the adjusting entry but with the debits and credits reversed. **Reversing entries serve only one purpose, that is, to facilitate (or simplify) a subsequent related entry.** Reversing entries are always optional; the same result is obtained whether or not they are used. If used, only certain of the adjusting entries are reversed.

Although it is impossible to provide rigid rules for selecting adjusting entries that may be reversed, some guidelines can be given.

1. **Adjusting entries usually reversed**—As a general rule, only the following adjusting entries should be reversed: *(a)* entries for accrued expenses and accrued revenues, and *(b)* entries for deferred expenses and deferred revenues that were originally recorded in a temporary (i.e., income statement) account.

2. **Adjusting entries not reversed**—As a general rule, the following adjusting entries should not be reversed: *(a)* internal cost allocations (e.g., depreciation, depletion, and amortization), and *(b)* deferred expenses and revenues initially recorded in permanent (i.e., balance sheet) accounts.

The purpose and application of reversing entries are illustrated in **Exhibit 2–9.** In that exhibit, a series of entries related to accrued wages is analyzed using two options: (1) with a reversing entry and (2) without a reversing entry. The two options demonstrate the **facilitating** feature of reversing entries and also suggest the kinds of adjusting entries that may be reversed.

To summarize, the primary characteristics of reversing entries are as follows:

1. Reverses (i.e., backs out) the debits and credits of one or more immediately preceding adjusting entries; relates only to adjusting entries.
2. Dated the first day of the next accounting period, then journalized and posted.
3. Purpose—only to facilitate a subsequent entry in the next accounting period.
4. Follows adjusting and closing entries.
5. Same end results whether used or not.
6. Only selected adjusting entries are reversed.

INFORMATION PROCESSING FOR INTERIM REPORTS

Most companies prepare monthly (i.e., interim) financial statements for internal use only. In addition, some companies distribute highly summarized and selected information from their interim financial statements. These monthly and quarterly financial statements are prepared by using **worksheets;** however, the **closing process** is not used until the end of the accounting year. Assuming an annual accounting year that ends December 31, the interim financial statements can be prepared as follows:

January 31—Enter the unadjusted trial balance (provided by the general ledger accounts) on a worksheet. Next, enter the adjusting entries on the worksheet and complete the worksheet as illustrated in this chapter. Prepare the January income statement, balance sheet, and statement of retained earnings. Do not journalize or post any adjusting or closing entries.

EXHIBIT 2–9

Reversing Entries Illustrated

KNOX CORPORATION
Annual Accounting Period Ends December 31, 19A

With reversing entry	Without reversing entry

a. **Adjusting entry**—The last payroll of Knox Corporation was paid on December 28, 19A; the next payroll will be on January 4, 19B. Therefore, at December 31, 19A, accrued wages (i.e., not yet paid or recorded) for three days amounted to $15,000. The following adjusting entry is required:

December 31, 19A:
 	
Wage expense 15,000
  Wages payable   15,000
	December 31, 19A:
	
	Wage expense 15,000
	  Wages payable 15,000

b. **Closing entry**—The revenue and expense accounts are closed to Income Summary.

December 31, 19A:
 	
Income summary* 215,000
  Wage expense   215,000
	December 31, 19A:
	
	Income summary* 215,000
	  Wage expense 215,000

c. At this time the adjusting and closing entries have been journalized and posted to the ledger. The information processing cycle for 19A has been completed. On Janauary 1, 19B, the accountant must decide what adjusting entries are to be **reversed** (if any). **Question:** Would a reversing entry for accrued wages on January 1, 19B, simplify or facilitate making the **next payroll entry** on January 4, 19B?

Decision—make a reversing entry, January 1, 19B	Decision—no reversing entry to be made
Wages payable . . . . 15,000 Wage expense . . . . 15,000 (Note that this entry exactly reverses the adjusting entry made above on 12/31/19A.)	
Effect: The Wages Payable account now reflects a **zero** balance; Wage Expense reflects a **credit** balance of $15,000.	Effect: The Wages Payable account continues to reflect a **credit** balance of $15,000; Wage Expense reflects a **zero** balance.

d. **Subsequent payroll entry**—Payment of $36,000 payroll on January 4, 19B. This amount includes the $15,000 liability (wages payable) carried over from December 19A.

January 4, 19B, payroll entry (disregarding payroll taxes):	

Wage expense 36,000
  Cash   36,000
	Wages payable 15,000
	Wage expense 21,000
	  Cash 36,000

Did the prior reversing entry simplify this subsequent entry? The answer is yes. The last entry, on the left, required only one debit, and, most importantly, preparation of the January 4 payroll entry did not

Exhibit 2-9 *(continued)*

require reference to the December 31, 19A, adjusting entry. To illustrate the importance of not having to refer to the adjusting entry, assume Knox Corporation made 75 adjusting entries and that accountant X supervised the adjusting process. Assume that accountant Z supervises payroll accounting. Therefore, on January 4, 19B, when accountant Z must record the $36,000 payment of the weekly payroll, the credit in the entry is to Cash. Accountant Z realizes that the payroll period spanned two accounting periods and wonders how much of the $36,000 should be debited to Wages Payable from 19A and how much should be debited to 19B Wage Expense. The only way to learn this fact is to scan, possibly all of, the 75 adjusting entries made December 31, 19A. To avoid such a waste of time and cost, accountant X can make a reversing entry at the same time the adjusting entry is made, but postdate it to be effective on January 1, 19B. Then on January 4, 19B, the next payroll date, accountant Z can record the payroll entry by debiting Wage Expense and crediting Cash for $36,000 with no need to refer to the December 31, 19A, adjusting entry. With or without a reversing entry, the Wage Expense account reflects a debit balance of $21,000 and Wages Payable reflects a zero balance. When the payroll processing is **computerized,** and no reversing entry is made, a special routine must be written for the first payment entry which is different from the remaining 51 payroll entries during the year.

* Includes $200,000 wages paid during the period.

February 28—Complete a worksheet as in January by using the *(a)* February 28 unadjusted trial balance (it will represent the **cumulative** amounts for January and February), and *(b)* only the February 28 adjusting entries (they will also be cumulative). The worksheet then will provide financial statements for January–February **combined.** Prepare the **February** only income statement by **subtracting out** the January amounts previously reported. The February balance sheet needs no change because a balance sheet reports cumulative amounts of assets and liabilities at a point in time. Do not journalize or post any adjusting or closing entries.

March 31—Repeat the process, as in February, using the *(a)* March 31 unadjusted trial balance, and *(b)* the March 31 adjusting entries. The worksheet will provide the **quarterly** financial statements. The March only income statement can be developed by subtracting **both** the January and February amounts. The quarterly and March balance sheets are identical.

SUMMARY

Most companies process a large quantity of accounting data each day. This work can be time consuming and costly. Therefore, a well-designed information processing system is needed to provide an efficient flow of information from the collection of raw economic data to the financial statements. **Exhibit 2–10** summarizes the major sequential phases of the information processing cycle as they are discussed in this chapter.

The means of processing accounting information necessarily will vary with

EXHIBIT 2–10

Summary of the Accounting Information Processing Cycle

Phase (order)	Identification	Objective
During the period (Phases 1–4):		
1	Collection of economic data.	To gather inputs to the accounting system. The inputs are supported by source documents as a basis for *(a)* transaction analysis and *(b)* subsequent verification.
2	Transaction analysis.	To identify, assess, and measure the economic impact on the entity of each transaction recognized. To provide the basis for developing the accounting entry in the journal.
3	Journalizing.	To provide a chronological record (i.e., by date) of the entries in the accounting system that reflect the increases and decreases in each account.
4	Posting.	To transfer the economic effects from the journal to the ledger; to reclassify and accumulate the economic effects for each asset, liability, owners' equity, revenue, expense, gain, and loss.
End of the period (Phases 5–10):		
5	Prepare unadjusted trial balance.	To provide, in a convenient form, a listing of the accounts and their balances in the general ledger after all current entries have been posted. It serves to *(a)* check the debit-credit equality and *(b)* provide data for use in developing the worksheet and the adjusting entries.
6*	Prepare worksheets.	To provide an organized and systematic approach at the end of the accounting period for developing *(a)* the adjusting entries, *(b)* the financial statements, and *(c)* the closing entries. One worksheet suffices for the income statement and balance sheet. Another worksheet is needed to develop the statement of changes in financial position.
7	Prepare financial statements.	To communicate summarized financial information to decision makers.
8	Journalize and post adjusting entries.	To update the general ledger and to separate the "mixed" balances into their permanent (i.e., balance sheet) and temporary (i.e., income statement) components so the temporary accounts will be ready for the closing process. This phase brings the general ledger account balances into agreement with the amounts reported on the financial statements.
9	Journalize and post closing entries.	To close the temporary accounts to retained earnings so they will be ready for reuse during the next period for accumulating and classifying revenues and expenses.
10*	Prepare post-closing trial balance.	To verify the debit-credit accuracy of the general ledger after the closing entries are posted.
Start of next period:		
11*	Reversing entries.	To facilitate subsequent entries by reversing certain adjusting entries. They are journalized and posted on the first day of the new period.

* Optional.

the size and complexity of the entity. Information processing may be accomplished (1) manually, when the work is performed by hand; (2) mechanically, when the information is processed by sorting equipment, tabulating machines, and so on; and (3) electronically, when electronic computers (i.e., mainframes and PCs) are used. Typically, an accounting system will use each of these approaches in varying degrees depending upon the situation. Consideration of all of these information approaches is not within the scope of this book. For instructional convenience, the manual approach is used because the steps are essentially the same regardless of the means. A thorough understanding of the accounting process is critical to the successful use of any information system.

SUPPLEMENT 2–A: CONTROL ACCOUNTS, SUBSIDIARY LEDGERS, AND SPECIAL JOURNALS

An accounting system usually includes application of the information processing devices known as control accounts, subsidiary ledgers, and special journals. This supplement discusses and illustrates these elements of an information processing system.

CONTROL ACCOUNTS AND SUBSIDIARY LEDGERS

The general ledger is the main ledger. It includes an account for each asset, liability, owners' equity, revenue, expense, gain, and loss. To facilitate record-keeping for accounts that involve a large amount of detail, selected general ledger accounts are designated as **control accounts** to which only summary information is posted. The details related to each control account are maintained in a separate **subsidiary ledger** (one for each control account). Thus, each control account is supplemented by its specially designated subsidiary ledger. To illustrate, accounts receivable usually is designated as **Accounts Receivable Control** in the general ledger and is supported by a separate **accounts receivable subsidiary ledger** that is composed of individual customer accounts. This arrangement will be illustrated below.

JOURNALS

Both **general** and **special** journals are used in most accounting systems. Even when extensive use is made of special journals, a need still exists for a general journal **(Exhibit 2–11)** in which to record (a) those transactions that do not apply to any of the special journals, (b) nonrepetitive current transactions, and (c)

EXHIBIT 2–11
General Journal

Date 19]	Accounts and Explanation	Ledger Folio	Debit	Credit
Jan.2	Equipment — trucks	140	9,000	
	Notes payable	214		9,000
	Purchased truck for use in			
	the business. Gave $9,000, 60-			
	day note, interest at 10% per			
	year, payable at maturity.			

General Journal   Page J-14

the adjusting, closing, and reversing journal entries. Occasionally, there will be a complex entry with characteristics that would, in part, qualify for entry in a special journal and, in part, in the general journal. Such entries may be entered only in the general journal or, alternatively, "split" between the general journal and a special journal.

Special Journals

A special journal serves the same purpose as a general journal except that it is designed to handle **only one type of transaction** because of the large volume of transactions of a particular type. Each special journal, therefore, is designed specifically to simplify the data processing tasks involved in journalizing and posting a particular type of transaction. The format of each special journal and the number used depend upon the types of frequent transactions recorded by the entity. Commonly used special journals are the following:

1. Merchandise sales on credit—designed for credit sales entries only.
2. Merchandise purchases on credit—designed for credit purchases only.
3. Cash receipts—designed for all cash receipts (including cash sales).
4. Cash payments—designed for all cash payments (including cash purchases).
5. Voucher system journals (replaces **2** and **4** above when the voucher system is used)—
    a. Voucher register—designed to record vouchers payable only. A voucher payable is prepared for each cash payment regardless of the purpose of the payment.

b. Check register—designed to record all checks written in payment of vouchers.

Special Journal for Merchandise Sales on Credit. This journal is designed to accommodate entries for credit sales of regular merchandise only. Therefore, it would handle only the following type of entry (cash sales would not be entered in this journal):

January 2, 19J:

Accounts receivable ($1,000 × 98%)	980	
Sales revenue		980
Credit sale to Adams Company; invoice price, $1,000; terms 2/10, n/30.[12]		

Credit sales should be recorded at **net of discount** (rather than at gross) amount, as illustrated above. Theoretically, net of discount is correct; however, for various reasons, credit sales sometimes are recorded at the gross amount (see Chapter 7).

Exhibit 2–12 shows a typical special journal for credit sales for a business that has two sales departments. The general ledger contains an Accounts Receivable Control account. Observe that this special journal provides a convenient format to record all of the relevant data on each credit sale. Also, it can be designed to differentiate sales by department. Clearly, it is easier to enter a credit sale in this format than in the general journal.

The mechanics of **posting** amounts from the special sales journal to the general and subsidiary ledgers also are simplified. There are two phases of posting a special journal:

1. **Daily posting**—The amount of **each** credit sale is posted daily to the appropriate individual account in the **accounts receivable subsidiary ledger.** Daily posting is essential so that each customer's account will be up-to-date when the customer pays. Posting is indicated by entering the account number in the Ledger Folio column. For example, the number 112.13 entered in the Ledger Folio column in Exhibit 2–12 is the account number assigned to Adams Company and signifies that $980 was posted as a debit to the appropriate customer's account in the subsidiary ledger.

2. **Monthly posting**—At the end of each month, the Amount column is summed. This **total is posted to two accounts in the general ledger;** that is, in Exhibit 2–12, the $9,360 was posted (1) as a debit to account No. 112 (Accounts Receivable Control) and (2) as a credit to account No. 500 (Sales Revenue Control). The T-accounts shown in **Exhibit 2–16** illustrate how these postings are reflected in the general ledger and the subsidiary ledger. Observe that the two ledgers show the **journal page** (i.e., folio) from which each amount was posted.

---

[12] Terms 2/10, n/30, mean that if the account is paid within 10 days after date of sale, a 2% discount is permitted to encourage early payment. If not paid within the 10-day discount period, the full amount is past due after the end of 30 days.

EXHIBIT 2–12:   Special Journal—Sales on Credit

Date 19J	Sales Invoice No.	Accounts Receivable (name)	Terms	Ledger Folio	Receivable and Sale Amount	Dept. Sales	
						Dept. A	Dept. B
Jan.2	93	Adams Co.	2/10, n/30	112.13	980		
3	94	Sayre Corp.	2/10, n/30	112.80	490		
11	95	Cope & Day Co.	net	112.27	5,734		
27	96	XY Mfg. Co.	2/10, n/30	112.91	1,960	(Not illustrated; the total of each column would also be posted to a sales subsidiary ledger.)	
30	97	Miller, J. B.	2/10, n/30	112.42	196		
31	—	Totals			9,360		
31	—	Posting			(112/500)		

Special Journal-Merchandise Sales on Credit   Page __S-23__

Special Journal for Merchandise Purchases on Credit.   In situations where there are numerous credit purchases of merchandise for resale, data processing may be facilitated by using a special journal designed only for this type of transaction:[13]

January 3, 19J:

Purchases ($1,000 × 99%)   990
    Accounts payable (PT Mfg. Co.)   990
    Purchased merchandise for resale; invoice price, $1,000; terms 1/20, n/30.

This transaction, rather than being entered in the general journal, would be entered in the purchases journal as in **Exhibit 2–13.** In this illustration, the purchases are recorded at net of discount, which is the theoretically correct approach. During the month, each amount would be posted daily as a credit to the accounts of the individual creditors in the **accounts payable** subsidiary ledger.

At the end of the month, the total of the Amount column (i.e., $6,760) would be posted to the general ledger as *(a)* a debit to the Purchases account No. 612 (if a periodic inventory system is used) and *(b)* a credit to the Accounts Payable Control account No. 210.

Special Journal for Cash Receipts.   Because a large volume of transactions for cash receipts is typical, a special cash receipts journal often is used. This special journal is designed to accommodate **all cash receipts** including cash sales. There-

---

[13] This entry assumes periodic inventory procedures. Alternatively, if perpetual inventory procedures are used, the debit would be to the inventory account.

EXHIBIT 2–13

Special Journal—Purchases on Credit

Special Journal-Merchandise Purchases on Credit						Page P-19
Date 19J	Purchase Order No.	Accounts Payable (name)	Terms	Ledger Folio	Purchase and Liability Amount
Jan.3	41	PT Mfg. Co.	1/20,n/30	210.61	990
7	42	Able Suppliers, Ltd.	net	210.12	150
31	—	Totals	—	—	6,760
31	—	Posting	—	—	(612/210)

fore, it must have a column for **cash debit** and several credit columns. Credit columns are designated for recurring credits, and a Sundry Accounts column is used to accommodate infrequent credits. A typical special cash receipts journal is shown in **Exhibit 2–14.**

During the month, each amount in the Accounts Receivable column is posted daily as a credit to the individual customer accounts in the **accounts receivable**

EXHIBIT 2–14:   **Special Journal—Cash Receipts**

Special Journal-Cash Receipts							Page CR-19
				Credits			
Date 19J	Explanation	Debits Cash	Account Title	Ledger Folio	Accounts Receivable	Sales Revenue	Sundry Accounts
Jan.4	Cash Sales	11,200		—		11,200	
7	On acct.	4,490	Sayre Corp.	112.80	4,490		
8	Sale of land	10,000	Land	123			4,000
			Gain on sale of land	510			6,000
10	On acct.	1,000	Adams Co.	112.13	1,000		
19	Cash sales	43,600		—		43,600	
20	On acct.	5,734	Cope & Day Co.	112.27	5,734		
31	Totals	116,224		—	11,224	71,000	34,000
31	Posting	(101)		—	(112)	(500)	(NP)*

* NP—Not posted as one total because the individual amounts are posted as indicated in the Ledger Folio column.

EXHIBIT 2–15

Special Journal—Cash Payments

					Debits				
				Special Journal-Cash Payments				Page CP-31	
Date 19J	Check No.	Explanation	Credits Cash	Account Name	Ledger Folio	Accounts Payable	Purchases	Sundry Accounts
Jan.2	141	Pur. mdse.	3,000				3,000	
10	142	On acct.	990	PT Mfg. Co.	210.61	990		
15	143	Jan. rent	660	Rent exp.	612			660
16	144	Pur. mdse.	1,810				1,810	
31	—	Totals	98,400		—	5,820	90,980	1,600
31	—	Posting	(101)		—	(210)	(612)	(NP)

subsidiary ledger. At the end of the month, (a) the individual amounts in the Sundry Accounts column are posted as credits to the appropriate general ledger accounts and (b) the totals (for Cash, Accounts Receivable, and Sales Revenue) are posted to the general ledger as indicated by the folio numbers. The total of the Sundry Accounts column is not posted because the individual amounts have already been posted.

Special Journal for Cash Payments.   Because of the large volume of cash disbursements, most companies use a special journal designed to accommodate **all cash payments** including cash purchases of merchandise. The special journal must have a column for **cash credits** and a number of debit columns. Debit columns are set up for frequently recurring debits, and a Sundry Accounts column is used for infrequent debits. A typical special cash payments journal, with some common entries, is shown in **Exhibit 2–15.** Posting follows the same procedures explained above for the cash receipts special journal.

Reconciling a Subsidiary Ledger

The sum of all account balances in a subsidiary ledger must agree with the overall balance reflected in the related control account in the general ledger. To assure that this correspondence exists, frequent reconciliations should be made. Clearly, a reconciliation cannot be accomplished unless all posting is complete, both to the control account and to the subsidiary ledger. To illustrate, a reconciliation based upon the information in **Exhibit 2–16** for **Accounts Receivable Control** and the **accounts receivable subsidiary ledger** would be as follows:

EXHIBIT 2–16

General Ledger and Subsidiary Ledger

General Ledger (partial)

Cash — No.101

19J			19J		
Jan.1	balance	18,700	Jan.31	CP-31	98,400
31	CR-19	116,224			

Accounts Receivable Control — No.112

19J			19J		
Jan.1	balance	5,000	Jan.31	CR-19	11,224
31	S-23	9,360			

Equipment — No.140

19J		
Jan.2	J-14	9,000

Notes Payable — No.214

			19J		
			Jan.2	J-14	9,000

Sales Revenue Control — No.500

			19J		
			Jan.31	S-23	9,360
			31	CR-19	71,000

Subsidiary Ledger for Accounts Receivable (Accts. No. 112)

Adams Company — Acct. No. 112.13

Date	Folio	Explanation	Debit	Credit	Balance
19J Jan.1		balance			1,000
2	S-23		980		1,980
10	CR-19			1,000	980

Cope & Day Company — Acct. No. 112.27

Jan.11	S-23		5,734		5,734
20	CR-19			5,734	-0-

Miller, J.B. — Acct. No. 112.42

Jan.30	S-23		196		196

Sayre Corporation — Acct. No. 112.80

Jan.1		balance			4,000
3	S-23		490		4,490
7	CR-19			4,490	-0-

XY Manufacturing Company — Acct. No. 112.91

Jan.27	S-23		1,960		1,960

Reconciliation of Accounts Receivable Subsidiary Ledger (at January 31, 19J)

	Amount
Subsidiary ledger balances:	
112.13 Adams Co.	$ 980
112.42 Miller, J. B.	196
112.91 XY Manufacturing Co.	1,960
Total—agrees with the balance in Accounts Receivable Control ($14,360–$11,224)	$3,136

The above discussion reviewed the concepts underlying special journals, control accounts, and subsidiary ledgers. Their design and use depend upon the characteristics of the company. They do not involve new accounting principles because they are only data processing techniques. The above discussion also emphasized the four primary efficiencies that may result from their use: (1) journalizing is simplified, (2) posting is simplified, (3) subdivision of work is simplified, and (4) a highly trained person is not needed to maintain a special journal or a subsidiary ledger that involves only one type of transaction.[14]

QUESTIONS

PART A

1. What are the three required financial statements? Give a brief explanation of what each statement reports.
2. List and briefly explain the five components of the basic accounting model.
3. Broadly explain the primary purpose of an accounting information processing system.
4. Explain the dual balancing feature of the fundamental accounting model.
5. Complete the following matrix by entering "debit" or "credit" in each cell.

Item	Increase	Decrease
Liabilities		
Revenues		
Assets		
Expenses		
Owners' equity		

[14] Voucher system journals are not discussed because they involve essentially the same procedures as illustrated. The voucher system journals are known as (a) the voucher register and (b) the check register.

(handwritten margin notes: External + Internal / Verified, tangible record / sales invoice / freight bills / recording effects of transactions / transfer to ledger/trial / Verifies D=C on be / used in WKSheet + Adj ent)

6. What kind of transactions and events are recorded in an accounting system? Explain.
7. With respect to the collection of economic data for the accounting system, why are source documents important? Give some examples of typical source documents.
8. Explain the nature and purpose of transaction analysis. *(handwritten: need it to develop accts)*
9. What is meant by journalizing? What purpose does it serve? *(handwritten: entry to record in accts system)*
10. What is meant by posting? What purpose does it serve?
11. What is a trial balance? What are the two primary purposes of a trial balance? Distinguish between unadjusted, adjusted, and post-closing trial balances. *(handwritten: Perm – BS Accts)*
12. Distinguish between permanent, temporary, and mixed accounts. *(handwritten: Temp – IS Accts)*
13. Classify the following accounts, before the adjusting entries, as permanent, temporary, or mixed (explain any assumptions you make):

Accounts receivable *P*	Prepaid insurance *P*
Supplies inventory *P*	Notes payable *P*
Retained earnings *P*	Interest revenue *T*
Patents *P*	Common stock *P*
Interest expense *T*	Property tax expense *T*

(handwritten: T = Rev / I + P / Gains + Loss)

14. Distinguish between the general ledger, control accounts, and subsidiary ledgers. What is the basic purpose of each?
15. Explain the difference between special journals and the general journal.

(handwritten: SJ = CR, CP, SJ, PJ, √ S)

PART B

(handwritten: increase efficiency + minimize processing errors)

16. Why is a worksheet a facilitating technique? What does it facilitate?
17. What are the purpose and nature of adjusting entries? Explain why adjusting entries usually must be made. Explain why the adjusting entries must be considered prior to developing the financial statements.
18. Why are the adjusting entries journalized and posted?
19. Complete the following tabulation to indicate the relationship between cash flow and accounting recognition of the four items to the left:

Item	Cash flow precedes (P) or follows (F) recognition
Deferred expense	*P*
Deferred revenue	*P*
Accrued expense	*F*
Accrued revenue	*F*

(handwritten: Bad Debt, Depreciation, COGS,)

20. Give four examples of internal cost allocations that require adjusting entries.
21. At the end of 19A, Baker Corporation had the following situations:

 a. Prepaid insurance, $150; the policy was acquired on January 1, 19A, and expires on December 31, 19B.

 b. Wages earned on December 29–31, 19A, not yet recorded or paid, $2,400.

(handwritten bottom: I E / P P I)

(handwritten: W E / W Payable)

c. Rent collected for January 19B, $400, that was credited to Rent Revenue when collected.

d. Interest expense of $200 for November–December 19A that will be paid April 30, 19B.

e. An asset that cost $10,000 (residual value, $1,000); being depreciated over five years, straight line.

Give the adjusting entry for each situation. If none is needed explain why.

22. The following accounts were recorded in the 19X adjusting entries of Jackson Corporation. Classify each account as an asset, liability, revenue, gain, expense, or loss, and explain the classification for each:

a. Prepaid insurance.
b. Property taxes payable.
c. Rent receivable.
d. Interest payable.
e. Rent revenue collected in advance.
f. Accumulated depreciation.
g. Allowance for doubtful accounts.

23. Briefly explain the differences between a perpetual and periodic inventory system.

24. The following data are available under a periodic inventory system: Purchases, $70,000; Sales, $150,000; Returned sales, $5,000; Returned purchases, $4,000; Freight-in, $7,000; Beginning inventory, $32,000; Selling expenses, $18,000; and Ending inventory, $29,000 (by count). Compute cost of goods sold.

25. Number the following phases in the accounting information processing cycle to indicate their normal sequence of completion:

___Journalize and post reversing entries.
___Posting.
___Transaction analysis.
___Collection of data.
___Journalize and post adjusting entries.
___Journalize and post closing entries.
___Prepare financial statements.
___Journalize current transactions.
___Prepare post-closing trial balance.
___Prepare worksheets.
___Prepare unadjusted trial balance.

26. What are the purpose and nature of closing entries?

27. What are the purpose and nature of reversing entries? Why are they journalized and posted?

28. X Company owes a $4,000, three-year, 9% note payable. Interest is paid each November 30. Therefore, at the end of the accounting period, December 31, the following adjusting entry was made:

Interest expense 30
    Interest payable   30

Would you recommend using a reversing entry in this situation? Explain.

EXERCISES

PART A: EXERCISES 2–1 TO 2–6

Exercise 2–1

Given below to the left is a series of journal entries. You are to analyze each entry and then respond to the right to indicate the *(a)* account classification and *(b)* type of transaction. The first entry is used as an example.

Typical entries (AB Corporation)			a. Account classification — A = Asset, L = Liability, OE = Owners' equity	P = Permanent, T = Temporary, M = Mixed	b. Type of transaction — R = Reciprocal, NR = Nonreciprocal	E = External, I = Internal
Example: Cash	9,000		A (+)	P	R	E
Sales		9,000	OE (rev.)	T		
a. Prepaid insurance	300		A–M	P	R	I
Cash		300	A	P		
b. Merchandise inventory	7,000		A	P	R	E
Accounts payable		7,000	L	P		
c. Retained earnings	400		OE	P	R	E
Cash		400	A	P		
d. Insurance expense	150		OE	T	—	I
Prepaid insurance		150	A–M	P	R	
e. Patent	1,000		A	P		E
Cash		1,000	A	P		
f. Depreciation expense	3,000		OE	T	—	I
Accumulated depreciation		3,000	A	P		
g. Accounts receivable	6,000		A	P	R	E
Sales		6,000	OE	T		
h. Cash	5,000		A	P	R	I
Capital stock		1,000	OE	P		
Contributed capital		4,000	OE	P		
i. Investment, stock of TK Corp.	900		A ?	P	—	E
Donated capital		900	OE ?	P–?		
j. Extraordinary loss	300		OE	T	—	I
Plant (fire loss)		300	A–?	P		I
k. Expense	200		OE	T	—	I
Wages payable		200	L	P		
l. Expense	50		OE	T	—	I
Office supplies inventory		50	A	P		

Exercise 2–2

The following selected transactions were completed during the current year by Rose Corporation:

a. Sold 60,000 shares of its own common stock, par $1 per share, for $80,000 cash.
b. Borrowed $20,000 cash on a six-month, 12% note payable (interest is payable at maturity date).
c. Purchased real estate for use in the business at a cash cost of $50,000. The real estate consisted of a small building ($35,000) and the lot on which it was located.
d. Purchased merchandise for resale at a cash cost of $28,000. Assume periodic inventory system; therefore, debit Purchases.
e. Purchased merchandise for resale on credit; terms 3/10,n/30. If paid within 10 days, the cash payment would be $485; however, if paid after 10 days, the payment would be $500. Because the company takes all discounts, credit purchases are recorded at net of the discount.
f. Sold merchandise for $20,000; collected 60% in cash, and the balance is due in 30 days.
g. Paid the balance due on the purchase in (e) within the 10-day period.
h. Paid the note and interest in full for the loan in (b) above on due date.
i. Recorded income tax for the current year, $2,000; will be paid early next year.
j. Recorded straight-line depreciation for one year on the building; 10-year useful life and estimated residual value, $5,000.

Required:

Analyze each of the above transactions and enter each in a general journal. Use the letter to the left to indicate the date.

Exercise 2–3

During the accounting year ended December 31, 19B, Felix Corporation completed the following selected transactions:

a. Sold 20,000 shares of its own common stock, par $5, for $11 cash per share.
b. Borrowed $100,000 cash on a one-year, 12% interest-bearing note, interest payable at maturity date March 31, 19C.
c. Purchased a small office building for $150,000 cash, of which the land cost was $20,000. Estimated useful life 10 years and $10,000 residual value. The company will use straight-line depreciation.
d. Service revenues, $200,000, of which 20% was on credit.
e. Declared and paid a $10,000 cash dividend.
f. Collected half of the credit revenues (item [d] above).
g. Incurred total expenses of $160,000, of which 15% was on credit.
h. Purchased an electric typewriter that had an invoice price of $1,500 for $1,200 cash.
i. Paid two thirds of the credit expenses (item [g]).
j. Recorded interest expense on the note (item [b]).

k. Recorded depreciation expense on the office building for six months because it was purchased on July 1, 19B.

Required:

Analyze each of the above transactions and enter each in a general journal.

Exercise 2–4

The 11 phases that comprise the accounting information processing cycle are listed to the left in scrambled order. To the right is a brief statement of the objective of each phase, also in scrambled order. You are to present two responses.

Required:

1. In the blanks to the left, number the phases in the usual sequence of completion.
2. In the blanks to the right, use the letters to match each phase with its objective.

Sequence (order)	Phases	Matching (with objective)	Objective
_____	Journalizing.	_____	*a.* Verification after closing entries.
_____	Journalize and post reversing entries.	_____	*b.* Communication to decision makers.
_____	Transaction analysis.	_____	*c.* Verification before adjusting entries.
_____	Prepare financial statements.	_____	*d.* Transfer from journal to ledger.
_____	Journalize and post closing entries.	_____	*e.* An activity that is based on source documents.
_____	Collection of raw data.		
_____	Posting.	_____	*f.* Update general ledger by separating "mixed" account balances.
_____	Journalize and post adjusting entries.	_____	*g.* Assess economic impact of each transaction.
_____	Prepare worksheets.		
_____	Prepare unadjusted trial balance.	_____	*h.* An original input into the accounting system.
_____	Prepare post-closing trial balance.	_____	*i.* To facilitate subsequent entries.
			j. To obtain a zero balance in the revenue and expense accounts.
			k. A logical and systematic technique that is used in completing the end-of-period procedures.

Exercise 2–5

Darby Corporation completed the three transactions given below:

a. January 1, 19A—sold 10,000 shares of its own unissued common stock, par $1 per share, for $46,000 cash.
b. January 3, 19A—purchased a machine that cost $50,000. Payment was $10,000 cash plus a $5,000, one-year, 15% interest-bearing note payable and a $35,000, three-year, 16% interest-bearing note payable. Interest on each note is payable each January 2.
c. February 1, 19A—sold two lots that would not be needed for $8,500. Received $3,500 cash down payment and a $5,000, 90-day, 15% interest-bearing note (interest payable at maturity date). The two lots had a book value of $6,500.

Required:

1. Analyze each of the above transactions and enter each in the general journal.
2. Set up T-accounts and post the entries in 1 above. For posting purposes, set up a

numbering system for both the journal pages and the ledger accounts. Use these numbers in your posting process.

Exercise 2–6

A clerk for Century Company prepared the following unadjusted trial balance which the clerk was unable to balance:

Account	Debit	Credit
Cash	$ 35,563	
Accounts receivable	31,000	
Allowance for doubtful accounts	(2,000)	
Inventory		$ 18,000
Equipment	181,500	
Accumulated depreciation		12,000
Accounts payable	18,000	
Notes payable		25,000
Common stock, par $10		180,000
Retained earnings (correct)		14,000
Revenues		75,000
Expenses	60,000	
Totals (out of balance by $63)	$324,063	$324,000

Assume you are examining the accounts and have found the following errors:

a. Equipment purchased for $7,500 at year-end was debited to Expenses.
b. Sales on credit of $829 were debited to Accounts Receivable for $892 and credited to Revenues for $829.
c. A $6,000 collection on accounts receivable was debited to Cash and credited to Revenues.
d. The inventory amount is understated by $2,000 (cost of goods sold is included in expenses).

Required:
Prepare a corrected trial balance. Show computations.

PART B: EXERCISES 2–7 TO 2–20

Exercise 2–7

Savin Company entered the following adjusting and closing (but no reversing) entries in its accounts at December 31, 19B, end of its accounting period:

a. Wage expense 1,400
     Wages payable 1,400

b. Warranty (guarantee) expense 950
     Estimated warranty liability 950

N c. Insurance expense ....*debit*........................   600
        Prepaid insurance   600

Y d. Interest expense   1,200
        Interest payable   1,200

Y e. Interest receivable   900
        Interest revenue   900

   f. Rent revenue ....*debit*.......   750
        Unearned rent revenue   750

   g. Income summary   5,000
        Retained earnings   5,000

Required:

For each entry give the following: whether accrued or deferred, type of entry, and explanation of the entry.

Exercise 2–8

Mavis Corporation adjusts and closes its accounts each December 31. The following situations require adjusting entries at the current year-end. You are requested to prepare the adjusting entries in the general journal for each situation. If no entry is required for any item, explain why.

a. Machine A is to be depreciated for the full year. It cost $167,000, and the estimated useful life is five years, with an estimated residual value of $12,000. Use straight-line depreciation.
b. Credit sales for the current year amounted to $190,000. The estimated bad debt loss rate on credit sales is ½%.
c. Property taxes for the current year have not been recorded or paid. A statement for the current year was received near the end of December for $3,000; if paid after February 1 in the next year, a 10% penalty is assessed.
d. Office supplies that cost $800 were purchased during the year and debited to Office Supplies Inventory. The inventories of these supplies on hand were as follows: $100 at the end of the prior year, and $300 at the end of the current year.
e. Mavis rented an office in its building to a tenant for one year, starting on September 1. Rent for one year amounting to $6,000 was collected at that date. The total amount collected was credited to Rent Revenue.
f. Mavis received a note receivable from a customer dated November 1 of the current year. It is an $18,000, 10%, note, due in one year. At the maturity date, Mavis will collect the amount of the note plus interest for one year.

Exercise 2–9

On December 31, 19D, Star Corporation had the following situations that might affect its annual report. You are to analyze each item and give any required adjusting entries. If none is required for any item, explain why.

a. At the end of the year, unpaid and unrecorded wages amounted to $4,500.
b. The company owns a building that is to be depreciated for the full year. It cost $284,000,

has an estimated useful life of 20 years, and a residual value of $54,000. Accumulated depreciation at the beginning of the current year was $60,000.

c. The company rented some space in its building to a tenant on August 1 of the current year and collected $7,200 cash, which was rent for six months in advance. Rent Revenue was credited for $7,200 on August 1.

d. The company paid a two-year insurance premium in advance on July 1 of the current year amounting to $1,000. The $1,000 was debited to Prepaid Insurance at payment date.

e. Credit sales for the current year amounted to $145,000. The estimated bad debt loss rate is ⅓% of credit sales.

f. On July 1 of the current year, the company received a $30,000, one-year, 15% note from a customer. At maturity date, the company will receive the principal amount plus interest for one year.

Exercise 2–10

1. Analyze the relationships and amounts for each of the four cases and complete the following schedule to compute cost of goods sold:

	Case A	Case B	Case C	Case D
Sales revenue	$100,000	$136,000	$128,000	$110,000
Beginning inventory ...	20,000	25,000	?	26,000
Net income (loss)	10,000	25,000	16,000	(10,000)
Ending inventory	30,000	?	32,000	?
Total expenses	40,000	41,000	44,000	48,000
Purchases	?	60,000	70,000	73,000
Cost of goods sold	?	?	?	?

2. Give the adjusting entry for the inventory and cost of goods sold assuming a periodic inventory system is used in Case A.

Exercise 2–11

a. On December 31, 19A, the Maintenance Supplies Inventory account showed a balance on hand amounting to $350. During 19B, purchases of office supplies amounted to $1,000. An inventory of maintenance supplies on hand at December 31, 19B, reflected unused supplies amounting to $500. Give the adjusting journal entry that should be made on December 31, 19B, assuming that: Case A—the purchases were debited to the Maintenance Supplies Inventory account, and Case B—the purchases were debited to Maintenance Supplies Expense.

b. On December 31, 19A, the Prepaid Insurance account showed a debit balance of $900, which was for coverage for the three months, January–March. On April 1, 19B, the company took out another policy covering a two-year period from that date. The two-year premium amounting to $9,600 was paid and debited to Prepaid Insurance. Give the adjusting journal entry that should be made on December 31, 19B, to adjust for the entire year.

Exercise 2–12

Voss Company adjusts and closes its accounts each December 31. Below are two typical situations involving adjusting entries.

a. During the current year, office supplies were purchased for cash, $750. The inventory of office supplies at the end of the prior year was $150. At the end of the current year, the inventory showed $240 unused supplies remaining on hand. Give the adjusting entry assuming at the time of the purchase that: Case A—$750 was debited to Office Supplies Expense, and Case B—$750 was debited to Office Supplies Inventory.

b. On June 1, the company collected cash, $8,400, which was for rent collected in advance for the next 12 months. Give the adjusting journal entry assuming at the time of the collection that: Case A—$8,400 was credited to Rent Revenue, and Case B—$8,400 was credited to Rent Revenue Collected in Advance.

Exercise 2–13

Jodie Company adjusts and closes its books each December 31. It is now December 31, 19A, and the adjusting entries are to be made. You are requested to prepare, in general journal format, the adjusting entry that should be made for each of the following items:

a. Credit sales for the year amounted to $200,000. The estimated loss rate on bad debts is ⅜%.

b. Unpaid and unrecorded wages incurred at December 31 amounted to $2,100.

c. The company paid a two-year insurance premium in advance on April 1, 19A, amounting to $3,000, which was debited to Prepaid Insurance.

d. Machine A that cost $37,000 is to be depreciated for the full year. The estimated useful life is 10 years, and the residual value, $2,000. Use straight-line depreciation.

e. The company rented a warehouse on June 1, 19A, for one year. They had to pay the full amount of rent one year in advance on June 1, amounting to $4,800, which was debited to Rent Expense.

f. The company received a 15% note from a customer with a face amount of $6,000. The note was dated September 1, 19A; the principal plus the interest is payable one year later. Notes Receivable was debited, and Sales Revenue credited on September 1, 19A.

g. On December 30, 19A, the property tax bill was received in the amount of $2,000. This amount applied only to 19A and had not been previously recorded or paid. The taxes are due, and will be paid, on January 15, 19B.

h. On April 1, 19A, the company signed a $30,000, 16% note payable. On that date, Cash was debited and Notes Payable credited for $30,000. The note is payable on March 31, 19B, for the face amount plus interest for one year.

i. The company purchased a patent on January 1, 19A, at a cost of $5,950. On that date, Patent was debited and Cash credited for $5,950. The patent has an estimated useful life of 17 years and no residual value.

j. The worksheet is being completed, and pretax income has been computed to be $40,000 after all the above adjustments. Assume an average income tax rate of 31.75%.

Exercise 2–14

The adjusted trial balance for ABC Company showed the following on December 31, 19E, which is the end of the annual accounting period:

Sales revenue	$92,000
Interest revenue	1,000
Purchases	44,000
Purchase returns	500
Freight-in (on purchases)	1,500
Beginning inventory (periodic)	17,800
Selling expenses	23,000
Administrative expenses	13,000
Interest expense	400
Income tax expense	1,000
Additional data:	
Ending inventory	19,000

Required:

Set up T-accounts for each of the above; enter the balance in each account, and then draw in lines to diagram and identify any adjusting and closing entries. Use Cost of Goods Sold, Income Summary, and Retained Earnings accounts.

Exercise 2–15

At December 31, 19B (end of the accounting period), Sara Corporation reflected the following amounts on its worksheet:

Sales revenue	$95,000
Interest revenue	2,000
Beginning inventory (periodic inventory system)	15,000
Ending inventory	17,000
Freight-in (on purchases)	3,000
Purchases	54,000
Sales returns	4,000
Purchase returns	1,000
Operating expenses (including income tax)	26,000

Required:
1. Compute cost of goods sold.
2. Give the adjusting entry for inventory and cost of goods sold. If none, explain why.
3. Give the closing entries for *(a)* revenues, *(b)* expenses, and *(c)* net income.

Exercise 2–16

Jans Corporation has just completed the worksheet at December 31, 19D (end of the accounting period). The following amounts were reflected on the worksheet:

Sales revenue	$93,000
Service revenue	27,000
Beginning inventory (periodic inventory system)	36,000
Ending inventory	32,000
Operating expenses	26,000
Sales returns and allowances	4,000

Purchases	54,000
Income tax expense	8,000
Purchase returns and allowances	2,000
Freight-in (on purchases)	6,000

Required:
1. Compute cost of goods sold.
2. Give the adjusting entry for inventory and cost of goods sold. If none, explain why.
3. Give the closing entries for *(a)* revenues, *(b)* expenses, and *(c)* net income.

Exercise 2–17

Franklin Company has completed its worksheet at December 31, 19B (end of its accounting period). The following accounts and amounts were reflected on the worksheet:

Sales revenue	$97,000
Service revenue	2,000
Operating expenses	22,000
Income tax expense	5,000
Cost of goods sold	53,000
Interest expense	4,000
Ending inventory (perpetual inventory system)	11,000

Required:
1. Give the adjusting entry for inventory and cost of goods sold. If none, explain why.
2. Give the closing entries for *(a)* revenues, *(b)* expenses, and *(c)* net income.

Exercise 2–18

At the end of the annual accounting period, Ross Corporation made the following adjusting entries:

December 31, 19B:

a. Wage expense	7,500	
Wages payable		7,500
b. Bad debt expense	600	
Allowance for doubtful accounts		600
c. Income tax expense	9,000	
Income tax payable		9,000
d. Depreciation expense	20,000	
Accumulated depreciation		20,000

Required:
Give the reversing entries that you think would be preferable on January 1, 19C. For each adjusting entry, explain the analysis you used to decide whether to reverse it.

Exercise 2–19

At the end of the annual accounting period, Kramer Corporation made the following adjusting entries:

December 31, 19A:

a. Property tax expense 750
     Property taxes payable 750
   (These are paid once each year.)

b. Rent receivable 3,600
     Rent revenue 3,600
   (Rent revenue is collected at various dates each month.)

c. Patent amortization expense 2,500
     Patents 2,500

d. Warranty expense 500
     Estimated warranty liability 500

e. Wage expense 4,000
     Wages payable 4,000

Required:

Give the reversing entries that should be made on January 1, 19B. Explain, for each adjusting entry, the analysis you used to determine whether to reverse it.

Exercise 2–20

Tuffy Corporation prepares monthly interim financial statements for internal use. Its accounting period ends December 31. At the end of each month, the company accountant prepares a cumulative worksheet that uses the (a) unadjusted trial balance at the end of the month and (b) adjusting entries based on cumulative amounts to the end of the month.

It is February 28 of the current year, and the worksheet has been completed. Therefore, the following data are available for the income statement (summarized to simplify):

	Reported in January	Reflected on February 28 worksheet
Sales revenue	$150,000	$365,000
Cost of goods sold	80,000	220,000
Total operating expenses	30,000	63,000
Interest revenue	2,000	3,400
Interest expense	5,000	11,100
Gain (loss) on disposal of assets	7,000	(9,000)
Income tax expense	11,000	16,325

Required:

Prepare a summarized income statement for the month of February. Show computations.

PROBLEMS

PART A: PROBLEMS 2–1 TO 2–4

Problem 2–1

Requirement 1:
Develop a diagram (using the T-account format) that indicates application of the financial position equation and the debit-credit concept for assets, liabilities, and owners' equity (including investments by owners, distribution to owners, revenues, expenses, gains, and losses).

Requirement 2:
Enter the following transaction amounts for Year 1 (coded by letter) into the T-accounts set up in Requirement 1:

a. Issued capital stock for cash, $90,000.
b. Borrowed $10,000 cash on long-term note.
c. Purchased equipment on credit for use in the business, $6,000.
d. Earned service revenue, $30,000, ⅙ on credit.
e. Paid all expenses in cash, $16,000.
f. Paid $2,000 cash on the equipment (purchased in [c]).

Requirement 3:
Does your diagram reflect a double-entry system? Explain the basis for your answer.

Requirement 4:
Complete the following schedule:

Items	Computations	Amount
a. Total assets	_____	$ _____
Total liabilities	_____	_____
Total owners' equity	_____	_____
b. Total debits	_____	_____
Total credits	_____	_____
c. Total revenues	_____	_____
Total expenses	_____	_____
Income	_____	_____
d. Total cash inflow	_____	_____
Total cash outflow	_____	_____
Ending cash balance	_____	_____

Problem 2–2

The following selected transactions were completed during Year 1 of operations by Vicar Corporation:

a. Sold 20,000 shares of its own common stock, par $1 per share, for $15 per share and received cash in full.
b. Borrowed $100,000 cash on a 12%, one-year note, interest payable at maturity on April 30, Year 2.
c. Purchased equipment for use in operating the business at a net cash cost of $164,000; paid in full.

d. Purchased merchandise for resale at a cash cost of $140,000; paid cash. Assume a periodic inventory system; therefore, debit Purchases.

e. Purchased merchandise for resale on credit terms 2/10, n/60. The merchandise will cost $9,800 if paid within 10 days; after 10 days, the payment will be $10,000. The company always takes the discount; therefore, such purchases are recorded at net of the discount.

f. Sold merchandise for $180,000; collected $165,000 cash, and the balance is due in one month.

g. Paid $30,000 cash for operating expenses.

h. Paid ¾ of the balance for the merchandise purchased in (e) within 10 days; the balance remains unpaid.

i. Collected 50% of the balance due on the sale in (f); the remaining balance is uncollected.

j. Paid cash for an insurance premium, $600; the premium was for two years' coverage (debit Prepaid Insurance).

k. Purchased a tract of land for a future building for company operations, $63,000 cash.

l. Paid damages to a customer who was injured on the company premises, $10,000 cash.

Required:

1. Enter each of the above transactions in a general journal; use J1 for the first journal page number. Use the letter to the left to indicate the date.

2. Set up appropriate T-accounts and post the journal entries. Use folio numbers in posting process. Assign each T-account appropriate title, and number each account in balance sheet order, followed by the income statement accounts; start with Cash, No. 101.

3. Prepare an unadjusted trial balance.

Problem 2–3

The following selected transactions were completed during Year 1 of operations by Delphi Corporation.

a. At date of organization, sold and issued 50,000 shares of its common stock, par $1 per share, for $90,000 cash.

b. Purchased a plant site for $100,000. The site included a building valued at $82,000 and land valued at $18,000. Payment was made, $70,000 cash and a $30,000 one-year, 12% note, interest payable at maturity.

c. Borrowed $70,000 cash from City Bank; signed a 15% interest (payable at maturity) note due in six months.

d. Purchased equipment for use in the business for $25,000; paid cash.

e. Purchased merchandise for resale at a cost of $80,000; paid $70,000 cash, balance on credit. Assume perpetual inventory system; therefore, debit Merchandise Inventory.

f. Sold merchandise for cash, $62,000; the perpetual inventory records showed that this merchandise cost $30,000 (you should make two entries).

g. Paid operating expenses, $35,000.

h. Sold merchandise for cash, $48,000; cost, $23,000.

i. Purchased merchandise for cash, $22,000.

j. Paid $7,000 of the balance for the merchandise purchased in (e).

k. Sold and issued 30,000 shares of its common stock for $53,000.

l. On due date, paid the local bank the note given in entry (c) in the amount of $70,000 plus the interest to maturity date.

m. Paid a two-year premium of $1,400 for an insurance policy on the building and equipment.

Required:

1. Journalize the above transactions in a general journal; use J1 for the first journal page. Use the letters to the left to indicate dates.
2. Set up appropriate T-accounts and post the entries. Use folio numbers in your posting process. Assign each T-account an appropriate descriptive title, and number each account in balance sheet order, followed by the income statement accounts; start with Cash, No. 101.
3. Prepare an unadjusted trial balance.

Problem 2–4

On January 1, 19E, the ledger accounts of Reo Service Corporation provided the following trial balance:

Acct. No.	Accounts	Debit	Credit
101	Cash	$ 12,000	$
102	Accounts receivable	16,000	
103	Allowance for doubtful accounts		700
104	Prepaid insurance		
105	Notes receivable, long term, 15%	6,000	
106	Investment in stock of AT Corporation	4,000	
107	Land	12,000	
108	Building	150,000	
109	Accumulated depreciation, building		30,000
110	Patent		
120	Accounts payable		4,000
121	Income tax payable (from 19D)		1,300
122	Notes payable, short term, 12%		10,000
130	Common stock, par $1		40,000
131	Contributed capital in excess of par		80,000
132	Retained earnings		34,000
140	Service revenue		
141	Interest revenue		
150	Operating expenses		
151	Interest expense		
152	Income tax expense		
160	Gain on sale of assets		
	Total	$200,000	$200,000

The following selected transactions (summarized) were completed during 19E (the accounting period ends December 31):

a. Paid the income tax liability from 19D.
b. Borrowed $30,000 cash on a six-month, 12% interest-bearing note (maturity date July 31, 19E).
c. Service revenue, $200,000; 20% on credit.
d. Declared and paid a $20,000 cash dividend.
e. Paid a two-year premium on a new insurance policy on the assets of the company, $400.

f. Sold an additional 1,000 shares of the company's unissued common stock, $8,000 cash.

g. Incurred operating expenses, $110,000; 10% on credit.

h. Purchased a patent for $13,000 cash.

i. Paid accounts payable, $14,000.

j. Collected accounts receivable, $38,000.

k. Sold half of the investment in stock of AT Corporation for $5,000 cash.

l. Paid the note payable and interest on maturity date July 31, 19E (see [*b*] above).

m. Collected interest for one year on the long-term note receivable (credit Interest Revenue).

Required:

1. Set up a general ledger, using T-accounts, for those accounts listed above in the trial balance and enter the beginning balances.

2. Give the general journal entries for the above transactions. Use journal page J9, and let the letters, *a–m,* represent dates.

3. Post the journal entries to the ledger, including all posting folio numbers.

4. Prepare an unadjusted trial balance dated December 31, 19E.

PART B: PROBLEMS 2–5 TO 2–14

Problem 2–5

Below are some unrelated adjusting and closing (but no reversing) entries. Write a suitable explanation for each of the following end-of-period entries:

a. Salary expense	7,000	
Salaries payable		7,000
b. Rent revenue	800	
Unearned rent revenue		800
c. Ending inventory	10,000	
Cost of goods sold	72,000	
Purchases		70,000
Beginning inventory		12,000
d. Interest receivable	900	
Interest revenue		900
e. Supplies expense	400	
Supplies inventory		400
f. Income summary	79,000	
Operating expenses		21,000
Administrative expenses		16,000
Interest expense		2,000
Cost of goods sold		40,000
g. Interest expense	750	
Interest payable		750
h. Income summary	12,500	
Retained earnings		12,500

i. Investment revenue	600	
Unearned investment revenue		600
j. Warranty (guarantee) expense	500	
Estimated warranty liability		500
k. Income tax expense	3,700	
Income taxes payable		3,700
l. Property tax expense	360	
Property taxes payable		360
m. Sales revenue	90,000	
Rent revenue	2,000	
Interest revenue	1,000	
Sales returns		1,500
Income summary		91,500

Problem 2–6

Becker Company adjusts and closes its accounts each December 31. It is December 31, 19D. You are requested to prepare, in general journal format, the adjusting entry that should be made for each of the following items:

a. The company owns a building and the site on which it is situated. The Building account reflects a cost of $467,000; and the Land account, $80,000. The estimated useful life of the building is 20 years, and the residual value, $57,000. Accumulated depreciation to January 1, 19D, was $61,500. Use straight-line depreciation.

b. Property taxes for the city fiscal year, which ends June 30, 19E, have not been recorded or paid. A tax statement was received near the end of December 19D for $6,000. The taxes are due, and will be paid, on February 15, 19E. Property tax expense for the city fiscal year ended June 30, 19D, was $4,800. No property tax expense has been recorded in 19D.

c. The company received a $9,000, 15% note from a customer on May 1, 19D. On that date, Notes Receivable was debited and Sales Revenue credited for $9,000. The face of the note plus interest for one year is payable on April 30, 19E.

d. At December 31, 19D, the Supplies Inventory account showed a debit balance of $1,600. An inventory of unused supplies taken at year-end reflected $300.

e. Sales revenue for the year amounted to $1,500,000, of which $270,000 was on credit. The estimated bad debt loss rate, based on credit sales, was $\frac{1}{3}$% for the year.

f. On August 1, 19D, the company rented some space in its building to a tenant and collected $4,200 cash rent in advance. This was for the 6 months starting August 1, 19D, and was credited to Rent Revenue.

g. At December 31, 19D, unrecorded and unpaid salaries amounted to $8,000.

h. On April 1, 19D, the company borrowed $20,000 on a one-year, 14% note. On that date, Cash was debited and Notes Payable credited for $20,000. At maturity date the face amount plus interest for one year must be paid.

i. On January 1, 19D, the company purchased a patent for use in the business at a cash cost of $3,000, which was debited to Patent. The patent has an estimated remaining economic life of 10 years and no residual value.

j. Inventory: December 31, 19C, $20,000; December 31, 19D, $35,000; Purchases, $790,000; and Purchase returns, $5,000. The company uses the periodic inventory system.

k. The worksheet is being completed; all of the above adjusting entries have been recorded on it. Pretax income has been computed to be $60,000. Assume the average income tax rate is 30%.

Problem 2–7

The following situations relate to the Mason Corporation. The fiscal accounting year ends December 31. The situations relate to the year 19D. Mason Corporation is a manufacturer rather than a retailer. The accounts are adjusted and closed each December 31.

In each instance, you are to give only the adjusting entry (or entries) that would be made on December 31, 19D, incident to adjusting and closing the books and preparation of the annual financial statements. State clearly any assumptions that you make. If an adjusting entry is not required, explain why. Give each adjusting entry in general journal format.

a. Machine A used in the factory cost $225,000; it was purchased on July 1, 19A. It has an estimated useful life of 15 years and a residual value of $15,000. Straight-line depreciation is used.

b. Sales for 19D amounted to $2,000,000, including $300,000 credit sales. It is estimated, based on experience of the company, that bad debt losses will be ¼% of credit sales.

c. At the beginning of 19D, Office Supplies Inventory amounted to $300. During 19D, office supplies amounting to $4,400 were purchased; this amount was debited to Office Supplies Expenses. An inventory of office supplies at the end of 19D showed $200 on the shelves. The January 1 balance of $300 is still reflected in the Office Supplies Inventory account.

d. On July 1, 19D, the company paid a three-year insurance premium amounting to $1,080; this amount was debited to Prepaid Insurance.

e. On October 1, 19D, the company paid rent on some leased office space. The payment of $3,600 cash was for the following 6 months. At the time of payment, Rent Expense was debited for the $3,600.

f. On August 1, 19D, the company borrowed $60,000 from Sharpstown Bank. The loan was for 12 months at 14% interest payable at maturity date.

g. Finished goods inventory on January 1, 19D, was $100,000; and on December 31, 19D, it was $130,000. The perpetual inventory record provided the cost of goods sold amount of $1,200,000.

h. The company owned some property (land) that was rented to B. R. Speir on April 1, 19D, for 12 months for $4,200. On April 1, the entire annual rental of $4,200 was credited to Rent Revenue Collected in Advance and Cash was debited.

i. On December 31, 19D, wages earned by employees but not yet paid (nor recorded in the accounts) amounted to $9,000. Disregard payroll taxes.

j. On September 1, 19D, the company loaned $30,000 to an outside party. The loan was at 15% per annum and was due in six months; interest is payable at maturity. Cash was credited for $30,000, and Notes Receivable debited on September 1 for the same amount.

k. On January 1, 19D, factory supplies on hand amounted to $100. During 19D, factory supplies that cost $2,000 were purchased and debited to Factory Supplies Inventory. At the end of 19D, a physical inventory count revealed that factory supplies on hand amounted to $400.

l. The company purchased a gravel pit on January 1, 19B, at a cost of $30,000; it was estimated that approximately 60,000 tons of gravel could be removed prior to exhaustion. It was also estimated that the company would take five years to exploit this natural resource. Tons of gravel removed and sold were: 19B—3,000; 19C—7,000; and 19D—5,000.

m. At the end of 19D, it was found that postage stamps that cost $90 were on hand (in a "postage" box in the office). When the stamps were purchased, Miscellaneous Expense was debited and Cash credited.

n. At the end of 19D, property taxes for 19D amounting to $29,500 had been assessed on property owned by the company. The taxes are due no later than February 1, 19E. The taxes have not been recorded on the books because payment has not been made.

o. The company borrowed $60,000 from the bank on December 1, 19D. A 60-day note payable was signed that called for 12% interest payable on maturity date. On December 1, 19D, Cash was debited and Notes Payable credited for $60,000.

p. On July 1, 19D, the company paid the city a $500 license fee for the next 12 months. On that date, Cash was credited and License Expense debited for $500.

q. On March 1, 19D, the company made a loan to the company president and received a $15,000 note receivable. The loan was due in one year and called for 10% annual interest payable at maturity date.

r. The company owns three company cars used by the executives. A six-month maintenance contract on them was signed on October 1, 19D, whereby a local garage agreed to do "all the required maintenance." The payment was made for the following six months in advance. On October 1, 19D, Cash was credited and Maintenance Expense was debited for $4,500.

Problem 2–8

Ace Service Corporation has been in operation since January 1, 19A. It is now December 31, 19B, the end of the annual accounting period. The company has never been audited by an independent CPA. The annual statements given below were prepared by the company bookkeeper at December 31, 19B (additional accounts needed in the solution are provided without amounts):

Income Statement

Revenues:	
Service revenue	$250,000
Interest revenue	1,000
Total revenues	251,000
Expenses:	
Salary expense	75,000
Wage expense	60,600
Depreciation expense	
Interest expense	2,400
Remaining expenses	50,000
Total expenses	188,000
Pretax income	63,000
Income tax expense	
Net income	$ 63,000
EPS	$3.50

Balance Sheet

Assets

Cash	$ 40,000
Note receivable (10%)	12,000
Interest receivable	
Inventory, office supplies	2,000
Prepaid insurance	1,500
Equipment...............................	200,000
Accumulated depreciation	(22,500)
Remaining assets	85,500
Total assets	$318,500

Liabilities

Accounts payable	$ 18,000
Wages payable	
Unearned service revenue	
Interest payable	
Income taxes payable	
Notes payable (16%)	40,000
Total liabilities	58,000

Stockholders' Equity

Capital stock, par $10	180,000
Retained earnings	80,500
Total stockholders' equity	260,500
Total liabilities and stockholders' equity	$318,500

An outside accountant was engaged to adjust the statements for any items omitted. As a consequence, the following additional information was developed:

a. No depreciation has been recognized for 19B. The equipment has an eight-year life and residual value of $20,000.
b. Prepaid insurance at the end of 19B was $500. Use "Remaining expenses."
c. Wages unpaid and unrecorded at the end of 19B amounted to $15,000.
d. Interest on the note receivable was collected on the last interest date, October 31, 19B.
e. The inventory count of office supplies at year-end showed $300. Use "Remaining expenses."
f. On December 31, 19B, service revenues collected but unearned amounted to $8,000.
g. Interest on the note payable is paid each August 31.
h. Assume the income tax rate is 20 percent.

Required:

1. Prepare adjusting entries for the above items in general journal form for December 31, 19B.
2. Restate the above statements after taking into account the adjusting entries made in 1 above. Key each adjustment. You need not use additional subclassifications on the statements. Suggestion: Use the following solution format:

Items	Reported amounts	Changes from adjusting entries (use + and −)	Correct amounts
(list the two statements here)			

Problem 2–9

The summarized adjusted trial balance for Barrett Corporation reflected the following on December 31, 19A, end of the annual accounting period:

Cash	$ 60,700	
Inventory (periodic system)*	12,000	
Accounts receivable	21,000	
Allowance for doubtful accounts		$ 400
Prepaid insurance......................	300	
Accounts payable		17,600
Wages payable		1,000
Income taxes payable		2,000
Common stock, par $10		50,000
Retained earnings		17,300
Sales revenue		88,000
Sales returns	2,000	
Purchases ...,.........................	45,000	
Freight-in (on purchases)	1,000	
Purchase returns		700
Operating expenses	18,400	
General expenses (including interest)	14,600	
Income tax expense	2,000	
	$177,000	$177,000

*Inventory (ending), 12/13/19A, $19,800.

Required:
1. Set up T-accounts for the inventory and cost of goods sold accounts, and those accounts that are to be closed. Enter the above balances. Use Cost of Goods Sold, Income Summary, and Retained Earnings accounts.
2. Give the adjusting entry for inventory and cost of goods sold and post it to the T-accounts.
3. Give the closing entries and post them to the T-accounts.

Problem 2–10

The adjusted trial balance for Bryan Corporation reflected the following on December 31, 19A, end of the annual accounting period:

Cash	$ 27,900	
Accounts receivable	32,000	
Allowance for doubtful accounts		$ 500
Inventory (periodic system)*	18,000	
Prepaid insurance	600	
Equipment	100,000	
Accumulated depreciation, equipment		20,000
Accounts payable		13,400
Wages payable		800
Income taxes payable		5,000
Notes payable, long term		20,000
Common stock, par $10		100,000
Retained earnings		12,400
Sales revenue		116,000
Interest revenue		1,000
Sales returns	3,000	
Purchases	70,000	
Freight-in (on purchases)	2,500	
Purchase returns		900
Operating expenses	18,000	
General expenses (including interest)	13,000	
Income tax expense	5,000	
	$290,000	$290,000

*Inventory, 12/31/19A, $23,000.

Required:

1. Set up T-accounts only for the inventory and cost of goods sold accounts, and the accounts that will be closed. Enter the balances given above. Diagram the adjusting entry for inventory and cost of goods sold and all of the closing entries. Use both Cost of Goods Sold and Income Summary accounts.
2. The company uses the periodic inventory system. Give the adjusting entry for inventory and cost of goods sold.
3. Give the closing entries.

Problem 2–11

The post-closing trial balance of the general ledger of VAT Corporation at January 1, 19F, reflected the following (VAT uses the periodic inventory system):

Acct. No.	Account	Debit	Credit
101	Cash	$28,000	
102	Accounts receivable	18,000	
103	Allowance for doubtful accounts		$ 400
104	Inventory (periodic system)*	10,000	
105	Equipment (20-year life; no residual value)	20,000	
106	Accumulated depreciation		6,000
200	Accounts payable		9,000
201	Wages payable		
202	Income tax payable		
300	Common stock, par $1		50,000
301	Retained earnings		10,600
302	Income summary		
400	Revenues		
500	Operating expenses		
501	Purchases		
505	Cost of goods sold		
600	Income tax expense		
		$76,000	$76,000

*Ending inventory, $17,000 (at 12/31/19F).

The following is a summary of selected transactions during 19F (use the number to the left to indicate the date):

Date

1. Sales revenue, $90,000, of which $20,000 was on credit.
2. Purchases, $40,000, of which $10,000 was on credit.
3. Collections on accounts receivable, $35,000.
4. Payments on accounts payable, $17,000.
5. Paid operating expenses, $25,800.
6. On January 1, 19F, sold VAT unissued common stock, 2,000 shares at par, collected cash in full.
7. On the last day of the year, purchased a new machine at a cost of $12,000; paid cash. Estimated useful life, 10 years; residual value, $2,000.

Required:

1. Set up T-accounts in the general ledger for the accounts listed above; they are all you will need. Enter the beginning balances.
2. Journalize each of the above transactions in the general journal.
3. Post each transaction. Use folio notations.
4. Prepare an unadjusted trial balance.
5. Journalize and post the adjusting entries; include the adjusting entry to set up cost of goods sold. Accrued (unpaid) wages at year-end amounted to $800. Bad debt expense is estimated to be 1% of credit sales for the period. Use straight-line depreciation and a 22% income tax rate.
6. Prepare an adjusted trial balance.
7. Prepare an income statement and balance sheet (subclassifications are not required).

8. Journalize and post the closing entries (use Cost of Goods Sold, Income Summary, and Retained Earnings accounts).
9. Prepare a post-closing trial balance.

Problem 2–12

The post-closing trial balance of the general ledger of Wilson Corporation at December 31, 19I, reflected the following:

Acct. No.	Account	Debit	Credit
101	Cash	$ 27,000	
102	Accounts receivable	21,000	
103	Allowance for doubtful accounts		$ 1,000
104	Inventory (perpetual inventory system)*	35,000	
105	Prepaid insurance (20 months remaining)	900	
200	Equipment (20-year estimated life; no residual value)	50,000	
201	Accumulated depreciation		22,500
300	Accounts payable		7,500
301	Wages payable		
302	Income taxes payable (for 19I)		4,000
400	Common stock, par $1		80,000
401	Retained earnings		18,900
500	Sales revenue		
600	Cost of goods sold		
601	Operating expenses		
602	Income tax expense		
700	Income summary		
		$133,900	$133,900

* Ending inventory, $45,000 (at 12/31/19J).

The following transactions occurred during 19J in the order given (use the number at the left to indicate the date):

Date

1. Sales revenue of $30,000, of which $10,000 was on credit; cost provided by perpetual inventory record, $19,500. Hint: When the perpetual system is used, make two entries to record a sale—first, debit Cash and credit Sales Revenue; and second, Debit Cost of Goods Sold and credit Inventory.
2. Collected $17,000 on accounts receivable.
3. Paid income taxes payable (19I), $4,000.
4. Purchased merchandise, $40,000, of which $8,000 was on credit.
5. Paid accounts payable, $6,000.
6. Sales revenue of $72,000 (in cash); cost, $46,800.
7. Paid operating expenses, $19,000.
8. On January 1, 19J, sold and issued 1,000 shares of common stock, par $1, for $1,000 cash.
9. Purchased merchandise, $100,000, of which $27,000 was on credit.

10.   Sales revenue of $98,000, of which $30,000 was on credit; cost, $63,700.
11.   Collected cash on accounts receivable, $26,000.
12.   Paid cash on accounts payable, $28,000.
13.   Paid various operating expenses in cash, $18,000.

Required:

1. Set up T-accounts in the general ledger for each of the accounts listed in the above trial balance and enter the December 31, 19I, balances.
2. Journalize each of the transactions listed above for 19J; use only a general journal.
3. Post the journal entries; use folio notations.
4. Prepare an unadjusted trial balance.
5. Journalize the adjusting entries and post them to the ledger. Assume a bad debt rate of ½% of credit sales for the period and an average 40% income tax rate. Hint: Income tax expense is $11,784. At December 31, 19J, accrued wages were $300. Use straight-line depreciation.
6. Prepare an adjusted trial balance.
7. Prepare an income statement and balance sheet (subclassifications are not required).
8. Journalize and post the closing entries.
9. Prepare a post-closing trial balance.

Problem 2–13

Major Corporation adjusts and closes its books each December 31. At December 31, 19C, the following unadjusted trial balance has been developed from the general ledger shown on the following page:

| | Balances (unadjusted) | |
Account	Debit	Credit
Cash	$139,960	
Accounts receivable	34,000	
Allowance for doubtful accounts		$ 5,400
Inventory (periodic system)	62,000	
Prepaid insurance (15 months remaining as of 1/1/19C)	600	
Long-term note receivable (14%)	12,000	
Investment revenue receivable		
Land	27,000	
Building	240,000	
Accumulated depreciation, building		130,000
Equipment	90,000	
Accumulated depreciation, equipment		50,000
Accounts payable		23,000
Salaries payable		
Income taxes payable		
Interest payable		
Unearned rent revenue		
Note payable, 10%, long term		120,000
Common stock, par $10		200,000
Contributed capital in excess of par		10,000
Retained earnings		27,900
Sales revenue		300,000
Investment revenue		1,260
Rent revenue		6,000
Purchases	164,000	
Purchase returns		4,000
Cost of goods sold		
Selling expenses	51,000	
General and administrative expenses	35,000	
Interest expense	7,000	
Extraordinary loss (pretax)	15,000	
Income tax expense		
	$877,560	$877,560

Additional data for adjustments and other purposes:

a. Estimated bad debt loss rate is ½% of credit sales. Ten percent of 19C sales were on credit. Classify as a selling expense.

b. The company uses the periodic inventory system—ending inventory (December 31, 19C), $70,000.

c. Interest on the long-term note receivable was last collected on September 30, 19C.

d. Estimated useful life on the building was 20 years; residual value, $40,000. Allocate 10% of depreciation expense to administrative expense and the balance to selling expenses. Assume straight-line depreciation (for proportionate usage).

e. Estimated useful life of the equipment was 10 years; residual value, zero. Allocate 10% of depreciation expense to administrative expense and the balance to selling expenses. Assume straight-line depreciation.

f. Unrecorded and unpaid sales salaries at December 31, 19C, were $7,500.

g. Interest on the note payable, long-term, was paid last on July 31, 19C.

h. On August 1, 19C, the company rented some space in its building to a tenant and collected $6,000 for 12 months rent in advance, which was credited to Rent Revenue.

i. Adjust for expired insurance. Classify as selling expense.

j. Assume an average 30% corporate income tax rate on all items including the extraordinary loss. Hint: Income tax expense is $3,615.

Required:

1. Enter the above unadjusted trial balance on a worksheet.
2. Enter the adjusting entries (including the adjusting entry for inventory and cost of goods sold) on the worksheet and complete it.
3. Prepare a summary income statement and balance sheet (subclassifications are not required).
4. Journalize the closing entries.

Problem 2–14

DAR Corporation currently is completing the end-of-the-period accounting process. At December 31, 19D, the following unadjusted trial balance was developed from the general ledger:

Account	Balances (unadjusted)	
	Debit	Credit
Cash	$ 60,260	
Accounts receivable	38,000	
Allowance for doubtful accounts		$ 2,000
Inventory (perpetual inventory system)..	105,000	
Sales supplies inventory	900	
Long-term note receivable, 14%	12,000	
Equipment	180,000	
Accumulated depreciation, equipment ...		64,000
Patent.............................	8,400	
Interest receivable		
Accounts payable.....................		23,000
Interest payable		
Income taxes payable		
Property taxes payable		
Unearned rent revenue		
Mortgage payable, 12%		60,000
Common stock, par $10		100,000
Contributed capital in excess of par		15,000
Retained earnings		32,440
Sales revenue		700,000
Investment revenue		1,120
Rent revenue		3,000
Cost of goods sold....................	380,000	
Selling expense	164,400	
General and administrative expenses	55,000	
Interest expense	6,600	
Income tax expense		
Extraordinary gain (pretax)		10,000
	$1,010,560	$1,010,560

Additional data for adjustments and other purposes:

a. Estimated bad debt loss rate is ¼ % of credit sales. Credit sales for the year amounted to $200,000; classify as a selling expense.

b. Interest on the long-term note receivable was last collected August 31, 19D.

c. Estimated useful life of the equipment is 10 years; residual value, $20,000. Allocate 10% of depreciation expense to general and administrative expense and the balance to selling expenses to reflect proportionate use. Use straight-line depreciation.

d. Estimated remaining economic life of the patent is 14 years (from January 1, 19D) and no residual value. Use straight-line amortization and classify as selling expense (used in sales promotion).

e. Interest on the mortgage payable was last paid on November 30, 19D.

f. On June 1, 19D, the company rented some office space to a tenant for one year and collected $3,000 rent in advance for the year; the entire amount was credited to Rent Revenue on this date.

g. On December 31, 19D, received a statement for calendar year 19D property taxes amounting to $1,300. The payment is due February 15, 19E. Assume it will be paid on that date and classify it as a selling expense. The $1,300 has not been recorded during 19D.

h. Sales supplies on hand at December 31, 19D, amounted to $300; classify as a selling expense.

i. Assume an average 40% corporate income tax rate on all items including the extraordinary gain. Hint: Income tax expense is $35,132.

Required:

1. Enter the above unadjusted trial balance on a worksheet.
2. Enter the adjusting entries and complete the worksheet.
3. Prepare an income statement and balance sheet (subclassifications are not required).
4. Journalize the closing entries.

SUPPLEMENT 2–A: PROBLEMS 2–15 TO 2–18

Problem 2–15

Kane Company uses special journals for credit sales, credit purchases, cash receipts, and cash payments. For each of the following transactions, indicate the appropriate journal:

Transactions	Appropriate journal
a. Sold common stock of Kane for cash.	_____
b. Purchased merchandise for resale; terms 2/10, n/60.	_____
c. Borrowed $5,000 on an 8% note.	_____
d. Recorded depreciation expense.	_____
e. Sold merchandise for cash.	_____
f. Purchased merchandise for cash.	_____
g. Purchased equipment for cash.	_____
h. Sold operational asset for cash.	_____
i. Purchased machinery on credit.	_____
j. Collected an account receivable.	_____
k. Paid a note payable.	_____

Transactions	Appropriate journal
l. Recorded accrued wages payable.	_____
m. Paid a cash dividend on common stock.	_____
n. Recorded estimated bad debt expense.	_____
o. Recorded amortization expense on a patent.	_____
p. Sold machinery on credit.	_____

Problem 2–16

Hall Retailers uses special journals. Following is a special cash receipts journal with several selected transactions.

Required:

1. Sum the special journal (below) and post it to the appropriate accounts in the general ledger and subsidiary ledger. Use control accounts and subsidiary ledgers for credit sales and accounts receivable. Assign systematic numbers to the accounts. Beginning customer balances were: Riley Corporation, $8,400; Brown, Inc., $1,240; and Watson Company, $10,000.
2. Reconcile the subsidiary ledger with its control account.

		Debits	Credits				
			Special Journal—Cash Receipts				Page CR-8
Date	Explanation	Cash	Account title	Folio	Accounts receivable	Sundry accounts	Sales
19E: Jan. 1	Cash sales	30,000					30,000
2	On account	4,200	Riley Corp.		4,200		
5	Cash sales	10,000					10,000
6	On account	1,240	Brown, Inc.		1,240		
8	Sale of short-term investment	7,000	Short-term investments Gain on sale of investments			4,000 3,000	
11	Cash sales	41,000					41,000
12	Borrowed cash	10,000	Notes payable			10,000	
15	On account	5,500	Watson Co.		5,500		
18	Collected interest	600	Interest revenue			600	
31	Cash sales	52,000					52,000

Problem 2–17

Jackson Wholesalers uses special journals. Following is the special credit sales journal with several representative transactions.

Required:

1. Sum the special journal (below) and post it to the appropriate accounts in the general ledger and the two subsidiary ledgers. Use control accounts and subsidiary ledgers for sales and accounts receivable; assign systematic numbers to the accounts.
2. Reconcile each subsidiary ledger with its respective control account.

Special Journal—Merchandise Sales on Credit						Page S-9	
Date	Sales invoice no.	Account receivable	Terms	Folio	Amount	Dept. sales	
						A	B
19D:							
Jan. 1	21	Fly Corp.	2/10, n/30		498	440	58
5	22	B. T. Co.	2/10, n/30		490	290	200
7	23	Easton Co.	2/10, n/30		294	104	190
11	24	Fly Corp.	2/10, n/30		588	288	300
13	25	Wells Co.	2/10, n/30		686	300	386
18	26	Fly Corp.	2/10, n/30		147	100	47
21	27	Easton Co.	2/10, n/30		784	554	230
28	28	B. T. Co.	2/10, n/30		245	200	45
31	29	Wells Co.	2/10, n/30		637	407	230

Problem 2–18

Bluebonnet Company is a small department store. The accounting system is maintained manually. Control accounts and subsidiary ledgers are used. The following information was selected from the accounting system at January 1, 19J:

Journals	Page number to be used
General journal	J-27
Special journals:	
Merchandise sales on credit	S-13
Merchandise purchases on credit	P-9
Cash receipts	CR-22
Cash payments	CP-34

General ledger accounts	Balance 1/1/19J	Acct. No.
Cash	$ 72,000	101
Accounts receivable	38,000	105
Inventory (periodic system)	45,000	110
Equipment	25,000	204
Accounts payable	21,000	303
Notes payable	10,000	305
Common stock, par $10	100,000	400
Contributed capital in excess of par		401
Retained earnings	49,000	410
Sales revenue		500
Sales returns		501
Purchases		600
Purchase returns		601
Expenses		700

Subsidiary ledgers

Accounts receivable (No. 105):

Ames, C. P.	7,000	105.1
Graves Co.	16,000	105.2
Mason Corp.	5,000	105.3
White Co.	10,000	105.4

Accounts payable (No. 303):

Buford Wholesale Co.	11,000	303.1
Dawn Suppliers, Inc.	7,000	303.2
Paul Wholesale Co.	3,000	303.3

The following transactions were completed during January 19J.

Date

1. Purchased merchandise for cash, $18,000.
2. Paid $11,000 owed to Buford Wholesale Company within the discount period.
3. Sold merchandise for cash, $26,000.
4. Purchased a new truck for use in the business; paid cash, $4,200.
5. Sold merchandise to XY Corporation on credit; terms 2/10, n/60; $9,800 if paid within 10 days; otherwise $10,000 (record net of discount at $9,800).
6. Paid expenses, $4,500.
7. Purchased merchandise on credit from Sauls Company; terms 2/10, n/60; $20,000, if paid within 10 days; otherwise add the 2% charge; record at $20,000.
8. Sold merchandise for cash, $37,000.
8. Collected on accounts receivable within the discount period as follows: Ames, $7,000; Graves, $16,000; and White, $10,000.
9. Purchased merchandise for cash, $21,000.
9. Collected in full from XY Corporation for the sale of January 5.
9. Paid accounts payable within the discount period: Dawn, $7,000; and Paul, $2,000.
10. Collected accounts receivable from Mason Corporation, $5,000, within the discount period.
10. Returned merchandise purchased from Paul Wholesale Company because its specifications were incorrect; received a credit for $1,000.
14. Paid expenses, $9,600.
15. Sold merchandise for cash, $11,400.
16. Paid balance due to Sauls within the discount period.
19. Borrowed $30,000 cash on a one-year, 16% interest-bearing note.
22. Sold merchandise on credit terms 2/10, n/30, as follows (net amount): Ames, $6,000; Graves, $13,000; Mason, $9,000; and White, $4,000.
23. A customer returned merchandise, purchased a few days earlier; because the correct size was unavailable, customer was given a cash refund of $175.
24. Collected the balance due from White Company within the discount period.
25. Returned damaged merchandise to a wholesale supplier and received a cash refund of $450.
26. Purchased merchandise on credit from Buford Wholesale Company; terms 2/10, n/60; net amount, $35,000.
27. Purchased merchandise on credit from Dawn Suppliers, Inc.: terms 2/10, n/60; net amount, $12,000.

28.   Cash sales, $47,000.
29.   Sold merchandise on credit to XY Corporation on the usual terms; net amount, $16,500.
30.   Collected in full for the credit sale to Mason on January 22.
31.   Sold common stock of Bluebonnet Company to a new shareholder, 1,000 shares for $20,000 cash.

Required:
1. Set up a general journal and special journals for credit sales, credit purchases, cash receipts, and cash payments, similar to those illustrated in Supplement 2–A. Sales and purchases on credit are recorded at net of discount.
2. Set up T-accounts for the general ledger and two subsidiary ledgers, accounts receivable and accounts payable. Enter the beginning balances in the T-accounts.
3. Journalize the above transactions in the appropriate journals.
4. Post to the subsidiary and general ledgers; use the folio numbers given above.
5. Prepare reconciliation of each subsidiary ledger with its respective control account.
6. Prepare a trial balance from the general ledger.

CASES

Case 2–1

Nu-Tech Company was organized during 19A by three technical experts to assemble (parts to be purchased from suppliers) and market an electronic device that they had previously patented. No products were sold during 19A; however, 19B and 19C produced significant sales, but modest profits. During 19B, the company hired a bookkeeper who, although industrious, had very little knowledge of accounting. Realizing this competency problem, the company is considering engaging an outside independent CPA to, as they said, "straighten things out and make recommendations." Among numerous other accounting problems, adjusting entries have never been made. The bookkeeper stated that "the transactions are recorded in the right way when they occur."

The following 19E transactions, and the way in which the bookkeeper recorded or explained them, are being discussed:

a. Inventory—ending 19D, $30,000; ending 19E, $47,000 (by inventory count).

     Inventory of parts 17,000
        Purchases   17,000

b. Depreciation—equipment (purchased at the beginning of 19D) cost, $80,000; estimated useful life, 10 years; manufacturer's recommended value at end of 5 years, $10,000.

     Depreciation expense 7,000
        Equipment   7,000

c. Unpaid wages at year-end 19D, $3,000; 19E, $11,000.

     Record when paid, because that is when the wages require
     the payment of resources and "it all evens out anyway."

d. Note payable, $60,000, five-year, 15%, interest payable each October 31; signed November 1, 19D.

Interest expense	9,000	
Cash		9,000

Because this is the correct amount of interest each year.

e. Contract to deliver six electronic devices, signed October 15, 19E, pending assembly, $45,000.

Due from customers	45,000	
Sales		45,000

f. Property taxes for 19E, billed in November 19E, payable without penalty up to February 15, 19F, $9,000. Paid on February 14, 19F.

February 14, 19F:

Property taxes	9,000	
Cash		9,000

g. Advertising costs for December 19E, Christmas season, $17,000. Paid, within the 30-day credit period, on January 26, 19F.

January 26, 19F:

Advertising	17,000	
Cash		17,000

Required:
1. Draft an accounting policy statement for Nu Tech that focuses primarily on "adjusting entries."
2. Evaluate the bookkeeper's way of recording the above transactions. Give your recommended adjusting entry, or other action, related to each of the transactions.

Case 2–2

Careless Corporation has just completed its third year of operations, December 31, 19C. The newly selected president was amazed, to say the least, when told that the "company's books have never been in balance." In fact, he has learned that they are $14,800 out of balance. Consequently, he has decided to ask an independent CPA to "get things straightened out." You are the lucky CPA! While getting an overview of the situation you learn that the bookkeeper journalizes and posts all of the daily transactions, but the adjusting and closing entries are entered directly into the ledger accounts. A worksheet is not used. After recording the adjusting entries, the bookkeeper prepares an adjusted trial balance, which is then used to prepare the financial statements.

At your request the bookkeeper prepared the following post-closing trial balance following his usual procedures:

CARELESS CORPORATION
Post-Closing Trial Balance
December 31, 19C

Accounts	Debit	Credit
Cash	$ 17,800	
Accounts receivable	55,000	
Note receivable	6,000	
Merchandise inventory (periodic system)	120,000	
Prepaid insurance	2,400	
Equipment	240,000	
Land (future plant site)	40,000	
Accounts payable		$ 20,000
Income tax payable		10,000
Mortgage payable		100,000
Common stock, par $10 (20,000 shares outstanding)		320,000
Dividends declared and paid	4,000	
Retained earnings		50,000
To balance	14,800	
Totals	$500,000	$500,000

After spending considerable time digging into the records and files of the company, you discovered the following:

a. Estimates of bad debt expense that total $5,000 have been credited directly to Accounts Receivable.
b. Accrued interest expense of $4,000 was recorded, but the credit was omitted.
c. Depreciation expense, on a straight-line basis (no residual value), is $30,000 per year. Depreciation for 19A and 19B was credited directly to the asset account.
d. The 19C ending inventory of $140,000 was not recorded; the beginning inventory was $120,000.
e. Prepaid insurance of $2,400 was for two full years, 19C and 19D.
f. Depreciation was not recorded in 19C.
g. Accounts payable of $2,000 were paid, but the debit was not recorded.
h. The common stock account needs scrutiny.
i. How should the account, Dividends Declared and Paid, be reported?

Required:
1. Based upon your findings prepare a corrected trial balance. Show corrections. Hint: Add the following accounts: Allowance for Doubtful Accounts, Accumulated Depreciation, Interest Payable, and Contributed Capital in Excess of Par.
2. Aside from the lack of accounting knowledge by the bookkeeper, explain why so many continuing mistakes were made in implementing the accounting process.
3. What recommendations would you make concerning the accounting process? Yes, the bookkeeper is no longer on the company payroll!

Case 2–3

Fannie Corporation started operations on January 1, 19C. It is now December 31, 19C, the end of the annual accounting period. A company clerk, who maintained the accounting records, has just prepared the following financial statements:

Profit and Loss Statement
December 31, 19C

Service income		$100,000
Costs:		
Salaries and wages	$30,000	
Repairs and maintenance	5,000	
Service	25,000	
Other miscellaneous	10,000	70,000
Profit		$ 30,000

Balance Sheet
December 31, 19C

Assets

Cash	$	7,500
Note receivable (16%)		1,200
Inventory, supplies		6,000
Equipment		90,000
Other miscellaneous assets		7,300
Total		$112,000

Debts

Accounts payable	$	8,000
Note payable (15%)		24,000
Total		32,000

Capital

Capital stock, par $10		50,000
Retained earnings		30,000
Total		80,000
Grand total		$112,000

    The above statements (unaudited) were presented to a local bank, at the bank's request, to support a major loan. The bank requested that the statements be "examined" by an independent CPA. You are the independent CPA, and among other accounting issues, you found that the following items were not considered by the company in preparing the income statement and balance sheet:

a. Service revenue amounting to $2,000 had been collected but not earned at December 31, 19C.
b. At December 31, 19C, wages earned by employees but not yet paid or recorded amounted to $9,000.
c. A count of the inventory of supplies at December 31, 19C, showed $4,000 supplies on hand.
d. Depreciation on the equipment acquired on January 3, 19C, was not recorded. The estimated residual value was $10,000, and the estimated useful life 10 years.
e. The note receivable received from a customer was dated November 1, 19C; the principal plus interest is payable April 30, 19D.

f. The note payable to the local bank was dated June 1, 19C; the principal plus interest is payable May 31, 19D.

g. Assume an average income tax rate of 20% for Fannie Corporation and that no income tax has been recorded.

h. Although you did not do a complete audit of the accounting results, your judgment is that the daily recording of transactions was appropriate.

Required:

1. Recast the income statement, using modern terminology, after giving effect to your findings. Use a format similar to the following to develop the statements:

Items	Reported amount	Changes due to findings				Correct amount
		Key	+ or −	Amount	Comments	
Income statement: (list the appropriate items here) Balance Sheet: (list the appropriate items here)						

2. Write a brief narrative addressed to Fannie Corporation to explain the two corrected statements (not an auditor's opinion).

3. Give any recommendations that you would make to Fannie Corporation concerning its accounting function.

Case 2–4

This is a continuing case that covers the entire accounting information processing cycle. Although it can be used at any time in the textbook, it is designed to be started in Chapter 2 and completed by the end of Chapter 4. In these two latter chapters, it is referred to as Cases 3–5 and 4–8. All of the case data and solutions are given in Chapter 2 and are not repeated later.

On January 2, 19C, Randal Company had the following trial balance:

Acct. no.	Account	Debit	Credit
101	Cash	$ 96,000	
102	Accounts receivable	45,000	
103	Allowance for doubtful accounts		$ 670
104	Office supplies inventory	800	
105	Inventory (periodic inventory system)	60,000	
106	Short-term investments		
107	Investment revenue receivable		
108	Fund to construct future plant	30,000	
109	Machinery	120,000	
110	Accumulated depreciation, machinery		72,000
111	Land (future plant site)	15,000	
112	Patent	4,000	
113	Other assets	55,000	
201	Accounts payable		35,000
202	Interest payable		
203	Income tax payable (19B)		12,330
204	Long-term mortgage note		
301	Common stock (par $10)		150,000
302	Contributed capital in excess of par		30,000
303	Retained earnings		125,800
400	Income summary		
500	Sales revenue		
501	Investment revenue		
600	Purchases		
601	Freight-in, purchases		
602	Purchase returns and allowances		
700	Selling expenses		
701	General and administrative expenses		
702	Interest expense		
703	Depreciation expense		
704	Income tax expense		
801	Extraordinary items		
802	Prior period adjustments		
		$425,800	$425,800

Transactions completed during the current reporting period, which ends on December 31, 19C (the entries are numbered for reference purposes):

1. Paid 19B income taxes payable on 3/3/19C, in full.
2. The following purchase transactions were completed:
   - Purchases of merchandise ...... $350,000 ($50,000 was on credit)
   - Purchase returns .... 1,000 (of unpaid credit purchases)
   - Freight on purchases .... 2,000 (cash)
3. The following selling expenses were incurred and paid during 19C:
   - Advertising .... $ 10,000
   - Salaries 130,000
   - Other selling 15,000

4. The following general and administrative expenses were incurred and paid during 19C:

Salaries $100,000
Office supplies (purchased) . . . . .   500 (debit account No. 104)
Rent expense   24,000

5. A 12% mortgage note payable was dated and signed on 3/1/19C, for $75,000; this amount of cash was received. Interest will be paid annually on this date.

6. A short-term investment in bonds was acquired for cash on 6/1/19C, at par, $20,000. Interest at 14% is payable annually on June 1.

7. Suffered severe flood loss amounting to $40,000. Assume that this is an extraordinary item; credit Cash because this amount was spent to restore the damaged assets.

8. Correction of a $30,000 accounting error in prior period resulting from a 19A understated billing for credit sales to a customer. Received $30,000 cash from the customer during 19C. Assume an income tax effect of $6,000.

9. At 12/31/19C, interest on the building fund amounting to $1,500 was added to the fund balance.

10. Cash collections on accounts receivable, $85,000.

11. Cash payments on accounts payable, $65,000.

12. Cash paid for dividends amounting to $2 per share (debit Retained Earnings).

13. Sales were $700,000 of which 15% was on credit.

Data for the 19C adjusting entries (lettered for reference purposes):

a. Bad debt expense is estimated to be 1% of total credit sales (debit Selling Expense).
b. Office supplies inventory at December 31, 19C, determined by count, $600.
c. Accrue the short-term investment revenue at 14% per year.
d. The machinery has an estimated life of 10 years and no residual value; assume straight-line depreciation and a full year's depreciation for 19C.
e. On January 1, 19C, the patent had eight years remaining life; assume straight-line amortization. Record amortization as general and administrative expenses.
f. Accrue interest on the mortgage note.
g. Assume an average income tax rate of 20% on all items.
h. Ending inventory, determined by count and valued at cost, $70,000.

Required:

1. Set up a general journal and T-accounts (with account numbers). Enter 19C beginning balances in the ledger accounts. All of the ledger accounts needed are listed in the above trial balance.

2. Journalize and post the current entries. Use posting notations in both the journal and ledger.

3. Set up a worksheet with a minimum of eight columns (or more if you prefer). Develop the unadjusted trial balance from the ledger and enter it into the first two money columns of the worksheet.

4. Enter the adjusting entries on the worksheet and complete it (label the adjusting entries with the letters to the left).

5. Prepare a single-step income statement and statement of retained earnings.

6. Prepare a classified balance sheet.

7. Journalize and post the adjusting entries.

8. Journalize and post the closing entries.

9. Prepare a post-closing trial balance.

10. Which adjusting entries would you reverse?

Suggested completion schedule (unless changed by your professor):

Requirement completed	Chapter	Key figures
Requirements 1–3, through the unadjusted trial balance on the worksheet	2 (Case 2–4)	Unadjusted trial balance total, $1,174,970
Requirements 4–5, through the income statement	3 (Case 3–5)	EPS, Net income, $1.14
Requirements 6–10	4 (Case 4–8)	Balance sheet total, $428,683

Chapter 3

Review—The Income Statement and Statement of Retained Earnings

OVERVIEW AND PURPOSE

An entity communicates financial information to decision makers primarily by using a complete set of financial statements at the end of each accounting year. A complete set of financial statements **must** include (a) an income statement, (b) a balance sheet (reviewed in Chapter 4), and (c) a statement of changes in financial position (discussed in Chapter 23). Also, to be in conformity with the **full-disclosure principle** the financial report almost always includes a statement of retained earnings (or owners' equity) and a series of **supporting** notes and schedules.

The relationships (sometimes called articulation) among the basic financial statements are illustrated in **Exhibit 3–1.** It shows that the income statement and the statement of changes in financial position (SCFP) are the connecting links between the beginning and ending balance sheets. The income statement and SCFP explain the **causes** of the changes in financial position during the current period. The income statement explains the changes due to **operations** (i.e., revenues, expenses, gains, and losses). In contrast, the SCFP explains the reasons for changes in the financial position of the entity in terms of **fund inflows and outflows** during the period.

The purpose of this chapter is to review the **income statement** from the perspective of both the decision makers who use it and the accountants who prepare it. Therefore, this chapter is subdivided as follows:

Part A: Concepts Underlying the Income Statement

1. Concepts.
2. Preparing the income statement.
3. Disclosure guidelines for the income statement.
4. Extraordinary items.
5. Unusual or nonrecurring items.

Part B: Specific Issues Directly Related to the Income Statement and Statement of Retained Earnings

1. Prior period adjustments.
2. Disclosure of income taxes.
3. Earnings per share.
4. Accounting changes.
5. Statement of retained earnings.

EXHIBIT 3–1:   Relationships Among Financial Statements

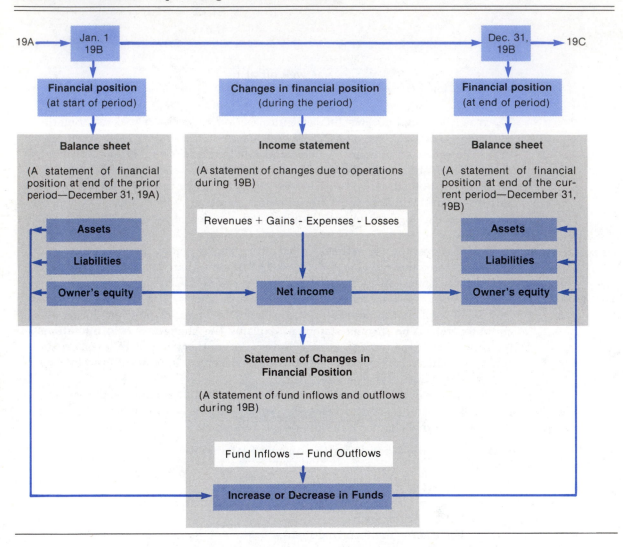

PART A: CONCEPTS UNDERLYING THE INCOME STATEMENT

CONCEPTS OF INCOME

The income statement[1] reports **net income** measured on the **accrual basis** in conformity with the conceptual framework and its application guidelines pre-

---

[1] A more descriptive title, statement of operations, is being used more often than previously.

sented in Chapter 1. This concept of income, commonly called accounting income, is a **transactions approach** because each revenue, expense, gain, and loss transaction is recorded when it occurs. Therefore, accounting income is measured in conformity with the revenue, cost, and matching principles.

Another concept of income, often called **economic income,** measures the income of a business as the amount of "real wealth" that the entity could consume, or use up, during a period and be as well off at the end of that period as it was at the beginning.[2] This definition is often referred to as a capital maintenance approach. Implementation of the concept of economic income would require the use of market values adjusted for the effects of inflation or deflation because real wealth means purchasing power.

In the broadest sense, accounting income and economic income are consistent. However, the measurement approaches are significantly different because economic income is based exclusively on wealth changes, whereas accounting income

EXHIBIT 3–2

Income Statement Elements

Definition of element

Revenues are inflows or other enhancements of assets of an enterprise or settlements of its liabilities (or a combination of both) during a period from delivering or producing goods, rendering services, or other activities that constitute the entity's ongoing major or central operations.

Gains are increases in equity (net assets) from peripheral or incidental transactions of an entity and from all other transactions and other events and circumstances affecting the entity during a period except those that result from revenues or investments by owners.

Expenses are outflows or other using up of assets or incurrences of liabilities (or a combination of both) during a period from delivering or producing goods, rendering services, or carrying out other activities that constitute the entity's ongoing major or central operations.

Losses are decreases in equity (net assets) from peripheral or incidental transactions of an entity and from all other transactions and other events and circumstances affecting the entity during a period except those that result from expenses or distributions to owners.

Source: FASB, *Statement of Financial Accounting Concepts No. 3,* "Elements of Financial Statements of Business Enterprises" (Stamford, Conn., December 1980), pars. 63–73.

[2] See J. R. Hicks, *Value and Capital,* 2d ed. (London: Oxford University Press, 1946), p. 172.

is measured using a transactions approach that involves detailed and continuous measurements throughout the reporting period. To provide reliable information to decision makers, the measurements should be verifiable and not subjective. Therefore, an appropriate accounting approach to income measurement is the transactions approach.

The transactions approach was used in your fundamentals of financial accounting course. It is discussed in this textbook because it is in conformity with GAAP. It measures accounting income in terms of the income statement elements—revenues, expenses, gains, and losses.

FASB Concepts Statement 3 defines the **income statement elements** as those shown in **Exhibit 3–2.** Observe that gains and losses cannot be included in the "ongoing major or central operations" of the entity.

PREPARING THE INCOME STATEMENT

The presentation of financial information on a typical income statement is consistent with the elements defined in Exhibit 3–2. Thus, the primary classifications on an income statement can be summarized as follows:

1. Revenues—such as sales, service, rent, and investment revenue.
2. Expenses—such as wages, services, rent, cost of goods sold, and income tax expense.
3. Gains and losses that are **either** (but not both) unusual **or** infrequent—such as from the disposal of equipment, sale of investments, and casualties.
4. Gains and losses that are **extraordinary** because they are **both** unusual **and** infrequent—such as damage losses from an earthquake.
5. Net income—the algebraic sum of revenues, expenses, gains, and losses.
6. Earnings per share—income divided by the average number of common shares outstanding during the year.

Format of the Income Statement

The accounting profession has not specified a particular **format,** sometimes referred to as display, that must be used for the income statement because reasonable flexibility to fit various situations is considered more important than a standard format. Therefore, considerable variation in practice exists.

The income statement reports all revenues, gains, expenses, and losses **for a specific period of time.** It is "dated" to indicate the period, such as **"For the Year Ended December 31, 19xx."** This dating identifies the length and ending date of the **reporting period.**

In addition, a number of *ARBs, APB Opinions,* and *FASB Statements* specify certain **disclosure** requirements that influence income statement presentation.

Although there is wide variation in income statement formats, two formats dominate in practice (and there are numerous forms of each). These formats

EXHIBIT 3–3

Single-step Income Statement Format

GRAHAM RETAIL COMPANY
Income Statement
For the Year Ended December 31, 19D

Revenues and gains:		
Sales (less returns and allowances of $20,000)		$670,000
Rent revenue		1,200
Interest and dividends revenue		4,800
Gain on sale of operational assets		6,000
Total revenues and gains		682,000
Expenses and losses:		
Cost of goods sold*	$264,000	
Distribution expense*	153,500	
Administrative expense*	73,500	
Depreciation expense	54,000	
Interest expense	6,000	
Loss on sale of investments	5,000	
Income tax expense ($126,000 × 30%)†	37,800	
Total expenses and losses		593,800
Income before extraordinary item		88,200
Extraordinary item:		
Loss due to earthquake	10,000	
Less: Income tax saving ($10,000 × 30%)	3,000	7,000
Net income		$ 81,200
EPS of common stock (20,000 shares outstanding):		
Income before extraordinary item ($88,200 ÷ 20,000)		$4.41
Extraordinary loss ($7,000 ÷ 20,000)		(.35)
Net income ($81,200 ÷ 20,000)		$4.06

* These expenses may be detailed in the statement or separately in the **notes** to the financial statements.
† Assumed average income tax rate, 30%.

usually are designated as (1) single step and (2) multiple step. A recent survey of 600 major companies reported that 52% of them essentially used a single-step format while 48% essentially used a multiple-step format.[3]

Single-Step Format. The single-step format uses two broad classifications: (1) revenues and gains and (2) expenses and losses. It is called a single-step statement because only one step is involved in arriving at net income. That is, revenues and gains minus expenses and losses equal net income. However, if the company

---

[3] AICPA, *Accounting Trends & Techniques, 1984* (New York, 1984). This is an excellent reference to determine how various companies report the multitude of different items on financial statements.

has extraordinary gains or losses (or other types of gains and losses that warrant separate disclosure), the steps increase.[4]

A single-step income statement is shown in **Exhibit 3–3** for Graham Retail Company. Observe that it includes an extraordinary item. Numerous variations exist in practice. For example, income tax expense related to operations sometimes is reported as a separate item below "Expenses and losses" but preceding "Income before extraordinary items."

Multiple-Step Format.   The multiple-step format provides multiple classifications and multiple intermediate differences (i.e., multiple steps). It is more informative than the single-step format. A multiple-step income statement, using the same data as in Exhibit 3–3, is illustrated in **Exhibit 3–4.** The differences between the single-step and multiple-step formats are that the multiple-step format (Exhibit 3–4), but not the single-step format (Exhibit 3–3), reports amounts for the following "income" captions:

1. Gross margin on sales (also called gross profit).
2. Income from continuing operations.
3. Income before extraordinary items.
4. Net income.

Study Exhibit 3–4 in order to learn the typical classifications in a multiple-step income statement. These classifications will be frequently used in subsequent chapters.

DISCLOSURE GUIDELINES FOR THE INCOME STATEMENT

An income statement must conform with the **revenue, cost, matching,** and **full-disclosure principles** presented in Chapter 1, Part B.

The **full-disclosure principle** requires that all relevant information relating to the economic affairs of the entity must be reported on the statement or in the supporting notes and schedules. Therefore, the typical income statement is supplemented with a number of **notes to the financial statements.** Typically, these notes contain schedules and written explanations to explain more fully the amounts reported in the tabular portions of the statements. For example, **Exhibit 3–5** presents a detailed expense schedule to supplement the income statement of Graham Retail Company illustrated in Exhibit 3–4.

---

[4] Extraordinary items and earnings per share (EPS) are discussed in Part B. Other income statement items that must be disclosed separately in a manner similar to extraordinary gains and losses include (a) cumulative effects of changes in accounting principles and (b) gains and losses on discontinued operations. These items are discussed in Chapters 20 and 21, respectively.

EXHIBIT 3–4
Multiple-step Income Statement Format

GRAHAM RETAIL COMPANY
Income Statement
For the Year Ended December 31, 19D

Sales revenue			$690,000
Less: Sales returns and allowances			20,000
Net sales			670,000
Cost of goods sold:			
Beginning inventory (periodic)		$ 52,000	
Purchases of inventory	$268,000		
Freight-in	1,200		
Cost of purchases	269,200		
Less: Purchase returns and allowances	2,700	266,500	
Total goods available for sale		318,500	
Less: Ending inventory		54,500	
Cost of goods sold			264,000
Gross margin on sales			406,000
Operating expenses:			
Distribution expense*		153,500	
Administrative expense*		73,500	
Depreciation expense		54,000	
Total operating expenses			281,000
Income from continuing (or primary) operations†			125,000
Other revenues and gains:			
Rent revenue	1,200		
Interest and dividend revenue	4,800		
Gain on sale of operational assets	6,000	12,000	
Other expenses and losses:			
Interest expense	6,000		
Loss on sale of investment	5,000	11,000	1,000
Income before income tax and extraordinary item			126,000
Income tax expense ($126,000 × 30%)‡			37,800
Income before extraordinary item			88,200
Extraordinary item:			
Loss due to earthquake		10,000	
Less: Income tax saving ($10,000 × 30%)		3,000	7,000
Net income			$ 81,200
EPS of common stock (20,000 shares outstanding):			
Income before extraordinary item ($88,200 ÷ 20,000)			$4.41
Extraordinary loss ($7,000 ÷ 20,000)			(.35)
Net income ($81,200 ÷ 20,000)			$4.06

* These expenses may be detailed in the statement or separately in the **notes** to the financial statements.
† Also, variously labeled, such as "Income from primary operations" and "Income from operations."
‡ Assumed average income tax rate, 30%.

(handwritten margin notes: 1), 2), 3), 4), "Earnings Per Share")

EXHIBIT 3–5
Expense Schedule

GRAHAM RETAIL COMPANY
Schedule of Operating Expenses
For the Year Ended December 31, 19D

Operating expenses:
Distribution expenses:

Advertising	$58,500	
Salaries	45,000	
Commissions	31,000	
Freight-out (on sales)	10,000	
Insurance on inventory	1,000	
Other selling expenses	8,000	$153,500
Administrative expenses:		
Office expenses	24,800	
Office payroll	42,100	
Rent	3,600	
Bad debt expense	3,000	73,500
Depreciation expense		54,000
Total operating expense		$281,000

APB Opinion 22, "Disclosure of Accounting Policies," August 1972, paragraph 8, states that "a description of all significant accounting policies of the reporting entity should be included as an integral part of the financial statements." Examples are those policies related to the basis of consolidation, depreciation methods, amortization of intangibles, inventory costing, accounting for research and development costs, translation of foreign currencies, recognition of profit on long-term construction contracts, and revenue from leasing transactions.

The objective of disclosure notes is the presentation of information that cannot be effectively communicated in another way. **Disclosure notes are an integral part of the financial statements.** Generally, pronouncements of the profession on reporting specific items specify that they may, or in some cases must, be disclosed in disclosure notes when it is impractical to present the information in the tabular portions of the statements. Two specific income statement items that must be disclosed separately are *(a)* depreciation expense and *(b)* income tax expense.

Disclosure of Depreciation

APB Opinion 12, paragraph 5, requires that *(a)* the amount of depreciation expense for the period and *(b)* the method or methods of depreciation used, be disclosed either in the financial statements or in the notes thereto. This requirement was specified because depreciation often is a major **noncash** expense. The amount of depreciation expense depends, in part, upon the depreciation policies of the enterprise rather than solely on external transactions; therefore, the amount of depreciation is subject to considerable latitude. To realistically assess probable future cash flows, statement users need to know both the amount of depreciation expense and the depreciation method(s) used.

In manufacturing enterprises, much of the depreciation expense may be included in the ending inventory and cost of goods sold amounts (it is not specifically identified). Therefore, reporting total depreciation by footnote is characteristic for these companies.

Disclosure of income tax is discussed in Part B of this chapter.

REPORTING EXTRAORDINARY ITEMS

For accounting purposes, an extraordinary item is **a transaction or event that is both unusual in its nature and infrequent in its occurrence.**

Extraordinary items are reported under a separate classification on the income statement to alert users of the financial statements about the extraordinary nature of these gains or losses. Separate reporting signals to users that these gains or losses cannot be expected to recur regularly and, therefore, should have little influence on predictions about the future income and cash flows of the entity.

Extraordinary items are controversial because they are difficult to define precisely. Prior to *APB Opinion 30* (1973), companies often classified gains and losses as ordinary or extraordinary, depending upon their motivations at the end of the accounting period. For example, a company with a low net income would select one or more large losses on the income statement and reclassify them as extraordinary in order to report a high income **before** extraordinary items. In other situations, large extraordinary gains would be classified as **ordinary** gains to increase income **before** extraordinary items. The tendency was to classify gains as ordinary and losses as extraordinary.

To prevent such manipulations, the APB issued *Opinion 30* (1973), which attempted to define extraordinary items very precisely; however, the result was to almost eliminate their existence. Extraordinary items are defined in *APB Opinion 30* as follows (emphasis added):

> Extraordinary items are events and transactions that are distinguished by their **unusual nature and by the infrequency of their occurrence.** Thus, **both** of the following criteria should be met to classify an event or transaction as an extraordinary item:
>
> *a.* **Unusual nature**—The underlying event or transaction should possess a high degree of abnormality and be of a type clearly unrelated to, or only incidentally related to, the ordinary and typical activities of the entity, taking into account the environment in which the entity operates.
> *b.* **Infrequency of occurrence**—The underlying event or transaction should be of a type that would not reasonably be expected to recur in the foreseeable future, taking into account the environment in which the entity operates.[5]

---

[5] AICPA, *APB Opinion No. 30,* "Reporting the Results of Operations" (New York, June 1973), par. 20.

Two aspects of the above definition should be emphasized. First, **both** criteria, unusual and infrequent, must be met. Thus, an item that meets **either,** but not both, is not an extraordinary item. Second, the **environment in which the entity operates** often is controlling. For example, earthquake damage usually would be extraordinary—it is unusual and occurs infrequently in most parts of the world. However, if one were to locate a plant on a fault where earthquakes occur regularly, earthquake damage would not be extraordinary in that **particular environment;** the damage would be considered "usual **or** frequent." Thus, whether an event or transaction is extraordinary depends not only on the characteristics of the event or transaction itself, but also on the environment in which it occurs. The *Opinion* cites only three different kinds of events that may be classified as extraordinary: (1) a major casualty, such as an earthquake; (2) expropriation by a foreign government; and (3) prohibition under a newly enacted law or regulation. However, this list was not intended to be exclusive.

The *Opinion* states that the following **should not** be considered as extraordinary items because they are expected during the customary and continuing business activities of any entity:

a. Write-down or write-off of receivables, inventories, equipment leased to others, or other intangible assets.
b. Gains or losses from exchange or translation of foreign currencies, including those related to major devaluations or revaluations.
c. Gains or losses on disposal of a segment of a business.
d. Other gains or losses from sale or abandonment of property, plant, or equipment used in the business.
e. Effects of a strike, including those against competitors and major suppliers.
f. Adjustments of accruals on long-term contracts.[6]

Extraordinary items must be reported on the income statement under a separate classification net of any income tax effect caused by their occurrence. If subject to income tax, an extraordinary gain causes an increase in income tax, and an extraordinary loss creates a tax saving. In both situations, the tax effect is subtracted from the gain or loss. Exhibits 3–3, 3–4, and 3–8 illustrate the required reporting of extraordinary items between the captions "Income before extraordinary items" and "Net income," and their inclusion in EPS reporting.

The reporting of extraordinary items is simple and straightforward; however, in practice the classification decision still involves subjectivity as is shown in actual financial statements.

Also, the APB and the FASB have made exceptions to the above definition to specify that certain items be classified as extraordinary; these are certain gains and losses from (1) extinguishment of debt (discussed in Chapter 17) and (2) income tax loss carryforwards (discussed in Chapter 10). These exceptions require that certain items be reported as extraordinary, although they may not meet both of the criteria—unusual and nonrecurring.

---

[6] Ibid., par. 23.

Finally, the **amount** of a loss or gain is not a criteria for determining whether an item should be designated as extraordinary. The only criteria are that the item be *(a)* unusual in nature and *(b)* infrequent in occurrence. However, as with other amounts, an extraordinary gain or loss that **clearly is not material in amount** (in conformity with the materiality threshold; see Chapter 1, Part B) is not required to be reported as an extraordinary item. However, lack of materiality does not preclude the opportunity to appropriately report an item.

REPORTING UNUSUAL OR INFREQUENT ITEMS

We have referred to events or transactions that are **either** unusual or infrequent, but not both. They do not qualify as extraordinary items; however, the prevailing view is that they should be called to the attention of the statement user to fulfill the **full-disclosure principle.** Therefore, *APB Opinion 30* requires that the effects

---

EXHIBIT 3–6

Reporting Unusual or Infrequent Items and Extraordinary Items

LUCKY OIL CORPORATION
Income Statement (partial)
For the Year Ended December 31, 19X

Revenues (not detailed in this example)		$990,000
Expenses (not detailed in this example)		878,000
Income from normal operations (pretax)		112,000
Unusual or infrequent items (Note 10):		
Loss on disposal of long-term investment	$ 43,000	
Gain on disposal of farming equipment	31,000	12,000
Income before income tax and extraordinary items.		100,000
Income tax expense		40,000
Income before extraordinary item		60,000
Extraordinary item:		
Gain, offshore drilling salvage (Note 11)	500,000	
Less: Income tax	200,000	300,000
Net income		$360,000
EPS (10,000 common shares outstanding):		
Income before extraordinary items	$ 6.00	
Extraordinary gain	30.00	
Net income	$36.00	

Note 10. The loss on disposal is due to the sale of the only long-term investment held by the company in the timber industry. The company has no plans to reinvest in this industry. The company has discontinued the use of farm equipment that originally was acquired for rent to landowners with whom the company had leasing activities.
Note 11. The extraordinary gain is due to discovery of a sunken ship during offshore drilling operations. The artifacts salvaged were sold.

of such events or transactions be **reported separately on the income statement** as follows (emphasis supplied):

> A material event or transaction that is unusual in nature or occurs infrequently, but not both, and therefore does not meet both criteria for classification as an extraordinary item, should be **reported as a separate component of income from continuing operations.** Such items should **not** be reported . . . net of income taxes.[7]

The *Opinion* stated that these items should not be reported net of income tax because *(a)* reporting net of tax is a feature of extraordinary items, *(b)* other items above "Income before extraordinary items" are not usually reported net of tax, and *(c)* intraperiod income tax allocation might become overly complex (discussed in Part B).

Exhibit 3–6 (page 155) illustrates one way to report unusual or infrequent items.

PART B: SPECIFIC ISSUES DIRECTLY RELATED TO THE INCOME STATEMENT AND STATEMENT OF RETAINED EARNINGS

PRIOR PERIOD ADJUSTMENTS

Prior period adjustments must be reported on the statement of retained earnings. This GAAP requirement means that prior period adjustments **never** flow through the income statement.

FASB Statement 16, paragraph 11, defines and prescribes the accounting for prior period adjustments in terms of only two items, as follows (emphasis added):

> Items of gain and loss related to the following shall be accounted for and reported as prior period adjustments and excluded from the determination of net income for the current period:
>
> *a.* **Correction of an error** in the financial statements of a prior period and
> *b.* **Adjustments** that result from realization of income tax benefits of preacquisition operating loss carryforwards of purchased subsidiaries.

FASB Statement 16 requires that all other items of revenue, expense, gain, and loss recognized during the period be included in the determination of reported net income for that period.

To illustrate the **recording** of a prior period adjustment for an error correction,

---

[7] Ibid., par. 26.

assume a machine that cost $10,000 (with a 10-year estimated useful life and no residual value) was purchased on January 1, 19A. Further, assume that the total cost was erroneously debited to an expense account in 19A. The error was discovered December 29, 19D. The following correcting entry would be required in 19D, assuming any income tax effects are recorded separately.

December 29, 19D:

Machinery	10,000	
Depreciation expense, straight line (for 19D)	1,000	
Accumulated depreciation (19A through 19D)..............		4,000
Prior period adjustment, error correction		7,000

Any income tax effect of the prior period adjustment could be included in the above entry or recorded separately. Assuming the same error was made on the income tax return, the entry to record the income tax effect of the prior period adjustment, assuming a 30% income tax rate, would be:

Prior period adjustment, error correction ($7,000 × 30%)	2,100	
Income tax payable		2,100

The Prior Period Adjustment, Error Correction account balance would be closed directly to Retained Earnings on December 31, 19D.

A prior period adjustment (net of its income tax effect) is **reported** on the statement of retained earnings as a **correction of the beginning balance** of retained earnings as illustrated in **Exhibit 3–7.**

EXHIBIT 3–7

Statement of Retained Earnings

GRAHAM RETAIL COMPANY
Statement of Retained Earnings
For the Year Ended December 31, 19D

Retained earnings, 1/1/19D		$378,800
Prior period adjustments:		
Correction of error from prior period, a credit	$7,000	
Less: Income tax effect	2,100*	4,900
Balance as adjusted		383,700
Add: Net income, 19D (per income statement,		
Exhibit 3–3)		81,200
		464,900
Deduct: cash dividends declared in 19D		30,000
Retained earnings, 12/31/19D (Note 7)		$434,900

Notes to financial statements:
Note 7. Retained earnings—Of the $434,900 ending balance in retained earnings, $280,000 is restricted from dividend availability under the terms of the bond indenture. When the bonds are retired, the restriction will be removed.
* This reporting of income tax is an example of intraperiod tax allocation; average income tax rate, 30%.

DISCLOSURE OF INCOME TAXES

Income taxes are assessed on profit-making corporations (but not on sole proprietorships or partnerships as separate entities). Also, stockholders must pay income taxes on dividends received; therefore, it is often pointed out that corporate income is subject to double taxation.

Income taxes paid by corporations are viewed as an expense (as opposed to a distribution of income). Because of the significant amounts, the matching and full disclosure principles must be fully satisfied. To meet these requirements, *APB Opinion 11* prescribed **two separate and distinctly different types of income tax allocations.** These are:

1. **Intraperiod tax allocation**—This is an allocation of total income tax expense for the **current accounting period** to various components on the current financial statements.
2. **Interperiod tax allocation**—This is an allocation of income taxes on taxable items **among accounting periods.** It occurs when there are items of revenue and/or expense on the income statement for the current period that, because of the tax laws, are reported on the income tax return for an earlier or later accounting period. Interperiod tax allocation causes **deferred income taxes,** which are **reported on the balance sheet.** This kind of allocation is discussed in Chapter 10.

Although intraperiod and interperiod tax allocation are different types, they are **not mutually exclusive. Both types are required because each serves a different reporting purpose.**

Intraperiod Income Tax Allocation[8]

The concept underlying **intraperiod** income tax allocation is that, in conformity with the matching principle, **all income tax consequences should be reported along with the transaction, or group of transactions, that caused the tax effect.** Thus, total income tax for the current period must be allocated to (1) income before extraordinary items, (2) extraordinary items, and (3) prior period adjustments.[9]

The need for **intraperiod** income tax allocations arises because financial statement users want information useful for **predicting the future cash flows of an entity.** Because extraordinary gains and losses are not as predictable as income before extraordinary items, investors may evaluate a company on the basis of its **income before extraordinary items.** Therefore, it is important to report separately the amounts of income tax expense applicable to (1) income before extraordinary items, (2) extraordinary items, and (3) prior period adjustments.

Revenues, gains, and prior period adjustments (if credits) usually increase income tax expense. In contrast, expenses, losses, and prior period adjustments (if

---

[8] Intraperiod tax allocation is discussed in this early chapter because it is used in illustrations and problems prior to Chapter 10, where tax allocation is discussed in detail.

[9] Although rare, certain direct entries to stockholders' equity accounts also may have income tax effects requiring intraperiod tax allocation.

EXHIBIT 3–8

Intraperiod Income
Tax Allocation

Situation: X Corporation's accounts provided the following data for 19B:

1. Income before income tax and before extraordinary items, $115,000.
2. Extraordinary gain (specified), $40,000 (taxable).
3. Beginning balance, retained earnings, $130,000.
4. Dividends declared and paid, $50,000.
5. Prior period adjustment, error correction, $7,000 debit (subject to income tax).
6. Income tax rates: First $25,000, 20%; all above $25,000, 40%.

Requirement 1—Compute total income tax for 19B.

Response:
Taxable income: $115,000 + $40,000 − $7,000 = $148,000.
Total income tax: ($25,000 × 20%) + [($148,000 − $25,000) × 40%] = $54,200.

Requirement 2—Prepare (1) a partial income statement starting with "income before income tax and before extraordinary items" and (2) a complete statement of retained earnings, both of which include **intraperiod** income tax allocation.

Response:
1. Partial income statement:

Income before income tax and extraordinary items	$115,000
Less: Applicable income tax expense*	41,000
Income before extraordinary items	74,000

Extraordinary items:		
Extraordinary gain (specified)	$40,000	
Less: Applicable income tax expense†	16,000	
Extraordinary gain, net of applicable		
income tax		24,000
Net income		$ 98,000

2. Statement of retained earnings:

Beginning balance (1/1/19B)		$130,000
Prior period adjustment:		
Error correction, a debit	$ 7,000	
Less: Income tax saving‡	2,800	4,200
Balance as corrected		125,800
Add: 19B net income (from income statement)		98,000
		223,800
Deduct: Cash dividends		50,000
Ending balance (12/31/19B)		$173,800

Requirement 3—Prove the intraperiod income tax allocation.

Response:
$41,000 + $16,000 − $2,800 = $54,200 (total tax).

* Computation of intraperiod tax allocation:
  Tax on ordinary income:

$25,000 × 20% =	$ 5,000	
$90,000 × 40% =	36,000	$41,000

† Tax on extraordinary gain:

$40,000 × 40% =	16,000
Total income tax allocated on the income statement	$57,000

‡ $7,000 × 40% = $2,800.

debits) usually reduce income tax expense. The amount of such a tax reduction often is called a **tax saving.**

Exhibit 3–8 illustrates **intraperiod** income tax allocation for X Corporation. In this illustration, **total** income tax for 19B was $54,200, which is allocated to three items: (1) income before extraordinary items, $41,000; (2) extraordinary gain, $16,000; and (3) prior period adjustment, $2,800 (a tax saving because this was a debit).

In this example, it would be misleading to allocate total income tax of $54,200 to income before extraordinary items (which would cause Income before extraordinary items to be $60,800) because $16,000 of the income tax expense arose from the extraordinary gain, and the prior period adjustment caused a $2,800 tax saving. If an investor were to evaluate X Corporation based on the $60,800 instead of the $74,000, the predicted income potential of the company probably would be understated.

Intraperiod income tax allocation also can be observed in the financial statements of Graham Retail Company as follows:

Exhibit	Item	Amount
3–4	Income before extraordinary item	$37,800
3–4	Extraordinary loss (tax saving)	(3,000)
3–7	Prior period adjustment	2,100
	Total income tax ($126,000 − $10,000 + $7,000) × 30% ...	$36,900

The combined journal entry to record 19D income tax by Graham Retail Company could be as follows:

Income tax expense (on the income statement)	34,800	
Prior period adjustment, income tax (on the statement of retained earnings)	2,100	
Income tax payable		36,900

EARNINGS PER SHARE

Earnings per share (EPS) is the relationship obtained by dividing *(a)* reported income (available to the holders of common stock) by *(b)* the average number of common shares outstanding (during the year). EPS is not computed on preferred stock; therefore, to compute EPS on the common stock only, income must be reduced by any preferred stock dividend claim (a priority).

EPS is important to decision makers because it *(a)* relates the income of the entity to a single share of stock, *(b)* helps investors in making relevant profit performance comparisons among companies with diverse numbers of common shares outstanding, and *(c)* makes possible comparisons of relative profitability of companies on the basis of a single share of stock.

Reporting EPS was optional prior to the issuance of *APB Opinion 15* in 1969. *Opinion 15* requires companies to report per share data for *(a)* income before extraordinary items and *(b)* net income.[10]

Calculation of Earnings per Share (EPS)

In this chapter, we will review only the fundamentals of EPS for companies with **simple capital structures.**[11]

To illustrate the calculation of EPS in simple situations, four separate cases are presented in **Exhibit 3–9.** These cases will provide sufficient background for the discussions and homework prior to the detailed EPS discussion in Chapter 22.

The four cases are summarized as follows:

Case A—This is the least complex case. It involves only common stock with no changes in the number of common shares outstanding during the year and no extraordinary items on the income statement. In such a situation, calculation of EPS involves dividing net income by the number of shares outstanding, as illustrated in Exhibit 3–9.

Case B—A slight complexity occurs when there is an extraordinary gain or loss on the income statement. In this case, EPS amounts are calculated and reported for *(a)* income before extraordinary items, *(b)* extraordinary items, and *(c)* net income, as illustrated in Exhibit 3–9.

Case C—Another complexity occurs when there is a change during the period in the number of shares outstanding because of the sale and issuance of common stock or the purchase of such shares as treasury stock. This complexity requires calculation of the **weighted-average** number of shares outstanding during the year. The weighted average, calculated as illustrated in Exhibit 3–9, is divided into the income amounts.

Case D—Another complexity occurs when the company issues more shares of its common stock because of a stock dividend or stock split. In these cases the shares issued are treated in EPS computations as though they had been outstanding for the entire period, as illustrated in Exhibit 3–9.

Another level of complexity occurs when both common and nonconvertible preferred stock are outstanding. Additional complexities arise when outstanding

---

[10] AICPA, *APB Opinion No. 15,* "Earnings per Share" (New York, May 1969), does not require reporting of EPS for extraordinary items. EPS for *(a)* income before extraordinary items and *(b)* net income are required. In this textbook, we usually illustrate reporting EPS for the three amounts, for completeness and because most companies follow this practice.

[11] Under certain conditions (i.e., complex capital structures), *APB Opinion 15* requires two presentations of EPS on the income statement: (1) primary EPS and (2) fully diluted EPS. Primary EPS relates income to the company's outstanding common stock, and fully diluted EPS relates income to the maximum number of shares of common stock that could conceivably become outstanding. Therefore, fully diluted EPS is an estimate of the company's **minimum** EPS under its existing capital structure.

EXHIBIT 3–9: Calculation of Earnings Per Share (EPS)

Assumptions	Calculating and reporting of EPS	
Case A: 30,000 common shares outstanding throughout the year; net income for the year, $96,000.	Net income	$96,000
	Earnings per common share ($96,000 ÷ 30,000 shares)	$ 3.20

Case B:
30,000 common shares outstanding throughout the year; income before extraordinary item, $96,000; extraordinary loss less applicable tax saving, $21,000; net income for the year, $75,000.

Income before extraordinary item	$96,000
Extraordinary loss less applicable tax saving	21,000
Net income	$75,000
Earnings per common share:	
Income before extraordinary item	$ 3.20
Extraordinary loss	(.70)
Net income	$ 2.50

$96,000 ÷ 30,000 shares = $3.20
(21,000) ÷ 30,000 shares = (.70)
75,000 ÷ 30,000 shares = 2.50

Case C:
30,000 common shares outstanding from January 1 through April 1, on which date an additional 10,000 common shares were sold and issued; other data as in Case B.

Income before extraordinary item	$96,000
Extraordinary loss less applicable tax saving	21,000
Net income	$75,000
Earnings per common share:	
Income before extraordinary item	$ 2.56
Extraordinary loss	(.56)
Net income	$ 2.00

Calculation of weighted-average number of shares:

Dates	Months	Shares	Weighted Shares
Jan. 1–Apr. 1	3	× 30,000 =	90,000
Apr. 1–Dec. 31	9	× 40,000 =	360,000
	12		450,000

Average: 450,000 ÷ 12 = 37,500.

$96,000 ÷ 37,500 shares = $2.56
(21,000) ÷ 37,500 shares = (.56)
75,000 ÷ 37,500 shares = 2.00

Case D:
30,000 common shares outstanding from January 1 through April 1, on which date an additional 20,000 common shares were issued as a **stock dividend;** other data as in Case B (no additional shares were sold).

Income before extraordinary item	$96,000
Extraordinary loss less applicable tax saving	21,000
Net income	$75,000
Earnings per common share:	
Income before extraordinary item	$ 1.92
Extraordinary loss	(.42)
Net income	$ 1.50

As provided in *APB Opinion 15,* when there is a stock dividend, the divisor is the average number of shares outstanding at year-end (including all stock dividends, as if they had been outstanding for the entire year). In this case, this is 30,000 + 20,000 = 50,000.

$96,000 ÷ 50,000 shares = $1.92
(21,000) ÷ 50,000 shares = (.42)
75,000 ÷ 50,000 shares = 1.50

preferred stock or bonds payable are convertible into common stock. These complexities involve the concepts of common stock equivalents and fully diluted EPS, which are discussed in Chapter 22.

FASB Statement 21, "Suspension of Earnings per Share and Segment Information by Nonpublic Enterprises," exempts corporations that are not publicly held from the EPS disclosure requirement.

ACCOUNTING CHANGES

APB Opinion 20 defines three types of accounting changes essentially as follows:[12]

1. **Changes in estimates**—The use of estimates (such as in determining depreciation expense or bad debt expense) is a natural consequence of the accounting process. However, experience and additional information may make it possible to improve estimates. For example, the estimated useful life of an operational asset, after having been used (and depreciated) for 6 years, may be changed from the original 10-year estimated life to a 15-year estimated life. Changes of this type are referred to as **changes in estimates** and are clearly distinguished from the next type of change— changes in accounting principle.

2. **Changes in accounting principle**—Because of a change in circumstances, or the development of a new accounting principle, a change in the recording and reporting approach for a particular transaction may be necessary. For example, a change in circumstances may make it desirable to change from straight-line depreciation to sum-of-the-years'-digits (SYD) depreciation. This would be a change in accounting principle, **a change from one acceptable principle to another acceptable principle.**

3. **Change in the accounting entity** (see Chapter 20).

Accounting changes are important because of the **comparability** quality, which holds that the financial data of an enterprise should be comparable among entities and from period to period. When a company changes the estimated useful life of a depreciable asset, changes from one depreciation method to another depreciation method for the asset, or engages in any other type of accounting change, both intercompany and interperiod comparability of the financial statements of the enterprise are affected. The provisions of *APB Opinion 20* emphasize interperiod comparability.

Accounting changes are discussed in detail in Chapter 20. **Changes in estimates** occur frequently in the discussions prior to Chapter 20; therefore, this type of change will be reviewed in order to provide background for the interim topics and homework.

---

[12] Accounting changes **are not** due to accounting errors. They are approved accounting approaches for the three situations described. Correction of **accounting errors** will be discussed later.

Changes in Estimates

Revisions of estimates, such as useful lives and/or residual value of depreciable assets, the loss rate for bad debts, and warranty costs, are called **changes in estimates** and are accorded special treatment. As a company gains experience in such areas as its depreciable assets, receivables, and warranties, it may have a sound basis for revising one or more of its prior accounting estimates. *APB Opinion 20* states that, in such instances, the **prior accounting results are not to be disturbed. Instead, the new estimate should be used over the current and remaining periods.** Thus, a change in estimate is made on a **prospective** (i.e., future-oriented) basis.

To illustrate the accounting for a change in estimate, assume a machine that cost $24,000 is being depreciated on a straight-line basis over a 10-year estimated useful life with no residual value. Early during the 7th year, on the basis of more experience with the machine, it is determined that the total useful life should have been 14 years (and no residual value). Thus, the remaining life becomes eight years from the start of the year in which the revised estimate was made (year 7 in the example). This change in estimate does not require an entry to correct the prior depreciation already recorded (years 1–6 in the example). Rather new depreciation amounts will be recorded at the end of the current year (year 7) and each year during the remaining useful life of the asset. The new depreciation amounts would be based upon *(a)* the **undepreciated** amount of the asset and *(b)* the new **remaining** useful life of the asset.

To illustrate, the new depreciation amounts would be computed and recorded as follows:

End of years 7–14 (8 years):

Depreciation expense	1,200	
Accumulated depreciation, machinery		1,200
Computations:		
Original cost		$24,000
Accumulated depreciation to date ($24,000 × 6/10)		14,400
Difference—depreciated over 8 years remaining life		$ 9,600
Annual depreciation over remaining life: ($9,600 ÷ 8 years)		$ 1,200

STATEMENT OF RETAINED EARNINGS

A statement of retained earnings often is presented as a supplement to the income statement and balance sheet because it is needed to comply with the full-disclosure requirement. However, many companies present a **statement of owners' equity** instead. This statement details all changes in owners' equity, including retained earnings. For example, see Chapter 14, "Reporting Stockholders' Equity—An Actual Situation."

The purposes of the statement of retained earnings are to report all changes in retained earnings during the accounting period, to reconcile the beginning and ending balances of retained earnings, and to provide a connecting link between the income statement and the balance sheet. The ending balance of retained earnings is reported on the balance sheet as one element of owners' equity (refer to Chapter 4). In conformity with *APB Opinion 9* and *FASB Statement 16,* the major segments of a statement of retained earnings are (1) prior period adjustments, (2) net income or loss for the period, and (3) dividends.

Appropriations and Restrictions of Retained Earnings

Appropriations of, and restrictions on, retained earnings limit the availability of retained earnings for dividend purposes to the unappropriated and unrestricted balance.

Restrictions may result from *(a)* **legal requirements,** as when a state statute requires that retained earnings be restricted for dividend purposes by the cost of any treasury stock held; or *(b)* **contractual agreements,** as when a bond agreement requires that retained earnings of a specified amount be withheld from dividend purposes until the bonds are retired.

Appropriations of retained earnings result from decisions by the corporation to set aside, or appropriate, a specific amount of retained earnings (temporarily or permanently). The effect of an appropriation is to remove the specified amount of retained earnings from dividend availability. For example, corporations often set up appropriations such as "retained earnings appropriated for future plant expansion."

The primary purposes of restrictions and appropriations are to *(a)* "protect" the cash position of the company by constraining cash dividends, *(b)* reduce the risk of nonpayment to creditors, and *(c)* inform statement users that a portion of retained earnings is set aside for a specific purpose (usually long term).

Exhibit 3–7 illustrates a restriction of $280,000 on the retained earnings of Graham Retail Company. In this situation, the unrestricted balance of retained earnings is $154,900 (i.e., $434,900 − $280,000 = $154,900). Graham recorded the restriction, on the date that it was imposed, as follows:

Retained earnings (unappropriated)	280,000	
Retained earnings appropriated (as required by		
the bond indenture)		280,000

When a restriction or appropriation is removed, the amount is returned to the Retained Earnings (unappropriated) account. Restrictions and appropriations usually are reported in a note (as illustrated in Exhibit 3–7). Retained earnings is discussed in detail in Chapter 15.

COMBINED STATEMENT OF INCOME AND RETAINED EARNINGS

The income statement and statement of retained earnings may be presented together in the form of a **combined statement.** The advantage of such a format

EXHIBIT 3–10

Combined Statement of Income and Retained Earnings

GRAHAM RETAIL COMPANY
Statement of Income and Retained Earnings
For the Year Ended December 31, 19D

Details of income statement as illustrated in Exhibit 3–3 (single step) or Exhibit 3–4 (multiple step).

Net income	$ 81,200
Retained earnings, January 1, 19D	378,800
Prior period adjustment, correction of error	
(net of income tax of $2,100) (Note 6)	4,900
Cash dividends declared and paid during 19D	(30,000)
Retained earnings, December 31, 19D (Note 7)	$434,900*

Notes to financial statements:
   Note 6. Prior period adjustments—During the year, the company discovered that an expenditure made in 19A was incorrectly expensed. This error caused net income of that period to be understated. The prior period adjustment of $7,000 corrects the error.
   Note 7. Restrictions—Of the $434,900 ending balance in Retained Earnings, $280,000 is restricted from dividend availability under the terms of the bond indenture. When the bonds are retired, the restriction will be removed.
   * Observe that this amount agrees with the ending balance in Exhibit 3–7.

is that it brings together related and relevant information for the statement user. A combined statement is illustrated in **Exhibit 3–10.**

ACTUAL FINANCIAL STATEMENTS ILLUSTRATED

Throughout this chapter, hypothetical examples were used for instructional purposes. To enable you to gain confidence in understanding financial statements, the **Appendix following Chapter 24** presents a complete set of actual financial statements for a well-known company. We suggest that you carefully examine these statements and relate them to the topics discussed in this chapter.

QUESTIONS

PART A

1. Briefly explain how the income statement is a connecting link between the beginning and ending balance sheets.
2. Briefly explain the difference between economic income and accounting income.
3. It is said that accounting income and economic income are broadly consistent, although the results are different. Explain this statement because it appears to be inconsistent.
4. Explain the basic distinction between revenues and gains.

5. Explain the basic difference between expenses and losses.
6. Briefly explain the two formats used for income statements. Explain why actual income statements usually are somewhere between these two formats.
7. Explain how gross margin is computed for a retail business. How would gross margin be computed for a service organization?
8. Explain how cost of goods sold is reported on a single-step income statement and on a multiple-step income statement.
9. List the four major "income" captions, in their order of appearance, on a typical multiple-step income statement.
10. Briefly explain the full-disclosure principle.
11. Explain the difference between the two expense accounts—Freight-In and Freight-Out.
12. Explain why the total amount of depreciation expense should be disclosed in the financial statements.
13. Define an extraordinary item. How should extraordinary items be reported on (a) a single-step and (b) a multiple-step income statement?
14. How are items that are either unusual or infrequent, but not both, reported on the income statement?
15. Outline a situation when a large hurricane or tornado loss could (a) be extraordinary and (b) not be an extraordinary item.
16. Does the amount of a gain determine whether it is an extraordinary item or not? Explain.

PART B

17. Briefly define a prior period adjustment. How is a prior period adjustment reported?
18. Briefly distinguish between intraperiod and interperiod tax allocation.
19. TK Corporation computed total income tax for 19B of $16,640. The following pretax amounts were used: (a) income before extraordinary loss, $60,000; (b) extraordinary loss, $12,000; and (c) prior period adjustment, $4,000 (a credit). The average income tax rate on all items was 32%. Compute the intraperiod income tax allocation amounts.
20. Explain why the matching principle requires intraperiod tax allocation.
21. Define earnings per share (EPS). Why is it required as an integral part of the income statement?
22. What EPS amounts must be reported on the income statement?
23. Fluke Company reported the following amounts at the end of 19D:

Extraordinary gain $90,000
Net income 50,000

Average number of common shares outstanding, 25,000.

Prepare the EPS presentation. Which EPS amount is likely to be the most relevant? Explain.
24. What are the three types of accounting changes discussed in *APB Opinion 20?* Explain what is meant by a change in estimate. Explain the basic approach used to account for and report a change in estimate.
25. VEE Company has a machine that cost $21,000 when acquired at the beginning of year 1. It has been depreciated using straight line, on the basis of a 10-year useful life and a $1,000 residual value. At the start of year 5, the residual value was changed to $3,000. Compute the amount of depreciation expense per year that should be recorded for the remaining useful life of the machine.

26. What items are reported on a statement of retained earnings? Explain how it provides a link between the current income statement and the balance sheet.
27. What is meant by appropriations and restrictions on retained earnings? How are such items usually reported?

EXERCISES

PART A: EXERCISES 3–1 TO 3–8

Exercise 3–1

Furst Corporation has been operating for five years in a dynamic industry. The 19E detailed income statement, prepared in conformity with generally accepted accounting principles (i.e., the transactions approach on the accrual basis), reported income of $17,600. The principal owner, who is the chief executive officer (CEO), believes that the company earned much more than that amount. To support his contention he developed the following schedule:

	Market values	
Items	End 19D	End 19E
Total assets (70% plant and equipment)	$270,000	$325,000
Total liabilities	130,000	125,000
Contributions of owners during 19E		20,000

Required:
1. Prepare a 19E income statement using the CEO's data.
2. How would you label this income amount?
3. What reservations would you have about this way of measuring income?

Exercise 3–2

Fifteen transactions are listed below (left) that may or may not affect the income statement. Income statement classifications are listed by letters to the right. You are to match each transaction with the appropriate letter to indicate the usual classification that should be used.

Answer	Selected transactions	Income statement classification
A	1. Sales.	A. Revenues.
I	2. Prepaid insurance.	B. Expenses.
E	3. Loss on disposal of service trucks.	C. Gains (ordinary).
C	4. Dividends received on an investment in African diamond mine.	D. Gains (unusual or infrequent).
		E. Loss (ordinary).
B	5. Wages accrued (unpaid and unrecorded).	F. Loss (unusual or infrequent).
E	6. Cost of moving the only plant the company owns from the northeast to the southwest (a major expenditure).	G. Gain (extraordinary).
H		H. Loss (extraordinary).
		I. None of the above.

Answer	Selected transactions	Income statement classification
B	7. Cost of goods sold.	
A	8. Services rendered.	
D	9. Gain (characterized as unusual or infrequent).	
I	10. Rent collected in advance.	
F	11. Fire loss (characterized as unusual).	
H	12. Loss due to a rare freeze which destroyed the citrus trees in the Rio Grande Valley.	
A — C	13. Gain on sale of short-term investments.	
I	14. Cash dividend declared and paid.	
H	15. Loss due to meteor which completely destroyed the plant.	

Exercise 3–3

The following items were taken from the adjusted trial balance of Kasper Manufacturing Corporation at December 31, 19B:

Sales revenue	$950,000
Cost of goods manufactured (including depreciation, $52,000)	580,000
Dividends received on investment in stocks	6,500
Finished goods inventory, 1/1/19B (periodic inventory system)	48,000
Interest expense	4,200
Extraordinary item: fire loss (pretax)	48,000
Distribution expenses	135,300
Common stock, par $10	200,000
General and administrative expenses	113,000
Interest revenue	2,500
Finished goods inventory, 12/31/19B	53,000
Income tax, assume average 30% tax rate	?

Required:
1. Prepare a single-step income statement (include EPS). Set up cost of goods sold as a separate schedule to include the inventory amounts and cost of goods manufactured.
2. Prepare a multiple-step income statement. Set up cost of goods sold within the statement.

Exercise 3–4

The following selected transactions were completed by Avis Company during the year 19C. The accounting period ends December 31.

a. On December 21, 19C, merchandise was sold for $15,000 cash. The customer took possession of two thirds of the merchandise on that date. The balance will be picked up on January 3, 19D.
b. Services were rendered to a customer starting on December 27, 19C. The services will be completed around January 8, 19D, at which time $32,000 cash in full will be collected. Assume eight working days are involved of which two were in 19C.
c. During 19C, the company sold 10 TV sets and collected $6,000 cash in full. The company gives a one-year guarantee. It is estimated that the average warranty cost per set under the guarantee is $20. Assume by the end of 19C, half of the guarantees on the 10 sets have been satisfied.

d. On December 31, 19C, a used truck was sold by the company. The truck had been used in operating the business and had a book value of $1,000. The sales price was $2,400, which was payable six months from date of the sale plus 15% interest per annum.

e. On December 27, 19C, the company received an income tax refund of $1,000 after four years of negotiations with the Internal Revenue Service.

Hint: Restudy the revenue, cost, and matching principles in Chapter 1, Part B.

Required:
For each transaction, give the following:

1. When revenue and/or expense should be recognized.
2. The amount(s) that should be recognized in 19C.
3. The basis for your decision.

Exercise 3–5

Friendly Company's records provided the following information at December 31, 19B (end of the accounting period):

Sales revenue	$95,000
Service revenue	35,000
Gain on sale of short-term investments	11,000
Distribution expense	18,000
General and administrative expense	12,000
Depreciation expense	6,000
Interest expense	4,000
Income tax expense (40% rate on all items)	?
Rare tornado loss on building (infrequent and unusual)	15,000
Loss on sale of store fixtures (infrequent but not unusual)	3,000
Beginning inventory (periodic inventory system)	20,000
Ending inventory	23,000
Purchases (including freight-in)	50,000
Purchase returns	2,000

Common stock shares outstanding, 10,000 shares.

Required:
1. Prepare a single-step income statement (show cost of goods sold computations in a separate supporting schedule).
2. Prepare a multiple-step income statement.

Exercise 3–6

AAA Sales and Service Company's accounts provided the following information at December 31, 19C (end of the accounting period):

Sales revenue	$199,000
Service revenue	33,000
Sales returns and allowances	1,500
Interest revenue	2,500
Gain on sale of short-term investments	1,000
Distribution expenses	56,700
General and administrative expenses	32,500
Depreciation expense	18,500

Income tax expense (40% rate on all items)	?
Loss on disposal of service trucks (assume infrequent but not unusual)	4,000
Gain (assume both unusual and infrequent)	10,000
Cost of goods sold (perpetual inventory system)	54,000
Interest expense	4,300
Common stock, par $5	100,000

Required:
1. Prepare a single-step income statement.
2. Prepare a multiple-step income statement.

Exercise 3–7

The following selected transactions were completed by JB Company during the year 19J; the accounting period ends December 31:

a. On December 30, 19J, sold $10,000 merchandise; terms 3/10, n/30.
b. On December 29, 19J, paid $3,000 for advertising in the local paper. The ads related only to a clearance sale that would run from January 1–31, 19K.
c. Performed services each working day for a customer from December 27, 19J, through January 5, 19K. Assume eight working days are involved, of which four were in 19J. Cash collected was $2,000 (in full) on December 27, 19J.
d. Sold a used TV set for $200 on December 28, 19J, and collected $125 cash. The balance is due in six months; however, collection of the balance is very doubtful, and the set will not be worth repossessing again. It is now carried in the inventory of used sets at $80. Credit Inventory because the perpetual inventory system is used.
e. On December 1, 19J, borrowed $6,000 cash and gave a one-year, 18% note payable for $6,000. Interest is payable at maturity.

Hint: Restudy the revenue, cost, and matching principles in Chapter 1, Part B.

Required:
For each transaction, give the following:

1. When revenue and/or expense should be recognized.
2. The amount that should be recognized in 19J.
3. The basis for your decision.

Exercise 3–8

The following items were taken from the adjusted trial balance of Big T Trading Corporation on December 31, 19K. Assume an average 30% income tax rate on all items (including the casualty loss). The accounting period ends December 31.

Sales revenue	$645,200
Rent revenue	2,400
Interest revenue	900
Gain on sale of operational assets (an ordinary item)	2,000
Distribution expenses	136,000
General and administrative expenses	110,000
Interest expense	1,500
Depreciation for the period	6,000
Extraordinary item: casualty loss (pretax)	22,000
Common stock (par $10)	100,000
Cost of goods sold (perpetual inventory system)	330,000

Required:

1. Prepare a single-step income statement.
2. Prepare a multiple-step income statement.

PART B: EXERCISES 3–9 TO 3–15

Exercise 3–9

The following pretax amounts were taken from the adjusted trial balance of Ball Corporation on December 31, 19B, end of the annual accounting period:

Balance, retained earnings, 1/1/19B	$ 40,000
Sales revenue	300,000
Cost of goods sold (perpetual inventory system)	105,000
Distribution expenses	36,000
Administrative expenses	34,000
Extraordinary gain (pretax)	10,000
Prior period adjustment, correction of error from prior period, pretax (a debit)	20,000
Dividends declared and paid	16,000

For problem purposes, assume the income tax rate for all items is 30%. The average number of common shares outstanding during the year was 10,000.

Required:

1. Prepare a complete multiple-step income statement.
2. Prepare a statement of retained earnings.
3. Give the entry to record income taxes payable (assume not yet paid).

Exercise 3–10

The following pretax amounts were taken from the adjusted trial balance of Zapata Corporation at December 31, 19C, end of the annual accounting period:

Dividends declared and paid	$ 30,000
Sales revenue	320,000
Cost of goods sold (perpetual inventory system)	110,000
Operating expenses	65,000
Extraordinary loss (pretax)	22,000
Prior period adjustment, correction of error from prior period, pretax (a credit)	10,000
Common stock (par $5)	150,000
Beginning retained earnings, 1/1/19C	50,000

Required:

1. Prepare a complete single-step income statement assuming the income tax rate is 40% on all items.
2. Prepare a statement of retained earnings.
3. Give the entry to record income taxes payable (assume not yet paid).

Exercise 3–11

The following pretax amounts were taken from the adjusted trial balance of DIBA Corporation at December 31, 19J, end of the annual accounting period:

Sales revenue	$250,000
Cost of goods sold (perpetual inventory system)	120,000
Operating expenses	80,000
Extraordinary gain (pretax)	20,000
Prior period adjustment, correction of error from prior period, pretax (a debit)	32,000
Retained earnings, balance 1/1/19J	40,000
Dividends declared and paid	10,000

Common stock (par $10):	Shares
Outstanding 1/1/19J	15,000
Sold and issued 4/1/19J	5,000
Sold and issued 10/1/19J	7,000
Outstanding 12/31/19J	27,000

Required:
1. Prepare a complete single-step income statement. Assume an average 30% tax rate on all items.
2. Prepare a statement of retained earnings.

Exercise 3–12

The following pretax amounts were taken from the adjusted trial balance of Goode Corporation at December 31, 19B, end of the annual accounting period:

Sales revenue	$200,000
Service revenue	50,000
Cost of goods sold (perpetual inventory system)	100,000
Operating expenses	80,000
Unusual item, gain on sale of operational asset (pretax)	25,000
Extraordinary item, loss (pretax)	20,000
Prior period adjustment, correction of error from prior period, pretax (a debit)	5,000

Common stock (par $1), 10,000 shares outstanding.

Assume an average 40% corporate tax rate on all items.

Required:
1. Prepare a single-step income statement that meets the full-disclosure requirements with respect to unusual items, extraordinary items, prior period adjustments, intraperiod tax allocation, and EPS.
2. Give the journal entry to record income tax (assume not yet paid).

Exercise 3–13

Knight Company purchased a machine that cost $40,000 on January 1, 1981. The estimated useful life was 12 years, and the estimated residual value was $4,000. Straight-line depreciation is used. On December 31, 1986, prior to the adjusting entry, the company's chief accountant decided that the machine should be depreciated over a 15-year total useful life and that the estimated residual value at the end of the 15th year should be $1,000.

Required:
1. Give the adjusting entry at the end of 1986 for depreciation expense. Show computations.
2. Give the correcting entry required at the end of 1986. If none is required, so state and give the reasons.

Exercise 3–14

It is December 31, 1986, and Laval Company is preparing adjusting entries at the end of the accounting year. The company owns two trucks of different types. The following situations confront the company accountant:

Truck No. 1 cost $7,700 on January 1, 1984. It is being depreciated on a straight-line basis over an estimated useful life of 10 years with a $700 residual value. At December 31, 1986, it has been determined that the total useful life should have been 6 years instead of 10, with a revised residual value of $900.

Truck No. 2 cost $4,550 on January 1, 1983. It is being depreciated on a straight-line basis over an estimated useful life of seven years with a $350 residual value. At December 31, 1986, it was discovered that no depreciation had been recorded on this truck for 1983 or 1984.

Required:
1. For each truck, give the required adjusting entry for depreciation expense at December 31, 1986. Show computations.
2. For each truck, give the appropriate correcting entry and show computations. If no correcting entry is needed, give the reasons.

Exercise 3–15

The following pretax amounts were taken from the accounts of Scott Corporation at December 31, 19C, end of the annual accounting period:

Sales revenue	$170,000
Cost of goods sold (perpetual inventory system)	85,000
Distribution and administrative expenses	45,000
Extraordinary gain (pretax)	15,000
Prior period adjustment, correction of error from prior period, pretax (a debit)	8,000
Interest expense	1,000
Cash dividends declared and paid	5,000
Retained earnings, 1/1/19C	51,400

Common stock (par $5), 10,000 shares outstanding.

Assume an average 40% tax rate on all items, including the extraordinary gain.

Required:
Prepare a combined single-step income statement and statement of retained earnings, including intraperiod income tax allocation and EPS.

PROBLEMS

PART A: PROBLEMS 3–1 TO 3–6

Problem 3–1

The following pretax information was taken from the adjusted trial balance of Braun Corporation at December 31, 19D, end of the accounting period:

Sales revenue	$999,000
Inventory, 12/31/19C	80,000
Inventory, 12/31/19D	92,000
Sales returns	4,000
Gain on sale of equipment (unusual but not infrequent)	8,000
Depreciation expense	25,000
Distribution expenses	140,000
General and administrative expenses	92,300
Rent revenue	15,000
Investment revenue	7,000
Gain on sale of land (pretax)	6,000
Interest expense	9,000
Extraordinary gain (pretax)	80,000
Loss on sale of long-term investments, ordinary item (pretax)	10,000
Cost of goods sold	547,000
Loss due to leak in roof (infrequent but not unusual)	4,000
Extraordinary loss (pretax)	10,000

The company uses a periodic inventory system. Assume an average 40% income tax rate on all items. There are 50,000 shares of common stock outstanding.

Required:

1. Prepare a single-step income statement.
2. Prepare a multiple-step income statement.

Problem 3–2

The following data were taken from the adjusted trial balance of Dover Retail Corporation at December 31, 19B, end of the accounting period:

Merchandise inventory, 1/1/19B (periodic inventory system)	$ 71,000
Purchases	121,400
Sales revenue	405,000
Purchase returns	3,400
Sales returns	5,000
Common stock (par $10)	200,000
Depreciation expense (70% administrative expense,	
30% distribution expense)	50,000
Rent revenue	4,000
Interest expense	6,000
Investment revenue	2,500
Distribution expenses (exclusive of depreciation)	105,500
General and administrative expenses (exclusive of depreciation)	46,000
Gain on sale of noncurrent asset (an ordinary gain)	6,000
Loss on sale of long-term investments (ordinary)	3,600
Income tax expense (not including the extraordinary item)	?
Extraordinary item: Flood loss (pretax)	10,000
Freight paid on purchases	1,000
Merchandise inventory, 12/31/19B	88,000

Assume an average 40% income tax rate on all items, including gains and losses on assets sold and extraordinary items.

Required:

1. Prepare a single-step income statement and a separate schedule of cost of goods sold to support it.
2. Prepare a multiple-step income statement (include cost of goods sold computation within the statement).

Problem 3–3

Listed below are the primary financial statement classifications coded with letters. Also, a list of 25 selected transactions is given along with a space for your response.

For each transaction enter one code letter to indicate the usual classification. Comment on doubtful items.

Code	Financial statement classification

Income Statement

A . . . . Revenue
B . . . . Expense
C . . . . Unusual or infrequent (but not both) gain or loss
D . . . . Extraordinary item

Statement of Retained Earnings

E . . . . An addition or deduction
F . . . . Addition to retained earnings
G . . . . Deduction from retained earnings
H . . . . Note to the financial statements

Balance Sheet

I . . . . Appropriately classified

Response   **Transaction (summarized)**

1. __I__ Estimated warranties payable.
2. __I__ Allowance for doubtful accounts.
3. __A__ Gain on sale of operational asset.
4. __D__ Hurricane damages.
5. __G__ Payment of $30,000 additional income tax assessment (on prior year's income).
6. __D__ Earthquake damages.
7. __B__ Distribution expenses.
8. __A__ Total amount of cash and credit sales for the period.
9. __C__ Gain on disposal of long-term investments in stocks.
10. __E__ Net income for the period.
11. __C__ Insurance gain on casualty (fire)—insurance proceeds exceeded the book value of the assets destroyed.
12. __G__ Cash dividends declared and paid.
13. __A__ Rent collected on office space temporarily leased.
14. __B__ Interest expense of the year paid plus interest accrued on liabilities.
15. __A__ Dividends received on stocks held as an investment.

16. __C__ Damages paid as a result of a lawsuit by an individual injured while shopping in the store; the litigation covered three years.
17. __D__ Loss due to expropriation of a plant in a foreign country.
18. __I__ A $10,000 bad debt is to be written off—the receivable had been outstanding for five years. Use the allowance method.
19. __E__ Adjustment due to correction during current year of an error; the error was made two years earlier (discussed in Part B of the chapter).
20. __B__ On December 31 of current year, paid rent expense in advance for the next year.
21. __B__ Cost of goods sold.
22. __A__ Interest collected on November 30 of the current year from a customer on a 90-day note receivable, dated September 1 of the current year.
23. __B__ Year-end bonus of $50,000 paid to employees for performance during the year.
24. __I__ Depreciation on a machine used in operations.
25. __D__ A meteor smashes the plant to smithereens ($5 million book value, no insurance).

Problem 3–4

Buffer Company prepared the following income statement at the end of its annual accounting period, December 31, 19C:

Profit and Loss Report
BUFFER COMPANY
December 31, 19C

Sales income		$ 98,000
Inventory	$ 12,000	
Merchandise	34,000	
Freight	1,000	
Inventory	(15,000)	
Cost of sales		32,000
Gross profit		66,000
Costs:		
Labor	15,000	
Depreciation	6,000	
Sales	21,000	
Overhead	8,000	
Interest	3,000	
Extraordinary	5,000	
Sale of used equipment	4,300	(61,400)
Other incomes:		
Service	3,600	
Interest	1,400	5,000
Taxable profit		9,600
Tax (25%)		2,400
Net profit		$ 7,200

EPS—$7,200 ÷ 5,000 shares = $1.40.

Required:
1. List all of the defects that you can identify on the above statement.
2. Recast the above statement in good format and terminology. Use the multiple-step format.

Problem 3–5

During the current year, 19X, Bishop Company completed the selected transactions given below that posed questions as to when revenue and/or expense should be recognized. The annual accounting period ends December 31.

a. Merchandise (TV sets) was sold on credit during 19X for $200,000. The terms were 25% down payment plus six monthly payments. The collection experience on such sales, although not as good as on regular credit sales (due at end of month of sale), has been consistently satisfactory.

b. On December 24, 19X, the company sold a used TV set for $110, which had been repossessed and was set up in used goods inventory at $60. At the date of sale, $70 cash was collected with the balance due in six months. There is a high probability that collection will not be made, and the TV set probably will not be worth repossessing again.

c. During 19X, the company sold 30 TV sets for a total of $12,000 and collected cash in full. The sets were guaranteed for 12 months from date of sale. It was estimated that the guarantee will cost the company, on the average, $15 per set. At year-end, it was estimated that half of the guarantees were still outstanding.

d. On December 14, 19X, received a $20,000 income tax refund from prior years. The negotiations extended over a three-year period.

e. Services were rendered to a customer starting on December 28, 19X, and will be completed January 15, 19Y. Cash in full ($6,000) will be collected at date of completion of the services. Assume 12 working days, of which 4 were in 19X.

f. On July 1, 19X, paid a two-year insurance premium in advance, $600.

g. On December 30, 19X, sold merchandise for $5,000; terms 2/10, n/30 (i.e., 2% discount if paid within 10 days).

h. On December 1, 19X, sold a customer merchandise for $1,000. Collected $600 cash and received a $400, 18% note for the remainder, principal plus interest due in three months.

i. On November 15, 19X, the court assessed damages against the company amounting to $25,000 cash. The suit was filed in 19W, as a result of an accident in the company store. Payment in full will be made on January 10, 19Y.

j. On December 23, 19X, purchased merchandise for resale that cost $18,000; terms, 2/10, n/30.

Hint: Restudy the revenue, cost, and matching principles in Chapter 1.

Required:
For each transaction, give the year in which revenue and/or expense should be recognized. Give the basis for your decision. Based on your analysis, also give the appropriate entry, if any, in 19X for each transaction.

Problem 3–6

Analyze the relationships and amounts for each case and complete the following schedule by entering the appropriate amount in each blank space:

1.

Case	Owners' equity at start of period	Additional investment by owners	Withdrawals by owners	Owners' equity at end of period	Net income (loss)
A	$10,000	$2,000	$1,000	$17,400	$_____
B	28,000	3,000	_____	22,000	4,700
C	_____	1,200	800	30,000	(2,200)
D	15,500	600	_____	12,950	(2,000)
E	18,000	_____	2,700	22,000	4,700

2.

Case	Sales revenue	Beginning inventory	Purchases	Ending inventory	Cost of goods sold	Gross margin	Total expenses	Net income
F	$_____	$25,000	$60,000	$_____	$67,000	$23,000	$_____	$1,000
G	80,000	_____	48,000	2,000	_____	23,000	18,000	_____
H	_____	20,000	_____	36,000	59,000	18,000	_____	8,000

PART B: PROBLEMS 3–7 TO 3–12

Problem 3–7

The following amounts were taken from the accounting records of Walker Corporation at December 31, 19B, end of the annual accounting period:

Sales revenue	$340,000
Service revenue	64,000
Cost of goods sold (perpetual inventory system)	170,000
Distribution and administrative expenses	86,000
Investment revenue	6,000
Interest expense	4,000
Infrequent item: Loss on sale of long-term investment (pretax)	10,000
Extraordinary item: Earthquake loss (pretax)	14,000
Cash dividends declared and paid	8,000
Prior period adjustment, correction of error from prior period, pretax (a debit)	12,000
Balance, retained earnings, 1/1/19B	80,300

Common stock (par $5), 30,000 shares outstanding.
Restriction on retained earnings, $50,000 per bond payable indenture.

Assume an average 45% income tax rate on all items.

Required:
Prepare a combined single-step income statement and statement of retained earnings, including tax allocation and EPS. Show computations.

Problem 3–8

Unitas Corporation is undergoing its annual audit by the independent CPA at December 31, 1986 (end of the annual accounting period). During the audit, the following situations were found that needed attention:

a. On December 29, 1984, an asset that cost $12,000 was debited in full to 1984 Operating Expenses. The asset has a six-year estimated life and no residual value. The company uses straight-line depreciation.

b. Late in 1986, the company constructed a small warehouse using their own employees at a total cost of $90,000. However, before the decision was made to self-construct it, Unitas obtained a $100,000 bid from a contractor. Upon completion of the warehouse, Unitas made the following entry in the accounts:

Cost

Warehouse (an operational asset)	100,000	
Cash		90,000
Other income (nonoperating)		10,000

c. Prior to recording 1986 depreciation expense, the management decided that a large machine that originally cost $128,000 should have been depreciated over a useful life of 14 years instead of 20 years. The machine was acquired January 2, 1981. Assume the residual value of $8,000 was not changed. Give the 1986 adjusting entry and any other entries incident to the change in useful life.

d. During December 1986, the company disposed of an old machine for $6,000 cash. Annual depreciation was $2,000. At the beginning of 1986, the accounts reflected the following:

Machine (cost)	$18,000
Accumulated depreciation	13,000

At date of disposal, the following entry was made:

Cash	6,000	
Machine		6,000

No depreciation has been recorded for 1986.

e. A patent that originally cost $3,400 is being amortized over its legal life of 17 years at $200 per year. After the 1985 adjusting entry, it had been amortized down to a book value of $800. At the end of 1986, it was determined in view of a competitor's patent, that the patent will have no economic value to the company by the end of 1987. Straight-line amortization is used.

Required:
For each of the above situations, briefly explain the type of accounting for each item and what should have been recorded in the accounts. If a journal entry is needed to correct the accounts in conformity with your decision in each case, provide it along with supporting computations. Ignore income tax considerations.

Problem 3–9

The following pretax amounts were taken from the adjusted trial balances of AAA Corporation at December 31, 19B, and 19C, end of the annual accounting periods:

	19C	19B
Sales and service revenues	$200,000	$170,000
Cost of goods sold (perpetual inventory system)	80,000	70,000
Operating expenses	67,000	58,000
Extraordinary item: Casualty loss (pretax)	37,500	–0–
Prior period adjustment, correction of error from prior period, pretax (a credit)		10,000
Cash dividends declared	36,000	4,000
Stock dividend (7/1/19B, see below; no income tax effect)		120,000*
Balance, retained earnings 1/1/19B		159,800

	Shares
Common stock (par $10); shares outstanding:	
1/1/19B	15,000
Stock dividend, 7/1/19B	5,000
12/31/19B, total	20,000
10/1/19C, sold and issued	10,000
12/31/19C, balance	30,000

    * Amount debited to Retained Earnings.

Assume an average 40% income tax rate on all items, including the casualty and prior period adjustment.

Required:
1. Prepare a comparative income statement, using the single-step format, with columns for 19C and 19B. Include EPS and intraperiod tax allocation.
2. Prepare a comparative statement of retained earnings with columns for 19C and 19B.
3. Give the entry to record income taxes at the end of 19B.

Problem 3–10

The following pretax amounts were taken from the accounts of Jarvis Corporation at December 31, 19C, end of the annual accounting period:

Sales revenue	$550,000
Cost of goods sold (perpetual inventory system)	280,000
Distribution expenses	100,000
Administrative expenses	70,000
Interest revenue	1,000
Interest expense	3,000
Unusual item: Gain from sale of noncurrent asset (pretax; an ordinary gain)	20,000
Extraordinary item: Casualty (pretax loss)	40,000
Balance, retained earnings, 1/1/19C	95,000
Cash dividends declared and paid	15,000
Prior period adjustment, correction of error from prior period, pretax (a debit)	8,000

Common stock (par $1), 40,000 shares outstanding.

Restriction on retained earnings amounting to $25,000 as required by the indenture agreement on bonds payable.

Assume an average 35% income tax rate on all items.

Required:

Prepare a combined multiple-step income statement and statement of retained earnings including intraperiod income tax allocation and EPS. Show computations.

Problem 3–11

The following financial statements have come to you for review:

FAST PRODUCTION COMPANY
Profit and Loss Statement
December 31, 19K

Incomes:			
Gross sales		$256,800	
Less: Sales returns		5,120	
Net sales			$251,680
Costs and expenses:			
Cost of goods sold:			
Inventory, Jan. 1		98,500	
Purchases	$132,600		
Less: Purchase returns	2,780	129,820	
		228,320	
Inventory, Dec. 31		102,300	
Cost of goods sold			126,020
Gross profit			125,660
Operating costs:			
Selling		38,000	
General and administrative:			
General	20,000		
Depreciation	8,800		
Bad debts	1,080	29,880	
Total operating costs			67,880
Profit from operations			57,780
Other income:			
Interest income			970
Profit			58,750
Less taxes			28,720
Net			$ 30,030

FAST PRODUCTION COMPANY
Earned Surplus Statement
At December 31, 19K

Balance from last year		$267,600
Corrections:		
Additions:		
Depreciation overstated		3,400
Adjusted		271,000
Additions:		
Profit	$30,030	
Profit on sale of land	8,200	38,230
		309,230
Deductions:		
Dividends	30,000	
Loss on sale of machinery	9,650	39,650
Earned surplus (to balance sheet)		$269,580

Required:

Critically evaluate the above financial statements. Cite items to support your response. List and explain all of the aspects of the above statements that you would change in order to conform to appropriate reporting, terminology, and format.

Problem 3–12

The following income statement and statement of retained earnings were prepared by the bookkeeper for Lax Corporation:

LAX CORPORATION
Statement of Profit
December 31, 19W

Sales income		$123,000
Service income		20,000
Total		143,000
Cost of sales (periodic inventory system):		
Inventory	$ 34,000	
Purchases (net)	71,000	
Inventory	(40,000)	65,000
Gross profit		78,000
Costs:		
Salaries, wages, etc.	35,000	
Depreciation and write-offs	7,000	
Rent	3,000	
Taxes, property	500	
Utilities	2,100	
Promotion	900	
Sales returns	2,000	
Sundry..................................	6,700	(57,200)
Special items:		
Profit on asset sold		6,000
Inventory shortage		(2,800)
Pretax profit		24,000
Income tax		3,200
Net profit		$ 20,800

LAX CORPORATION
Earned Surplus
December 31, 19W

Balance, earned surplus		$27,000
Add:		
Profit		20,800
Correction of inventory error of 19V (pretax)		5,000
Total		52,800
Deduct:		
Earthquake loss (pretax)	$13,000	
Dividends	10,000	
Earned surplus to capital	5,000	27,000
Balance		$25,800

Required:

1. List each item on the above statements that you believe should be changed and give your recommendations on each with respect to appropriate reporting, terminology, and format. The average income tax rate is 20%, and 10,000 shares of common stock are outstanding. For problem purposes assume the earthquake loss is extraordinary.
2. Prepare a complete multiple-step income statement and a complete statement of retained earnings.

CASES

Case 3–1

The conceptual model (or equation) that underlies the income statement can be expressed as follows:

$$(\text{Revenues} - \text{Expenses}) + (\text{Gains} - \text{Losses}) = \text{Income}$$

This expression requires that each of the four components be carefully defined in order that the measurement of each accounting element can be reliable and relevant. This case examines each of the four components in conceptual terms with special emphasis on measuring an entity's periodic income.

Required:
1. What principle, or principles, primarily govern identification and measurement of revenues? Briefly explain each principle.
2. What principle, or principles, primarily govern identification and measurement of expenses? Briefly explain each principle.
3. Identify and explain some of the more troublesome problems encountered in applying the principles identified in 1 and 2 above.
4. What guidelines govern identification of extraordinary items? What is the primary problem in applying these guidelines?
5. What guidelines govern identification of prior period adjustments?
6. What guidelines primarily govern reporting of items that are either unusual or infrequent, but not both? What is the primary problem in applying these guidelines?

Case 3–2

During the 19D audit, the independent CPA encountered the following situations that caused serious concern as to proper classifications on the financial statements of selected clients. Assume all amounts are material.

a. A client was assessed additional income taxes of $100,000 plus $36,000 interest related to the past three years.
b. A client suffered a casualty loss (a fire) amounting to $500,000. The client occasionally experiences a fire, but this was significantly more than any such loss ever experienced by the client company.
c. A client company paid $175,000 damages assessed by the courts as a result of an injury to a customer on the company premises three years earlier.
d. A client sold a large operational asset and reported a gain of $70,000.
e. The major supplier of raw materials to a client company experienced a prolonged strike. As a result, the client company reported a loss of $150,000. This is the first such loss; however, the client has three major suppliers and strikes are not unusual in those industries.
f. A client owns several large blocks of common stock of other corporations. The shares have been held for a number of years and are viewed as a long-term investment. During the past year, 20% of the stock was sold to meet an unusual cash demand. Additional sales of the stock are not anticipated.

Required:

1. Briefly define *(a)* ordinary business operations, *(b)* unusual or infrequent gains and losses, *(c)* extraordinary gains and losses, and *(d)* prior period adjustments. Explain how the effects of each should be reported.
2. For each transaction, indicate how the financial effects should be classified; that is, classify as *(a)* ordinary business operations; *(b)* unusual or infrequent (but not both) gains and losses; *(c)* extraordinary; or *(d)* prior period adjustments. Explain the basis for your decision for each situation.

Case 3–3

J. B. Jacobsen started the JBJ Grocery as a sole proprietorship on January 1, 19A. He invested $25,000 cash and rented suitable space for $2,400 per month. Jacobsen spent $15,000 cash for fixtures and an additional $4,000 to paint and renovate the interior. He borrowed $180,000 cash from City Bank and signed a 10-year, 15%, mortgage note with his debt-free residence as security. The monthly loan payments (for interest and principal combined) are $2,904. Jacobsen spent $160,000 of the loan proceeds for inventory and the remaining $20,000 was "for working capital as needed." He uses the periodic inventory system.

It is December 31, 19A, and one full year of merchandising groceries has ended. The bank loan officer requested that Jacobsen come in for a discussion of JBJ's financial situation. When asked by the bank loan officer about his profits for the year, Jacobsen replied that he started with zero cash and ended with $26,000 cash, which was the best way to measure real profit. In response to another question, Jacobsen said, "Yes, I have a bookkeeping system in my files composed of the bank statements, purchase invoices, unpaid bills, payroll records (three employees), and other business documents."

Because the monthly loan payments for November and December were paid about two weeks late, the bank loan officer was somewhat concerned. The loan amortization schedule indicated that the 12 monthly payments had reduced the loan principal by $8,413. Because of his concern, the loan officer asked Jacobsen to provide a list of assets and liabilities as of December 31 and an income statement for 19A that relates only to the JBJ Grocery. Approximately 10 days later the bank loan officer received (by mail) the following data:

JBJ Grocery—19A

Assets:

Cash	$ 26,000
Due from special customers	6,000
Inventory (quantities on shelves held constant by regular replacement as sold)	160,000
Store fixtures	15,000
Renovation costs	4,000
Personal residence (pledged)	250,000
Miscellaneous assets	3,000
Total	$464,000

Liabilities:

Grocery wholesalers	$ 42,000
Personal loan by owner ($25,000 − $24,000 salary)	1,000
Mortgage note [$180,000 − ($2,904 × 12 mos.)]	145,152
Miscellaneous debts (taxes, etc)	5,000
Total	$193,152

Profit and Loss Statement

Income from sales		$184,000
Grocery purchases	$90,000	
Labor costs	30,000	
Utilities	7,800	
Rent ($2,400 per month)	28,800	
Miscellaneous (property taxes, insurance, etc.)	1,400	158,000
Profit		$ 26,000

Required:

1. The loan officer has some doubts about the above data and has asked you to prepare "an unaudited balance sheet and income statement, and to use your own judgment on questionable items." Provide explanations when needed.
2. The loan officer also asked you to provide relevant comments and recommendations. The stipend is quite adequate so you agreed to do the job immediately. You are not to contact Jacobsen.

Case 3–4

The Appendix following Chapter 24 gives an actual set of financial statements. Examine them carefully and respond to the following questions (for 1984 only, unless otherwise specified):

a. Are the statements comparative? Why are comparative statements usually presented?
b. Are the statements consolidated? What do you understand this to mean?
c. Is this a retail, financial, or a manufacturing company? Explain.
d. How many different kinds of revenue were reported? How many different kinds of expenses were reported?
e. How were interest expense and interest revenue reported on the income statement?
f. Was the total amount of depreciation expense separately reported on the income statement? If not, where was it presented?
g. Were any unusual or infrequently occurring (but not both) items reported on the income statement in 1983 or 1984?
h. Were any extraordinary items reported on the 1983 or 1984 income statement? What were they? Were they net of tax?
i. Was there any indication of an accounting change? If so, explain how it was reported and what type of change it was.
j. How many EPS amounts were reported?
k. What "differences" were reported on the income statement? Gross margin? Income from continuing operations? Income before extraordinary items? Net income? Others (list)?
l. What were the profit margins (net income divided by revenue) for 1983 and 1984?
m. What basis was used for valuing inventories?
n. List all unusual features of the income statement. What aspects of it would you criticize? Explain.
o. How does this company define "funds" in the SCFP? What amount of "funds" was provided from operations in 1984?
p. What was the primary depreciation method used?
q. What was the amount of income tax expense for 1984?
r. In 1984, what was the total amount of cash dividends declared on (a) common stock and (b) preferred stock?

s. In 1984, what was the amount of income from foreign activities?

t. What were the total amounts of net sales and net income reported for the first quarter of 1984?

u. Did the auditor's report express any reservations about the financial statements? Explain.

v. Overall, do you believe the balance sheet and the income statement could be improved with respect to format and terminology? Explain each change that you would suggest for consideration.

w. What has been the long-term trend of net income?

Case 3–5: A special continuing case from Chapter 2 (Case 2–4) and continuing through Chapter 4 (Case 4–8)

This case is a mini-practice set. The basic situation and the 10 requirements given in Chapter 2 (Case 2–4) start with the journal entries and T-accounts and continue through the accounting information processing cycle. A viable use of this case involves starting it in Chapter 2 and completing it by the end of Chapter 4. Students should attain the following schedule:

Requirements completed	Chapter	Key figures
Requirements 1–3, through the unadjusted trial balance on the worksheet.	2 (Case 2–4)	Unadjusted trial balance total, $1,174,970
Requirements 4–5, through the income statement	3 (Case 3–5)	EPS, net income, $1.14
Requirements 6–10	4 (Case 4–8)	Balance sheet total, $428,683

Case 3–6

The following information was taken from an article in the *Journal of Accountancy:* *

Case A:

"XYZ Company's fruit crop was destroyed by a severe freeze. The loss was $40,000. A freeze in XYZ's location is very rare. . . . ABC Company's fruit crop was also destroyed by a severe freeze. The loss was $40,000. A severe freeze in ABC's locale occurs about every two years."

Case B:

"Company A sold 100 shares of XYZ Company common stock for a gain of $5,000. This is the only stock that Company A owned or will ever own. . . . Company B also sold 100 shares of XYZ Company common stock for a gain of $5,000. Company B has several other investments in its common stock portfolio and is frequently involved in stock transactions."

Required:

1. Give the definition of an extraordinary item.

2. For Case A, explain how, and why, XYZ Company and ABC Company should report the $40,000 loss.

3. For Case B, explain how, and why, Company A and Company B should report the $5,000 gain.

---

* Bill D. Jarnigan, "Extraordinary Items: An Update," *Journal of Accountancy*, April 1984, pp. 42–44.

Chapter 4

Review—The Balance Sheet and Statement of Changes in Financial Position

OVERVIEW AND PURPOSE

Chapter 3 reviewed the income statement and statement of retained earnings. This chapter reviews the two remaining required financial statements—the balance sheet and the statement of changes in financial position (SCFP). The balance sheet is a statement of financial position at a specific date. The income statement and the SCFP are **change statements** (i.e., connecting links) between two successive balance sheets. That is, as change statements, the income statement and the SCFP present the **reasons why** the financial position of an enterprise changed during the current accounting period.

The purpose of this chapter is to discuss the concepts, characteristics, and formats (i.e., display) of the balance sheet and the statement of changes in financial position. To accomplish this purpose, this chapter is organized as follows:

Balance Sheet: — *Statement of financial position*
1. Concepts that underlie the balance sheet.
2. Characteristics of the balance sheet.
3. Review of the balance sheet classifications.

Statement of Changes in Financial Position:
1. Concepts that underlie the statement of changes in financial position (SCFP).
2. Interpreting the SCFP.

Additional Reporting Issues

BALANCE SHEET

Concepts that Underlie the Balance Sheet

Financial statements provide information about an entity's economic resources, claims against those resources, and the interests of the owners at specific dates. This information allows investors, creditors, and other interested parties to assess the **financial strength, flexibility, and liquidity** of the enterprise. This assessment is useful to decision makers for projecting the **future cash flows** of the entity.

The balance sheet is designed to provide this information by reporting the assets, liabilities, and owners' equity of the entity at the end of each reporting (i.e., accounting) period. Because it presents the current **financial position** of an entity, it also is referred to as the **statement of financial position.** The designation **balance sheet** refers to the fact that the statement "balances" according to the fundamental accounting model: Assets = Liabilities + Owners' equity. The designation "balance sheet" is not descriptive; therefore, progressive accountants increasingly are using the descriptive title, statement of financial position.[1]

The **financial strength** of a company is reflected primarily by *(a)* the relationship between its assets and liabilities, and *(b)* its credit standing with financial institutions and other lenders. **Financial flexibility** refers to the ability of a company to effectively respond to unexpected cash demands and new opportunities to enhance its earnings and assets. **Financial liquidity** refers to the time required by the entity to *(a)* convert noncash assets to cash and *(b)* pay maturing liabilities. As a position statement, the balance sheet must be dated at a specific date, such as "At December 31, 19xx." In contrast, the income statement and the SCFP are dated to cover a specific period of time, such as "For the Year Ended December 31, 19xx." This date identifies the end of the **reporting period.**

Fundamentally, a balance sheet *(a)* **lists** the assets, liabilities, and components of owners' equity, and *(b)* **reports** a specific dollar amount (i.e., valuation) for each item listed. Assigning a valuation to each item poses a basic conceptual issue. The issue is: Should those valuations at each balance sheet date represent *(a)* **current market** values or *(b)* **historical cost** values determined at transaction dates? Some accountants and financial analysts argue that market values are more **relevant** to decision makers—investors, creditors, and other interested parties— because current values are more useful than historical cost values in assessing financial strength and in projecting future cash flows of the entity.

Despite the relevance of market values, balance sheets primarily report **historical cost** values to satisfy the qualitative characteristic of **reliability** (see Chapter 1, Part B, including Exhibit 1–3). The market value of an asset often can be known reliably only when the asset is bought or sold in a completed transaction. This transaction involves parties that have **different economic interests** (i.e., an arm's-length transaction where the seller wants a high price and the purchaser wants a low price). At balance sheet date, this situation does not exist; therefore, determination of market values generally is viewed as subjective and susceptible to manipulation, bias, and misrepresentation. Thus, **reliability is the basis for the use of historical cost values in accounting.** Such values are objective, measurable, and verifiable. It is important that decision makers, and you as a student of accounting, clearly understand what balance sheet valuations mean, and equally important, what they do not mean.

In reference to the conceptual foundation presented in Chapter 1, Part B, the primary concepts and principles that apply to the balance sheet are: (1) reliability, (2) comparability, (3) the cost principle, and (4) the full-disclosure principle.

FASB Concepts Statement 3 defines the three major **elements** reported on a balance sheet as shown in **Exhibit 4–1.**

---

[1] The 1984 edition of *Accounting Trends & Techniques,* AICPA, reported that 91% of the 600 companies used the title "balance sheet," and the remainder used more descriptive titles.

EXHIBIT 4–1

Balance Sheet
Elements

Definition of element
Assets are probable future economic benefits obtained or controlled by a particular entity as a result of past transactions or events.
Liabilities are probable future sacrifices of economic benefits arising from present obligations of a particular entity to transfer assets or provide services to other entities in the future as a result of past transactions or events.
Equity [i.e., owners' equity] is the residual interest in the assets of an entity that remains after deducting its liabilities. In a business enterprise, the equity is the ownership interest.

Source: FASB, *Statement of Financial Accounting Concepts No. 3,* "Elements of Financial Statements of Business Enterprises" (Stamford, Conn., December 1980), pars. 19–55.

Characteristics of the Balance Sheet

Valuations Reported on the Balance Sheet. The discussion above indicated that historical cost values are reported on the balance sheet. That statement requires elaboration. Assets are reported at their **book or carrying value,** which may be *(a)* their cost determined in the originating transaction in conformity with the **cost principle,** or *(b)* an amount less than cost due to market value impairment, depreciation, depletion, and amortization of the original cost caused by use, exploitation, or expiration. In general, cash is reported at its current value, and accounts receivable at expected **net realizable value** (amount of the receivables less the allowance for doubtful accounts). Inventories and marketable equity securities usually are reported at cost (lower of cost or market is discussed later), and plant and equipment are reported at cost less accumulated depreciation.

Liabilities are reported on the balance sheet at their carrying, or book, value which is their maturity value or discounted present value.

Owners' equity is a residual amount. It does not report the current market value of the business; rather, it is a measurement of the owners' interests that follows directly from the measurements used for the assets and liabilities in conformity with GAAP.

Format and Classifications in the Balance Sheet. The full-disclosure principle (see Chapter 1, Part B) requires a complete balance sheet with relevant subclassifications of assets, liabilities, and owners' equity. However, detailed specification of the format of the balance sheet is not prescribed by GAAP. Current practice reflects two overall formats: *(a)* the account, or horizontal, format that lists the assets on the left and the liabilities plus owners' equity on the right, and *(b)* the report, or vertical, format. The report form dominates in current practice. Several variations are: Assets = Liabilities + Owners' equity; Assets − Liabilities = Owners' equity; and Working capital + Noncurrent assets − Noncurrent liabilities = Owners' equity.

To aid decision makers, balance sheet items usually are grouped according to common characteristics. **Assets usually are grouped in decreasing order of liquidity (i.e., nearness to cash), liabilities by time to maturity, and owners' equity in decreasing order of permanence.** Classifications of information used in a balance sheet, and the array of items under each classification, are determined by GAAP. However, they are strongly influenced by the characteristics of each industry and of the enterprise. For example, the balance sheet of a financial institution, such as a bank, will reflect classifications different from those of a manufacturing company. Format and classifications should be designed for a particular enterprise and comply with the full-disclosure principle, which specifies that reporting be informative and not misleading. Therefore, flexibility in format and classifications is desirable. Nevertheless, there is a reasonable degree of uniformity. The following classifications represent current reporting practices and terminology:

Assets:
  1. Current assets.
  2. Investments and funds.
  3. Operational (or fixed) assets—tangible (often called property, plant and equipment).
  4. Operational assets—intangible.
  5. Other assets.
  6. Deferred charges.

Liabilities:
  1. Current liabilities (including short-term deferred credits).
  2. Long-term, or noncurrent, liabilities (including long-term deferred credits).

Owners' equity:
  1. Contributed capital (or paid-in capital):
     a. Capital stock.
     b. Contributed (or paid in) capital in excess of the par or stated value of capital stock (or premium on capital stock).
     c. Other contributed capital.
  2. Retained earnings.
  3. Unrealized losses and gains.

The above classification scheme provides a major caption for each balance sheet element—assets, liabilities, and owners' equity. Under each element caption, several subclassifications commonly are used. **Exhibit 4–2** illustrates a typical balance sheet.

EXHIBIT 4–2:   Statement of Financial Position (Balance Sheet)

JOY CORPORATION
Statement of Financial Position (Balance Sheet)
At December 31, 19X

Assets

Current assets:

Cash		$ 35,200
Short-term investments (current market value, $35,000)		20,000
Accounts receivable (trade)	$ 43,100	
Less: Allowance for doubtful accounts	1,300	41,800
Merchandise inventory (FIFO, LCM)		120,000
Prepaid expenses:		
Prepaid insurance		3,000
Total current assets		220,000

Investments and funds:

Investment in stock of Y Corporation (at cost)	$ 77,000	
Less: Allowance to reduce to market value	7,000	70,000
Plant expansion fund	80,000	150,000

Land, building, and equipment:

Land		24,000	
Building	200,000		
Less: Accumulated depreciation	80,000	120,000	
Equipment and fixtures	140,000		
Less: Accumulated depreciation	56,000	84,000	228,000

Intangible assets:

Patent (cost, $42,500, less accumulated amortization, $17,500)		25,000

Other assets:

Land held for future building site		37,000

Deferred charges:

Rearrangement costs		8,000
Total assets		$668,000

Liabilities

Current liabilities:

Accounts payable (trade)		$ 48,700
Notes payable		30,000
Rent revenue collected in advance		1,800
Wages payable		2,000
Income taxes payable		12,500
Total current liabilities		95,000

Long-term liabilities:

Bonds payable, 6%, due 19Z	175,000	
Less: Unamortized discount	4,000	171,000
Total liabilities		266,000

(continued on next page)

EXHIBIT 4–2 *(concluded)*

Stockholders' Equity

Contributed capital:

Preferred stock, par $10, 9% cumulative, nonparticipating, authorized
    20,000 shares, issued and outstanding 5,000 shares   50,000

Common stock, nopar, authorized 100,000 shares, issued and outstanding
    75,000 shares   150,000

Additional contributed capital:

  In excess of par value of preferred stock   40,000

      Total contributed capital   240,000

Retained earnings (Note A)   169,000

      Total contributed capital and retained earnings   409,000

Less: Unrealized loss on long-term investment   7,000

      Total stockholders' equity   402,000

Total liabilities and stockholders' equity $668,000

Notes to financial statements:

Note A. Under the terms of the bond indenture (i.e., agreement), a part of retained earnings, determined by a formula, is restricted from dividend availability. The formula, computed for 19X, restricts retained earnings in the amount of $61,000. This amount will be increased each year as provided by the bond indenture formula. When the bonds are retired, the restriction will be automatically removed.

REVIEW OF BALANCE SHEET CLASSIFICATIONS

Current Assets

Current assets are composed of (1) cash and (2) other assets that are **reasonably expected** to be realized in cash, or to be sold or consumed during the normal operating cycle of the business or within one year from the balance sheet date, whichever is longer.

The **normal operating cycle** of a business is the average period of time between the expenditure of cash for goods and services and the date those goods and services are converted into cash. Thus, it is the average length of time from cash expenditure, to inventory, to sale, to accounts receivable, and back to cash.

Most companies use one year as the time period for classifying items as current or long-term because *(a)* the operating cycle usually is less than one year, or *(b)* the length of the operating cycle may be difficult to measure reliably.

Current assets usually are presented on the balance sheet in order of **decreasing liquidity** (i.e., nearness to cash conversion). The major items comprising current assets, in order of liquidity are cash, short-term investments, receivables, inventories, and prepaid expenses.

Assets that are similar to but **not** classified as current assets are: (1) cash and claims to cash that are **restricted for uses other than current operations,** (2) receivables with an **extended** maturity date, and (3) **long-term** prepayments of expenses.

The definition of current assets is clear-cut. However, problems are encountered in implementation. The phrases "normal operating cycle" and "reasonably expected to be realized in cash" involve judgments. Companies can "use" this judgment to incorrectly classify certain items as current assets to produce a desired effect on working capital (i.e., the difference between current assets and current liabilities). For example, a stock investment may be classified as a current or noncurrent asset, depending upon the **stated intention** of management as to the planned holding period. An intention to hold the investment beyond the period specified for current assets would require its classification as a noncurrent asset. Thus, a simple change in **intention** of management may be used to justify an arbitrary change in the classification of the investment.

Prepaid expenses is another area with variation in classification. A short-term prepayment should be classified as a current asset (i.e., a prepaid expense), whereas a long-term prepayment should be classified as noncurrent (i.e., a deferred charge). Prepaid expenses are current assets because, having "invested" by paying expenses in advance, cash outlays for the next reporting period are reduced.

Some companies and industries do not use a current asset category. For example, financial institutions, such as banks and mutual funds, have no current asset caption because it would be pointless due to the nature of their asset structures.

Cash set aside in savings accounts or other investments should be reported as short-term or long-term investments (discussed later in this chapter). Restrictions that require minimum cash balances in checking accounts must be disclosed.

Short-term investments must be valued on a lower-of-cost-or-market (LCM) basis (discussed in Chapter 6).

Merchandise inventories usually must be reported at LCM (discussed in Chapter 7).

Current Liabilities

The definition of current liabilities parallels the definition of current assets. **Current liabilities are short-term liabilities "whose liquidation is reasonably expected to require the use of existing resources properly classified as current assets, or the creation of other current liabilities."**[2] This definition relates to current assets as a total rather than to specific current assets (e.g., a specific customer's account receivable).

Current liabilities include the following items:

1. Accounts payable (trade) for goods and services that enter into the operating cycle of the business.
2. Special short-term payables for nonoperating items and services.
3. Short-term notes payable.

---

[2] AICPA, *Accounting Research and Terminology Bulletins, Final Edition* (New York, 1961), p. 21.

4. Current maturities of long-term liabilities.
5. Collections in advance for unearned revenue (such as rent revenue collected in advance).
6. Accrued expenses for payrolls, interest, and taxes (e.g., income taxes and property taxes).

Liabilities that are similar to but are not classified as current liabilities include long-term notes, bonds, and obligations that will not be paid out of current assets. For example a bond issue payable during the next reporting period would not be classified as a current liability if it is paid out of a special noncurrent cash fund. Similarly, currently maturing bonds payable that are to be refunded (i.e., paid off by issuing a new series of bonds) usually should not be classified as a current liability, as specified in *FASB Statement 6*.

Working Capital

Working capital, as a separate designation, occasionally is reported on the balance sheet. It is discussed here because **working capital is defined as current assets minus current liabilities.** The computation of working capital, and the working capital ratio, for Joy Corporation (Exhibit 4–2) would be as follows:

Current assets $220,000
Current liabilities 95,000
Difference—working capital $125,000

Working capital ratio: $220,000 ÷ $95,000 = 2.32

Notice that the definition of working capital only explains how it is computed. More explicitly, if the current assets were converted to cash at their **book value** and the current liabilities paid at their **book value,** working capital would be the amount of cash remaining.

Although the concept of working capital is widely used in the business community, no one ever receives or pays working capital. In fact, a company may report an excellent working capital position and at the same time have a serious cash deficiency. Therefore, many business persons believe that cash flow statements are more informative than working capital statements. Nevertheless, the amount of working capital and the working capital ratio are viewed as measures of liquidity, that is, the ability of the enterprise to meet its short-term obligations.[3] For example, the working capital **ratio** computed for Joy Corporation shows that at book value the current assets were 2.32 times the current liabilities, or that for each $1 of current liabilities, there was $2.32 in current assets. Because of the

---

[3] For a criticism of working capital as a measure of liquidity, see R. Greene, "Are More Chryslers in the Offing?" *Forbes,* February 2, 1981, pp. 69–73, esp. p. 72, "Cash Flow Made Easy."

use of working capital as an index of liquidity, the independent auditor sometimes encounters attempts to misclassify some noncurrent assets as current and some current liabilities as noncurrent. These manipulations would make it possible for the company to report a better working capital position than actually exists.

In financial reporting, offsetting of current assets and liabilities is improper. This practice avoids full disclosure and would permit a business to show a more favorable current ratio than actually exists. For example, if Joy Corporation were to offset a current liability of $45,000 against current assets, the current ratio would be computed as follows: ($220,000 − $45,000 = $175,000) ÷ ($95,000 − $45,000 = $50,000) = 3.5 instead of the correct ratio of 2.32.

Offsetting is permissible only when a legal right to offset exists. For instance, it would be permissable to offset a $5,000 overdraft in one bank account against another account reflecting $8,000 on deposit in **that same bank** because the bank can offset the two deposit accounts.

Investments and Funds

The investments and funds classification includes **noncurrent** investments and cash set aside in special-purpose funds for long-term use as needed. This classification usually is reported directly under current assets. The long-term assets reported under this caption are:

1. Long-term investments in the capital stock of another company.
2. Long-term investments in the bonds of another company; any unamortized premium is added to the investment, and any unamortized discount is subtracted (see Chapter 17).
3. Investments in subsidiaries, including long-term receivables from subsidiaries.
4. Funds set aside for long-term future use, such as bond sinking funds (to retire bonds payable), expansion funds, stock retirement funds, and long-term savings deposits.
5. Cash surrender value of life insurance policies carried by the company.
6. Long-term investments in tangible assets, such as land and buildings, which are not used in current operations (but not operational assets that are temporarily idle).

The important distinctions between current investments and funds and the above long-term assets are that (a) the long-term items are not used in the central ongoing and major operations of the entity, and (b) management plans to retain the long-term items beyond one year from the balance sheet date, or the operating cycle if it is longer.

Long-term investments reported under this caption usually are shown at their original cost. Funds included under this caption are shown at the accumulated amount in the fund. This valuation amount usually includes all contributions to the fund plus all interest accumulations added to the fund balance to date.

Operational Assets

Operational assets are long-term, noncurrent assets used in the continuing operations of the entity; they are not held for resale. Thus, operational assets are different from inventories (e.g., of raw materials, work in process, finished goods, and supplies). Historically, operational assets were labeled as **fixed assets** because of their relative permanence or long-term nature. Operational assets are subclassified as follows:

1. **Tangible**—Those assets with **physical substance,** such as land, buildings, machinery, equipment, furniture, fixtures, and natural resources.
2. **Intangible**—Those assets with no physical substance but which have value **because of the rights that their ownership confers.** Examples include patents, copyrights, trademarks, brand names, leaseholds, and goodwill.

Operational Assets—Tangible.   This group of operational assets is reported on the balance sheet under various captions depending upon the business. Manufacturing enterprises use a caption such as **Property, plant, and equipment.** Other companies use a caption such as **Property and equipment,** or simply **Property.**

Tangible operational assets include items that are *(a)* depreciable, such as buildings, machinery, and fixtures, and *(b)* not subject to depreciation, such as land. Therefore, land should be reported separately.

APB Opinion 12 requires that the balance sheet, or the related notes, report *(a)* balances of major classes of depreciable assets by nature or function; *(b)* accumulated depreciation, either by major classes of depreciable assets or in total; and *(c)* a description of the methods used in computing depreciation for the major classes of operational assets. The term **reserve for depreciation** should not be used to refer to accumulated depreciation because no "reserve" exists; instead, the appropriate term is "Accumulated depreciation." Exhibit 4–2 illustrates reporting tangible operational assets.

Tangible operational assets are shown on the balance sheet at original cost, in conformity with the **cost principle,** less any accumulated depreciation or depletion, determined in conformity with the **matching principle.**

Operational Assets—Intangible.   This classification is reported separately on the balance sheet under the title **Intangible assets.** Major items should be listed separately, and the accumulated amount of **amortization** also should be disclosed. By convention, the contra account, accumulated amortization, seldom is separately listed. This contrasts to the usual treatment given tangible operational assets (see Exhibit 4–2).

Intangible operational assets are reported on the balance sheet at original cost, in accordance with the **cost principle,** less accumulated amortization, determined in conformity with the **matching principle.**

Although deferred charges are intangible, they differ from "operational assets—intangible." The latter represent **exclusive rights,** whereas deferred charges are long-term prepaid expenses (see the deferred charge discussion later in this chapter).

Other Assets

The **other assets** classification is used for assets that cannot be included under alternative asset classifications. Examples include long-term receivables from employees and idle operational assets (such as an idle plant). An item should be analyzed carefully before it is classified as "other assets" because there is often a logical basis for classifying it elsewhere. If an asset has no future economic benefit, it should be written off and reported on the income statement as a loss in the period in which the write-off occurs.

Deferred Charges

Deferred charges are caused by the **prepayment** of long-term expenses. These expenses have reliably determinable future economic benefits useful in earning future revenues. Thus, long-term prepaid expenses are deferred in conformity with the matching principle. The **only** conceptual difference between a prepaid expense (classified as a current asset) and a deferred charge is the **length of time** over which the deferred amount will be amortized.

The following accounts typify the "Deferred charges" caption: Machinery Rearrangement Costs, Organization Costs, Pension Costs Paid in Advance, and Insurance Prepayments (long-term prepayments not properly classified as a current asset). Deferred charges sometimes are inappropriately reported as "Other assets."

Long-Term Liabilities

A long-term liability is an obligation that will not require the use of current assets for payment during the next operating cycle or during the next reporting year, whichever is longer. Long-term liabilities initially are recorded at their "cost" (i.e., the value received) in conformity with the cost principle. If such cost cannot be determined reliably, then the long-term liability is recorded at the discounted present value of all of its required future cash flows. The "cost" and maturity amount of a long-term liability may coincide (see discussion in Chapters 10 and 17). A liability issued at more than its maturity amount is issued at a premium; if issued for less than its maturity amount, it is issued at a discount. Any unamortized debt premium should be added to the debt. Any unamortized debt discount should be subtracted (see Chapter 17).

All liabilities not appropriately classified as current liabilities are reported under this caption. Typical long-term liabilities are bonds payable, long-term notes payable, and long-term lease obligations.

Deferred Credits

A company may include the caption "Deferred credits" between long-term liabilities and owners' equity. This caption is not an appropriate classification because the financial position equation (Assets = Liabilities + Owners' equity) does not include it. At best, "Deferred credits" is a catchall balance sheet classification of long-term credit balance accounts that are difficult to classify elsewhere. Typical deferred credits are long-term deferred income taxes, deferred revenues (i.e., revenues collected in advance), and deferred investment tax credits. Most of the items reported under this caption are long-term liabilities or proper components of owners' equity (deferred credits are discussed in detail in Chapter 10).

Owners' Equity

Owners' equity for a corporation is called stockholders' equity; for a partnership, partners' equity; and for a sole proprietorship, proprietor's equity. Owners' equity is the owners' residual interest in the entity; it is the difference between total assets and total liabilities. This classification is used to report the various kinds of capital of an entity, such as contributed capital and accumulated earnings.

Because of legal requirements, owners' equity is subclassified to reflect detailed **sources.** For a corporation, the following sources commonly are reported:

1. Contributed capital (or paid-in capital):
   a. Capital stock.
   b. Contributed (or paid in) capital in excess of the par or stated value of capital stock (or premium on capital stock).
   c. Other contributed capital.
2. Retained earnings.
3. Unrealized losses and gains.

Contributed Capital (or Paid-In Capital)

Capital stock.   This caption reports the **sources** of owners' equity that are represented by the stated or legal capital (i.e., usually the par value of the outstanding preferred and common stock) of the corporation. **Legal capital** is specified by state law and in the Articles of Incorporation (i.e., the Charter) of the corporation. Each class of stock, common and preferred, must be reported at its par or stated amount, or in the case of nopar stock, the total amount paid in (these specifications vary depending upon the law of the state of incorporation). Details of each class of capital stock should be reported separately. These details include number of shares authorized, issued, outstanding, and subscribed; conversion features; callability; preferences; and any other special features.

Contributed capital in excess of par or stated value.   This source sometimes is called **additional paid-in capital** or premium on stock. It reports the amounts received by the corporation in excess of the par or stated value of the capital stock outstanding. These amounts usually arise when the corporation sells its stock above its par or stated amount per share, or issues stock dividends (discussed in Chapters 14 and 15).

Other contributed capital.   This source of contributed capital arises from such transactions as assets donated to the company (i.e., donated capital), treasury stock, and retirements and conversion of stock (discussed in Chapter 15).

Retained Earnings.   Retained earnings is the corporation's accumulated earnings, less accumulated losses and dividends. It reports the amount of resources (from undistributed earnings) that the corporation has retained for use in the enterprise. In most corporations, retained earnings is the major **source** of owners' equity. In the long term, most corporations distribute dividends to the stockholders amounting to less than the corporation's earnings. This policy establishes a continuing source of internally generated funds. Indirectly, retained earnings represents additional investments by the stockholders because they have foregone dividends equal to the cumulative balance of retained earnings. A negative balance in retained earnings usually is called a **deficit.**

A portion of the total amount of retained earnings may be **restricted or appropriated.** This means that during the period of restriction or appropriation, the restricted or appropriated amount is not available for dividends. For example, Joy Corporation (Exhibit 4–2) had total retained earnings of $169,000. However, $61,000 of that amount was restricted for a specific period of time. After the restriction is removed, the $61,000 may be included in the amount available for dividends.

A restriction on retained earnings may be **contractual,** as in Exhibit 4–2, in which the bond indenture restricts the amount of retained earnings available for dividend declaration. Alternatively, a restriction may result from a **legal requirement,** such as a restriction by state law equal to the cost of any treasury stock held. The purpose of such laws is to protect the creditors of the corporation. Finally, the board of directors may exercise its **discretion** and **appropriate** a portion of retained earnings, as in the case of "retained earnings appropriated for future plant expansion."

Restrictions or appropriations of retained earnings may be reported in two ways. One way is to report restrictions or appropriations in notes, such as Note A in Exhibit 4–2. Another approach is to make an **entry** in the accounts to reflect the restriction or appropriation. For example, the $61,000 restriction on retained earnings reported by Joy Corporation (Exhibit 4–2) could be recorded and reported as follows:

Entry to **record** the appropriation in the accounts:

Retained earnings	61,000	
Retained earnings restricted by bond indenture		61,000

Reporting on the balance sheet then could be:

Retained earnings, unappropriated	$108,000
Retained earnings, restricted by bond indenture	61,000
Total retained earnings	$169,000

Each additional appropriation, or increase in a prior appropriation, reduces the unappropriated balance and increases the total appropriated by the same amount.

Unrealized Capital.   This component of owners' equity is used mainly for recording and reporting **unrealized** losses resulting from the application of the LCM rule to long-term equity investments in capital stock, under the requirements of *FASB Statement 12*. This *Statement* requires that the cumulative amount of unrealized loss be reported separately as an **unrealized element of owners' equity** (i.e., a reduction in owners' equity as shown in Exhibit 4–2). A **realized gain** or loss is recognized only when an actual transaction occurs. In contrast, an **unrealized gain** or loss is recognized in the absence of an actual transaction. Assume a company owns a tract of land that cost $50,000. If it sells the land for $80,000, a $30,000 **realized** gain is recognized. Assume instead that the land is not sold but is written up to its market value of $80,000. Then a $30,000 **unrealized** gain would be recognized. This discussion is not intended to imply that write-ups of assets to market value currently are in accordance with GAAP. However, there are a few exceptions as explained in Chapters 6, 11, 16, and 24.

STATEMENT OF CHANGES IN FINANCIAL POSITION

Concepts that Underlie the Statement of Changes in Financial Position

This review of the statement of changes in financial position (SCFP) will enhance your understanding of what and how information on the flow of funds is reported during each reporting period. At this time we will not consider the approaches used to develop the SCFP in complex situations (see Chapter 23). *APB Opinion 19* **requires** a SCFP, in addition to an income statement and a balance sheet.

The SCFP reports the **sources** (i.e., inflows) and the **uses** (i.e., outflows) of funds during the reporting period. Therefore, it is dated the same as the income statement (e.g., "For the Year Ended December 31, 19X"). The SCFP is a **change statement,** as diagrammed in Exhibit 3–1. It reports **changes** in the assets, liabilities, and owners' equity accounts that caused funds to flow into and out of the company during the reporting period.

On the SCFP, funds are measured as either cash (usually cash plus short-term investments) or working capital (current assets minus current liabilities).[4] This review of the SCFP will measure funds as cash, rather than working capital, for four fundamental reasons:

1. Cash as a measure of funds is easy to comprehend. This is not always true for working capital because there is no such common denomination.

---

[4] For SCFP purposes, short-term investments usually are considered to be cash because by definition they *(a)* have a ready market, *(b)* will be converted to cash during the next year, or operating cycle if longer, and *(c)* have the highest liquidity other than cash.

Working capital is an arithmetical difference that involves a number of different assets and liabilities.

2. The major objective of financial statements is to assist decision makers to predict future **cash** flows of the entity (not working capital flows).
3. Cash often is a critical asset in a company.
4. Recent actions by the FASB and the FEI (Financial Executives Institute) suggest that ultimately only the cash basis will be required.

The SCFP concept is indicated by the following format, or display, in this required statement:

Sources of cash:
From continuing operations   } (i.e., from the income
From extraordinary items   }   statement)
From other sources:
    Borrowing
    Sale of the company's capital stock
    Sale of noncash assets
Total cash inflow during the period

Uses of cash:
Payment of liabilities
Purchase of assets
Payment of cash dividends
Contributions to charitable causes
Total cash outflow during the period

Increase (decrease) in cash during the period

INTERPRETING THE SCFP

Exhibit 4–3 presents a typical statement of changes in financial position, **cash basis.** Notice the three major captions: (1) sources of cash, (2) uses of cash, and (3) net increase (decrease) in cash during the reporting period. The first two captions report the individual items that caused *(a)* cash inflows and *(b)* cash outflows. The net increase (decrease) in cash during the reporting period must agree with the change (increase or decrease) in the Cash account for that period. Now, examine the **sources of cash** in Exhibit 4–3.

Cash inflow from operations. The first, and primary, source of cash is from operations (i.e., $77,000). This is the amount of cash inflow from the operating activities as reflected on the income statement. This **source** begins with income (or loss) before extraordinary items. In accrual accounting, income from continuing operations usually includes items that did not use (or provide) cash, such as

EXHIBIT 4–3

Statement of
Changes in Finan-
cial Position, Cash
Basis

ALLSTAR CORPORATION
Statement of Changes in Financial Position, Cash Basis
For the Year Ended December 31, 19X (the current reporting period)

Sources of cash:

From operations:

Income before extraordinary items (accrual basis)	$ 80,000	
Add (deduct) items to convert to cash basis:		
Depreciation expense	30,000	
Increase in accounts receivable	(25,000)	
Increase in inventory	(36,000)	
Decrease in prepaid expense	2,000	
Increase in accounts payable	28,000	
Decrease in income tax payable	(2,000)	
Net cash inflow from operations		$ 77,000
From extraordinary items (net of income tax)		20,000
From other sources:		
Borrowing on short-term note	47,000	
Sale of Allstar's common stock	45,000	
Sale of operational assets*	25,000	117,000
Total cash inflow from all sources		214,000

Uses of cash:

Payment of long-term notes	30,000	
Purchase of operational assets	100,000	
Purchase of long-term investment, Y Corp	50,000	
Payment of cash dividends	40,000	
Total cash outflow for all purposes		220,000
Net increase (decrease) in cash during the reporting period		$ (6,000)†
Direct exchanges not affecting cash (Note A)		$140,000

Note A: The company purchased land at a cost of $140,000; full payment was made by issuing 10,000 shares of Allstar common stock, par $1, to the seller (market value $14 per share).
* Sold at book value.
† Proof: Beginning cash balance, $35,000, minus the ending cash balance, $29,000, equals a $6,000 decrease.

depreciation or an increase in accounts payable. Therefore, such **items** must be added back to (or deducted from) income from continuing operations. That is, these additions and deductions are used to **convert** the accrual basis income amount (i.e., $80,000) to a purely cash basis (i.e., $77,000). In the example in Exhibit 4–3, **six** such items were added or deducted. The need for each of these additions or deductions can be explained as follows:

1. Depreciation expense, $30,000—added to accrual income because it was deducted to compute income (i.e., $80,000), but it **did not require the payment of any cash** during the current reporting period.

2. Increase in accounts receivable, $25,000—deducted because this amount of sales was **not collected in cash** during the current reporting period.

3. Increase in inventory, $36,000—deducted because this amount of additional **cash was spent** to increase inventory during the current reporting period.

4. Decrease in prepaid expense, $2,000—added because this amount of expense was deducted to compute income (i.e., $80,000), but it **did not require the payment of cash** during the current reporting period.

5. Increase in accounts payable, $28,000—added because this amount of purchases (or operating expenses) **did not require the payment of cash** during the current reporting period.

6. Decrease in income tax payable, $2,000—Deducted because this amount of **cash was paid** for income tax in addition to the income tax expense reported on the income statement during the current reporting period.

In this manner the net cash source (inflow) from operations was determined to be $77,000.

Notice that the data used to compute "net cash inflow from operations" was provided by *(a)* the current income statement (i.e., net income before extraordinary operations and depreciation expense), and *(b)* a comparison of the beginning and ending balance sheets (i.e., increase or decrease in the **balances** of accounts receivable, inventory, prepaid expense, accounts payable, and income tax payable).

Cash inflow from extraordinary items. An examination of the accounting records showed that an **extraordinary** transaction was recorded that included a **debit to cash,** net of income tax, of $20,000.

Cash inflow from other sources. An examination of the accounting records showed that Allstar *(a)* borrowed $47,000 cash on a short-term note, *(b)* sold some of its common stock for $45,000 cash, and *(c)* sold some of its operational assets for $25,000 cash. To simplify this illustration, it was assumed that these operational assets were sold at book value. Therefore, there was no gain or loss on disposal. Had the cash sale price been different than the book value, a gain would be deducted, or a loss added, as an adjustment to income before extraordinary items. The adjustment would be necessary to remove the gain or loss effect from "net cash inflow from operations" because the disposal transaction is reported under "other sources" (see Chapter 23).

An examination of the accounting records showed that the above transactions were the only **sources** of cash during the reporting period. Therefore, total cash inflow from all sources during the reporting period was $214,000 (Exhibit 4–3).

Uses of cash. Now consider the **uses of cash** reported by Allstar Corporation on the SCFP. An examination of the accounting records showed that **all cash expenditures** during the current reporting period could be grouped into four major uses: (1) payment of long-term notes, $30,000; (2) purchase of operational assets, $100,000; (3) purchase of long-term investments, $50,000; and (4) payment of a cash dividend, $40,000. Thus, **total cash outflow** during the current reporting period was $220,000 (Exhibit 4–3).

Observe that total cash outflows (i.e., $220,000) **does not** include cash expenditures for expenses because those expenditures were included in computing **net cash inflow from operations** (i.e., $77,000).

Given total **cash inflows** of $214,000 and total **cash outflows** of $220,000, the **cash balance necessarily decreased** by $6,000, as reported in Exhibit 4–3. This decrease can be verified by comparing the beginning and ending balances in the Cash account.

Direct Exchanges. The last item reported on the SCFP (Exhibit 4–3) is "Direct exchanges not affecting cash." This transaction is disclosed in Note A, which explains that Allstar Corporation purchased land, and instead of paying cash for it, the company paid for it in full by issuing 10,000 shares of its own common stock. Notice that in conformity with the **cost principle,** the cost of the land was recorded at the **market value** of the consideration given for it (i.e., 10,000 shares × $14 per share market value = $140,000). This item should be reported, although no cash was paid, because the SCFP must report on an **all-resources basis.** Under this basis, the land transaction is called a **direct exchange** (i.e., a noncash trade). The all-resources basis **assumes** that a direct exchange implicitly involves two transactions. In this case, the transactions are (1) a sale of the common stock (for $140,000) and (2) a purchase of the land for cash.

APB Opinion 19 requires that direct exchanges be reported on the SCFP on an as-if basis. This means that, although no cash was received or paid, a direct exchange is reported "as if" cash was received (from sale of the stock in the example) and "as if" cash was immediately paid (for the land in the example). Rather than reporting a direct exchange in a separate section (as in Exhibit 4–3), some companies report it as both a cash inflow and a cash outflow on the SCFP. The effect of this reporting would be to increase both total cash inflows and total cash outflows by $140,000. However, the net decrease in cash during the period would remain the same (i.e., a $6,000 decrease).

Without the all-resources requirement, significant resource inflows and outflows would not be reported on the SCFP.

An actual SCFP, prepared on the **cash basis,** is shown in the Appendix following Chapter 24. Chapter 23 discusses the preparation and interpretation of the SCFP on both the cash and working capital bases.

ADDITIONAL REPORTING ISSUES

We will conclude the review of information processing and the financial statements with a brief discussion of additional reporting issues that often are encountered.

Terminology

Accounting has developed its own jargon. Often the same word or phrase is used to mean different things. In preparing reports, accountants should refrain from using vague terminology. Captions and titles should be selected carefully because the statements will be used by a wide range of decision makers. From time to time, pronouncements such as the *ARBs, APB Opinions,* and *FASB Statements* recommend improved terminology. For example, *FASB Concepts Statement 3* created a new term, **comprehensive income.** This term encompasses a wider range of revenues, expenses, gains, and losses than is contemplated by conventional net income. At some time in the future, the FASB may define this term more precisely and incorporate it in the income statement.

An example of careless terminology is using the term **reserve** to refer to *(a)* a contra asset account, such as "reserve for depreciation," instead of the more descriptive term "accumulated depreciation"; *(b)* an estimated liability, such as "reserve for warranties" instead of "estimated warranty liability"; and *(c)* an appropriation of retained earnings, such as "reserve for future expansion" instead of "Retained earnings appropriated for future expansion." *Accounting Terminology Bulletin No. 1* recommended that the term be restricted to the last usage. Even in this context, the authors do not believe that the word *reserve* is suitable to describe the nature of a restriction or appropriation of retained earnings.

Similarly, the terminology bulletin recommended using the terms **retained earnings** instead of earned surplus and **net income** instead of net profit. *APB Opinion 19* recommended using the title **statement of changes in financial position (SCFP),** instead of the vague title, funds flow statement. Confusion of the terms **cost** and **expense,** discussed in Chapter 3, is another example of careless terminology. **Throughout this textbook we discuss and use preferred terminology because the effectiveness of accounting communication and precision in discussing accounting concepts and their implementation depends largely upon consistent use of precise and descriptive terminology.**

Comparative Statements

To predict the future success, or failure, of an enterprise, one should assemble comparable financial information for two or more periods. For prediction purposes, trends are much more revealing than information for only one period. In recognition of this fact, *ARB 43* states:

> The presentation of comparative financial statements in annual and other reports enhances the usefulness of such reports and brings out more clearly the nature and trends of current changes affecting the enterprise. Such presentation emphasizes the fact that statements for a series of periods are far more significant than those for a single period and that the accounts for one period are but an installment of what is essentially a continuous history.[5]

Comparative financial statements for the current and prior reporting periods are essential to meet the **full-disclosure principle.** In 1980, the SEC began requiring three-year comparative statements, in lieu of the customary two-year state-

---

[5] AICPA, *Accounting Research Bulletin No. 43,* "Restatement and Revision of Accounting Research Bulletins" (New York, 1953), chap. 2, sec. A.

ments, for "listed" companies. The actual statements shown in the Appendix following Chapter 24 display comparative amounts.

In addition to comparative statements, many companies present a special tabulation of selected financial items for time spans of 5 to 20 or more years. Items often included are total revenues, income before extraordinary items, net income, depreciation expense, EPS, dividends, total assets, total owners' equity, and average number of shares of common stock outstanding. These long-term summaries are particularly useful in trend analysis.

Subsequent Events

Subsequent events are important events or transactions that occur **subsequent** to the balance sheet date but **prior** to the actual issuance of the financial statements (ordinarily one to four months later), and that have a material effect on the financial statements. Subsequent events must be reported in the financial statements of the current reporting period. They involve information that could influence the statement users' interpretation and evaluation of the future prospects of the enterprise. Auditing standards define these events and specify that they must be reported either in the (1) tabular portion of the statements or (2) notes to the statements, depending upon their nature.

The effects of subsequent events should be reported in the **tabular portion of the statements** if they *(a)* provide additional evidence about conditions **that existed at balance sheet date,** *(b)* affect estimates inherent in the process of preparing the financial statements, and *(c)* require adjustments to the financial statements resulting from the estimates. An example would be a material loss on an uncollectible receivable because of a customer's deteriorating financial condition. The deteriorating financial condition presumably was occurring at balance sheet date, but recent information made it more evident.

Subsequent events should be **disclosed in the notes** to the statements if they *(a)* result from conditions that did not exist at balance sheet date, *(b)* arose subsequent to the balance sheet date, and *(c)* do not merit adjustment to the current financial statements. Examples listed in *Codification of Statements on Auditing Standards,* AU Sec. 560.06, are sale of a bond or capital stock issue, litigation based on an event subsequent to the balance sheet date, inventory losses due to casualty, and losses caused by a condition that arose subsequent to balance sheet date (such as a fire or flood). The fire or flood did not "exist" at the balance sheet date.

This topic is considered in depth in auditing texts and courses.

Full Disclosure

The **full-disclosure principle** requires complete reporting of all information relating to the economic affairs of the enterprise to avoid **misleading** financial statements. Full disclosure requires, in addition to the information reported in the tabular portions of the financial statements, additional information in the notes and schedules that supplement the financial statements.

Disclosure notes are narrative explanations relating to such items as accounting policies used by the company, pension plans, maturity dates on payables and receivables, restrictions relating to long-term debt, and the effects of subsequent events and contingencies (e.g., lawsuits pending). A note may refer to a single amount on one of the three basic statements or to several amounts on two or more of them, or to a situation that is not directly reflected on any of them. The guideline for deciding when a note is required, other than when specifically required, is largely judgmental.

A number of *APB Opinions* and *FASB Statements* require disclosures in the notes to the financial statements. For example, *APB Opinion 22*, "Disclosure of Accounting Policies," requires that information about **important** accounting policies adopted by the enterprise, including their identification and description, be disclosed "in a separate *Summary of Significant Accounting Policies* preceding the notes to the financial statements or as the initial note." The summary should include policies that involve *(a)* a selection from existing alternatives, *(b)* principles and methods peculiar to the industry, and *(c)* unusual or innovative applications of GAAP.

Supporting schedules often are presented separately or are incorporated into the notes. Supporting schedules are typical for large and complex companies, and in situations where a particular item involves a number of complex changes during the period. We mentioned in Chapter 3 that when there have been numerous changes in owners' equity, the statement of retained earnings often is replaced with a more comprehensive schedule. For example, the 1984 financial statements of The Quaker Oats Company given in the Appendix following Chapter 24 presents a "Consolidated Statement of Common Shareholders' Equity."

Parenthetical notes are often used in the tabular portions of the financial statements to disclose information such as the method of inventory costing and valuation; for example, Inventory (FIFO, applied on LCM basis). **Contra items,** such as accumulated depreciation and allowance for doubtful accounts, are reported as separate line deductions or parenthetically.

Quaker Oats' statements presented in the Appendix following Chapter 24 include typical disclosures.

Auditors' Report

The auditors' report also is called the accountants' report or the independent accountants' report. It often is the last item in the financial statements.

The independent auditors' primary function is to express the **auditors' professional opinion** on the financial statements. Although the auditors have sole responsibility for their opinion expressed in the auditors' report, **the management of the enterprise** has the **primary responsibility for the financial statements** (including the supporting notes). The financial statements are management's; the auditors affirm or disaffirm the statements in the **opinion.**

The auditors' report includes (1) a **scope** paragraph and (2) an **opinion** paragraph. The standard format of the auditors' report is as follows:

(Scope paragraph)

We have examined the balance sheet of X Company as of (at) December 31, 19xx, and the related statements of income, retained earnings and changes in financial position for the year then ended. Our examination was made in accordance with generally accepted auditing standards and, accordingly, included such tests of the accounting records and such other auditing procedures as we considered necessary in the circumstances.

(Opinion paragraph)

In our opinion, the financial statements referred to above present fairly the financial position of X Company as of (at) December 31, 19xx, and the results of its operations and the changes in its financial position for the year then ended, in conformity with generally accepted accounting principles applied on a basis consistent with that of the preceding year.[6]

Signed, CPAs

Eight key elements in the auditors' report have special significance:[7]

1. Date.
2. Salutation.
3. Identification of the statements examined.
4. Statement of scope of the examination.
5. Opinion introduction.
6. Reference to fair presentation in conformity with generally accepted accounting principles.
7. Reference to consistency.
8. Signature of the CPAs.

When the audit is finished, the auditors are required to draft the **opinion** paragraph to communicate their professional opinion about the financial statements by giving one of the following types of opinions.

1. **Unqualified opinion**—An unqualified opinion is given when the CPA has formed the opinion that the statements (1) "present fairly" the results of operations, financial position, and changes in financial position; (2) conform to GAAP, applied on a consistent basis; and (3) meet full-disclosure requirements so that the statements are not misleading.
2. **Qualified opinion**—A qualified opinion is given when the requirements for an unqualified opinion are not met and the auditor has limited exceptions to the client's financial statements. A qualified opinion must clearly explain the reasons for the "exception" and its effect on the financial statements.
3. **Adverse opinion**—An adverse opinion is given when the financial statements do not "fairly present." Also, material exceptions require an adverse opinion on the statements.

---

[6] AICPA, *Codification of Statements on Auditing Standards* (New York, 1977), AU Sec. 509.07.

[7] AICPA, *The Auditors' Report—Its Meaning and Significance* (New York, 1967), p. 2.

4. **Disclaimer of opinion**—When the auditors have not been able to obtain sufficient competent evidential matter, auditors must state that they are unable to express an opinion (i.e., they issue a disclaimer). Auditors must explain the reasons for not giving an opinion.

A comprehensive discussion of the responsibilities of independent auditors is beyond the scope of this book. The above summary is provided to describe the range of possible auditors' opinions regarding the extent to which the financial statements of a client company conform to GAAP.

The auditors' opinion is intended to assure that the financial statements conform to the qualitative characteristics of accounting information (i.e., relevancy, reliability, and comparability), as specified in *FASB Concepts Statement 2,* and otherwise conform to GAAP. The importance of this assurance can be seen in the context of the investment or lending decision of an outside party. For example, without assurance that the financial statements conform to GAAP, the investor or creditor could be misled by such actions as the omission of certain liabilities, inclusion of nonexistent assets, or misclassification of current and long-term items. Likewise, the auditors' report provides assurance that the elements of the company's financial statements conform to the basic definitions of assets, liabilities, and so on, as given in *FASB Concepts Statement 3.* In conclusion, the auditors' report should be viewed as a critical part of an annual financial report because it indicates whether the report is **reliable.**

QUESTIONS

1. What is the basic purpose of a balance sheet?
2. What is a balance sheet? Why is it dated differently from an income statement and an SCFP?
3. Basically, what "values" are reported on the balance sheet?
4. Define assets.
5. Define liabilities.
6. Explain the relationship between the balance sheet and the full-disclosure principle.
7. Contrast the two balance sheet formats.
8. Define current assets and current liabilities emphasizing their interrelationship.
9. Define working capital. What is the current ratio?
10. Distinguish between short-term investments and the investments classified as investments and funds. Under what conditions could an investment be reclassified from current assets to investments and funds and vice versa?
11. Is it proper to offset current liabilities against current assets? Explain.
12. Define the "Investments and funds" caption on a balance sheet.
13. What are operational assets? Distinguish between tangible and intangible operational assets.
14. Why is it sometimes necessary to use the caption "Other assets"? Give two examples of items that might be reported under this classification.
15. Explain a deferred charge and contrast it with a prepaid expense.

16. Distinguish between current and noncurrent liabilities. Under what conditions would a noncurrent liability amount be reclassified as a current liability?

17. What is a deferred credit? Explain why this classification, reported on a balance sheet between liabilities and owners' equity, is difficult to defend conceptually.

18. What is owners' equity? What are the main components of owners' equity?

19. What is a restriction or appropriation of retained earnings? How are restrictions and appropriations reported?

20. What is the purpose of the SCFP?

21. Explain the SCFP all-resources concept.

22. What two methods of measuring funds can be used in the SCFP?

23. Explain the position of the accounting profession with respect to use of the terms reserves, surplus, and net profit. Why is careful attention to terminology important in financial statements?

24. What are comparative statements? Why are they important?

25. What is meant by subsequent events? Why are they reported? How are they reported?

26. In general, why are notes in the financial statements important? How does the accountant determine when a note should be included?

27. What is the auditors' report? Basically, what does it include? Why is it especially important to the statement user?

28. Are the financial statements the representations of the management of the enterprise, the independent accountant, or both? Explain.

EXERCISES

Exercise 4–1

Indicate the best answer for each of the following (explain any qualifications):

1. Which of the following is not a current asset?
   a. Office supplies inventory.
   b. Short-term investment.
   c. Petty cash (undeposited cash).
   d. Cash surrender value of life insurance policies.

2. The distinction between current and noncurrent assets and liabilities is based primarily upon—
   a. One year; no exceptions.
   b. One year or operating cycle, whichever is shorter.
   c. One year or operating cycle, whichever is longer.
   d. Operating cycle; no exceptions.

3. Under GAAP, unexpired insurance usually is a—
   a. Noncurrent asset.
   b. Deferred charge.
   c. Prepaid expense.
   d. Short-term investment.

4. Working capital means—
   a. Excess of current assets over current liabilities.
   b. Total current assets.

    c. Capital contributed by stockholders.

    d. Capital contributed by stockholders plus retained earnings.

5. Which of the following is not a current liability?

    a. Accrued interest on notes payable.

    b. Accrued interest on bonds payable.

    c. Rent revenue collected in advance.

    d. Premium on bonds payable, a credit (unamortized).

6. A deficit is synonymous with—

    a. A net loss for the current reporting period.

    b. A cash overdraft at the bank.

    c. Negative working capital at the end of the reporting period.

    d. A debit balance in retained earnings at the end of the reporting period.

7. A balance sheet is an expression of the model—

    a. Assets = Liabilities + Owners' equity.

    b. Assets = Liabilities − Owners' equity.

    c. Assets + Liabilities = Owners' equity.

    d. Working capital + Operational assets − Long-term liabilities = Contributed capital.

8. Acceptable usage of the term *reserve* is reflected by—

    a. Deduction from an asset to reflect accumulated depreciation.

    b. Description of a known liability for which the amount is estimated.

    c. Restriction or appropriation of retained earnings.

    d. Deduction on the income statement for an expected loss.

9. Which terminology essentially is synonymous with "balance sheet"?

    a. Operating statement.

    b. SCFP.

    c. Statement of financial value of the business.

    d. Statement of financial position.

10. The "operating cycle concept"—

    a. Causes the distinction between current and noncurrent items to depend upon whether they will affect cash within one year.

    b. Permits some assets to be classed as current even though they are more than one year removed from becoming cash.

    c. Is becoming obsolete.

    d. Affects the income statement but not the balance sheet.

Exercise 4–2

Below left is a list of items from a typical balance sheet for a corporation. Below right is a list of brief statements of the valuations usually reported on the balance sheet for specific items.

Required:

Use the code letters to the right to indicate, for each balance sheet item listed, the **usual** valuation reported on the balance sheet. Comment on any doubtful items. Some code letters may be used more than once or not at all. The first item is an example.

Balance sheet items	Valuations usually reported
1. __C__ Land (held as investment).	A. Amount payable when due (usually no interest because short term).
2. _____ Merchandise inventory, FIFO.	
3. _____ Short-term investments.	B. Lower of cost or market.
4. _____ Accounts receivable (trade).	C. Original cost when acquired.

Balance sheet items	Valuations usually reported

Balance sheet items

5. _____ Long-term investment in bonds of another company (purchased at a discount; the discount is a credit balance).
6. _____ Plant site (in use).
7. _____ Plant and equipment (in use).
8. _____ Patent (in use).
9. _____ Accounts payable (trade).
10. _____ Bonds payable (sold at a premium; the premium is a credit balance).
11. _____ Common stock (par $10 per share) sold at par.
12. _____ Contributed capital in excess of par.
13. _____ Retained earnings.
14. _____ Land (future plant site).
15. _____ Idle plant (awaiting disposal).
16. _____ Natural resource.

Valuations usually reported

D. Market value at date of the balance sheet, whether it is above or below cost.
E. Original cost less accumulated amortization over estimated economic life.
F. Par value of the issued shares.
G. Face amount of the obligation plus unamortized premium.
H. Realizable value expected.
I. Principal of the asset less unamortized discount.
J. Cost when acquired less accumulated depreciation.
K. Accumulated income less accumulated losses and dividends.
L. Excess of issue price over par or stated value of common stock.
M. No valuation reported (explain).
N. Expected net disposal proceeds, if below book value, otherwise net book value.
O. Cost less accumulated depletion.
P. None of the above (when this response is used, explain the valuation usually used).

Exercise 4–3

A typical balance sheet has the following subcaptions:

    A. Current assets.
    B. Investments and funds.
    C. Operational assets (property, plant, and equipment).
    D. Intangible assets.
    E. Other assets.
    F. Deferred charges.
    G. Current liabilities.
    H. Long-term liabilities.
    I. Capital stock.
    J. Additional contributed capital.
    K. Retained earnings.

Required:

Use the code letters above to indicate, for each balance sheet item listed, the **usual** classification. If an item is a contra amount (i.e., a deduction) under a caption, place a minus sign before the lettered response.

1. _−C_ Accumulated depreciation (example).
2. _H_ Bonds payable (due in 10 years).
3. _G_ Accounts payable (trade).
4. _B_ Investment in stock of X Company (long term).
5. _C_ Plant site (in use).

6. __K__ Restriction or appropriation of retained earnings. K
7. __A__ Office supplies inventory. A
8. __E__ Loan to company president (collection not expected for two years). F
9. __K__ Accumulated income less accumulated dividends. K
10. __-H__ Unamortized bond discount (on bonds payable; a debit balance). H-
11. __B__ Bond sinking fund (to retire long-term bonds). B
12. __A__ Prepaid insurance. A
13. __A__ Accounts receivable (trade). A
14. __A__ Short-term investment. A
15. __-A__ Allowance for doubtful accounts. -A
16. __C__ Building (in use). C
17. __I__ Common stock (par $10). I
18. __A__ Interest revenue earned but not collected. A
19. __D__ Patent. D
20. __B__ Land, held for investment. B
21. __E__ Land, idle plant site held for sale. E

Exercise 4–4

A typical balance sheet has the following subcaptions:

    A. Current assets.
    B. Investments and funds.
    C. Operational assets (property, plant, and equipment).
    D. Intangible assets.
    E. Other assets.
    F. Deferred charges.
    G. Current liabilities.
    H. Long-term liabilities.
    I. Capital stock.
    J. Additional contributed capital.
    K. Retained earnings.

Required:

Use the code letters above to indicate, for each balance sheet item listed, the **usual** classification. If an item is a contra amount (i.e., a deduction) under a caption, place a minus sign before the lettered response.

1. __A__ Accounts receivable, trade (example).
2. __H__ Unamortized premium (on bonds payable; a credit balance).
3. __A__ Short-term investments.
4. __G__ Cash dividends payable (within six months).
5. __G__ Rent revenue collected in advance.
6. __-C__ Accumulated depreciation.
7. __J__ Premium on common stock issued.
8. __E__ Idle plant held for final disposal.
9. __F__ Deferred costs being amortized over five years.
10. __A__ Inventory of supplies.
11. __I__ Preferred stock.
12. __-B__ Unamortized discount on long-term investment in bonds of another company (the discount is a credit balance).
13. __G__ Installment payment due in six months on long-term note payable.

14. ___G___ Accrued interest on note payable.
15. ___A___ Rent revenue receivable.
16. ___A___ Allowance for doubtful accounts.
17. ___B___ Investment in bonds of another company (long term).
18. _____ Undeposited cash (for making change).
19. ___L___ Bonds payable, long term.
20. ___F___ Idle plant site (held for early sale).
21. ___K___ A deficit for the current reporting period.

Exercise 4–5

The following data, in no particular order, were provided by the accounts of Small Corporation, December 31, 19B, end of the current reporting year. All amounts are correct, all of the accounts have typical balances, and debits equal credits. The amounts are given in thousands of dollars.

Accounts payable	$ 3
Debt retirement fund (long term)	20
Accounts receivable	16
Income taxes payable	1
Short-term investments, marketable securities (cost)	5
Bonds payable (long term)	50
Accumulated depreciation, equipment and furniture	16
Common stock, par $1 (100,000 shares authorized)	70
Cash	11
Retained earnings, January 1, 19B	13
Allowance for doubtful accounts	1
Unearned rent revenue	2
Dividends payable	3
Inventory of merchandise (December 31, 19B)	30
Land held for future business site	18
Equipment and furniture	80
Net income for 19B	35
Dividends (cash) declared (a debit)	3
Prepaid expenses (short term)	1
Unamortized bond premium (bonds payable, a credit)	1
Patent	4
Deferred rearrangement costs	2
Investment in capital stock of T Corporation (long term)	10
Premium on common stock	5

Required:
Prepare a complete balance sheet (in thousands), assuming Small Corporation uses the captions illustrated in Exhibit 4–2. Use the account titles as given. Show computation of the ending balance of retained earnings.

Exercise 4–6

The ledger of Waco Manufacturing Company reflects obsolete terminology, but you find its books have been, on the whole, accurately kept. After the most recent closing of the books at December 31, 19B, the following accounts were submitted to you for the preparation of a balance sheet:

Accounts payable	$33,200
Accounts receivable	9,500
Accrued expenses (credit)	800
Bonds payable, 14%	25,000
Capital stock ($100 par)	70,000
Cash	13,000
Earned surplus	xx,xxx
Factory equipment	31,200
Finished goods	12,100
Investments	13,000
Office equipment	9,500
Raw materials	9,600
Reserve for bad debts	500
Reserve for depreciation	9,000
Rent expense paid in advance (a debit)	3,000
Sinking fund	7,000
Land held for future plant site	15,000
Note receivable	6,600
Work in process	18,300

You ascertain that two thirds of the depreciation relates to factory and one third to office equipment. Of the balance in the Investments account, $4,000 will be converted to cash during the coming year; the remainder represents a long-term investment. Rent paid in advance is for the next year. The note receivable represents a loan to the company president on October 1, 19B, and is due in 19D when the principal amount ($6,600) plus 16% interest per annum will be paid to the company. The sinking fund is being accumulated to retire the bonds at maturity.

Required:

1. Prepare a classified balance sheet using preferred format, classifications, and terminology.
2. Compute (a) the amount of working capital and (b) the current ratio.

Exercise 4–7

The following trial balance was prepared by Davco Corporation as of December 31, 19F. The adjusting entries for 19F have been made, except for any specifically noted below.

Cash	$19,000	
Accounts receivable	15,000	
Inventories	12,000	
Equipment	22,400	
Land	6,400	
Building	7,600	
Deferred charges	1,100	
Accounts payable		$ 5,500
Note payable, 15%		8,000
Capital stock (par $10)		38,500
Earned surplus		31,500
	$83,500	$83,500

You ascertain that certain errors and omissions are reflected in the above trial balance, including the following:

1. The $15,000 balance in accounts receivable represents the entire amount owed to the company; of this amount, $12,400 is from trade customers, and 5% of that amount is estimated to be uncollectible. The remaining amount owed to the company represents a long-term advance to its president.
2. Inventories include $1,000 of goods incorrectly valued at double their cost (i.e., reported at $2,000). No correction has been recorded. Office supplies on hand of $500 also are included in the balance of inventories.
3. When the equipment and building were purchased new in January 1, 19A (i.e., 6 years earlier), they had, respectively, estimated lives of 10 and 25 years. They have been depreciated using the straight-line method on the assumption of zero residual values, and depreciation has been credited directly to the asset accounts.
4. The balance of the Land account includes a $1,000 payment made as a deposit of earnest money on the purchase of an adjoining tract. The option to buy it has not yet been exercised and probably will not be exercised during the coming year.
5. The interest-bearing note matures March 31, 19G, having been drawn July 1, 19F. Interest on it has been ignored.
6. Common stock shares outstanding, 2,500.

Required:
Prepare a correct balance sheet with appropriate captions and subcaptions; use preferred terminology and the vertical format. Show the computation of the ending balance in retained earnings.

Exercise 4–8

The following adjusted trial balance was prepared by Western Corporation at December 31, 19X:

Debits

Cost of goods sold	$230,000
Distribution and administrative expenses (including interest)	130,000
Income tax expense	41,500
Cash	44,000
Short-term investments	12,000
Accounts receivable	70,000
Merchandise inventory*	72,000
Office supplies inventory	2,000
Investment in bonds of X Corp. (long term), cost (market value, $35,000)	33,000
Land (plant site in use)	10,000
Plant and equipment	120,000
Franchise (less amortization)	8,000
Rearrangement costs†	15,000
Idle equipment held for disposal	7,500
Dividends declared and paid during 19X	40,000
	$835,000

Credits

Sales revenue	$480,000
Accumulated depreciation, plant and equipment	40,000
Accounts payable	50,000
Income taxes payable	11,000
Bonds payable	50,000
Allowance for doubtful accounts	3,000
Premium on bonds payable (unamortized)	1,000
Common stock, par $10 (authorized 50,000 shares)	150,000
Excess of issue price over par of common stock	18,000
Retained earnings, 1/1/19X	32,000
	$835,000

* Perpetual inventory system.
† Amortization period three years; this is the unamortized balance.

Required:
1. Prepare a single-step income statement.
2. Prepare a balance sheet with appropriate captions and terminology.

Exercise 4–9

Based upon the following information, prepare the stockholders' equity section of the balance sheet for Raleigh Corporation at December 31, 19C.

Preferred stock, par $15, authorized 20,000 shares	$270,000
Cash received above par of preferred stock	15,000
Common stock, nopar, 60,000 shares issued (100,000 shares authorized)	200,000
Retained earnings:	
Unappropriated	80,000
Restricted by special contract	60,000

Exercise 4–10

Dawson Corporation is preparing the balance sheet at December 31, 19K. The following items are at issue:

a. Note payable, long-term, $80,000. This note will be paid in installments. The first installment of $10,000 will be paid August 1, 19L.

b. Bonds payable, 12%, $200,000; at December 31, 19K, unamortized premium amounted to $6,000.

c. Bond sinking fund, $40,000; this fund is being accumulated to retire the bonds at maturity. There is a restriction on retained earnings required by the bond indenture equal to the balance in the bond sinking fund.

d. Rent revenue collected in advance for the first quarter of 19L, $6,000.

e. After the balance sheet date, but prior to issuance of the 19K balance sheet, one third of the merchandise inventory was destroyed by flood (date, January 13, 19L); estimated loss, $150,000.

f. Ending balance of unappropriated retained earnings (December 31, 19K), $35,000.

Required:

Show, by illustration, with appropriate captions, how each of these items should be reported on the December 31, 19K, balance sheet.

Exercise 4–11

The records of Scott Corporation provided the following selected data on December 31, 19B:

Preferred stock, par $10, 100,000 shares authorized	$350,000
Common stock, nopar, 200,000 shares authorized of which 100,000 are outstanding...	300,000
Premium on preferred stock	90,000
Earned surplus (free) at end of 19B (excluding all appropriations)..	40,000
Reserves at end of 19B for:	
Bad debts	11,000
Depreciation	90,000
Patent amortization	6,000
Warranty obligations	14,000
Income tax obligations	31,000
Future plant expansion (management decision, plans are to remove this appropriation within five years after completion)	70,000
Retirement of bonds payable (required by the bond indenture; automatically ends when the bonds are paid)	60,000
Bond sinking fund	60,000

Required:

1. Prepare the stockholders' equity section of the balance sheet using preferred terminology and format.
2. If any of the above items do not belong in the stockholders' equity section, explain how they should be reported.

Exercise 4–12

Following are listed, in no particular order, the major and minor captions for a balance sheet and an SCFP (cash equivalent basis). Terminology given in the chapter is used.

1. Total assets.
2. Cash from other sources.
3. Contributed capital.
4. Add (deduct) adjustments to convert to cash basis.
5. Retained earnings.
6. Net cash inflow from operations.
7. Current liabilities.
8. Cash from extraordinary items (net of tax).
9. Uses of cash.
10. Unrealized capital.
11. Owners' equity.
12. Total cash outflow for all purposes.
13. Operational assets—tangible.
14. Petty cash.
15. Net increase (decrease) in cash during the period.
16. Long-term liabilities.
17. Assets.
18. Current assets.
19. Capital stock.
20. Sources of cash.
21. Other assets.
22. Cash inflow from operations.
23. From operations.
24. Contributed capital in excess of par.
25. Deferred charges.
26. Prior period adjustments.
27. Total cash inflow from all sources.
28. Liabilities.

29. Investments and funds.
30. Total liabilities.
31. Total liabilities and owners' equity.

32. Total owners' equity.
33. Direct exchanges (a separate caption).
34. Operational assets—tangible (or intangible).

Required:

Set up two captions: *(a)* Balance Sheet and *(b)* SCFP. For each caption, list the numbers given above in the order that they normally would be reported on the statements (do not renumber). Example:

a. Balance Sheet: 17, 18, and so on.
b. SCFP: 20, 22, and so on.

Comment on any doubtful items; two numbers will not be used.

Exercise 4–13

The records of Highland Company provided the selected data given below at December 31, 19C.

Net income	$100,000
Paid cash dividend	18,000
Established a construction fund (building)	50,000
Increased inventory of merchandise	14,000
Borrowed on a long-term note	25,000
Depreciation expense	20,000
Acquired five acres of land for a future site for the company; paid in full by issuing 3,000 shares of Highland capital stock, par $10, when the quoted market price per share was $15.	—
Increase in prepaid expenses	3,000
Decrease in accounts receivable	7,000
Payment of bonds payable in full	97,000
Increase in accounts payable	5,000
Cash from disposal of old operational assets (sold at book value)	12,000
Decrease in rent receivable	2,000
Cash from extraordinary item (net of income tax)	1,000

Required:

Prepare a complete SCFP, cash basis. Use thousands of dollars, preferred terminology, and appropriate format. Report any direct exchanges on an "as if basis" in order to reflect concurrent cash inflow and outflow.

Exercise 4–14

The following statement is being prepared by Akron Corporation.

AKRON CORPORATION
Funds Flow Statement
For the Year Ended December 31, 19B

Funds received:

From operations:

Net income before EO items*	$90,000	
Add (deduct):		
Depreciation expense	40,000	
Amortization of patent	9,000	
Decrease in accounts receivable balance	5,000	
Increase in inventory balance	(10,000)	
Increase in wages payable balance	4,000	$138,000
Extraordinary item, net (EO loss was $1,000)		12,000
Machinery, old (sold at book value)		7,000
Loan on long-term note		25,000
Total funds generated		$182,000

Funds spent:

Retirement of mortgage	$60,000	
Cash dividends	20,000	
Machinery (new)	50,000	
Acquired land; issued capital stock in full payment (6,000 shares, par $5)†	–0–	
Invested in capital stock of B Corporation	10,000	
Increase in cash balance	42,000	
Total funds spent		$182,000

* Extraordinary is abbreviated EO.
† Market price per share, $6.

Required:

1. How are funds measured in this statement—working capital or cash? How can you be sure?
2. Explain how there could be a $12,000 source for the EO item in view of the $1,000 loss.
3. Is a direct exchange reported in this statement? Explain.
4. Recast the above statement using preferred format and terminology.

PROBLEMS

Problem 4–1

Below left is a list of typical items from a balance sheet for a corporation. Below right is a list of brief statements of valuations usually reported on a balance sheet for different items.

Balance sheet items	**Valuations usually reported**

Balance sheet items

1. __N__ Cash (example).
2. __A__ Short-term investments.
3. __H__ Accounts receivable (trade).
4. __B__ Notes receivable (short term).
5. __A__ Merchandise inventory.
6. __J__ Prepaid expenses (such as prepaid insurance).
7. __M__ Long-term investment in bonds of another company (purchased at a premium).
8. __I__ Long-term investment in stock of another company (less than 20% of the outstanding shares purchased).
9. __Q__ Plant site (in use).
10. __Q__ Plant equipment (in use).
11. __S__ Patent (used in operations).
12. __G__ Deferred charge.
13. __O__ Accounts payable (trade).
14. __O__ Income taxes payable.
15. __B__ Notes payable (short term).
16. __A P__ Bonds payable (sold at a discount).
17. __A C__ Common stock (nopar).
18. __I__ Preferred stock (par $10 per share).
19. __E__ Contributed capital in excess of par.
20. __F__ Retained earnings.
21. __R__ Land held for speculation.
22. __K__ Land held for a future plant site.
23. __L__ Damaged merchandise (goods held for sale).

Valuations usually reported

A. Lower-of-cost-or-market.
B. Principal amount collectable at maturity.
C. Total amount paid in by stockholders when issued.
D. Cost to acquire the asset.
E. Excess of issue price over par value of stock.
F. Accumulated income less accumulated losses and dividends.
G. Cost to acquire, less amortization to date.
H. Estimated net realizable value (amount billed less estimated loss due to uncollectibility).
I. Par value of shares issued.
J. Cost less expired or used portion.
K. Cost at date of investment.
L. Replacement cost.
M. Principal amount plus unamortized premium.
N. Current market value.
O. Amount payable when due (short term).
P. Maturity amount of the obligation less unamortized discount.
Q. Cost to acquire less accumulated depreciation.
R. Market value at the date of the balance sheet, whether it is above or below cost.
S. No valuation reported (explain).
T. None of the above (when this response is used, explain the valuation usually used).

Required:

Use the code letters to the right to indicate, for each balance sheet item listed, the usual valuation reported on the balance sheet. Provide explanatory comments for each doubtful item. Some code letters may be used more than once or not at all.

Problem 4–2

Typical balance sheet classifications along with a code letter for each classification are as follows:

A. Current assets.
B. Investments and funds.
C. Operational assets, tangible (property, plant, and equipment).
D. Intangible assets.
E. Other assets.

F. Deferred charges.
G. Current liabilities.
H. Long-term liabilities.
I. Capital stock.
J. Additional contributed capital.
K. Retained earnings.

Typical balance sheet items are as follows:

1. __A__ Cash (example).
2. __B__ Cash set aside to meet long-term purchase commitment.
3. __C__ Land (used as plant site).
4. __G__ Accrued salaries.
5. __B__ Investment in the capital stock of another company (long term; not a controlling interest).
6. __A__ Inventory of damaged goods.
7. __E__ Idle plant being held for disposal.
8. __B__ Investment in bonds of another company.
9. __B__ Cash surrender value of life insurance policy.
10. __D__ Goodwill.
11. __C__ Natural resource (timber tract).
12. __-A__ Allowance for doubtful accounts.
13. __E__ Stock subscriptions receivable (no plans to collect in near future).
14. __F__ Organization costs.
15. __-H__ Discount on bonds payable.
16. __G__ Service revenue collected in advance.
17. __G__ Accrued interest payable.
18. __-D__ Accumulated amortization on patent.
19. __A__ Prepaid rent expense.
20. __A__ Short-term investment (common stock).
21. __G__ Rent revenue collected but not earned.

22. __K__ Net of accumulated revenues, gains, expenses, losses and dividends.
23. __G__ Trade accounts payable.
24. __G__ Current maturity of long-term debt.
25. __B__ Land (held for speculation).
26. __G__ Notes payable (short term).
27. __B__ Special cash fund accumulated to build plant five years hence.
28. __H__ Bonds issued—to be paid within six months out of bond sinking fund.
29. __B__ Long-term investment in rental building.
30. __D__ Copyright.
31. __-C__ Accumulated depreciation.
32. __E__ Deferred plant rearrangement costs.
33. __D__ Franchise.
34. __A__ Revenue earned but not collected.
35. __H__ Premium on bonds payable (unamortized).
36. __I__ Common stock (at par value).
37. __A__ Petty cash fund.
38. __-K__ Deficit. ~ Balance in retained earnings
39. __J__ Contributed capital in excess of par.
40. __K__ Earnings retained in the business.

Required:

Enter the appropriate code letter for each item to indicate its usual classification on the balance sheet. When it is a contra item (i.e., a deduction) in a caption, place a minus sign before it. Comment to justify your answer.

(AICPA adapted)

Problem 4–3

The balance sheet given below, which was submitted to you for review, has been prepared for inclusion in the published annual report of the Careless Company for the year ended December 31, 19X:

CARELESS COMPANY
Balance Sheet
December 31, 19X

Assets

Current:			
Cash			$ 1,900,000
Accounts receivable	$3,900,000		
Less: Reserve for bad debts	50,000		3,850,000
Inventories—at the lower of cost (determined by the first-in, first-out method) or market			3,500,000
Total current			9,250,000
Investment in raw land			250,000
Fixed:			
Land—at cost		200,000	
Buildings, machinery and fixtures—at cost	$4,200,000		
Less: Reserves for depreciation	1,490,000	2,710,000	2,910,000
Deferred charges and other assets:			
Cash surrender value of life insurance		15,000	
Prepaid costs of major plant rearrangements		12,000	
Plant assets held for early resale		20,000	47,000
Total assets			$12,457,000

Liabilities

Current:			
Notes payable to bank			$ 750,000
Current maturities of first-mortgage note			600,000
Accounts payable—trade			1,900,000
Reserve for income taxes for the year ended 12/31/19X			700,000
Accrued expenses			550,000
			4,500,000
Funded debt:			
9% first-mortgage bonds payable in annual installments of $600,000 .	$4,200,000		
Less: Current maturity	600,000		3,600,000
Reserves:			
Reserve for damages		50,000	
Reserve for possible future inventory losses		300,000	
Reserve for contingencies		500,000	
Reserve for additional federal income taxes		100,000	950,000
Capital:			
Capital stock—authorized, issued and outstanding 100,000 shares of $10 par value		1,000,000	
Capital surplus		300,000	
Earned surplus		2,107,000	3,407,000
Total liabilities			$12,457,000

Additional information:

1. The reserve for damages was set up by a debit to 19X expense and a credit to the reserve for damages possibly payable by the company as a defendant in a lawsuit in progress at the balance sheet date. The lawsuit was subsequently settled for $50,000 prior to issuance of the statement.

2. The reserve for possible future inventory losses was set up in prior years, by action of the board of directors, as debits to earned surplus and credits to the reserve. No change occurred in the account during the current fiscal year.

3. The reserve for contingencies was set up by debits to earned surplus and credits to the reserve over a period of several years by the board of directors to provide for a possible future recession in general business conditions.

4. The reserve for federal income taxes was set up in a prior year as a debit to earned surplus and a credit to the reserve. It relates to additional taxes which the Internal Revenue Service contended that the company owed. The company now has good evidence that settlement will be effected for the $100,000.

5. The capital surplus consists of the difference between the par value of $10 per share of capital stock and the price at which the stock was actually issued.

Required:

1. Redraft the above balance sheet using appropriate format, major captions, subcaptions, titles, and terminology. Use thousands of dollars. Report both appropriated and unappropriated retained earnings amounts on the balance sheet.

2. What is the *(a)* amount of working capital and *(b)* working capital ratio?

3. Explain when and how the four "reserves" will be zero.

(AICPA adapted)

Problem 4–4

The following data were provided by the accounts of Fuere Corporation, December 31, 19C, end of the current reporting year:

Cash	$ 21,000
Accounts receivable, trade	36,000
Short-term investment in marketable securities (cost $41,000)	40,000
Inventory of merchandise (cost, $92,000), FIFO	90,000
Prepaid expense (short term)	1,000
Bond sinking fund (to pay bonds at maturity)	35,000
Advances to suppliers (short term)	4,000
Dividends (cash) declared during 19C	15,000
Rent revenue receivable	2,000
Investment in stock of V Corporation (long term, at cost, which approximates market)	22,000
Unamortized discount on bonds payable	3,000
Loans to employees (company president; payment date uncertain)	25,000
Land (building site in use)	30,000
Building	400,000
Equipment	60,000
Franchise (used in operations)	12,000
Deferred equipment rearrangement cost (long term)	4,000
Total debits	$800,000

Mortgage payable, long term	$ 50,000
Accounts payable	6,000
Dividends payable (payable March 1, 19D)	15,000
Deferred rent revenue	3,000
Interest payable	4,000
Accumulated depreciation, building	160,000
Accumulated depreciation, equipment	20,000
Allowance for doubtful accounts	1,000
Bonds payable (maturity 19W)	100,000
Common stock, nopar (30,000 shares outstanding)	200,000
Preferred stock, par $10	80,000
Premium on preferred stock	16,000
Retained earnings, January 1, 19C	17,000
Net income for 19C	88,000
Appropriation of retained earnings for plant expansion (set up prior to 19C)	40,000
Total credits	$800,000

Required:

1. Prepare a complete statement of financial position, assuming the company uses the captions illustrated in Exhibit 4–2. Assume all amounts are correct and round to the nearest thousand dollars. Use the account titles as given. Show computation of the ending balance in retained earnings and include any restrictions on retained earnings on the statement.

2. Interpretation—Refer to your response to Requirement 1 and respond to the following:

   a. Give the amount of working capital and the working capital ratio.
   b. Give the amount of total retained earnings.
   c. By what percent was the building depreciated?
   d. What were the per share issue prices of the preferred and common stock?
   e. Give the entry that was made to record the 19C dividend declaration.
   f. Give the entry that was made for the appropriation of retained earnings.
   g. Give the entry that probably was made to record the issuance of the (1) preferred stock and (2) common stock. Assume cash transactions.
   h. Give the entry that was made for the advances to suppliers. Assume cash transactions.
   i. Give the adjusting entry that probably was made for rent revenue receivable.
   j. Give the adjusting entry that probably was made for deferred rent revenue.
   k. Give the probable closing entry for net income.

Problem 4–5

The adjusted trial balance for Bird Corporation, and other related data, at December 31, 19C, are given on page 230. Although the company uses obsolete terminology, the amounts are correct (but certain amounts may have to be reported separately). Assume that the perpetual inventory system is used.

Adjusted Trial Balance, December 31, 19C

Debits

Cash	$ 43,600
Land (used for building site)	29,000
Cost of goods sold	110,500
Short-term securities (stock of S Co.)	42,000
Goodwill (unamortized cost)	12,000
Merchandise inventory	30,000
Office supplies inventory	1,000
Patent	7,000
Operating expenses	55,000
Income tax expense	17,500
Bond discount (unamortized)	7,500
Prepaid insurance	900
Building (at cost)	150,000
Land (held for speculation)	31,000
Accrued interest receivable	300
Accounts receivable (trade)	17,700
Note receivable, 16% (long-term investment)	20,000
Cash surrender value of life insurance policy	9,000
Deferred store rearrangement costs (assume a deferred charge)	6,000
Dividends paid during 19C	15,000
Prior period adjustment (correction of error from prior year—no income tax effect)	16,000
	$621,000

Credits

Reserve for bad debts	$ 1,100
Accounts payable (trade)	15,000
Revenues	230,000
Reserve for income taxes	7,500
Note payable (short term)	12,000
Common stock, par $10, authorized 50,000 shares	100,000
Reserve for depreciation, building	90,000
Retained earnings, 1/1/19C	38,000
Accrued wages	2,100
Reserve for estimated damages (set up in 19B)	10,000
Premium on common stock	15,000
Reserve for patent amortization	4,000
Cash advance from customer	3,000
Accrued property taxes	1,300
Note payable (long term)	16,000
Rent revenue collected in advance	1,000
Bonds payable, 11% ($25,000 due 6/1/19D)	75,000
	$621,000

Additional information (no accounting errors are involved):
a. Market value of the short-term marketable securities, $46,000.
b. Merchandise inventory is based on FIFO, lower-of-cost-or-market (LCM).
c. Goodwill is being amortized (i.e., written off) over a 20-year period. The amortization for 19C has already been recorded (as a direct credit to the Goodwill account and a

debit to expense). Amortization of other intangibles is recorded in this manner except for the patent (a contra account is used for it).

d. Reserve for income taxes represents the estimated income taxes payable at the end of 19C. Reserve for estimated damages was recorded as a credit to this reserve account and a debit to Retained Earnings during 19B. The $10,000 was the estimated amount of damages that would have to be paid as a result of a damage suit against the company. At December 31, 19C, the appeal was still pending. The $10,000 represents an appropriation, or restriction, placed on retained earnings by management.

e. Operating expenses as given include interest expense, and revenues include interest and investment revenues.

f. The cash advance from customer was for a special order that will not be completed and shipped until March 19D; the sales price has not been definitely established because it is to be based upon cost (no revenue should be recognized for 19C).

Required:
1. Prepare a single-step income statement and a separate statement of retained earnings.
2. Prepare a balance sheet including appropriate disclosures. Use preferred terminology, captions, subcaptions, and format.

Problem 4–6

The adjusted trial balance for Truefit Manufacturing Corporation at December 31, 19X, is given below in no particular order. Debits and credits are not indicated; however, debits equal credits. All amounts are correct. Assume the usual type of balance in each account and a perpetual inventory system, FIFO, LCM.

Work in process inventory	$ 24,000
Accrued interest on notes payable	1,000
Accrued interest receivable	1,200
Accrued income on short-term investments	1,000
Common stock, nopar, authorized 100,000 shares, issued 40,000	150,000
Cash in bank	40,000
Trademarks (unamortized cost)	1,400
Land held for speculation	17,000
Supplies inventory	600
Goodwill (unamortized cost)	20,000
Raw material inventory	13,000
Bond sinking fund	10,000
Accrued property taxes	1,200
Accounts receivable (trade)	19,000
Accrued wages	2,300
Mortgage payable (due in three years)	10,000
Building	130,000
Prepaid rent expense	1,700
Organization expenses (unamortized cost—assume a deferred charge)	7,800
Deposits (cash collected from customers on sales orders to be delivered next quarter; no revenue yet recognized)	1,000
Long-term investment in bonds of K Corp. (at cost)	60,000
Patents (unamortized cost)	12,000
Reserve for bond sinking fund*	10,000
Reserve for depreciation, office equipment	1,600
Reserve for depreciation, building	5,000
Premium on preferred stock	8,000

Cash on hand for change	400
Preferred stock, par $100, authorized 5,000 shares, 10% noncumulative	60,000
Precollected rent income	900
Finished goods inventory	48,000
Note receivable (short term)	4,000
Bonds payable, 12% (due in 6 years)	50,000
Accounts payable (trade)	17,000
Reserve for bad debts	1,400
Notes payable (short term)	7,000
Office equipment	25,000
Land (used as building site)	8,000
Short-term investments (at cost)	15,500
Retained earnings, unappropriated (1/1/19X)	13,200
Cash dividends on preferred and common stock declared and paid during 19X	20,000
Revenues during 19X	400,000
Cost of goods sold for 19X	210,000
Expenses for 19X (including income taxes)	90,000
Income taxes payable	40,000

* This is a restriction on retained earnings required by the bond indenture equal to the bond sinking fund that is being accumulated to retire the bonds.

Required:

1. Prepare a single-step income statement; use preferred terminology. To compute EPS, deduct $6,000 of net income as an allocation to nonconvertible preferred stock.
2. Prepare a complete balance sheet; use preferred terminology, format, captions and sub-captions.
3. Assume that between December 31, 19X, and issuance of the financial statements, a flood damaged the finished goods inventory in an amount estimated to be $20,000. This event has not been and should not have been recorded in 19X. However, disclosure in the 19X statements is required. Prepare the necessary disclosure.

Problem 4–7

Acosta Corporation has just prepared the annual financial statements dated December 31, 19C. The stockholders' equity section of the balance sheet was appropriately and correctly reported as follows:

Stockholders' Equity

Contributed capital:	
Preferred stock, par $10, 5%, nonparticipating, cumulative; authorized 100,000 shares, issued and outstanding 60,000 shares (of which 3,000 are held as treasury stock)	$ 600,000
Common stock, nopar; authorized 500,000 shares, issued and outstanding 200,000 shares	1,249,000
Contributed capital in excess of par, preferred stock	115,000
Total contributed capital	1,964,000
Retained earnings	102,000
Total	2,066,000
Less: Treasury stock (preferred stock, 3,000 shares), at cost	38,000
Total stockholders' equity	$2,028,000

During 19C, the following transactions and data were correctly included in the above amounts reported in stockholders' equity:

a. Prior period adjustment: Accounting errors made in prior periods (net of
   income tax), a debit .... $ 15,000
b. Sold capital stock (1/3/19C):
   (1) Preferred stock 10,000 shares at $10 100,000
   (2) Common stock, 11,000 shares at $7.50 82,500
c. Treasury stock acquired, 2,000 shares of preferred at $11 per share 22,000
d. Shares issued for common stock dividend on common stock, 5,000 shares
   at $7 (debited to retained earnings) 35,000
e. Net income reported 165,000
f. Cash dividends:
   (1) Preferred stock 28,000
   (2) Common stock 50,000
g. On 12/31/19C, the board of directors voted to approve appropriation of $70,000 of retained earnings as a "Reserve for Future Expansion."

Required:

You have been requested to prepare a complete statement of changes in stockholders' equity. It must include changes in *(a)* shares and dollar amounts for each class of stock, *(b)* contributed capital in excess of par, *(c)* retained earnings, and *(d)* total. Start the schedule with the beginning balances, January 1, 19C. Refer to Exhibit 14–8 for one example to expand upon.

Problem 4–8

At the end of the current reporting year, December 31, 19K, Fisher Company's executives were very concerned about the ending cash balance of $2,500 (the beginning cash balance of $32,500 also had been considered serious at that time).

During 19K, the management undertook numerous actions to attain a better liquidity position. In view of the decreasing cash balance, they asked the chief accountant to prepare a cash-flow report (for the first time). Accordingly, the following information has been developed from the accounting records:

a. Net loss before extraordinary items, $125,000.
b. Debt:
   (1) Borrowing on long-term note, $10,000.
   (2) Payments on maturing long-term debt, $100,000.
   (3) Settled short-term debt of $50,000 by issuing Fisher capital stock at par (which approximated market value).
   (4) Increased accounts payable by $20,000.
c. Cash payments:
   (1) Regular cash dividends, $28,000.
   (2) Purchase of new operational assets, $22,000.
d. Cash received:
   (1) Sold and issued Fisher capital stock, $11,000.
   (2) Sold old operational assets at their book value, $1,000.
   (3) Sold investment (long term) in stock of T Corporation and made the following entry:

   Cash 90,000
   Loss on disposal of investment 30,000
       Investment in T Corporation stock   120,000

e. Relevant income statement data:
   (1) Depreciation expense, $58,000.
   (2) Patent amortization expense, $2,000.
f. Relevant balance sheet accounts:
   (1) Decrease in income tax payable, $10,000.
   (2) Decrease in inventory, $38,000.
   (3) Increase in accounts receivable, $5,000.

Required:
1. Based on the above data, prepare a statement of changes in financial position, cash basis (in thousands). Refer to Exhibit 4–3 for format and terminology.
2. Respond to the following:
   a. Briefly explain how the company, with a $125,000 loss, was able to report a positive net cash inflow from operations.
   b. Comment on what you consider to be the significant issues and problems reflected in the "adjustments to cash basis."
   c. What potential problem is indicated by the "other sources"?

Problem 4–9

Christina De La Fuente, the president of De La Fuente Corporation has asked the company controller for a statement of changes in financial position, cash basis, for the reporting year just ended, December 31, 19B. The company has not previously prepared such a statement. Accordingly, the following data has been obtained from the accounting records:

a. Cash account balances: January 1, 19B, $43,000; ending balance, $34,000.
b. Income before extraordinary items, $95,000. Sales revenue amounted to $295,000, and the balance in accounts receivable decreased by $5,000 during the year; the extraordinary item consisted of a $11,000 gain (net of income tax).
c. Depreciation expense, $12,000; amortization of patent, $1,000.
d. Inventory increased $9,000, and accounts payable increased $3,000 during the year.
e. Income tax payable increased $4,000 during the year.
f. During December 19B, the company settled a $10,000 note payable by issuing shares of its own capital stock with equivalent value.
g. Cash expenditures during 19B were: (1) payment of long-term debts, $64,000; (2) purchase of new operational assets, $79,000; (3) payment of a cash dividend, $16,000; and (4) purchase of land as an investment, $25,000.
h. Sale and issuance of shares of De La Fuente capital stock for $20,000 cash.
i. Issuance of a long-term mortgage note, $30,000.
j. Sale of some old operational assets; the following entry was made:

Cash	5,000	
Accumulated depreciation	12,000	
Operational asset		15,000
Gain on sale of operational assets		2,000

Instructional note: On the SCFP, the $5,000 cash received should be reported under "other sources" and the $2,000 gain should be deducted as an adjustment to net income. The gain must be deducted to remove its effect from net income because (1) it was added on the income statement to derive income, and (2) it must be excluded in the computation of "net cash inflow from operations" (it does not represent a cash inflow).

Required:

1. Prepare a complete SCFP, cash basis, in response to the president's request. Follow the format illustrated in Exhibit 4–3.
2. Now assume that the president has examined your SCFP and is very pleased with it, but comes back with the following questions to which you must respond:
   a. How much cash was generated by sales?
   b. What is the cash generated from operations (before the extraordinary items)?
   c. Explain the reasons for the adjustments to income before extraordinary items.
   d. Why was the $2,000 gain on the sale of old operational assets deducted from income? Why is the gain not reported as a cash inflow?
   e. Why is the debt/stock transaction reported on the statement; no cash was paid or received?

Problem 4–10

The following data were abstracted from the financial statements of King Merchandising Company:

Balance sheet data	12/31/19A	12/31/19B
Trade accounts receivable—net	$ 84,000	$ 78,000
Inventory	150,000	140,000
Payables for merchandise (credit)	(95,000)	(96,000)

Total sales for 19B were $1.2 million and for 19A were $1.1 million. Cash sales were 20% of total sales each year.

Cost of goods sold was $840,000 for 19B.

Variable general and administrative (G&A) total expenses for 19B were $120,000. They have varied in the same proportion to sales each year and have been paid 50% in the year incurred and 50% the following year.

Fixed G&A expenses, including $35,000 depreciation and $5,000 bad debt expense, totaled $100,000 each year. The amount of such expenses that required cash payments were paid 80% in the year incurred and 20% the following year. Each year (i.e., 19A and 19B) there were a $5,000 bad debt expense and a $5,000 write-off. No unpaid G&A expenses are included in the payables above.

Required:

1. How much cash was collected during 19B resulting from total sales in 19A and 19B?
2. How much cash was disbursed during 19B for purchases of merchandise?
3. How much cash was disbursed during 19B for variable and fixed G&A expenses?

(AICPA adapted)

CASES

Case 4–1

R. Applewhite & Sons is a family corporation operating a chain of seven retail clothing stores in the Southwest. The total owners' equity of $5 million (all shares are outstanding) is owned by R. Applewhite (president and founder) and eight members of the Applewhite family. Except for accounts payable, modest amounts of short-term bank credit, and the usual short-term liabilities, the entire resources of the enterprise came from contributed capital and retained earnings. The general reputation of the company is excellent, and there have never been complaints about slowness in paying its liabilities. The family now has an opportunity to undertake a profitable expansion from 7 to 10 stores and estimates that upward of $2.5 million will be required for the purpose. It will be necessary to borrow this sum, and the issuance of five- to eight-year mortgage notes is contemplated.

Because the business is closely held and has never borrowed to an extent that made issuance of financial statements to outsiders necessary, the only persons who have seen the corporation's statements are members of the family, a few top employees, and some governmental officials, chiefly tax agents. When R. Applewhite was told by a prospective lender that detailed financial statements for the past five years and audited statements for the most recent year as a basis for considering the loan would have to be provided, Applewhite's initial reaction was to "hit the ceiling." After consideration, however, Applewhite became willing to have the audit made and to release balance sheets as of the end of the most recent five years. Applewhite was, as yet, unwilling to release statements of income and changes in financial position, and a majority of the other owners agreed with this stand.

Required:

1. If these five balance sheets are quite detailed, what can prospective lenders ascertain from them?
2. In your opinion would the five balance sheets give enough information to warrant granting a $2.5 million secured intermediate-term loan? Explain the basis for your response.
3. If you were the lending officer of the prospective creditor and sought a compromise in the form of getting some added financial facts without receiving the other statements, what added information would be most useful to you?

Case 4–2

The president of Apple Manufacturing Company is a personal friend of yours, and she tells you the company has never had an audit and is contemplating having one principally because it is suspected that the financial statements are not well prepared. As an example, the president hands you the following balance sheet for review:

APPLE MANUFACTURING COMPANY
Balance Sheet
For the Year Ended December 31, 19X

Resources

Liquid assets:

Cash in banks	$12,500
Receivables from various sources net of reserve for bad debts ($200)	5,000
Inventories	6,000
Cash for daily use	500
Total	24,000

Permanent assets:

Treasury stock, par	4,000
Fixed assets (net of depreciation)	26,000
Grand total	$54,000

Obligations and Net Worth

Short-term:

Trade payables		$ 3,000
Salaries accrued		1,000
Total		4,000

Fixed:

Mortgage		8,000

Net worth:

Capital stock, par $10		30,000
Earned surplus		12,000
Total..		42,000
Grand total		$54,000

Required:

1. List and explain your criticisms of the above balance sheet.
2. Using the above data, prepare a balance sheet that meets your specifications in terms of format, terminology, and classification of data. If necessary make realistic assumptions. *Hint:* Total assets are $50,000.

Case 4–3

The following balance sheet has come to your attention:

EASY CORPORATION
Balance Sheet Statement
For Year Ended December 31, 19C

Assets

Liquid assets:

Cash		$ 31,000	
Receivables	$ 29,000		
Less: Reserve for bad debts	700	28,300	
Inventories		42,000	
			$101,300

Investments and funds:

Petty cash fund		200	
Sinking fund		70,000	
			70,200

Permanent assets:

Land and building	140,000		
Less: Reserve for depreciation	9,000	131,000	
Equipment	84,000		
Less: Reserve for depreciation	29,000	55,000	
			186,000

Deferred charges:

Prepaid expenses		2,700	
Accrued sinking fund income (interest)		600	
			3,300
Total..			$360,800

Obligations

Short term:

Accrued interest on mortgage payable		$ 700
Accounts payable		36,500
Reserve for income taxes	$ 13,000	
Less: U.S. government bonds	8,000	5,000

$42,200

Long term:

    Mortgage payable* 74,000

Net Worth

Capital stock	150,000
Earned surplus	52,400
Reserve for contingencies	66,400
	268,800
Less: Treasury stock	24,200

244,600

Total $360,800

* The mortgage payable matures 4/18/19D, and is funded by the sinking fund.

Required:

Constructively criticize the above balance sheet. Set up your responses in the following format:

Specific criticism (list)	Explanation of criticism	Recommended treatment
1.		
Etc.		

Case 4–4

The most recent balance sheet of Brown Corporation appears below:

BROWN CORPORATION
Balance Sheet
For the Year Ended December 31, 19B
Assets

Current:

Cash	$ 12,000	
Marketable securities	10,000	
Accounts receivable	30,000	
Merchandise	25,000	
Supplies	5,000	
Stock of Co. W (not a controlling interest)	17,000	$ 99,000

Investments:

Cash surrender value of life insurance	45,000	
Treasury stock (2,500 shares)	37,500	82,500

Tangible:

Building and land ($10,000)	$56,000		
Less: Reserve for depreciation	10,000	46,000	
Equipment	15,000		
Less: Reserve for depreciation	10,000	5,000	51,000

Deferred:

Prepaid expenses	2,000	
Discount on bonds payable	3,000	5,000
Total		$237,500

Debt and Capital

Current:

Accounts payable	$ 16,000	
Reserve for income tax	17,000	
Customers' accounts with credit balance	100	$ 33,100

Fixed (interest paid at year-end):

Bonds payable (due at end of 19L), 7%	45,000	
Mortgage, 11%	12,000	57,000
Reserve for bad debts		900

Capital:

Capital stock, authorized 10,000 shares, par $15	112,500	
Earned surplus	25,000	
Capital surplus	9,000	146,500
Total		$237,500

Required:

1. List and explain your criticisms of the above balance sheet.
2. Prepare a complete balance sheet; use appropriate format, captions, and terminology. The capital stock was sold above par. Deduct treasury stock from stockholders' equity.

Case 4–5

The president of Decca Corporation was concerned and surprised that the December 31, 19H, balance sheet (end of the current reporting period) reported a cash balance of $7,500; the December 31, 19G, balance sheet reported a cash balance of $87,500.

Consequently, for the first time in the history of the company (it is closely held and has never been audited), the president asked the company accountant to prepare a "report on the cash situation for 19H," with relevant comments. After reading two recently published discussions relating to the statement of changes in financial position, the accountant assembled the following 19H data from the accounting records (including the 19G and 19H balance sheets):

a. Balance sheet data (19H):
   (1) Decrease in income tax payable, $3,000.
   (2) Increase in prepaid expense, $8,000.
   (3) Cash borrowing, $20,000.
   (4) Decrease in merchandise inventory balance, $70,000.
   (5) Sale of Decca capital stock at par, $60,000 cash.
   (6) Purchase of new operational assets, $18,000 cash.
   (7) Increase in accounts payable, $50,000.
   (8) Payments on debt, $252,000.
   (9) Decrease in accounts receivable, $21,000.
b. Statement of retained earnings data (19H):
   (1) Payment of cash dividends, $30,000.
   (2) No prior period adjustments.
c. Income statement data (19H):
   (1) Net loss (no extraordinary items), $300,000.
   (2) Depreciation expense, $150,000.
d. Special transaction—During December, Decca sold a tract of raw land that it had acquired primarily for investment purposes. This infrequent transaction was appropriately recorded as follows:

Cash	130,000	
Loss on disposal of land investment	30,000*	
Land investment		160,000

* Reported as an infrequent loss on the 19H income statement.

Required:
1. Prepare a complete SCFP, cash basis, (in thousands of dollars); use a format similar to Exhibit 4–3.
2. Respond to the following questions, which will be used to develop the relevant comments requested by the president:
   a. What assurance can you give that the SCFP is correct?
   b. What is the reason for each of the "adjustments to cash basis"?
3. Based upon the SCFP developed in Requirement 1, pinpoint and assess the prospects for future net cash inflows from all sources.

Case 4–6

The following statement has just been prepared by Bryan Corporation:

BRYAN CORPORATION
Statement of Changes in Financial Position
For the Year Ended December 31, 19X

Sources of funds:

From operations:

Net income	$130,000	
Add (deduct) adjustments to convert to fund basis:		
Depreciation expense	30,000	
Accounts receivable increase	(15,000)	
Inventory increase	(17,000)	
Accounts payable increase	11,000	
Income taxes payable decrease	(4,000)	
Loss on sale of long-term investment	3,000	
Funds generated from continuing operations		$138,000
From other sources:		
Sale of long-term investment	21,000	
Issuance of common stock to acquire machinery (Note A)	50,000	
Sale of unissued common stock	15,000	
Issuance of long-term note payable	20,000	
Total funds from other sources		106,000
Total funds generated		244,000

Uses of funds:

Dividends	40,000	
Acquisition of machinery (Note A)	50,000	
Payment on bonds payable	100,000	
Total funds used		190,000
Increase in Cash account during the year		$ 54,000

Note A: Paid for new machinery with Bryan capital stock.

Required:

1. How are funds measured in this statement? Explain.
2. What was net income for the year? How much was net cash inflow from operations? Explain how management generated more net cash inflow from operations than net income.
3. What was the primary source of funds? What was the primary use of funds? What sources and uses would you rely upon for predictions of funds flow in this company? Explain.
4. Explain the long-term investment transaction. Why is it reflected in two places?
5. Write Note A with respect to the machinery.
6. Explain the reason for the addition or deduction of each adjustment to net income.
7. Some changes in terminology would be helpful. Identify them and suggest preferable terminology.

Case 4–7

The Appendix following Chapter 24 gives an actual set of financial statements. Examine them carefully and respond to the following questions (respond for 1984 unless directed otherwise):

a. Are they comparative statements? Briefly explain.

b. Are they consolidated statements?

c. What is the date of the end of the fiscal or reporting year?

d. How many years did the long-term summary cover?

e. What was the long-term trend of total assets?

f. What was the return on average common shareholders' ending equity for 1983 and 1984?

g. What classifications were used on the balance sheet?

h. What was the amount of (1) cash and (2) working capital reported at the end of the current year?

i. What was the income tax obligation at the end of the current year?

j. How many different long-term liabilities are outstanding?

k. What percent of total assets was provided by (1) creditors and (2) owners?

l. Was the SCFP prepared on a working capital basis or a cash equivalent basis? How was this made known in the statement?

m. What item represented the highest use of funds?

n. By how much did funds increase or decrease during 1982, 1983, and 1984?

o. What kind of opinion did the auditor give? Explain.

p. Who is responsible for the preparation and integrity of the company's financial statements? Support your answer.

q. What are the responsibilities of the Audit committee? Who serves on this committee?

Case 4–8: A special continuing case from Chapter 2 (Case 2–4) and Chapter 3 (Case 3–5).

This case is a mini-practice set. The basic situation and the 10 requirements, given in Chapter 2 (Case 2–4) start with the journal entries and T-accounts, and continue through the accounting information processing cycle. A viable use of this case involves starting it in Chapter 2 and completing it by the end of Chapter 4. Students should attain the following schedule:

Requirements completed	Chapter	Key figures
Requirements 1–3, through the unadjusted trial balance on the worksheet	2 (Case 2–4)	Unadjusted trial balance total, $1,174,970.
Requirements 4–5, through the income statement	3 (Case 3–5)	EPS, net income, $1.14.
Requirements 6–10, completed	4 (Case 4–8)	Balance sheet total, $428,683.

Chapter 5

Interest—Concepts of Future and Present Value

OVERVIEW AND PURPOSE

Interest on contractual obligations and certain assets is central to many accounting issues. **Interest is the cost of using money over time;** therefore, it often is referred to as the time value of money.

A dollar at a given date will represent different amounts of resources at earlier and later dates when interest is considered. For example, given a 10% interest rate, a person would prefer receiving $10,000 cash today rather than receiving that same amount 10 years from today (assuming no inflation or deflation). The strength of this preference would be based on the additional $15,937 compound interest one could earn on the $10,000 if it was received at the earlier date.

Measurement of the time value of money involves the basic concepts of the **future value** and **present value** of a dollar. Higher interest rates and longer time periods increase the interest amount. As a consequence, the accounting and reporting implications become more significant. Knowledge of these concepts is essential for accountants because they are applied to such diverse accounting topics as receivables, investments, funds, depreciation, goodwill, installment contracts, liabilities, bonds, pensions, leases, business combinations, and investment decisions.

The purpose of this chapter is to present *(a)* a complete, concise discussion of interest concepts; and *(b)* some typical illustrations of their application in accounting. To accomplish this purpose, the chapter is organized as follows:

Part A: Basic Interest Concepts and Future and Present Values of 1

1. Interest concepts.
2. Future value of 1.
3. Present value of 1.
4. Selecting an interest rate.

Part B: Annuities—Future and Present Values

1. Concept of an annuity.
2. Future value of an annuity.
3. Present value of an annuity.
4. Using multiple annuity values.

PART A: BASIC INTEREST CONCEPTS AND FUTURE AND PRESENT VALUES OF 1

CONCEPT OF INTEREST

Conceptually, interest is the time value of money. It is measured by the excess of resources (usually cash) received or paid over the amount of resources loaned or borrowed at a different date. The outflow of resources for the time value of money is called **interest expense.** The inflow of resources for the time value of money is called **interest revenue.** At various times, entities make decisions that involve either *(a)* receiving funds, goods, or services currently with a promise to make payments over one or more future periods, or *(b)* disbursing funds for operating assets or investments to obtain returns over one or more future periods. In both cases, the time value of money is fundamental to the decision-making process and in measuring and reporting the financial effects of those decisions.

To illustrate the measurement of interest in a simple situation, assume XY Company borrowed $10,000 cash and promised to repay $11,200 one period later, i.e., at maturity date. The total interest on this contract would be measured as the difference in resources as follows:

Resources borrowed	$10,000
Resources repaid at maturity	11,200
Interest (i.e., time value of money)	$1,200
Analysis:	
Interest in dollars	$1,200
Interest rate for the one period ($1,200 ÷ $10,000)	12%

Consistent Interest Periods and Rates

Interest usually is expressed as a **rate per year,** such as 12%. However, contracts that require interest often specify interest periods of less than one year, such as monthly, quarterly, or semiannually. Thus, a 12% annual interest rate would be 1% per month, 3% quarterly, or 6% semiannually assuming interest is paid monthly, quarterly, or semiannually, respectively. If an interest rate is specified with no indication of an interest **period** of less than one year, annual interest should be assumed.[1]

---

[1] Throughout this textbook and in the problem materials, short-term periods are used to facilitate comprehension. Also, amounts usually are rounded to the nearest dollar for instructional convenience.

SIMPLE VERSUS COMPOUND INTEREST

Contracts that require interest will specify either simple interest or compound interest.

Simple interest is computed for each interest period on the same amount of **principal** each period, regardless of any interest accrued in the past. For example, a $10,000 loan that specifies 12% simple interest would require the payment of $1,200 interest each year the loan is outstanding. If there are three interest periods, total interest would be $3,600. The equation for computing simple interest can be expressed as follows:

$$\text{Interest amount} = \text{Principal} \times \text{Interest rate} \times \text{Time}$$
$$\qquad\qquad\qquad\qquad (P) \qquad\qquad (i) \qquad\qquad (n)$$

Compound interest is computed on the amount of **principal** for the period **plus all prior interest accumulated** and not paid or withdrawn. Thus, in addition to interest on principal, compound interest includes interest on interest. Interest amounts that are more than the simple interest amount occur only when there are two or more interest periods. For example, the $10,000 loan, cited above, at 12% compound interest for three interest periods would produce $4,049 of interest, computed as follows:

Period 1—$10,000 × 12%	$1,200
Period 2—($10,000 + $1,200) × 12%	1,344
Period 3—($10,000 + $1,200 + $1,344) × 12%	1,505
Total compound interest	$4,049

Notice that the simple interest amount was $3,600; the difference of $449 (i.e., $4,049 − $3,600) is caused by the inclusion of interest on interest.

OVERVIEW OF FUTURE VALUE AND PRESENT VALUE INTEREST CONCEPTS

Future value (FV) and present value (PV) concepts relate to compound interest only; that is, they include interest on principal and interest on the prior accumulated interest. **Future value** involves a current amount that is **increased** in the future by interest **compounding. Present value** involves a future amount which is **decreased** from the future to the present by compound interest **discounting.**

Future value and present value concepts also include two different situations in regard to the principal. In the simplest situation, the FV or PV amount involves a **single** principal amount. In the other situation, called an **annuity,** the FV or

PV is represented by a series of consecutive equal principal amounts (usually called rents); that is, one such amount for each period.

As a result, there are four basic FV and PV **values.** These four values, based on $1, for a range of periods *(n)* and interest rates *(i)* are presented in Tables 5–1, 5–2, 5–3, and 5–4 (given at end of this chapter). These four values may be summarized as follows:

A. **Values of 1—a single principal amount:**
1. **Future value of 1**—the future value of a **single** principal amount of 1 after a specified number of periods *(n)* when increased at *i* compound interest rate. The symbol used is f, and the formula is: $f = (1 + i)^n$. Table 5–1 gives *f* values, based on $1, for various *n* and *i* values.

2. **Present value of 1**—the present value of a single principal amount of 1 due *n* periods in the future when discounted (i.e., decreased) back to the present time at *i* compound interest rate. The symbol used is *p* and the formula is: $p = \dfrac{1}{(1+i)^n}$. Table 5–2 gives *p* values, based on $1, for various *n* and *i* values.

B. **Annuities—a series of equal periodic amounts** (called rents):
3. **Future value of an annuity of 1**—the future value of a series of *n* equal periodic rents (or contributions) of 1 when **increased** at *i* compound interest rate. The symbol is *Fo,* and the formula is:[2]

$$Fo = \frac{(1+i)^n - 1}{i}$$

Table 5–3 gives F_o values, based on rents of $1 each period, for various *n* and *i* values.

4. **Present value of an annuity of 1**—the present value of a series of *n* equal periodic rents (or contributions) of 1 in the future when **discounted** (i.e., decreased) back to the present time at *i* compound interest rate. The symbol is *Po* and the formula is (see footnote 2):

$$Po = \frac{1 - \dfrac{1}{(1+i)^n}}{i}$$

Table 5–4 gives P_o values, based on rents of $1 each period, for various *n* and *i* values.

The remainder of this chapter will discuss and illustrate the application of each of these situations. However, briefly examine the four FV/PV tables given at the end of this chapter. They will be referred to frequently in the discussions that follow. Notice the following characteristics of each table:

---

[2] The subscript *"o"* refers to **ordinary** annuities as contrasted with annuities due. Also, notations used vary considerably. *FV* and *PV* often are used as abbreviations for future and present value, respectively.

1. Each table heading identifies the specific values presented and the formula.
2. Interest rates *(i)* are given as column headings. These are rates **per interest period** regardless of whether the interest period is annual, semiannual, quarterly, monthly, or daily.
3. Periods *(n)* are given in the left column. The *n* values may be viewed as annual, semiannual, quarterly, monthly, or daily periods.
4. The table values are based on 1 unit of currency (in the United States, this is $1).
5. The table values express the effect of **interest.** No allowance is made for inflation or deflation. The market interest rates are determined in part by expected inflation or deflation.

FUTURE AND PRESENT VALUE OF 1 COMPARED

Future value of 1 and present value of 1 are the same in one respect—they both relate to a **single** principal amount. The future value of 1 looks **forward** from present dollars to future dollars. The present value of 1 looks **back** from future dollars to present dollars. This distinction is shown by "time lines" in **Exhibit 5–1;** it is important to observe the direction of the arrows in each instance.

EXHIBIT 5–1

Future Value of 1 versus Present Value of 1

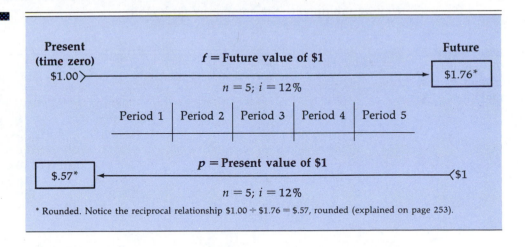

| Present (time zero) | | | f = Future value of $1 | | | | Future |

$1.00 ————————————————————→ $1.76*

$n = 5; i = 12\%$

Period 1 | Period 2 | Period 3 | Period 4 | Period 5

p = Present value of $1

$.57* ←———————————————————— $1

$n = 5; i = 12\%$

* Rounded. Notice the reciprocal relationship $1.00 ÷ $1.76 = $.57, rounded (explained on page 253).

FUTURE VALUE OF 1

The concept of future value of 1 (the symbol used herein is f) often is called compound interest. The future value is the single principal amount plus all subsequent accumulated compound interest. For example, $1,000 deposited in a savings account on January 1, 19A, compounded each interest period of one year at 12% interest, would amount (accumulate) to $1,762 at the end of the fifth year (December 31, 19E). The increase of $762 is the accumulated compound interest during the five years. The future value of 1 always will be more than 1 by the compound interest accumulation.

To increase our knowledge of the concept of a future value of 1 (a single amount), we will consider four ways that it can be computed. Assume we want to compute the future value of $1, invested for five years at 12% compound interest each year (i.e., PV of principal = $1, $n = 5$, $i = 12\%$). The future value can be computed as follows:

1. **By successive interest computations**—Multiply the principal ($1) by the interest rate (12%) and add to the principal the 12 cents interest for the first period; the sum ($1.12) is the amount at the end of the first period. This amount then becomes the **interest-bearing** amount for the second period. This sum is principal plus interest $(1 + i)$ and may be used as the multiplier of the balance at the start of the second period to determine the compound amount at the end of that period. The tabulation below in (1) uses this multiplier to illustrate successive interest computations to derive our answer, $1.76 (rounded). The FV of any amount can be computed in this way by substituting the amount in place of $1.

2. **By formula**—Substitute into a formula which states that for n interest periods at i rate of interest the future value of 1 is $f = (1 + i)^n$. Substituting, $1 invested at 12% annual compound interest for 5 years = $($1 + .12)^5$, or $1.76. See (2) in the tabulation for period 5. The FV of any amount can be computed in this way by multiplying the amount by $(1 + i)^n$.

Tabulation of Compound Interest Computations

	(1) By successive computations			(2) By formula
Period	Balance at start of period	Multiplier $(1+i)$	Amount at end of period	Alternate computation at end $(1+i)^n$
1	$1	1.12	$1.12	$(1.12)^1 = \$1.12$
2	1.12	1.12	1.2544	$(1.12)^2 = 1.2544$
3	1.2544	1.12	1.40493	$(1.12)^3 = 1.40493$
4	1.40493	1.12	1.57352	$(1.12)^4 = 1.57352$
5	1.57352	1.12	1.76234	$(1.12)^5 = 1.76234$

3. **By use of a table**—Tables showing the future and present values for various n and i combinations may be obtained from many sources. Partial tables are presented at the end of this chapter. Table 5–1 is based on the formula $f = (1 + i)^n$; therefore, it presents the future value of 1 values (for a limited number of periods and interest rates). Reference to Table 5–1, down the 12% column and across on the five-period line, shows the future value of 1 to be 1.76234 (the same as computed in the above tabulation). Table 5–1 is titled **Future Value of 1**, and the underlying formula is $f = (1 + i)^n$. Tables make computation of future and present values easier because any amount to be used is multiplied by the appropriate table value for $1. When the table value is to

be applied to a large amount, rounding of **table values** can cause a material error in the resulting amount computed. The tables presented in this chapter are carried to five places.

4. By use of a calculator—Many calculators are programmed to compute FV and PV. To compute an f value, the following inputs are used: n, i, and PV amount.

Each of the four approaches requires that the n and i values be consistent interest periods and rates (see page 246). For most accounting purposes you should be able to use approaches **3** and **4**.

Accounting Applications of Future Value of 1

Case A. On January 1, 19A, Able Company deposited $100,000 in a special construction fund. The fund will earn 10% interest, compounded annually. Interest earned each period will be added to the fund.
Required:
1. Compute the amount that will be in the fund at the end of 19C.

$$\$100,000 \times f_{n=3;\ i=10\%} \text{ (Table 5–1, 1.331)} = \$133,100.$$

2. What is the total amount of accumulated interest?

$$\$133,100 - \$100,000 = \$33,100.$$

3. Prepare a fund accumulation schedule.

	Fund Accumulation Schedule	
Date	Interest earned	Fund balance
January 1, 19A		$100,000
December 31, 19A	$100,000 × 10% = $10,000	110,000
December 31, 19B	110,000 × 10% = 11,000	121,000
December 31, 19C	121,000 × 10% = 12,100	133,100

4. Give the journal entries related to the fund.

January 1, 19A:

Special construction fund		100,000			
Cash					100,000

	19A		19B		19C
Each December 31:					
Special construction fund ...	10,000		11,000		12,100
Investment revenue		10,000		11,000	12,100

Case B. On January 1, 19A, Baker Company deposited $100,000 in a special savings account. The fund will earn 10% interest compounded quarterly. Interest earned will be added to the fund.
Required:
1. Compute the amount that will be in the fund at the end of 19C.

$$\$100,000 \times f_{n=12;\ i=2\ 1/2\%} \text{ (Table 5–1, 1.34489)} = \underline{\underline{\$134,489}}.$$

2. What is the total amount of accumulated interest?

$$\$134,489 - \$100,000 = \underline{\underline{\$34,489}}.$$

Determination of an Unknown Interest Rate or Unknown Number of Periods

Situations may be encountered when either the interest rate (i) or the number of periods (n) is not known, but sufficient data are available for their determination. For example, in Case A above, three values were provided: *(a)* principal, $100,000; *(b)* interest rate, 10%; and *(c)* periods, 3. These three values were used to compute the future value (f) of $133,100. Thus, there were a total of **four** variables. Now let's examine two situations, using the same case, where the unknown variable is not the future value (f).

Situation 1—the interest rate is unknown.

Given: Present value, $100,000; future value, $133,100, interest periods, 3. To compute the implicit **interest rate:**

  a. $133,100 ÷ $100,000 = 1.33100, which is the table value of $1, for three periods.
  b. Use Table 5–1 and read **across** for three interest periods to find this table value.
  c. Table value 1.33100 is found under the 10% column.
  d. The interest rate, therefore, is $\underline{\underline{10\%}}$.

Situation 2—the number of interest periods is unknown.

Given: Present value, $100,000; future value, $133,100, interest rate, 10%. To compute the **number of interest periods:**

  a. $133,100 ÷ $100,000 = 1.33100, which is the table value of $1, at 10% interest.
  b. Use Table 5–1 and read **down** the 10% column to find this table value.
  c. Table value 1.33100 is found on the line for three periods.
  d. The implied number of interest periods, therefore, is $\underline{\underline{3}}$.

Interpolation of Table Values. To determine an unknown interest rate, or number of periods, interpolation often is necessary. This is because the computed table values usually will be between two interest rates or two periods. Assume $5,000 is deposited in a savings account at compound interest, with an expected balance of $15,000 at the end of year 10. Question: What is the implicit interest rate, assuming annual compounding?

Computation:

    a. $15,000 ÷ $5,000 = 3.00000.

    b. Table 5–1 indicates that for $n = 10$; 11% = 2.83942; and for 12% = 3.10585. Therefore, the implicit rate is between 11% and 12%—a little closer to 12%— approximately six tenths of the way between them.

    c. We usually would use 12%, or 11.6%, as close approximations.

    d. If more precision is desired, we could use linear interpolation and derive 11.603% as follows:[3]

$$11\% = 2.83942$$
$$? \ = 3.00000 \quad 3.00000 - 2.83942 = .16058$$
$$12\% = 3.10585 \qquad\qquad\qquad\qquad 3.10585 - 2.83942 = .26643$$

$$11\% + \left[\left(\frac{.16058}{.26643} \right) \times (12\% - 11\%) \right] = \underline{\underline{11.603\%}}$$

PRESENT VALUE OF 1

The concept of present value of 1 (the symbol used herein is p) often is called compound discounting. The **present value** of a single principal amount is the future principal less all compound interest discounted to the present date at the specified interest rate. The present value of $1 always will be less than $1 by the amount of the compound interest discount. For example, a single principal amount of $10,000 discounted at 10% interest for three years is $7,513 (rounded).

All present value of 1 amounts are reciprocals of their comparable future value amounts because one (i.e., f) adds accumulated compound interest and the other (i.e., p) subtracts accumulated compound discount. That is, $f = (1 + i)^n$ and $p = \dfrac{1}{(1 + i)^n}$ as shown in the headings of Tables 5–1 and 5–2, respectively (this relationship was illustrated on page 249).

Calculation of Present Value of 1

Present value of $1 amounts can be computed four different ways as follows:

    1. Successive discounting by dividing each period's beginning f amount by $(1 + i)$.

---

[3] This is an illustration of linear interpolation. A more precise answer can be obtained by using a calculator and the following procedure:

$$\$5,000 (1 + i)^{10} = \$15,000$$
$$(1 + i)^{10} = \$15,000 \div \$5,000$$
$$(1 + i) \ = (3.0)^{1/10}$$
$$i \ = 11.612\%$$

2. Dividing the equivalent f value in Table 5–1 into 1 (p is a reciprocal to f).
3. Use of an available present value of 1 table such as Table 5–2.
4. Use of a pocket calculator programmed to compute FV and PV values.

For most accounting purposes you should be able to use approaches **3** and **4**.

Accounting Application of Present Value of 1

On January 1, 19A, Cary Company purchased a machine. Payment was $25,000 cash and a $50,000 note, due on December 31, 19B. The $50,000 includes all accumulated interest. The implied interest rate is 10%.

Required:

1. Compute the cost of the machine.

Cash paid	$25,000
Note at present value, $50,000 \times p_{n\,=2;\ i\,=10\%}$	
(Table 5–2, .82645)	41,323
Cost of the machine	$66,323

2. Give the entry to record the acquisition of the machine.

Machine	66,323	
Cash		25,000
Note payable		41,323*

* This note could be recorded at $50,000 with a debit for the interest of $8,677 to Discount on Note Payable. The results would be the same (discussed in Chapter 10).

3. Prepare a debt amortization schedule.

	Debt Amortization Schedule		
	Interest expense incurred	Liability (note payable)	
Date	**(payable at maturity)**	**Increase**	**Balance**
January 1, 19A			$41,323
December 31, 19A	$41,323 \times 10\% = \$4,132	$4,132	45,455
December 31, 19B	45,455 \times 10\% = 4,545	4,545	50,000

4. Give the entries related to this situation.

	December 31	
	19A	19B
Interest expense	4,132	4,545
Note payable	4,132	4,545
Note payable		50,000
Cash		50,000

SELECTING AN INTEREST RATE

The results of future and present value computations are significantly influenced by the interest rate used, particularly when the rates are high and the time period is long. For example, the future value of $100,000 for 20 periods at 10% per period is $672,750. If the interest rate is 8%, the future value is $466,096—a significant difference.

Generally, an interest rate has three components: (1) a pure no-risk component, (2) a risk component that varies among borrowers and types of loans, and (3) an expected inflation-rate component. These components are very difficult, if not impossible, to separate in a given situation.

In recognition of (1) the difficulty in selecting a realistic interest rate and (2) the opportunity to select an interest rate to manipulate FV and PV results for accounting purposes, *APB Opinion 21,* paragraphs 13 and 14, provides a general guideline. The guideline is that the rate selected should approximate "the rate which would have resulted if an independent borrower and an independent lender had negotiated a similar transaction under comparable terms and conditions with the option to pay the cash price upon purchase or to give a note for the amount of the purchase which bears the prevailing rate of interest to maturity." The rate described in this quotation usually is called the **going, prevailing,** or **market** rate for the transaction under consideration.

PART B: ANNUITIES—FUTURE AND PRESENT VALUES

ANNUITIES DEFINED

Annuities involve periodic payments or receipts of cash during a specified period of time. For all specific purposes, including accounting, annuities must be precisely defined.

Annuities involve the future and present value concepts discussed in Part A of this chapter. **Annuities differ from amounts of 1 (*f* or *p*) in one way; instead of a single amount, all annuities include a series of amounts. There is one amount for each period that the annuity is in existence.** These principal amounts usually are called **rents;** they may be cash payments or cash receipts. An annuity has three essential **characteristics:**[4]

1. Equal time periods.
2. Equal rents, either at the end or the beginning of each interim time period.
3. Equal interest rates compounded or discounted each interest period.

When one or more of these characteristics changes, a different annuity is created. These characteristics are **explicit** in all interest table values, including FV/PV computer programs. Observe that they are explicit in the table formulas given in the headings of Tables 5–3 and 5–4. For example, these three characteristics are encompassed in the equal monthly payments on an auto loan. An auto loan usually is an annuity that requires periodic cash payments by the borrower and provides periodic cash receipts for the lender.

The **future value** of an annuity is the sum of all of its principal amounts (i.e., its rents) **plus** all of the accumulated compound interest on those rents. The **present value** of an annuity is the sum of all of its principal amounts (i.e., its rents) **less** all of the accumulated compound discount on those rents.

Annuities are either **ordinary** or **due.** The classification depends upon the **timing of the rents** during each period that the annuity is in existence. An **ordinary annuity** (also called an annuity in arrears) is an end-of-period annuity. Its rents occur at the **end of each annuity period** that the annuity is in existence. An **annuity due** (also called an annuity in advance) is a beginning-of-period annuity. Its rents occur at the **beginning of each annuity period** that the annuity is in existence.

To illustrate the difference between an ordinary annuity and an annuity due, assume that a $15,000, 10%, three-year debt is incurred on April 1, Year 1. The debt is to be paid in three equal annual installments that include compound interest. Case A: Assume payments of $6,032 are to be made each March 31, for three annuity periods. This is an **ordinary annuity** because the payments are to be made at the **end** of each annuity period. Case B: Assume instead that payments of $5,483 are to be made April 1, Years 1, 2, and 3. This is an **annuity due** because the payments are to be made at the **beginning** of each interim annuity period. Notice the significant difference in the periodic payments (i.e., ordinary, $6,032 − due, $5,438 = $594). The annuity due involves less interest because each of the annual payments under the annuity due is paid one year earlier than under the ordinary annuity.

The characteristics and applications of the future value and present value of annuities are discussed and illustrated in the remainder of this chapter.

---

[4] These are sometimes called "standard or consistent" annuities. They conform to the formulas given in all annuity tables (e.g., Tables 5–3 and 5–4). In a broader sense, the term "annuities" often is used to refer to situations that involve principal and compound interest with periodic rents, but the interest rate, periodic rent, or interest periods, may be specified to change during the life of the annuity. These kinds of annuities require special computations.

FUTURE VALUE OF AN ANNUITY OF 1

The future value of an annuity, designated F herein, is the sum of all of its periodic rents **plus** the accumulated compound interest on each of those rents. The formula for the future value of an ordinary annuity is: $F_o = \dfrac{(1+i)^n - 1}{i}$.

If the rents are at the **end** of each annuity period, its future value is an ordinary annuity; if the rents are at the beginning of each annuity period, its future value is an annuity due. The difference between these two annuities is one period's compound interest. The timing of their respective rents is different by one period.

Exhibit 5–2 shows two time lines and compares the future value of an ordinary annuity with the future value of an annuity due of $1 at 10% compound interest for three annuity periods (and three rents). The symbol "F_o" is used to designate the future value of an **ordinary annuity** and "F_d" to designate an **annuity due.** Panel B of Exhibit 5–2 identifies the differences between F_o and F_d annuities.

Because of the difference in the timing of the periodic rents, the future value of the **ordinary annuity** illustrated in Exhibit 5–2 involves **three rents but only two compound interest periods.** In contrast, the **annuity due involves three rents and three interest periods.** Therefore, for each of the three annuity values illustrated, $F_o \times (1 + i) = F_d$. **This relationship means that if an F_o value is known, it can be multiplied by $(1 + i)$ to determine its comparable F_d value.**[5]

Determination of the Future Value of an Annuity of 1

The future value of an **ordinary** annuity can be determined by using any one of four approaches. To illustrate, assume rents of $1, $n = 3$, and $i = 10\%$. The four approaches, **each of which computes the future value as of the date of the last rent** (i.e., an ordinary annuity), are as follows:

1. Successive computations of the future value of 1 (Table 5–1):

Rent	×	Table value, "f"	=	F_o
1		$(n = 2; i = 10\%) = 1.210$	=	1.210
1		$(n = 1; i = 10\%) = 1.100$	=	1.100
1		$(n = 0; i = 10\%) = 1.00$	=	1.000
F_o—future value of ordinary annuity				3.310

---

[5] Another procedure frequently used when the **future value of an annuity due** is needed is to determine the future table value of an ordinary annuity for **one more rent** (i.e., $n + 1$) than the number of rents specified in the annuity problem, and then subtract 1.0 from that table value. The effect of this is to add one more period of compound interest while keeping the rents the same. This procedure frequently is expressed as: $(n + 1$ rents$) - 1.0$. If the **present value of an annuity due** is needed, the relationships are essentially the opposite; thus, the procedure is: $(n - 1$ rents$) + 1.0$. Calculators often are programmed to compute either an ordinary annuity or an annuity due.

EXHIBIT 5–2

Future Value of Ordinary Annuity Distinguished from Future Value of Annuity Due

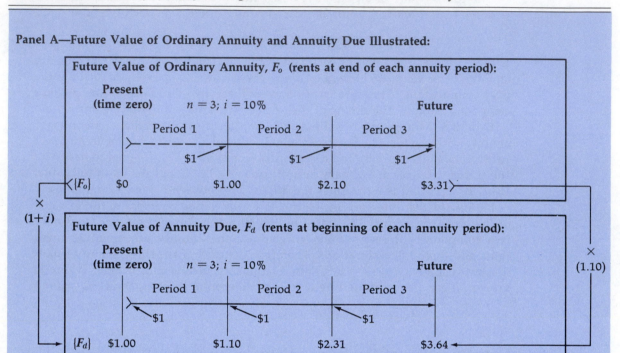

Panel A—Future Value of Ordinary Annuity and Annuity Due Illustrated:

Panel B—Future Value of Ordinary Annuity and Annuity Due Differentiated:

	Type of Future Value Annuity	
Characteristic	F_o—Ordinary	F_d—Due
1. Timing of each rent	End of each period	Beginning of each period
2. Number of rents (n)	Three} $n = 3$	Three} $n = 3$
3. Number of interest periods (j)	Two } $j = 2$	Three} $j = 3$
4. Point in time of the future value	On date of last rent	One interest period after the last rent

2. By formula:

$$F_o = \frac{(1+i)^n - 1}{i} = \frac{.331}{.10} = \underline{\underline{3.310}}$$

3. By using a prepared FV table of ordinary annuities:

Table 5–3, (n = 3; i = 10%) = 3.310, as of the date of the third and last rent.

4. Pocket calculator programmed for annuities:

Input: $n = 3$; $i = 10\%$, pmt. \$1; press FV $= \underline{\underline{3.310}}$

For all practical purposes, the last two approaches are used.

The future value of an **annuity due** usually is determined by (1) multiplying the comparable F_o value (Table 5–3) by $(1 + i)$, or (2) using a FV-programmed calculator that computes both ordinary and annuity due values.

Accounting Applications of Future Value of an Annuity of 1

Tables of future value of annuity of 1 are used to calculate the future value of a series of rents at a specific rate of compound interest. In most situations, the following are known: (1) the amount of the equal rent (R), (2) the number of rents *(n)*, and (3) the constant interest rate per period *(i)*. To determine the **future value,** the appropriate future value from Table 5–3 is multiplied by the amount of the periodic rent.

A typical accounting application of future value of an annuity is the accumulation of a fund by making equal annual contributions to it. Funds typically are established to be used in the future for such purposes as construction or expansion of a facility, or payment of a debt on its maturity date.

To illustrate the accumulation of such a fund, two cases will be presented. Case A is an ordinary annuity, and Case B is an annuity due (the usual situation for a fund).

Case A. On April 1, 19A, AB Company decided to accumulate a **fund** to pay a debt that matures on March 31, 19D. The company decided to deposit \$10,000 cash in this debt retirement fund each March 31, 19B, 19C, and 19D. The fund will earn 10% compound interest which will be added to the fund balance on March 31, 19C, and 19D. The company's accounting period ends December 31. Notice that the debt matures on the date of the **last** deposit, which is when the annuity terminates.

Required:
1. Is this an ordinary annuity or an annuity due?

   This is an ordinary annuity because the rents are deposited at the **end** of each of the three annuity periods. This is evident because the **last rent is deposited on the last day that the annuity is in existence**—March 31, 19D.

The time line for this **ordinary annuity** is:

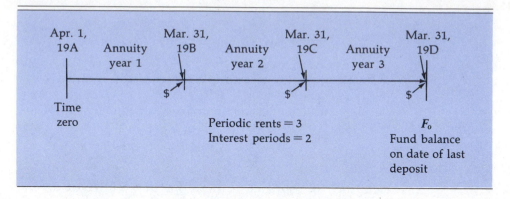

2. What amount will be in the fund at the end of the annuity's existence?

$$\$10,000 \times F_{o_{n=3;\ i=10\%}} \text{ (Table 5–3, 3.31000)} = \underline{\underline{\$33,100}}$$

3. Prepare the fund accumulation schedule.

			Fund	
Case A: Fund Accumulation Schedule—Ordinary Annuity				
Month and annuity year	**Cash deposit**	**Interest revenue**	**Change**	**Balance**
March 31, 19B	$10,000		+$10,000	$10,000
March 31, 19C	10,000	$10,000 × 10% = $1,000	+ 11,000	21,000
March 31, 19D	10,000	21,000 × 10% = 2,100	+ 12,100	33,100*
Totals	$30,000	$3,100	$33,100	

* Ordinary annuity balance, which is as of the date of the last deposit.

4. Give the journal entries required at each year-end, March 31.

	19B		19C		19D	
Debt retirement fund	10,000		11,000		12,100	
Cash		10,000		10,000		10,000
Interest revenue				1,000		2,100

5. Give the journal entry to record withdrawal of the fund balance on March 31, 19D.

Cash (or debt retired)	33,100	
Debt retirement fund		33,100

Case B. Assume the same facts as in Case A, except that the annual deposits are made at the beginning of each interim annuity period on April 1, 19A, 19B, and 19C.

Required:

1. Is this an ordinary annuity or an annuity due?

This is an annuity due because the rents are deposited at the beginning of each of the three annuity periods. This is evident because the last rent is deposited one interest period **prior** to the date on which the annuity ceases to exist, March 31, 19D.

The time line for this **annuity due** is:

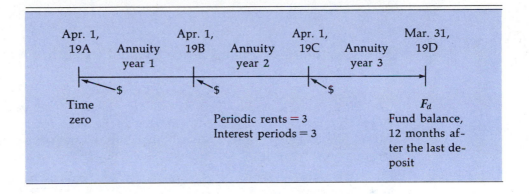

2. What amount will be in the fund at the end of the annuity's existence?

$10,000 \times F_{d_{n}=3;\ i=10\%}$ (Table 5–3, 3.31000, $\times$ 1.10 = 3.64100) = $36,410.

3. Prepare the fund accumulation schedule.

Case B: Fund Accumulation Schedule—Annuity Due

Month and annuity year	Cash deposit	Interest revenue	Fund Change	Fund Balance
April 1, 19A	$10,000		+$10,000	$10,000
March 31, 19B		$10,000 \times 10\% = $1,000	+ 1,000	11,000
April 1, 19B	10,000		+ 10,000	21,000
March 31, 19C		21,000 \times 10\% = 2,100	+ 2,100	23,100
April 1, 19C	10,000		+ 10,000	33,100
March 31, 19D		33,100 \times 10\% = 3,310	+ 3,310	36,410*
Totals	$30,000	$6,410	$36,410	

* Annuity due balance, which is 12 months after the last deposit.

4. Give the journal entries for this annuity due, for *(a)* April 1, 19A, and March 31, 19B, and *(b)* March 31, 19D, when the fund balance is withdrawn.

a. April 1, 19A:

Debt retirement fund	10,000	
Cash		10,000

March 31, 19B:

Debt retirement fund	1,000	
Interest revenue		1,000

b. March 31, 19D (maturity date):

Debt retirement fund	3,310	
Interest revenue		3,310
Cash (or debt retired)	36,410	
Debt retirement fund		36,410

Determination of Other Values Related to Future Value of an Ordinary Annuity

In the preceding example—Case A, ordinary annuity—**three** values were given: (1) periodic rent, $R = \$10,000$; (2) number of periodic rents, $n = 3$; and (3) periodic interest rate, $i = 10\%$. A fourth value, future value of an ordinary annuity was unknown; however, it was computed as follows:

$$\$10,000 \times F_{o_{n=3;\ i=10\%}} \text{ (Table 5–3, 3.31000)} = \underline{\underline{\$33,100}}.$$

Situations may be encountered when either the periodic rent *(R)*, interest rate *(i)*, or number of rents *(n)* is not known. If any three of the four variables are given, the fourth variable can be computed. Refer to the preceding example, Case A; determination of any value (other than the future value) can be computed as follows:[6]

1. Compute the periodic rent *(R):*

    Given: Future value of ordinary annuity, $33,100; $n = 3$; $i = 10\%$.

    $$R = \$33,100 \div F_{o_{n=3;\ i=10\%}} \text{ (Table 5–3, 3.310)} = \underline{\underline{\$10,000}}$$

2. Compute the periodic interest rate *(i):*

    Given: future value of ordinary annuity, $33,100; rent, $10,000; and $n = 3$.

    $33,100 \div \$10,000 = 3.310$, the Table 5–3 value for $n = 3$.

    Reference to the Table 5–3 **line** for $n = 3$ indicates a periodic interest rate of $\underline{\underline{10\%}}$. See the discussion below for an **annuity due.**

---

[6] The Case A data given above are used with one "given" changed in each instance to demonstrate the computational approaches and the correctness of the answers.

3. Compute the number of rents (n):

> Given: future value of an ordinary annuity, $33,100; rent, $10,000; and $i = 10\%$.

> $33,100 \div 10,000 = 3.310$, the Table 5–3 value for $i = 10\%$.

Reference to the Table 5–3 **column** for $i = 10\%$ indicates the number of rents to be 3. If this were an **annuity due,** the annuity due value would be divided by $(1 + i)$ to allow use of the ordinary annuity table.

PRESENT VALUE OF AN ANNUITY OF 1

The present value of an annuity, designated P herein, is the sum of all of the periodic rents **minus** the accumulated compound discount on each of those rents. The formula for the present value of an ordinary annuity is:

$$P_o = \frac{1 - \dfrac{1}{(1+i)^n}}{i}$$

If the rents are at the **end** of each annuity period, its present value is an ordinary annuity. If the rents are at the **beginning** of each interim annuity period, its present value is an annuity due. The difference between these two annuities is one period's compound discount because the timing of their respective rents is different by one period.

Exhibit 5–3 shows two time lines and compares the present value of an ordinary annuity with an annuity due of $1 at 10%. The symbol P_o is used to designate the present value of an **ordinary annuity** and P_d designates an **annuity due.** Panel B of Exhibit 5–3 identifies the four differences between P_o and P_d annuities.

Because of the difference in the timing of the periodic rents, the value of the **ordinary annuity** illustrated in Exhibit 5–3 involves **three rents and three interest discount periods.** In contrast, **the annuity due involves three rents but only two discount periods.** The annuity due is discounted for one less period than the ordinary annuity, which means that the ordinary annuity amount will be **less** than the comparable annuity due amount by $(1 + i)$; therefore, $P_o \times (1 + i) = P_d$. This relationship means that if a P_o value is known, it can be multiplied by $(1 + i)$ to determine its comparable P_d value. To repeat for emphasis, the P_d amount is more than the P_o amount because there is discounting for one less period.

Determination of the Present Value of an Annuity

The present value of an **ordinary annuity** can be determined by (1) successive discounting (using Table 5–2 p values), (2) by formula (see Table 5–4), (3) using

EXHIBIT 5–3

Present Value of Ordinary Annuity Distinguished from Present Value of Annuity Due

Panel A—Present Value of Ordinary Annuity and Annuity Due Illustrated:

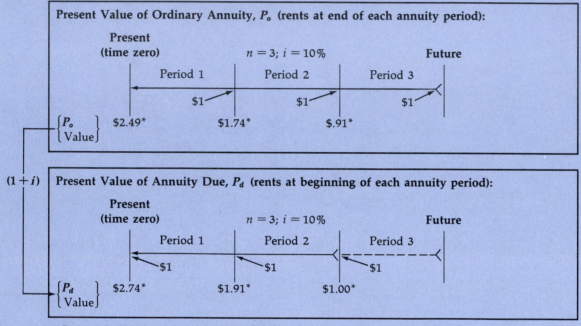

* Present values of the annuity on the date indicated.

Panel B—Present Value of Ordinary Annuity and Annuity Due Differentiated:

Characteristic	P_o—Ordinary	P_d—Due
1. Timing of each rent	End of each interim period	Beginning of each interim period
2. Number of rents (n)	Three $\quad n = 3$	Three $\quad n = 3$
3. Number of interest periods (j)	Three $\quad j = 3$	Two $\quad j = 2$
4. Point in time of the first rent	End of first interest period	Present date

a prepared present value of annuity of 1 table, such as Table 5–4, or (4) a PV-programmed calculator.

The present value of an **annuity due** usually is determined by: (1) multiplying the related "P_o" value (Table 5–4) by $(1 + i)$, or (2) a PV-programmed calculator that provides annuity due results.

Accounting Applications of Present Value of an Annuity of 1

Tables of present value of an annuity of 1 are used to calculate the present value of a series of future rents at a specific compound discount rate. In most cases, the following variables are known: (1) the amount of each equal rent (R), (2) the number of rents (n), and (3) the constant rate of interest per interest period (i). To determine the **present value** in a specific situation, the appropriate present value factor from Table 5–4 is multiplied by the amount of the periodic rent.

An accounting application of the present value of an annuity is the payment of a debt (incurred to purchase an asset on credit) in equal future installments (i.e., an annuity).

To illustrate such a situation, two cases will be presented. Case C is an ordinary annuity, and Case D is an annuity due.

Case C. On April 1, 19A, CD Company owed a $15,000 liability (a present value amount). Because of CD's liquidity problem, the creditor agreed to allow CD Company to pay the debt in three equal installments at 10% compound interest. The payments of $6,032 are payable March 31, 19B, 19C, and 19D.

Required:

1. Is this an ordinary annuity or an annuity due? Explain.

   This is an ordinary annuity because the rents are payable at year-end; the first payment is to be made 12 months after the debt was incurred.

   The time line for this **ordinary** annuity is:

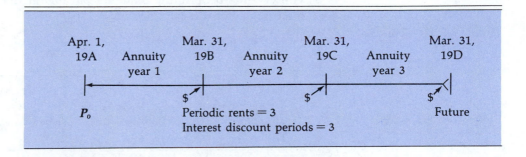

2. What is the present value of the three rents?

$$\$6,032 \times P_{o_{n=3;\ i=10\%}} \text{ (Table 5–4, 2.48685)} = \underline{\$15,000}$$

3. How was the amount of each equal annual payment computed?

$$\$15,000 \div P_{o_{n=3;\ i=10\%}} \text{ (Table 5–4, 2.48685)} = \underline{\$6,032}$$

4. Prepare the debt payment schedule.

Case C: Debt Amortization Schedule—Ordinary Annuity

Month and annuity year	Cash payment	Interest expense	Liability Change	Balance
April 1, 19A				$15,000
March 31, 19B	$ 6,032	$15,000 × 10% = $1,500	− $ 4,532	10,468
March 31, 19C	6,032	10,468 × 10% = 1,047	− 4,985	5,483
March 31, 19D	6,032	5,483 × 10% = 549*	− 5,483	−0−
Totals	$18,096	$3,096	$15,000	

* Rounded to come out even.

5. Give the entries required on each March 31.

	19B	19C	19D
Interest expense..........	1,500	1,047	549
Liability	4,532	4,985	5,483
Cash	6,032	6,032	6,032

Case D. Assume the same facts as in Case C, except that three equal annual payments of $5,483 are to be made on each April 1, years 19A, 19B, and 19C.

Required:

1. Is this an ordinary annuity or an annuity due? Explain.

   This is an annuity due because the rents are payable at the beginning of each year; the first payment is paid immediately.

   The time line for this annuity due is:

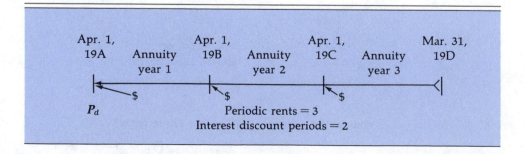

2. What is the present value of the three rents?

   $5,483 × P_{d_n =3; i =10\%}$ (Table 5–4, 2.48685; × 1.10 = 2.73554) = $15,000.

$$\$5{,}483 \times P_{d_n =3;\ i =10\%}\ (\text{Table 5–4, 2.48685};\ \times\ 1.10 = 2.73554) = \underline{\underline{\$15{,}000}}.$$

3. How was the amount of each equal annual payment computed?

$$\$15,000 \div P_{d_{n}=3;\ i=10\%}\ (2.73554, \text{ per 2 above}) = \$5,483$$

4. Prepare the debt amortization schedule.

Case D: Debt Amortization Schedule—Annuity Due Basis

Date	Cash payment	Interest expense	Liability Change	Balance
April 1, 19A........				$15,000
April 1, 19A........	$ 5,483		−$ 5,483	9,517
March 31, 19B......		$9,517 × 10% = $ 952	+ 952	10,469
April 1, 19B	5,483		− 5,483	4,986
March 31, 19C		4,986 × 10% = 497*	+ 497	5,483
April 1, 19C........	5,483		− 5,483	–0–
Totals	$16,449	$1,449	$15,000	

* Rounded to come out even.

5. Give the entries required on each April 1 and March 31.

April 1:	19A	19B	19C
Liability	5,483	5,483	5,483
Cash	5,483	5,483	5,483

March 31:		19B	19C
Interest expense		952	497
Liability		952	497

DETERMINATION OF OTHER VALUES RELATED TO AN ANNUITY DUE

Determination of any **implicit interest rate** that involves an **annuity due** is more complex when only ordinary annuity tables are available. Ordinary annuity tables can be used because the only difference is one period's compound interest (if FV) or compound discount (if PV). To illustrate, assume an overdue debt of $83,398 will be paid in five equal installments of $20,000 each. The first payment is to be paid immediately; therefore, this involves the **PV of an annuity due**. What is the implicit compound interest rate?

Solution:

$83,398 ÷ $20,000 = 4.1699, table value for PV of an annuity due, $n = 5$; $i = ?$

To use a PV ordinary annuity table: Subtract 1.0 from the annuity due value (i.e., 4.1699 − 1.0 = 3.1699; this gets the correct interest accumulation), then read on line $n − 1$ (i.e., 5 periods − 1 period = 4 periods).

Reference to Table 5–4 on line $n = 4$ shows 3.16987 under 10%; therefore, the approximate interest rate is 10% (reread footnote 5).

Proof: $20,000 $\times P_{d_{n=5;\ i=10\%}}$ (Table 5–4, 3.79079; × 1.10 = 4.16987)
   = $83,398 (rounded).

If the problem involves the **future value of an annuity due,** the procedure is the opposite. That is, to use an ordinary FV annuity table, add 1.0 to the annuity due value, then read on line $n + 1$ to get the implicit interest rate.

USING MULTIPLE PRESENT AND FUTURE VALUE AMOUNTS

There are situations that require the application of two or more future or present value amounts (i.e., table values for *f, p, F,* and *P*). Problems that use two or more of these values require a careful analysis of the situation and a precise knowledge of what each "table" value means.

Two situations are given below, with solutions, to illustrate the application of multiple future and present values.

Situation 1—On January 1, 19A, TG Company deposited $100,000 in a special fund to provide five annual equal payments in the future to Employee Doe who was injured while working. The fund will earn 11%, which will increase the fund starting on December 31, 19A. Doe is to receive the five annual payments each January 1, starting in 19E, the year in which Doe will retire.

Required:
1. Compute the amount of the annual payments that Doe will receive.
2. Prepare a fund schedule for the period January 1, 19A, through January 1, 19I.

Solution:
Requirement 1 (diagrammed for instructional purposes and computation):

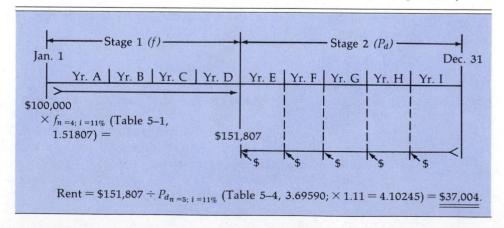

Rent = $151,807 ÷ $P_{d_{n=5;\ i=11\%}}$ (Table 5–4, 3.69590; × 1.11 = 4.10245) = $37,004.

Requirement 2:

Fund Schedule

Date	Interest revenue	Fund change	Fund balance
January 1, 19A	Single deposit	+$100,000	$100,000
December 31, 19A	$100,000 × 11% = $11,000	+ 11,000	111,000
December 31, 19B	$111,000 × 11% = 12,210	+ 12,210	123,210
December 31, 19C	$123,210 × 11% = 13,553	+ 13,553	136,763
December 31, 19D	$136,763 × 11% = 15,044	+ 15,044	151,807
January 1, 19E	Payment	− 37,004	114,803
December 31, 19E	$114,803 × 11% = 12,628	+ 12,628	127,431
January 1, 19F	Payment	− 37,004	90,427
December 31, 19F	$ 90,427 × 11% = 9,947	+ 9,947	100,374
January 1, 19G	Payment	− 37,004	63,370
December 31, 19G	$ 63,370 × 11% = 6,971	+ 6,971	70,341
January 1, 19H	Payment	− 37,004	33,337
December 31, 19H	$ 33,337 × 11% = 3,667	+ 3,667	37,004
January 1, 19I	Payment	− 37,004	–0–

Situation 2—ST Construction Company is negotiating to purchase 4 acres of land with a deposit of gravel that is suitable for exploitation. ST Company and the seller are negotiating the price. ST Company has completed an extensive study that provided reliable estimates as follows:

Expected net cash revenues over life of resource:	
End of year 1	$ 5,000
End of years 2–5 (per year)	30,000
End of years 6–9 (per year)	40,000
End of year 10 (last year—resource exhausted)	10,000
Estimated sales value of 4 acres after exploitation and net of land-leveling costs (end of 10th year)	2,000

Required:
   Compute the amount ST Construction Company should offer for the land assuming it expects a 12 percent return on the investment. Assume all amounts are at year-end and that the above amounts are net of income taxes.

Solution:
   This problem requires computation of the present value of the future expected cash inflows.
   The amount that should be offered is the sum of the present values of the

net cash revenues for the various years. The complexity in this situation arises because *(a)* $5,000 for year 1, $10,000 for year 10, and the $2,000 estimated value at the end of year 10 involve use of the present value of 1 concept; and *(b)* the equal annual revenues for years 2–5 and 6–9 involve the use of the present value of two different annuities.

Complex situations such as this one demonstrate the need to diagram most future and present value situations in terms of *(a)* the timing of the resource flows (rents), *(b)* the interest assumptions, and *(c)* the value to be derived. Moreover, this problem also illustrates the three basic decisions that must be made to solve all future and present value problems:

1. Identification of whether the situation involves future value or present value concepts.
2. Identification of whether the situation involves a single sum or an annuity. Situations often involve single sums and annuities in combination.
3. If the situation involves an annuity, do the rents occur at the end of each annuity period (an ordinary annuity) or at the beginning of each period (an annuity due)? Situations may involve ordinary annuities and annuities due in combination.

For ST Company the primary focus is on **present value** because future cash inflows are provided and the amount that the company should be willing to pay is the present value of those future expected cash inflows. Because equal future cash inflows are expected for years 2–5 and 6–9, two **annuities** are involved. Because these two cash inflows are assumed to be at year-end, annuities are ordinary.

Because of its complexities, this problem is best solved in two steps, one for each element in the solution, as follows:

Step 1—Prepare a time-line diagram, which reveals the *(a)* timing of the resource flows, *(b)* interest assumption, and *(c)* value to be derived. A time-line diagram of this situation can be drawn as follows:

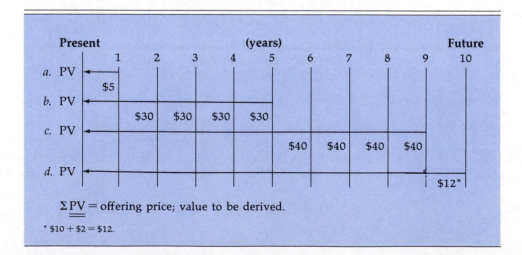

Step 2—Compute the present values of each annuity and single-sum amounts in order:

PV Item	Computation	Present value
a.	Year 1—PV of a single sum:	
	$5,000 $\times p_{n=1;\ i=12\%}$ (Table 5–2, .89286).	$ 4,464
b.	Years 2–5—PV of ordinary annuity, deferred one year:	
	$30,000 $\times (P_{o_{n=5;\ i=12\%}} - P_{o_{n=1;\ i=12\%}})$ (Table 5–4) [3.60478 $(n=5)$ − .89286 $(n=1)$] = 2.71192	81,358
c.	Years 6–9—PV of ordinary annuity, deferred 5 years:	
	$40,000 $\times P_{o_{n=9;\ i=12\%}} - P_{o_{n=5;\ i=12\%}}$) (Table 5–4) [5.32825 $(n=9)$ − 3.60478	68,939
	$(n=5)$] = 1.72347	
	* Subtract 5 for the five year deferral.	
d.	Year 10—PV of a single sum:	
	($10,000 + $2,000) $\times p_{n=10;\ i=12\%}$ (Table 5–2, .32197)	3,864
	Offering price (PV of all future cash flows)	$158,625

SUMMARY OF CONCEPTS

This chapter has presented the concepts of future and present value. It has illustrated their relevance in certain accounting problems. At the beginning of the chapter, the primary accounting applications were listed. Those applications often are required to conform to GAAP. Because of the wide range of accounting applications, accountants need a thorough understanding of FV and PV concepts. These concepts also have considerable relevance in financial analyses, capital budgeting, and alternative choice problems which accountants often encounter in public, private, and governmental accounting. Throughout the later chapters, and in subsequent business administration courses, the concepts of present and future value are widely used.

A summary of the interest concepts discussed in this chapter is presented on page 272.

Summary of Interest Concepts

Title	Symbol	Basic concept summarized	Formula	Table	Illustrative table values $n = 5; i = 10\%$	$n = 6; i = 10\%$
Simple interest	i	Interest on principal only regardless of any prior accrued interest.	$P \times i \times n$	—	—	—
FV of 1	f	FV of a single principal amount increased by compound interest i for n periods.	$(1+i)^n$	5–1	1.61051 (always more than 1)	1.77156 (more by compound i for 1 period)
PV of 1	p	PV of a single principal amount decreased by compound discount i for n periods. A reciprocal of FV of 1.	$\dfrac{1}{(1+i)^n}$	5–2	.62092 (always less than 1)	.56447 (less by i discount for 1 period)
FV of annuity of 1: Ordinary annuity	F_o	FV of a series of n equal **end-of-period** rents at compound interest i. One less interest period than rents.	$\dfrac{(1+i)^n - 1}{i}$	5–3	6.10510 (always more than sum of rents)	7.71561 (more by 1 rent, plus compound interest for 1 period)
Annuity due	F_d	FV of a n series of equal **beginning-of-period** rents at compound interest i. Same number of interest periods as rents.	$\dfrac{(1+i)^n - 1}{i} \times (1+i)$	$F_o \times (1+i)$	6.71561 (6.10510 × 1.10)	8.48717 (7.71561 × 1.10)
PV of annuity of 1: Ordinary annuity	P_o	PV of a series of n equal **end-of-period** rents in the future decreased at compound discount i. Same number of interest periods as rents.	$\dfrac{1 - \dfrac{1}{(1+i)^n}}{i}$	5–4	3.79079 (always less than sum of rents)	4.35526 (more by 1 rent, less discount for 1 period)
Annuity due	P_d	PV of a series of n equal **beginning-of-period** rents in the future decreased at compound discount i. One less interest period than rents.	$\dfrac{1 - \dfrac{1}{(1+i)^n}}{i} \times (1+i)$	$P_o \times (1+i)$	4.16987 (3.79079 × 1.10)	4.79079 (4.35526 × 1.10)

$$FV = (PV)\left(TV_1 \begin{matrix} N=5 \\ i=10\% \end{matrix}\right)$$

TABLE 5–1
Future Value of 1, $f = (1 + i)^n$

Periods	2%	2½%	3%	4%	5%	6%	7%	8%	9%	10%
1	1.02000	1.02500	1.03000	1.04000	1.05000	1.06000	1.07000	1.08000	1.09000	1.10000
2	1.04040	1.05063	1.06090	1.08160	1.10250	1.12360	1.14490	1.16640	1.18810	1.21000
3	1.06121	1.07689	1.09273	1.12486	1.15763	1.19102	1.22504	1.25971	1.29503	1.33100
4	1.08243	1.10381	1.12551	1.16986	1.21551	1.26248	1.31080	1.36049	1.41158	1.46410
5	1.10408	1.13141	1.15927	1.21665	1.27628	1.33823	1.40255	1.46933	1.53862	1.61051
6	1.12616	1.15969	1.19405	1.26532	1.34010	1.41852	1.50073	1.58687	1.67710	1.77156
7	1.14869	1.18869	1.22987	1.31593	1.40710	1.50363	1.60578	1.71382	1.82804	1.94872
8	1.17166	1.21840	1.26677	1.36857	1.47746	1.59385	1.71819	1.85093	1.99256	2.14359
9	1.19509	1.24886	1.30477	1.42331	1.55133	1.68948	1.83846	1.99900	2.17189	2.35795
10	1.21899	1.28008	1.34392	1.48024	1.62889	1.79085	1.96715	2.15892	2.36736	2.59374
11	1.24337	1.31209	1.38423	1.53945	1.71034	1.89830	2.10485	2.33164	2.58043	2.85312
12	1.26824	1.34489	1.42576	1.60103	1.79586	2.01220	2.25219	2.51817	2.81266	3.13843
13	1.29361	1.37851	1.46853	1.66507	1.88565	2.13293	2.40985	2.71962	3.06580	3.45227
14	1.31948	1.41297	1.51259	1.73168	1.97993	2.26090	2.57853	2.93719	3.34173	3.79750
15	1.34587	1.44830	1.55797	1.80094	2.07893	2.39656	2.75903	3.17217	3.64248	4.17725
16	1.37279	1.48451	1.60471	1.87298	2.18287	2.54035	2.95216	3.42594	3.97031	4.59497
17	1.40024	1.52162	1.65285	1.94790	2.29202	2.69277	3.15882	3.70002	4.32763	5.05447
18	1.42825	1.55966	1.70243	2.02582	2.40662	2.85434	3.37993	3.99602	4.71712	5.55992
19	1.45681	1.59865	1.75351	2.10685	2.52695	3.02560	3.61653	4.31570	5.14166	6.11591
20	1.48595	1.63862	1.80611	2.19112	2.65330	3.20714	3.86968	4.66096	5.60441	6.72750
21	1.51567	1.67958	1.86029	2.27877	2.78596	3.39956	4.14056	5.03383	6.10881	7.40025
22	1.54598	1.72157	1.91610	2.36992	2.92526	3.60354	4.43040	5.43654	6.65860	8.14027
23	1.57690	1.76461	1.97359	2.46472	3.07152	3.81975	4.74053	5.87146	7.25787	8.95430
24	1.60844	1.80873	2.03279	2.56330	3.22510	4.04893	5.07237	6.34118	7.91108	9.84973
25	1.64061	1.85394	2.09378	2.66584	3.38635	4.29187	5.42743	6.84848	8.62308	10.83471

Periods	11%	12%	14%	15%	16%	18%	20%	22%	24%	25%
1	1.11000	1.12000	1.14000	1.15000	1.16000	1.18000	1.20000	1.22000	1.24000	1.25000
2	1.23210	1.25440	1.29960	1.32250	1.34560	1.39240	1.44000	1.48840	1.53760	1.56250
3	1.36763	1.40493	1.48154	1.52088	1.56090	1.64303	1.72800	1.81585	1.90662	1.95313
4	1.51807	1.57352	1.68896	1.74901	1.81064	1.93878	2.07360	2.21533	2.36421	2.44141
5	1.68506	1.76234	1.92541	2.01136	2.10034	2.28776	2.48832	2.70271	2.93163	3.05176
6	1.87041	1.97382	2.19497	2.31306	2.43640	2.69955	2.98598	3.29730	3.63522	3.81470
7	2.07616	2.21068	2.50227	2.66002	2.82622	3.18547	3.58318	4.02271	4.50767	4.76837
8	2.30454	2.47596	2.85259	3.05902	3.27841	3.75886	4.29982	4.90771	5.58951	5.96046
9	2.55804	2.77308	3.25195	3.51788	3.80296	4.43545	5.15978	5.98740	6.93099	7.45058
10	2.83942	3.10585	3.70722	4.04556	4.41144	5.23384	6.19174	7.30463	8.59443	9.31323
11	3.15176	3.47855	4.22623	4.65239	5.11726	6.17593	7.43008	8.91165	10.65709	11.64153
12	3.49845	3.89598	4.81790	5.35025	5.93603	7.28759	8.91610	10.87221	13.21479	14.55192
13	3.88328	4.36349	5.49241	6.15279	6.88579	8.59936	10.69932	13.26410	16.38634	18.18989
14	4.31044	4.88711	6.26135	7.07571	7.98752	10.14724	12.83918	16.18220	20.31906	22.73737
15	4.78459	5.47357	7.13794	8.13706	9.26552	11.97375	15.40702	19.74229	25.19563	28.42171
16	5.31089	6.13039	8.13725	9.35762	10.74800	14.12902	18.48843	24.08559	31.24259	35.52714
17	5.89509	6.86604	9.27646	10.76126	12.46768	16.67225	22.18611	29.38442	38.74081	44.40892
18	6.54355	7.68997	10.57517	12.37545	14.46251	19.67325	26.62333	35.84899	48.03860	55.51115
19	7.26334	8.61276	12.05569	14.23177	16.77652	23.21444	31.94800	43.73577	59.56786	69.38894
20	8.06231	9.64629	13.74349	16.36654	19.46076	27.39303	38.33760	53.35764	73.86415	86.73617
21	8.94917	10.80385	15.66758	18.82152	22.57448	32.32378	46.00512	65.09632	91.59155	108.42022
22	9.93357	12.10031	17.86104	21.64475	26.18640	38.14206	55.20614	79.41751	113.57352	135.52527
23	11.02627	13.55235	20.36158	24.89146	30.37622	45.00763	66.24737	96.88936	140.83116	169.40659
24	12.23916	15.17863	23.21221	28.62518	35.23642	53.10901	79.49685	118.20502	174.63064	211.75824
25	13.58546	17.00006	26.46192	32.91895	40.87424	62.66863	95.39622	144.21013	216.54199	264.69780

TABLE 5–2

Present Value of 1, $p = \dfrac{1}{(1+i)^n}$

Periods	2%	2½%	3%	4%	5%	6%	7%	8%	9%	10%
1	.98039	.97561	.97087	.96154	.95238	.94340	.93458	.92593	.91743	.90909
2	.96117	.95181	.94260	.92456	.90703	.89000	.87344	.85734	.84168	.82645
3	.94232	.92860	.91514	.88900	.86384	.83962	.81630	.79383	.77218	.75131
4	.92385	.90595	.88849	.85480	.82270	.79209	.76290	.73503	.70843	.68301
5	.90573	.88385	.86261	.82193	.78353	.74726	.71299	.68058	.64993	.62092
6	.88797	.86230	.83748	.79031	.74622	.70496	.66634	.63017	.59627	.56447
7	.87056	.84127	.81309	.75992	.71068	.66506	.62275	.58349	.54703	.51316
8	.85349	.82075	.78941	.73069	.67684	.62741	.58201	.54027	.50187	.46651
9	.83676	.80073	.76642	.70259	.64461	.59190	.54393	.50025	.46043	.42410
10	.82035	.78120	.74409	.67556	.61391	.55839	.50835	.46319	.42241	.38554
11	.80426	.76214	.72242	.64958	.58468	.52679	.47509	.42888	.38753	.35049
12	.78849	.74356	.70138	.62460	.55684	.49697	.44401	.39711	.35553	.31863
13	.77303	.72542	.68095	.60057	.53032	.46884	.41496	.36770	.32618	.28966
14	.75788	.70773	.66112	.57748	.50507	.44230	.38782	.34046	.29925	.26333
15	.74301	.69047	.64186	.55526	.48102	.41727	.36245	.31524	.27454	.23939
16	.72845	.67362	.62317	.53391	.45811	.39365	.33873	.29189	.25187	.21763
17	.71416	.65720	.60502	.51337	.43630	.37136	.31657	.27027	.23107	.19784
18	.70016	.64117	.58739	.49363	.41552	.35034	.29586	.25025	.21199	.17986
19	.68643	.62553	.57029	.47464	.39573	.33051	.27651	.23171	.19449	.16351
20	.67297	.61027	.55368	.45639	.37689	.31180	.25842	.21455	.17843	.14864
21	.65978	.59539	.53755	.43883	.35894	.29416	.24151	.19866	.16370	.13513
22	.64684	.58086	.52189	.42196	.34185	.27751	.22571	.18394	.15018	.12285
23	.63416	.56670	.50669	.40573	.32557	.26180	.21095	.17032	.13778	.11168
24	.62172	.55288	.49193	.39012	.31007	.24698	.19715	.15770	.12640	.10153
25	.60953	.53939	.47761	.37512	.29530	.23300	.18425	.14602	.11597	.09230

Periods	11%	12%	14%	15%	16%	18%	20%	22%	24%	25%
1	.90090	.89286	.87719	.86957	.86207	.84746	.83333	.81967	.80645	.80000
2	.81162	.79719	.76947	.75614	.74316	.71818	.69444	.67186	.65036	.64000
3	.73119	.71178	.67497	.65752	.64066	.60863	.57870	.55071	.52449	.51200
4	.65873	.63552	.59208	.57175	.55229	.51579	.48225	.45140	.42297	.40960
5	.59345	.56743	.51937	.49718	.47611	.43711	.40188	.37000	.34111	.32768
6	.53464	.50663	.45559	.43233	.41044	.37043	.33490	.30328	.27509	.26214
7	.48166	.45235	.39964	.37594	.35383	.31393	.27908	.24859	.22184	.20972
8	.43393	.40388	.35056	.32690	.30503	.26604	.23257	.20376	.17891	.16777
9	.39092	.36061	.30751	.28426	.26295	.22546	.19381	.16702	.14428	.13422
10	.35218	.32197	.26974	.24718	.22668	.19106	.16151	.13690	.11635	.10737
11	.31728	.28748	.23662	.21494	.19542	16192	.13459	.11221	.09383	.08590
12	.28584	.25668	.20756	.18691	.16846	.13722	.11216	.09198	.07567	.06872
13	.25751	.22917	.18207	.16253	.14523	.11629	.09346	.07539	.06103	.05498
14	.23199	.20462	.15971	.14133	.12520	.09855	.07789	.06180	.04921	.04398
15	.20900	.18270	.14010	.12289	.10793	.08352	.06491	.05065	.03969	.03518
16	.18829	.16312	.12289	.10686	.09304	.07078	.05409	.04152	.03201	.02815
17	.16963	.14564	.10780	.09293	.08021	.05998	.04507	.03403	.02581	.02252
18	.15282	.13004	.09456	.08081	.06914	.05083	.03756	.02789	.02082	.01801
19	.13768	.11611	.08295	.07027	.05961	.04308	.03130	.02286	.01679	.01441
20	.12403	.10367	.07276	.06110	.05139	.03651	.02608	.01874	.01354	.01153
21	.11174	.09256	.06383	.05313	.04430	.03094	.02174	.01536	.01092	.00922
22	.10067	.08264	.05599	.04620	.03819	.02622	.01811	.01259	.00880	.00738
23	.09069	.07379	.04911	.04017	.03292	.02222	.01509	.01032	.00710	.00590
24	.08170	.06588	.04308	.03493	.02838	.01883	.01258	.00846	.00573	.00472
25	.07361	.05882	.03779	.03038	.02447	.01596	.01048	.00693	.00462	.00378

TABLE 5–3

Future Value of Annuity of n Rents of 1 Each (Ordinary), $F_o = \dfrac{(1+i)^n - 1}{i}$

Periodic Rents (n)	2%	2½%	3%	4%	5%	6%	7%	8%	9%	10%
1	1.00000	1.00000	1.00000	1.00000	1.00000	1.00000	1.00000	1.00000	1.00000	1.00000
2	2.02000	2.02500	2.03000	2.04000	2.05000	2.06000	2.07000	2.08000	2.09000	2.10000
3	3.06040	3.07563	3.09090	3.12160	3.15250	3.18360	3.21490	3.24640	3.27810	3.31000
4	4.12161	4.15252	4.18363	4.24646	4.31013	4.37462	4.43994	4.50611	4.57313	4.64100
5	5.20404	5.25633	5.30914	5.41632	5.52563	5.63709	5.75074	5.86660	5.98471	6.10510
6	6.30812	6.38774	6.46841	6.63298	6.80191	6.97532	7.15329	7.33593	7.52333	7.71561
7	7.43428	7.54753	7.66246	7.89829	8.14201	8.39384	8.65402	8.92280	9.20043	9.48717
8	8.58297	8.73612	8.89234	9.21423	9.54911	9.89747	10.25980	10.63663	11.02847	11.43589
9	9.75463	9.95452	10.15911	10.58280	11.02656	11.49132	11.97799	12.48756	13.02104	13.57948
10	10.94972	11.20338	11.46388	12.00611	12.57789	13.18079	13.81645	14.48656	15.19293	15.93742
11	12.16872	12.48347	12.80780	13.48635	14.20679	14.97164	15.78360	16.64549	17.56029	18.53117
12	13.41209	13.79555	14.19203	15.02581	15.91713	16.86994	17.88845	18.97713	20.14072	21.38428
13	14.68033	15.14044	15.61779	16.62684	17.71298	18.88214	20.14064	21.49530	22.95338	24.52271
14	15.97394	16.51895	17.08632	18.29191	19.59863	21.01507	22.55049	24.21492	26.01919	27.97498
15	17.29342	17.93193	18.59891	20.02359	21.57856	23.27597	25.12902	27.15211	29.36092	31.77248
16	18.63929	19.38022	20.15688	21.82453	23.65749	25.67253	27.88805	30.32428	33.00340	35.94973
17	20.01207	20.86473	21.76159	23.69751	25.84037	28.21288	30.84022	33.75023	36.97370	40.54470
18	21.41231	22.38635	23.41444	25.64541	28.13238	30.90565	33.99903	37.45024	41.30134	45.59917
19	22.84056	23.94601	25.11687	27.67123	30.53900	33.75999	37.37896	41.44626	46.01846	51.15909
20	24.29737	25.54466	26.87037	29.77808	33.06595	36.78559	40.99549	45.76196	51.16012	57.27500
21	25.78332	27.18327	28.67649	31.96920	35.71925	39.99273	44.86518	50.42292	56.76453	64.00250
22	27.29898	28.86286	30.53678	34.24797	38.50521	43.39229	49.00574	55.45676	62.87334	71.40275
23	28.84496	30.58443	32.45288	36.61789	41.43048	46.99583	53.43614	60.89330	69.53194	79.54302
24	30.42186	32.34904	34.42647	39.08260	44.50200	50.81558	58.17667	66.76476	76.78981	88.49733
25	32.03030	34.15776	36.45926	41.64591	47.72710	54.86451	63.24904	73.10594	84.70090	98.34706

Periodic Rents (n)	11%	12%	14%	15%	16%	18%	20%	22%	24%	25%
1	1.00000	1.00000	1.00000	1.00000	1.00000	1.00000	1.00000	1.00000	1.00000	1.00000
2	2.11000	2.12000	2.14000	2.15000	2.16000	2.18000	2.20000	2.22000	2.24000	2.25000
3	3.34210	3.37440	3.43960	3.47250	3.50560	3.57240	3.64000	3.70840	3.77760	3.81250
4	4.70973	4.77933	4.92114	4.99338	5.06650	5.21543	5.36800	5.52425	5.68422	5.76563
5	6.22780	6.35285	6.61010	6.74238	6.87714	7.15421	7.44160	7.73958	8.04844	8.20703
6	7.91286	8.11519	8.53552	8.75374	8.97748	9.44197	9.92992	10.44229	10.98006	11.25879
7	9.78327	10.08901	10.73049	11.06680	11.41387	12.14152	12.91590	13.73959	14.61528	15.07349
8	11.85943	12.29969	13.23276	13.72682	14.24009	15.32700	16.49908	17.76231	19.12294	19.84186
9	14.16397	14.77566	16.08535	16.78584	17.51851	19.08585	20.79890	22.67001	24.71245	25.80232
10	16.72201	17.54874	19.33730	20.30372	21.32147	23.52131	25.95868	28.65742	31.64344	33.25290
11	19.56143	20.65458	23.04452	24.34928	25.73290	28.75514	32.15042	35.96205	40.23787	42.56613
12	22.71319	24.13313	27.27075	29.00167	30.85017	34.93107	39.58050	44.87370	50.89495	54.20766
13	26.21164	28.02911	32.08865	34.35192	36.78620	42.21866	48.49660	55.74591	64.10974	68.75958
14	30.09492	32.39260	37.58107	40.50471	43.67199	50.81802	59.19592	69.01001	80.49608	86.94947
15	34.40536	37.27971	43.84241	47.58041	51.65951	60.96527	72.03511	85.19221	100.81514	109.68684
16	39.18995	42.75328	50.98035	55.71747	60.92503	72.93901	87.44213	104.93450	126.01077	138.10855
17	44.50084	48.88367	59.11760	65.07509	71.67303	87.06804	105.93056	129.02009	157.25336	173.63568
18	50.39594	55.74971	68.39407	75.83636	84.14072	103.74028	128.11667	158.40451	195.99416	218.04460
19	56.93949	63.43968	78.96923	88.21181	98.60323	123.41353	154.74000	194.25350	244.03276	273.55576
20	64.20283	72.05244	91.02493	102.44358	115.37975	146.62797	186.68800	237.98927	303.60062	342.94470
21	72.26514	81.69874	104.76842	118.81012	134.84051	174.02100	225.02560	291.34691	377.46477	429.68087
22	81.21431	92.50258	120.43600	137.63164	157.41499	206.34479	271.03072	356.44323	469.05632	538.10109
23	91.14788	104.60289	138.29704	159.27638	183.60138	244.48685	326.23686	435.86075	582.62984	673.62636
24	102.17415	118.15524	158.65862	184.16784	213.97761	289.49448	392.48424	532.75011	723.46100	843.03295
25	114.41331	133.33387	181.87083	212.79302	249.21402	342.60349	471.98108	650.95513	898.09164	1054.79118

Pymt

TABLE 5–4

Present Value of Annuity of n Rents of 1 Each (Ordinary), $P_o = \dfrac{1 - \dfrac{1}{(1+i)^n}}{i}$

Periodic Rents (n)	2%	2½%	3%	4%	5%	6%	7%	8%	9%	10%
1	.98039	.97561	.97087	.96154	.95238	.94340	.93458	.92593	.91743	.90909
2	1.94156	1.92742	1.91347	1.88609	1.85941	1.83339	1.80802	1.78326	1.75911	1.73554
3	2.88388	2.85602	2.82861	2.77509	2.72325	2.67301	2.62432	2.57710	2.53129	2.48685
4	3.80773	3.76197	3.71710	3.62990	3.54595	3.46511	3.38721	3.31213	3.23972	3.16987
5	4.71346	4.64583	4.57971	4.45182	4.32948	4.21236	4.10020	3.99271	3.88965	3.79079
6	5.60143	5.50813	5.41719	5.24214	5.07569	4.91732	4.76654	4.62288	4.48592	4.35526
7	6.47199	6.34939	6.23028	6.00205	5.78637	5.58238	5.38929	5.20637	5.03295	4.86842
8	7.32548	7.17014	7.01969	6.73274	6.46321	6.20979	5.97130	5.74664	5.53482	5.33493
9	8.16224	7.97087	7.78611	7.43533	7.10782	6.80169	6.51523	6.24689	5.99525	5.75902
10	8.98259	8.75206	8.53020	8.11090	7.72173	7.36009	7.02358	6.71008	6.41766	6.14457
11	9.78685	9.51421	9.25262	8.76048	8.30641	7.88687	7.49867	7.13896	6.80519	6.49506
12	10.57534	10.25776	9.95400	9.38507	8.86325	8.38384	7.94269	7.53608	7.16073	6.81369
13	11.34837	10.98318	10.63496	9.98565	9.39357	8.85268	8.35765	7.90378	7.48690	7.10336
14	12.10625	11.69091	11.29607	10.56312	9.89864	9.29498	8.74547	8.24424	7.78615	7.36669
15	12.84926	12.38138	11.93794	11.11839	10.37966	9.71225	9.10791	8.55948	8.06069	7.60608
16	13.57771	13.05500	12.56110	11.65230	10.83777	10.10590	9.44665	8.85137	8.31256	7.82371
17	14.29187	13.71220	13.16612	12.16567	11.27407	10.47726	9.76322	9.12164	8.54363	8.02155
18	14.99203	14.35336	13.75351	12.65930	11.68959	10.82760	10.05909	9.37189	8.75563	8.20141
19	15.67846	14.97889	14.32380	13.13394	12.08532	11.15812	10.33560	9.60360	8.95011	8.36492
20	16.35143	15.58916	14.87747	13.59033	12.46221	11.46992	10.59401	9.81815	9.12855	8.51356
21	17.01121	16.18455	15.41502	14.02916	12.82115	11.76408	10.83553	10.01680	9.29224	8.64869
22	17.65805	16.76541	15.93692	14.45112	13.16300	12.04158	11.06124	10.20074	9.44243	8.77154
23	18.29220	17.33211	16.44361	14.85684	13.48857	12.30338	11.27219	10.37106	9.58021	8.88322
24	18.91393	17.88499	16.93554	15.24696	13.79864	12.55036	11.46933	10.52876	9.70661	8.98474
25	19.52346	18.42438	17.41315	15.62208	14.09394	12.78336	11.65358	10.67478	9.82258	9.07704

Periodic Rents (n)	11%	12%	14%	15%	16%	18%	20%	22%	24%	25%
1	.90090	.89286	.87719	.86957	.86207	.84746	.83333	.81967	.80645	.80000
2	1.71252	1.69005	1.64666	1.62571	1.60523	1.56564	1.52778	1.49153	1.45682	1.44000
3	2.44371	2.40183	2.32163	2.28323	2.24589	2.17427	2.10648	2.04224	1.98130	1.95200
4	3.10245	3.03735	2.91371	2.85498	2.79818	2.69006	2.58873	2.49364	2.40428	2.36160
5	3.69590	3.60478	3.43308	3.35216	3.27429	3.12717	2.99061	2.86364	2.74538	2.68928
6	4.23054	4.11141	3.88867	3.78448	3.68474	3.49760	3.32551	3.16692	3.02047	2.95142
7	4.71220	4.56376	4.28830	4.16042	4.03857	3.81153	3.60459	3.41551	3.24232	3.16114
8	5.14612	4.96764	4.63886	4.48732	4.34359	4.07757	3.83716	3.61927	3.42122	3.32891
9	5.53705	5.32825	4.94637	4.77158	4.60654	4.30302	4.03097	3.78628	3.56550	3.46313
10	5.88923	5.65022	5.21612	5.01877	4.83323	4.49409	4.19247	3.92318	3.68186	3.57050
11	6.20652	5.93770	5.45273	5.23371	5.02864	4.65601	4.32706	4.03540	3.77569	3.65640
12	6.49236	6.19437	5.66029	5.42062	5.19711	4.79322	4.43922	4.12737	3.85136	3.72512
13	6.74987	6.42355	5.84236	5.58315	5.34233	4.90951	4.53268	4.20277	3.91239	3.78010
14	6.98187	6.62817	6.00207	5.72448	5.46753	5.00806	4.61057	4.26456	3.96160	3.82408
15	7.19087	6.81086	6.14217	5.84737	5.57546	5.09158	4.67547	4.31522	4.00129	3.85926
16	7.37916	6.97399	6.26506	5.95423	5.66850	5.16235	4.72956	4.35673	4.03330	3.88741
17	7.54879	7.11963	6.37286	6.04716	5.74870	5.22233	4.77463	4.39077	4.05911	3.90993
18	7.70162	7.24967	6.46742	6.12797	5.81785	5.27316	4.81219	4.41866	4.07993	3.92794
19	7.83929	7.36578	6.55037	6.19823	5.87746	5.31624	4.84350	4.44152	4.09672	3.94235
20	7.96333	7.46944	6.62313	6.25933	5.92884	5.35275	4.86958	4.46027	4.11026	3.95388
21	8.07507	7.56200	6.68696	6.31246	5.97314	5.38368	4.89132	4.47563	4.12117	3.96311
22	8.17574	7.64465	6.74294	6.35866	6.01133	5.40990	4.90943	4.48822	4.12998	3.97049
23	5.26643	7.71843	6.79206	6.39884	6.04425	5.43212	4.92453	4.49854	4.13708	3.97639
24	8.34814	7.78432	6.83514	6.43377	6.07263	5.45095	4.93710	4.50700	4.14281	3.98111
25	8.42174	7.84314	6.87293	6.46415	6.09709	5.46691	4.94759	4.51393	4.14742	3.98489

QUESTIONS

PART A

1. Explain what is meant by the time value of money.
2. Assuming the annual rate of interest is 9%, what would consistent interest rates be for the following periods: *(a)* semiannual, *(b)* quarterly, and *(c)* monthly?
3. What is the fundamental difference between simple interest and compound interest?
4. Briefly explain each of the following:

   a. Future value of 1.
   b. Present value of 1.
   c. Future value of annuity of *n* rents of 1 each.
   d. Present value of annuity of *n* rents of 1 each.

5. Assume $6,000 is borrowed on a two-year, 15% note payable. Compute the total amount of interest that would be paid on this note assuming *(a)* simple interest and *(b)* compound interest.
6. Match columns 2 and 3 with column 1 by entering the appropriate letter from column 1:

Column 1	Column 2	Column 3
A. Future value of 1.	F _____	$\dfrac{1}{(1+i)^n}$ _____
B. Present value of 1.	P _____	$(1+i)^n$ _____
C. Future value of annuity of 1.	p _____	$\dfrac{1-\dfrac{1}{(1+i)^n}}{i}$ _____
	f _____	
D. Present value of annuity of 1.		$\dfrac{(1+i)^n - 1}{i}$ _____

7. Match the following by entering the appropriate letter (*n* and *i* are the same for each value):

   A. Future value of 1.   17.51851 _____
   B. Present value of 1.   4.60654 _____
   C. Future value of   .26295 _____
      annuity of 1 (ordinary).   3.80296 _____
   D. Present value of
      annuity of 1 (due).

8. Contrast a future value of 1 with a present value of 1.
9. The future value of 1 at 13% interest for 15 years is 6.25427. What is the present value of 1 in this situation? If the present value of 1 at 17% interest for 12 years is .15197, what is the future value of 1 at 17% for 12 years?
10. If the table value for a future value of 1 is known, how may it be converted to the table value for present value of 1? Show the computations to convert the following future values of 1 to the equivalent present values of 1: 1.46933; 3.18547; and 216.54199.
11. If $10,000 is deposited in a savings account at 8% compound interest, what would be the balance in the savings account at the end of 9 years? 15 years? 25 years?

12. Assume you have a legal contract which specifies that you will receive $150,000 cash in the future. Assuming a 9% interest rate, what would be the present value of that contract if the amount will be received: *(a)* 7 years, *(b)* 15 years, or *(c)* 24 years from now?

PART B

13. What are the three characteristics of an annuity? Explain what would happen if any of these characteristics changed.
14. Table 5–3 gives a future value of an annuity of 1 (ordinary annuity) of 3.09 (rounded) for $n = 3$; $i = 3\%$. Explain the meaning of this table value.
15. If $10,000 is deposited in a savings account at the end of each of n annual periods and will earn 9%, what would be the balance in the savings account at the date of the last deposit (i.e., an ordinary annuity), assuming $n = 7$ years, 15 years, and 24 years?
16. Explain the difference between *(a)* future value of an ordinary annuity and *(b)* future value of an annuity due.
17. Explain the difference between *(a)* present value of an ordinary annuity and *(b)* present value of an annuity due.
18. Compute the present value of an annuity of five rents of $6,000 each using an 8% interest rate, assuming *(a)* an ordinary annuity and *(b)* an annuity due. Explain why the two amounts are different.
19. Compute the future value of an annuity of six rents of $4,000 each using an 8% interest rate, assuming *(a)* an ordinary annuity and *(b)* an annuity due. Explain why the two amounts are different.
20. XR Company will create a building fund by contributing $15,000 per year to it for 10 years; the fund will be increased each year at a 7% compound interest rate. Assume the current year is 19A. *(a)* Explain how you would determine whether this situation is an ordinary annuity or an annuity due. *(b)* In each instance, how many rents and interest periods would be involved?
21. If an annuity value of 1 is computed by formula or read from an annuity table, explain the implicit dates for both a future value and present value, assuming *(a)* an ordinary annuity and *(b)* an annuity due.

EXERCISES

PART A: EXERCISES 5–1 TO 5–14

(Round solutions to the nearest dollar. Also, assume annual compounding and discounting unless otherwise stated.)

Note: Exercises 5–1 through 5–14 do not involve annuities.

Exercise 5–1

Davy Company plans to deposit $60,000 today into a special building fund that will be needed at the end of six years. A financial institution will serve as the fund trustee and will pay 12% interest on the fund balance.

Required:
Compute the fund balance at the end of year 6, assuming:

Case A—Annual compounding.
Case B—Semiannual compounding.
Case C—Quarterly compounding.

Exercise 5–2

The two situations below are independent.

1. KW Company will need $200,000 cash to renovate an old machine five years from now. Assume a financial institution will increase a fund at 12% annual interest. Compute the amount of cash that must be deposited now to meet the future need assuming (show computations):

   Case A—Annual compounding.
   Case B—Semiannual compounding.
   Case C—Quarterly compounding.

2. On January 1, 19A, WT Company has a contract whereby the company is due to receive $50,000 cash on December 31, 19F. The company is short of cash and desires to discount (sell) this claim. WT is willing to accept a 16% annual discount. Under these conditions, how much cash would WT receive on January 1, 19A?

Exercise 5–3

Each of the following situations is independent.

1. You invested $5,000 in a savings account at 12% compound interest. What balance would be in your savings account at the end of six years assuming:

   a. Annual compounding?
   b. Semiannual compounding?
   c. Quarterly compounding?

   Explain why these amounts are different.

2. You have agreed to accumulate a fund of $40,000 at the end of six years by making a single deposit now. The fund will earn 8% compound interest. What amout must you deposit now to accumulate the $40,000 fund assuming:

   a. Annual compounding?
   b. Semiannual compounding?
   c. Quarterly compounding?

   Explain why these amounts are different.

Exercise 5–4

Each of the following situations is independent.

1. DB Corporation plans a plant expansion that will require approximately $300,000 at December 31, 19C. Because it has some idle cash on hand now, January 1, 19A, it desires to know how much it would have to invest as a lump sum now to accumulate

the required amount, assuming 14% annual compound interest is added to the fund each December 31.

Required:

1. Compute the amount that must be invested on January 1, 19A.
2. Prepare an accumulation schedule for the plant expansion fund.

2. On January 1, 19A, DB Corporation signed a $200,000 note that is due on December 31, 19D (the $200,000 includes both principal and interest). According to the agreement, DB has the option to pay the $200,000 at maturity date or to pay the obligation in full on January 1, 19A, with a 12% compound interest discount. What would be the amount of cash required on January 1, 19A, to settle the debt in full under the early payment option?

Exercise 5–5

Small Company has on hand $150,000 cash that will not be needed in the near future. However, the company will expand operations within the next three to five years. The company has decided to establish a savings account locally which will earn 10% interest compounded annually. The interest will be added to the fund each year. The deposit of $150,000 is made on January 1, 19A.

Required:

1. Compute the balance in the fund at the end of year 3.
2. Prepare a fund accumulation schedule.
3. Give the journal entries for the fund for 19A.

Exercise 5–6

B. Ball has a small child. Ball has decided to set up a fund to provide for the child's college education. A local financial institution will handle the fund and increase it each year on a 10% annual compound interest basis. Ball desires to make a single deposit on January 1, 19A, and specifies that the fund must have a $90,000 balance at the end of the 16th year.

Required:

1. Compute the amount of cash that must be deposited on January 1, 19A.
2. Prepare a fund accumulation schedule through December 31, 19C (three years).
3. Give the journal entries for the fund for 19A.

Exercise 5–7

AC Company purchased some additional equipment that was needed because of a new contract. The equipment was purchased on January 1, 19A. Because the contract would require two years to complete and AC was short of cash, the vendor agreed to accept a down payment of $10,000 and a two-year note for $45,000 (this amount includes the principal and all interest) due December 31, 19B. Assume the going rate of interest for this debt was 20%.

Required:

1. Compute the cost of the equipment in conformity with the cost principle. Show computations.
2. Give the entry at date of acquisition of the equipment.
3. Prepare a debt amortization schedule.
4. Give all additional entries related to the debt.

Exercise 5–8

Assume you deposit $25,000 in a special savings account on January 1, 19A; the interest rate is 9%.

Required:
1. Compute the balance in the savings account at the end of 19E, assuming *(a)* simple interest and *(b)* compound interest.
2. Calculate and explain the cause of the difference.

Exercise 5–9

The two following situations are independent.

1. DT Company, at the present date, has $40,000 which will be deposited in a savings account until needed. It is anticipated that $111,000 will be needed at the end of nine years to expand some manufacturing facilities. What approximate rate of interest would be required to accumulate the $111,000, assuming compounding on an annual basis? Show computations; no need to interpolate.
2. DT Company is planning an addition to its office building as soon as adequate funds can be accumulated. The company has estimated that the addition will cost approximately $250,000. At the present time $100,000 cash is on hand that will not be needed in the near future. A local savings institution will pay 14% interest (compounded annually). How many periods would be required to accumulate the $250,000? Show computations; no need to interpolate.

Exercise 5–10

The two following situations are independent.

1. On September 1, Year 1, BX Company decided to deposit $200,000 in a debt retirement fund. The company needs $337,000 cash to pay a debt on August 31, Year 5. What rate of compound interest must the fund earn to meet the cash requirement to pay the debt?
2. TV Company owes a $200,000 debt (this amount includes both principal and interest) that is payable three years from now. TV wants to pay the debt in full immediately. The creditor has agreed to settle the debt in full for $177,800 cash. What rate of compound discount is the creditor applying to the note?

Exercise 5–11

The two situations that follow are independent.

1. You have decided to invest $10,000 today in a mutual fund. You anticipate leaving this investment in the fund for 12 years. The fund will be increased each year-end by specified compound interest rates as follows: years 1–4 inclusive, 8%; 5–8 inclusive, 9%; and 9–12 inclusive, 10%.
   Compute the balance that will be in the fund at the end of year 12.

2. You own a special kind of property that cost $6,000 five years ago. Now you want to sell it for cash. You estimate reliably that this property will produce two net cash inflows as follows: End of year 5 from now, $120,000; and end of year 8 from now, $80,000. You deem it reasonable to use compound discount interest rates of 6% for the $120,000 cash inflow and 10% for the $80,000 cash inflow (it is more risky to the buyer). Given these estimates, compute the approximate selling price that you should expect.

Exercise 5–12

Each of the following situations is independent.

1. A compound interest table (or formula) value for $n = 9$ and $i = 9\%$ is .46043. Is this a future value of 1 or a present value of 1? Explain.
2. What table value should be used to compute the balance in a fund at the end of year 11, if $100,000 is deposited at the date the fund is established, assuming 12% annual compound interest, and semiannual compounding?
3. What table value should be used to compute the present value of $50,000, assuming 16% compound interest, quarterly compounding and six years of discounting?
4. A fund is established by depositing $5,000 at compound interest; the fund will have a balance of $19,980 at the end of 18 years. What is the approximate rate of interest?
5. A note payable of $20,000 (including both principal and interest) is due three years hence. Assuming a 14% compound interest rate, at what amount should this debt be settled today (i.e., three years before maturity) on a cash basis?

Exercise 5–13

Each of the following situations is independent.

1. Approximately how long will it take a $10,000 fund to double at 10% interest, assuming (a) simple interest and (b) compound interest?
2. A $100 utility deposit is made; the utility company must pay 5% compound interest on all such deposits. How much would the customer receive if the utility service was discontinued at the end of year 8?
3. What amount should be deposited in a savings account today, at 8% annual compound interest, to have a $30,000 balance in the account at the end of year 10?
4. On January 1, 19A, a machine is purchased with a "sticker price" of $8,000. Credit arrangements stated that the $8,000 (including any interest) is payable in full on December 31, 19B. The going rate of compound interest on this kind of credit is 15%. What is the cost of the machine in conformity with the cost principle?
5. VT Company owed a debt of $2,895, which is now due. Arrangements were made whereby VT can extend the debt by signing a four-year note of $6,000 (including principal and interest). What approximate rate of compound interest is implicit in the note?

Exercise 5–14

On January 1, 19A, you invested $10,000 cash in a special savings account. It will be increased by the compound interest each year-end. The fund will earn 6% for the first three years, 8% for the next three years, and 10% for the last four years.

Required:
Compute the balance in the fund at the end of year 10.

PART B: EXERCISES 5–15 TO 5–26

Exercise 5–15

Baker Company has decided to accumulate a fund by making equal periodic contributions. The fund will be increased each interest period by 12% compound interest. The current date is January 1, 19A.

Required:

1. Complete the following tabulation to compare an ordinary annuity with an annuity due:

   a. Ordinary (end-of-period) annuity:

Compounding	Rent	n	i	Table value	Fund balance
Annual	$5,000	5	12%	6.35285	$31,764.25
Semiannual	2,500	10	6	13.18079	32,951.93
Quarterly	1,250	20	4	29.77808	37,222.60

   b. Annuity due (beginning of period): $\times (1 + int)$

Compounding	Rent	n	i	Table value	Fund balance
Annual	$5,000	5	12%	7.115192	___
Semiannual	2,500	10	6	13.9716374	___
Quarterly	1,250	20	4	30.9692032	___

2. Explain why the ordinary annuity and annuity due fund balances are different.
3. Give the journal entry at the end of the first annuity period for each of the six situations above (indicate dates).

Exercise 5–16

Complete the following table assuming $n = 7$; $i = 16\%$:

Concept	Symbol	Formula	"Value" based on $1	Table
1. Future value of 1.	___	___	___	___
2. Present value of 1.	___	___	___	___
3. Future value of ordinary annuity of n rents of 1 each.	___	___	___	___
4. Present value of ordinary annuity of n rents of 1 each.	___	___	___	___
5. Future value of annuity due of n rents of 1 each.	___	___	___	___
6. Present value of annuity due of n rents of 1 each.	___	___	___	___

Exercise 5–17

The following two situations are independent.

Situation 1:

On January 1, year 1, SB Company decided to create an expansion fund by making equal annual deposits of $66,000. The fund is required on December 31, year 5. Interest at 12% compounded annually will be added to the fund. Five deposits are planned. Two alternative dates are under consideration:

Alternative A—Make the annual deposits on each December 31 starting in year 1.

Alternative B—Make the annual deposits on each January 1 starting in year 1.

Required:

Complete the following schedule:

Alternative	Type of annuity	Balance in the fund at end of 19E	
		Computations	Amount
A			
B			

Situation 2:

TV Company agreed on January 1, year 1, to deposit $120,000 cash with a trustee. The trustee will increase the fund on a 10% compound interest basis on the fund balance each successive year. The trustee is required to pay out the fund in 10 equal annual installments to a former employee of TV so that the fund is completely exhausted at the end of that time. Two alternative payment dates are under consideration:

Alternative A—Make the annual payments to the former employee each December 31 starting in year 1.

Alternative B—Make the annual payments to the former employee each January 1 starting in year 1.

Required:

Complete the following schedule:

Alternative	Type of Annuity	Amount of the equal annual payments	
		Computations	Amount
A			
B			

Exercise 5–18

VIT Company has decided to accumulate a debt retirement fund by making three equal annual deposits of $22,000 on each December 31, starting at the end of 19A. Assume the fund will accumulate annual compound interest at 14% per year which will be added to the fund balance.

Required:

1.. What kind of annuity is this? Why?
2. What will be the balance in the fund on December 31, 19C (immediately after the last deposit)?
3. Prepare an accumulation schedule for this fund.
4. Prepare the journal entries for the period January 1, 19A, through December 31, 19C.
5. What would be the balance in the fund if it were set up on an annuity due basis?

Exercise 5–19

On September 1, 19A, Sault Company incurred a $60,000 debt. Arrangements have been made to pay this debt in three equal annual installments starting on September 1, 19A; the compound interest rate is 15%.

Required:

1. Is this an ordinary annuity or annuity due? Explain.
2. Compute the amount of the equal annual payments.
3. Prepare a debt amortization schedule.
4. Give the journal entries related to the debt.
5. Compute the annual payment if the debt payments were made annually beginning on August 31, 19B.

Exercise 5–20

On May 1, 19A, WAT Company owes a $70,000 debt that will be paid in three equal annual payments. The first payment is to be made on April 30, 19B. The compound interest rate is 14%.

Required:

1. Is this an ordinary annuity or an annuity due? Explain.
2. Compute the amount of the equal annual payments.
3. Prepare a debt amortization schedule.
4. Give the journal entries related to the fund.
5. Compute the annual payment if the debt payments were made annually beginning on May 1, 19A.

Exercise 5–21

GNU Company has decided to establish a debt retirement fund with equal annual contributions of $15,000, starting on January 1, 19A. The fund will be increased at each year-end at 9% per annum. The $53,000 debt must be paid on December 31, 19C.

Required:

1. Is this an ordinary annuity or an annuity due? Explain.
2. What will be the balance of the fund on December 31, 19C?
3. Prepare a fund accumulation schedule.
4. Give the journal entries related to the fund.
5. What balance would be in the fund if it had been set up on an ordinary annuity basis, with the first annual contribution on December 31, 19A?

Exercise 5–22

The following two situations are independent.

Situation 1:

Oliver Company plans to establish a debt retirement fund, beginning December 31, 19A, to accumulate $90,120. End-of-period contributions of $20,000 will be made to a trustee each December 31, so that the desired amount will be available on December 31, 19D, the date of the last rent. Compute the required interest rate that must be earned by the fund on an annual compound basis to satisfy these requirements. Show your computations to demonstrate that your answer is correct.

Situation 2:

Polus Company has decided to create a plant expansion fund by making equal annual deposits of $30,000 on each January 1. Interest at 10% compounded annually will be added to the fund balance each year-end. The company wants to know how many deposits will be required to build a fund of $313,077. Show your computations to demonstrate that your answer is correct.

Exercise 5–23

The following two situations are independent.

Situation 1:

On January 1, 19A, Kay Company purchased a machine that cost $60,000. Kay paid $35,535 cash and incurred a debt for the difference. This debt is to be paid off in equal annual installments of $6,000 payable each December 31. The interest rate on the unpaid balance each period is 18% per annum. How many equal payments must be made at each year-end? Show computations to prove your answer.

Situation 2:

On January 1, 19A, Vic Company owes a past-due debt of $31,743. Arrangements have been made whereby Vic will pay this debt by making four equal installments of $10,000 that include both principal and compound interest. The payments will be made on January 1, 19A, 19B, 19C, and 19D. Compute the implicit interest rate in this agreement. Show computations to prove your answer.

Exercise 5–24

Each of the following situations is independent.

Situation 1:

You have $50,000 in a fund that earns 10% annual compound interest. If you desire to withdraw it in five equal annual amounts, starting today, how much would you receive each year?

Situation 2:

You will deposit $500 each semiannual period starting today; this savings account will earn 6% compounded each semiannual period. What will be the balance in your savings account at the end of year 10?

Situation 3:

You purchased a new automobile that cost $14,000. You received a $4,000 trade-in allowance for your old auto and signed a 12% note for $10,000. The note requires eight equal quarterly payments starting one quarter from date of purchase. What is the amount of each payment?

Situation 4:

You deposited $2,000 at the end of each year in a savings account for five years at compound interest. The fund had a balance of $12,456 at the date of the last deposit. What rate of interest did you earn?

Situation 5:

On January 1, 19A, you owed a debt of $15,131.14. An agreement was reached that you would pay the debt plus compound interest in 24 monthly installments of $800, the first payment to be made on January 31, 19A. What rate of annual interest are you paying?

Exercise 5–25

WV Company established a construction fund on July 1, 19A, by making a single deposit of $250,000. Also, at the end of each year, starting on June 30, 19B, the company will make $20,000 deposits in the fund. The fund will earn 9% compound interest each year, which will be added to the fund balance.

Required:
1. Compute the balance that will be in the fund at the end of five years (on June 30, 19F).
2. Give the journal entries that would be made for the first year starting on July 1, 19A, and through June 30, 19B.

Exercise 5–26

Rye Company is considering purchasing a used machine that is in excellent mechanical condition. The company plans to keep the machine for 10 years, at which time the residual value will be zero. An analysis of the capacity of the machine and the costs of operating it (including materials used in production) provided an estimate that the machine would increase aftertax net cash inflow by approximately $100,000 per year.

Required:
1. Compute the approximate amount that Rye should be willing to pay now for the machine assuming a target earnings rate of 15% per year. Assume also that the revenue is realized at each year-end. Show your computations.
2. What price should be paid assuming a $20,000 residual value?

PROBLEMS

PART A: PROBLEMS 5–1 TO 5–6

(Round solutions to the nearest dollar. Also, assume annual compounding and discounting unless otherwise stated.)

Problem 5–1

Avis Company deposited $300,000 in a special expansion fund on May 1, 19A, for future use as needed. The fund will accumulate 12% compound interest per year.

Required:
1. Complete the following table by entering, into each cell, the balance that would be in the fund at the end of the intervals indicated:

Compounding assumption	Periodic interest rate	Fund balance at end of	
		Two years	Four years
Annual			
Semiannual			
Quarterly			

2. Prepare a fund accumulation schedule based on the first cell (annual, for two years).
3. Give journal entries for the fund based on the first cell (annual, for two years).

Problem 5–2

Scott Company anticipates that it will need $200,000 cash for an expansion in the next few years. Assume an annual compound interest rate of 14%. The company desires to make a single contribution now, January 1, 19A, so that the $200,000 will be available when needed.

Required:

1. Complete the following schedule by entering into each cell the amount that must be deposited now to meet the above specifications:

		Amount to be deposited now			
		Two years		Three years	
Compounding assumption	Interest rate	n	$	n	$
Annual	_____	_____	$_____	_____	$_____
Semiannual	_____	_____	$_____	_____	$_____

2. Prepare a fund accumulation schedule based on $n = 2$; $i = 14\%$.
3. Give journal entries for 19A and 19B based on $n = 2$, $i = 14\%$.

Problem 5–3

The following three situations are independent.

1. On January 1, 19A, Investor A deposited $7,000 in a savings account that would accumulate at 12% annual compound interest for three years.

   Required:
   a. Compute the balance that would be in the savings account at the end of the third year.
   b. Prepare a fund accumulation schedule for this situation.

2. On March 1, 19A, Investor B deposited $7,000 in a savings account that would accumulate to $9,317 at the end of three years, assuming annual compound interest.

   Required:
   a. Compute the interest rate that would be necessary. Show computations.
   b. Prepare a fund accumulation schedule for this situation.

3. On September 1, 19A, Investor C deposited $7,000 in a savings account that would accumulate to $11,108, assuming 8% annual compound interest.

   Required:
   a. Compute the number of periods that would be necessary. Show computations.
   b. Prepare a fund accumulation schedule for this situation.

Problem 5–4

Day Company deposited $100,000 in a special expansion fund for use in the future as needed. The fund will accumulate at 12% annual compound interest. The fund was started on March 1, 19A, and the interest will be added to the fund balance on an annual compound interest basis.

Required:

1. Compute the balance that will be in the fund at the end of 3 years, 5 years, and 10 years, respectively.

2. Prepare a fund accumulation schedule for three years.
3. Give the journal entries for Day Company for the first three years. Disregard adjusting and closing entries.
4. What adjusting entry would be made on December 31, 19A, assuming this is the end of the accounting period for Day Company?

Problem 5–5

The following three situations are independent.

1. On September 1, year 1, Investor A deposited $40,000 in a savings account that would accumulate to $43,600 at August 31, year 1.

Required:
a. Compute the implicit compound annual interest rate.
b. What would be the balance in the fund at the end (i.e., August 31) of years 5, 10, and 20?

2. On May 1, year 1, Investor B deposited $100,000 in a savings account that would accumulate to $136,763 on April 30, year 3.

Required:
a. Compute the implicit compound annual interest rate.
b. Prepare the three-year fund accumulation schedule.

3. On October 1, year 1, Investor C deposited $10,000 in a savings account and expects the fund to have a balance of $25,000 at the end of year 10.

Required:
a. Compute the implicit interest rate. Show the interpolation that would be required to obtain the approximate interest rate to two decimal places.
b. What would be in the fund at the end of year 20? (Hint: Use calculator programmed for FV.)

Problem 5–6

Nix Company is trying to "clean up" some of its debts. On January 1, 1986, the company has savings accounts as follows:

Date established	Amount deposited (a single deposit for each)	Annual compound interest rate
1/1/75	$20,000	8%
1/1/81	30,000	10%

The outstanding debts on January 1, 1986, to be paid off are as follows:

Due date	Type of note	Face of note*
12/31/89	Noninterest bearing	$ 60,000
12/31/96	Noninterest bearing	200,000

* These amounts include both principal and all interest thereon. The amount given for each note is the single sum to be paid at maturity date.

Required:

1. Compute the amount of cash that Nix can get from the two savings accounts on January 1, 1986.
2. Compute the amount for which the two debts can be settled on January 1, 1986, assuming a going rate of interest of 18%.
3. Assuming all cash is withdrawn from the savings accounts and all payments are made on the debts, would Nix have a cash shortage or an excess? How much?

PART B: PROBLEMS 5–7 TO 5–19

Problem 5–7

Alvin Company will establish a special debt retirement fund amounting to $70,000. A trustee has agreed to handle the fund and to increase it each year on a 10% annual compound interest basis. Alvin will make equal annual contributions to the fund during the years 19A through 19D.

Required:

1. Compute the amount of the required annual deposit assuming they are made on *(a)* December 31 and *(b)* January 1. If your answers are different, explain why.
2. Prepare a fund accumulation schedule for each starting date; *(a)* and *(b)* above.
3. Give the journal entries related to each starting date for 19A through 19D. Date each entry. Hint: To save time you can use a tabulation similar to the following:

Date	Fund (debit)	Cash (credit)	Interest revenue (credit)

Problem 5–8

Tabor Company is contemplating the accumulation of a special fund to be used for expanding sales activities into the western part of the country. It is January 1, 19A, and the fund will be needed at the beginning of 19D, according to present plans. The fund will earn 12% interest compounded annually. Annual contributions will be $50,000. The management has not yet decided whether to start the deposits on January 1, 19A, or December 31, 19A.

Required:

1. Compute the amount of the fund balance at the beginning of 19D, assuming three annual deposits are made on *(a)* January 1 and *(b)* December 31. If your answers are different, explain why.
2. Prepare a fund accumulation schedule for each starting date; *(a)* and *(b)* above.
3. Give the journal entries related to each starting date for 19A through 19C. Date each entry. *Hint:* To save time you can use a tabulation similar to the following:

Date	Fund (debit)	Cash (credit)	Interest revenue (credit)

Problem 5–9

It is January 1, 19E, and RX Company owes an $80,000 past-due debt to City Bank. The bank has agreed to permit RX to pay the debt in three equal installments, each payment to include principal and compound interest at 18%. One issue has not yet been settled. The bank desires that the first installment be paid immediately; however, because of a cash liquidity problem, RX is asking to make the first payment at year end, December 31, 19E.

Required:

1. Compute the amount of the three equal annual payments if *(a)* the first payment is on January 1, 19E, and *(b)* the first payment is on December 31, 19E. If the amounts are different, explain why.
2. Prepare a debt amortization schedule for each payment starting date.
3. Give the journal entries related to each payment starting date through the last payment. Hint: To save time you can use a tabulation similar to the following:

Date	Interest expense (debit)	Liability (debit)	Liability (credit)	Cash (credit)

Problem 5–10

Quick Construction Company can purchase a used machine for $25,000. The machine will be needed on a new job that will continue for approximately three years. It is January 1, 19A, and the machine is needed immediately. Because of a shortage of cash, Quick has asked the vendor for credit terms. The vendor charges 20% annual compound interest. The machine can be purchased under these terms by making three equal payments.

Required:

1. Compute the amount of the three equal payments assuming they are to be paid on *(a)* January 1, 19A, B, and C; and *(b)* December 31, 19A, B, and C. If your answers are different, explain why.
2. Prepare a debt payment schedule for *(a)* and *(b)* above.
3. Give the journal entries for *(a)* and *(b)* through 19C. Date each entry. Hint: To save time you can use a tabulation similar to the following:

Date	Interest expense (debit)	Liability (debit)	Liability (credit)	Cash (credit)

4. What amount should be recorded as the cost of the machine in *(a)* and *(b)* above?

Problem 5–11

On January 1, 19A, Wick Company agreed with its president, J. Smith, to make a single deposit immediately, to establish a fund with a trustee that will pay Smith $50,000 per year for each of the three years following retirement. Smith will retire on January 1, 19K, and the equal annual payments are to be made by the trustee each December 31 starting in 19K. The trustee will add to the fund 12% annual compound interest each year-end. The fund is to have a zero balance on December 31, 19M, immediately after the last payment to Smith.

Required:

1. Compute the single amount that Wick Company must deposit in the fund on January 1, 19A, to meet the specified payments to Smith.
2. Prepare a fund schedule to show the use of the fund during the payout period from January 1, 19K, through December 31, 19M. Use captions similar to the following: Date; Cash payments to Smith; Interest revenue earned on the fund; Net fund decreases, and Fund balance.

3. How much of the amount paid to Smith during the payout period was provided by interest earned during the payout period?

Problem 5–12

Richie Student is considering the purchase of a Super Sail Boat which has a cash price of $6,500. Terms can be arranged for a $2,000 cash down payment and payment of the remaining $4,500, plus interest at 18% compound interest per annum, in three equal payments. Assume purchase on January 1, 19A, and payments on each December 31 thereafter.

Required:
1. Compute the amount of each annual payment.
2. What did Richie pay for the boat? What was the total amount of interest paid?
3. Prepare a debt amortization schedule using the following format:

Date	Cash payment	Interest expense	Liability	
			Decrease	Balance

4. Upon graduation (end of 19C) Richie sold the sailboat for three equal annual payments of $1,000 each; the first payment was paid on the date that the boat was transferred, January 1, 19D. Assume a 9% going rate of interest. What selling price did Richie get?

Problem 5–13

For each of the independent situations given below, assume the interest rate is 12% and compounding is semiannual.

Situation 1:
How much will accumulate by the end of six years, if $2,000 is deposited each interest period in a savings account at the *(a)* end of each period and *(b)* at the start of each period? Verify your answers, one with the other.

Situation 2:
What will be the periodic payments each period on a $35,000 debt that is to be paid in semiannual installments over a four-year period, assuming compound interest, if payments are made at the *(a)* beginning of each period and *(b)* end of each period?

Situation 3:
A special machine is purchased that had a list price of $38,000. Payment in full was: cash, $8,000; and five equal semiannual payments of $5,000 each. The first payment will be made at the end of the first semiannual period from purchase date. How much should be recorded in the accounts as the cost of the machine?

Situation 4:
A special investment is being contemplated. This investment will produce an estimated end-of-period income of $16,000 semiannually for five years. At the end of its productive life it will have an estimated recovery value of $3,500. Determine a reasonable estimate of the value of the investment.

Problem 5–14

Each situation that follows is independent of the other.

Situation 1:
On June 1, 19C, RV Company owed a $40,000 overdue debt. The bank agreed to allow payment of it over the next three years at 16% compound interest; payments to be

made each quarter. Compute the periodic payments assuming *(a)* the first payment is made August 31, 19C, and *(b)* the first payment is made June 1, 19C. If you get different answers, explain why they are different.

Situation 2:

RV Company rents a warehouse from Owner Jones for $12,000 annual rent, payable in advance on each January 1. RV Company proposed to sign a three-year lease and to pay the three years' rent in advance. The owner agreed to the proposal with the stipulation that the $36,000 be paid immediately (i.e., on January 1). RV Company has this proposal under consideration because it expected some discount in view of the fact that funds currently are earning about 9% per annum. Develop a counter proposal as to the amount that RV Company should pay. Give the entry that RV Company should make on January 1 to record your proposal, assuming it is accepted by Jones.

Problem 5–15

Refer to the tables of future and present values given in the chapter to respond to the following independent situations (no need to interpolate):

Situation 1:

XT Company deposited $12,500 cash in a fund that will increase at compound interest to $53,880 in 14 years. What is the approximate interest rate?

Situation 2:

XT Company owes a $20,400 noninterest-bearing note payable, which is due several years hence. The payee (i.e., creditor) has offered to settle the note today for $5,364 cash. Compute the approximate term to maturity (in years) from today, assuming a 16% interest rate.

Situation 3:

XT will deposit $5,000 in a fund at the end of each year for 20 years. Compound interest will be added to the fund at the end of each period. The balance of the fund on the date of the last deposit will be $228,810. Compute the approximate interest rate that the fund earned each year.

Situation 4:

XT Company owes a $17,950 debt that is being paid in equal installments at 15% compound interest. The annual year-end payments are $4,000 each (rounded to the nearest $). Compute the number of payments that XT Company will make.

Situation 5:

XT Company will deposit $4,000 in a fund at the beginning of each year for six years. Compound interest will be added to the fund each year-end. The balance in the fund at the end of year 6 will be $30,616. Compute the approximate interest rate that this fund will earn. Prove your answer.

Situation 6:

XT Company owes a $20,200 debt that is being paid off in equal beginning of the year payments of $3,192 (rounded). The payments include 12% compound interest. Compute the number of payments that XT Company will make. Prove your answer.

Problem 5–16

Daddy Lane has an industrious daughter, Lois, who is 15 years old today. For her birthday, Lane invests $20,000 toward her college education. Lane stipulates that Lois may withdraw four equal annual amounts from the fund, the first withdrawal to be made on her 18th birthday. The savings and loan association in which Lane placed the investment will add to the fund annual compound interest at the rate of 14% at the end of each year.

Required:

1. Compute the amount of each of the four withdrawals by Lois which will completely deplete the fund on the date of the final withdrawal. Hint: Diagram the problem situation.
2. Prepare a schedule that reflects the *(a)* accumulation of the fund balance and *(b)* withdrawal period (i.e., from the 15th birthday through the 21st birthday). *Hint:* Use captions similar to the following:

			Fund	
Date	Cash	Interest revenue	Changes	Balance

Problem 5–17

East Corporation is negotiating to purchase a plant from another company that will complement East's operations. They have just completed a careful study of the plant and have developed the following estimates:

Expected net cash inflow:	
End of years 1–5 (per year)	$50,000
End of years 6–10 (per year)	40,000
End of year 11	30,000
End of year 12	10,000
Expected net residual value at end of year 12	3,000

Required:

1. Compute the amount that East should be willing to pay for the plant assuming a 16% return on the investment. Assume all amounts are at year-end and are given net of expenses and income taxes.
2. Assume the down payment is $150,000. East will pay this, and the bank will lend East the balance at 16% per annum, payable in equal annual payments (including interest and principal) over five years. The payments will be at each year-end, starting one year after the date of purchase. Compute the amount of the equal annual payments on the loan. Compute the total interest that will be paid.
3. Give the entries (or entry) to record the purchase in 1 above, and the loan in 2 above using the amounts you computed.
4. Give entries at the end of year 1 to record *(a)* net revenue from the plant, assuming the estimate was correct, *(b)* interest expense, and *(c)* the loan payment.

Problem 5–18

Each of the following situations is independent.

Situation 1:

VW Company can purchase a heavy-duty mechanical switch for $100, which will last for three years on the average. The company uses 75 of these switches in its plant. A new type of electronic switch has been developed that will perform the same service; its cost is $200 and its expected useful life is 15 years. The company expects a 15% average earnings rate on its funds invested in plant equipment. How much would the company save or lose in present value dollars, by using one of the electronic switches?

Situation 2:

VW Company plans to establish a fund that will pay its retiring president $50,000 each year-end following retirement for a period of five years from retirement date.

How much cash must be deposited on the president's retirement date assuming 9% annual compound interest?

Situation 3:

VW Company owes a $75,000 debt that is due now. Arrangements have been made to pay the debt in six equal annual installments at 14% compound interest. The first installment is made immediately. Compute the amount of each payment.

Situation 4:

VW Company is negotiating to purchase an asset that has estimated net cash inflows at year-end as follows: year 1, $40,000; years 2–4; $30,000; and years 5–10, $20,000. At the end of year 10, the asset will have an estimated residual value of $25,000. Assuming 11% compound interest, compute the total cash price that VW should be willing to pay.

Problem 5–19 (Overview)

Compute each of the following amounts (each one is independent of the others). Round to the nearest dollar or percent.

a. On January 1, 19A, $20,000 is deposited in a fund at 8% compound interest. At the end of year 5, the fund balance will be, assuming—

    (1) Annual compounding $_____
    (2) Semiannual compounding $_____
    (3) Quarterly compounding $_____

b. On January 1, 19A, a machine is purchased at an invoice price of $10,000. The full purchase price is to be paid on December 31, 19E. Assuming 16% compound interest, what did the machine cost if compounding is:

    (1) Annual $_____
    (2) Semiannual $_____
    (3) Quarterly $_____

c. If $5,000 is deposited in a fund and it will increase to $13,598 by the end of year 13, the implicit compound interest rate is _____%.

d. If the present value of $15,000 is $5,864 at 11% compound annual discount, the number of periods is _____.

e. On January 1, 19A, a company decided to establish a fund by making 10 equal annual deposits of $4,000, starting on December 31, 19A. The fund will be increased by 8% compound interest. What will be the fund balance at the end of year 10 (i.e., immediately after the last deposit)?

f. On January 1, 19A, a company decided to establish a fund by making 10 equal annual deposits of $4,000, starting on January 1, 19A. The fund will be increased by 8% compound interest. What will be the balance in the fund at the end of year 10?

g. John Doe is at retirement and has a large amount of ready cash. He wants to deposit enough cash in a fund to receive back $20,000 each December 31 for the next five years, starting on December 31, 19A. Assuming 10% compound interest, how much cash must Doe deposit on January 1, 19A?

h. Ace Company is considering the purchase of a unique asset on January 1, 19A. The asset will earn $7,000 net cash inflow each January 1 for five years, starting January 1, 19A. At the end of year 5, the asset will have no value. Assuming a 14% compound interest rate, what should Ace be willing to pay for this unique asset on January 1, 19A?

i. In 19A, XT Company decided to build a fund by the end of 19G of $446,140 by making seven equal annual deposits of $50,000, starting on December 31, 19A. What is the implicit compound interest rate for this fund?

j. The present value of several future equal annual cash payments at year-end of $30,000 each is $141,366, assuming 11% compound discount. What is the implicit number of cash payments?

k. M. Moe will retire 10 years from now and wants to establish a fund now that will pay him $30,000 cash at the end of each of the first five years after retirement. Specific dates are: date of a single deposit by Moe, January 1, year 1; date of first cash payment from the fund to Moe, December 31, year 11. The fund will pay 10% compound interest. How much cash must Moe deposit on January 1, year 1, to provide the five equal annual year-end cash payments from the fund?

CASES

Case 5–1

You are an executive of VP Company and have earned a performance bonus. You have the option of taking the $15,000 bonus now, or to take $30,170 five years from now. Which option would you elect? Explain why.

Case 5–2

Ace Construction Company has just won a bid on a major contract. The contract will require the purchase of new equipment that has a quoted price of $200,000. The vendor, X Company, requires $50,000 cash down payment and will accept a two-year, $150,000, noninterest-bearing note (assume an interest rate on this type of note is 20% per annum). The face of the note includes both principal and interest.

Required:

1. Compute the cost of the equipment on January 1, 19A. Explain the accounting principle that you applied and justify your answer.
2. Give the entry to record the purchase of the equipment. Explain the approach you used to record the note.
3. Prepare a debt amortization schedule for the note.
4. Give the journal entries that Ace should make each year while the note is outstanding and for payment of the note on the maturity date. Should interest costs be included in the cost of the equipment because this is a noninterest-bearing note? Explain.
5. Assume that Ace was short of cash to make the $50,000 down payment. Ace has on hand a noninterest-bearing note of $90,000 received from a customer. The $90,000 includes both principal and interest and matures on December 31, 19C. Ace sold this note to HiCost Finance Company at a 24% compound discount. Compute the amount of cash Ace would receive on January 1, 19A.

Case 5–3

Caster Corporation had a $200,000 life insurance policy at the time of the death of its president. The company is the beneficiary and can receive the $200,000 cash immediately, or elect any one of the following options:

a. Withdraw the $200,000, plus 10% compound interest, in equal annual payments over the next five years. The first payment would be made immediately.
b. Withdraw $100,000 cash now, and withdraw the remainder, plus 10% compound interest, in equal annual payments over the next five years. The first payment would be made one year from now.
c. Withdraw $50,000 at years-end 1, 2, and 3, and then withdraw the balance at the end of year 5; all including 10% compound interest.

Required:
1. Complete the following schedule. Show all computations (round to the nearest $).

Option	Cash to be received in year					Total cash
	1	2	3	4	5	
a.	$	$	$	$	$	$
b.						
c.						

2. *a.* How much interest did each option earn?
   b. Give any logical reasons for withdrawing the $200,000 immediately.

Case 5–4

Viable Corporation purchases large machines for use in its plant. Machine Type A is typical of these machines. Currently, Viable is considering the purchase of a new Type A machine. Two different brand names are being considered as follows:

	Brand A	Brand B
Cost (cash basis)	$100,000	$85,000
Operating expense to operate the machine (per year) ..	$ 6,000	$ 8,000
Estimated useful life (years)	8	8
Estimated residual value (% of cost)	20%	10%

Viable expects a 20% return on its investments.

Required:
1. Prepare an analysis to compare the relative cost of the two brands (assume all variables, other than the four listed above, are the same for both brands).
2. Which machine should Viable purchase? Why (consider other factors along with your computations)?

Case 5–5

Slick Real Estate Tax Shelters, Inc., advertised that its special tax-shelter partnerships "earn 21% interest for the investor each year." An independent analysis of the actual figures (obtained from a prior partner after considerable effort) showed that an individual who invested $100,000 would receive a projected return of $310,000 at the end of year 10 (from investment date) (adapted from "How to Fool with Averages," *Forbes Magazine*, December 7, 1984, pp. 33–34).
Required:
1. Compute the actual interest rate implicit in the tax shelter (round to the nearest percent).
2. Was the advertised rate of return of 21% correct or was it misleading? Explain why.

Cash, Short-Term Investments and Receivables

OVERVIEW AND PURPOSE

The preceding chapters introduced most of the basic concepts and procedures of accounting. Chapters 6 through 9 will discuss the current assets. This chapter discusses the highly liquid assets; therefore, it is organized as follows:

Part A: Cash
1. Characteristics of cash.
2. Cash management and control.
3. Reconciling bank and book cash balances.

Part B: Short-Term Investments
1. Short-term investments defined.
2. Accounting for short-term equity investments.
3. Accounting for short-term debt investments.

Part C: Receivables
1. Accounts receivable.
2. Estimating bad debt expense.
3. Notes receivable.

Supplement 6–A: Comprehensive Bank Reconciliation

PART A: CASH

CHARACTERISTICS OF CASH AND CASH EQUIVALENTS

Cash is the medium of exchange; it is used to express most of the measurements in accounting. Because of its pervasive use by society, cash as a specific term is understood by nearly everyone. However, there are a number of legal documents, such as a check written against a bank deposit, that are more precisely called **cash equivalents.**

Cash inflows and outflows are recorded in an accounting system in one or more **cash accounts.** For **recording** purposes, cash should include **only** those items that are available for use as a medium of exchange. Thus, cash includes balances in bank checking accounts, currency, and certain formal negotiable instruments that are accepted by banks for immediate deposit and withdrawal. These negotiable documents include ordinary checks, bank drafts, cashier's checks, certified checks, and money orders. These documents are **recorded** as cash for accounting purposes. Other cash equivalents, such as balances in savings accounts and certificates of deposit (CDs), usually are **recorded** as short-term investments because there often is a penalty for early conversion to immediate cash. Cash also **excludes** such items as postage stamps (a prepaid expense), receivables from company employees, cash advances paid to employees and outsiders, and postdated checks.

For external **reporting purposes** (i.e., on the balance sheet), companies often combine cash and cash equivalents, such as short-term investments. Three typical 1983 examples of **cash reporting** (not recording) are as follows:

W. R. Grace & Company:
Cash and cash equivalents, including marketable
securities of $24.5 (millions) $163.7

Gannett Co., Inc.:
Cash . . . . $ 7,582,000
Marketable securities at cost, which approximates market   37,450,000

Liquid Air Corporation:
Cash (thousands of dollars) . . . . $ 5,166
Certificates of deposit   5,600

A continuing survey of the accounting practices of 600 large companies reported the following:

Cash—Balance Sheet Captions

	Number of companies			
	1983	1982	1981	1980
Cash	293	321	359	384
Cash and equivalents	86	75	60	38
Cash includes certificates of deposit or				
time deposits	59	62	63	71
Cash combined with marketable securities	162	142	118	107
Total companies	600	600	600	600

Source: AICPA, *Accounting Trends & Techniques, 1984* (New York, 1984), p. 105.

A **compensating balance** occurs when a bank lends funds to a customer and requires that a minimum balance be retained at all times in the customer's checking account. The practical effects are to *(a)* limit the amount of funds effectively borrowed and *(b)* increase the **effective** interest rate on the loan. Strictly viewed, a compensating balance should not be included in the cash balance. If compensating balances are not disclosed, misleading inferences about the company's liquidity and interest costs may occur. Therefore, compensating balances should be (a) reported on the balance sheet as a noncash current asset, or (b) clearly disclosed in the notes to the financial statements.[1]

Checks that have not been mailed or otherwise delivered to the payees by the end of the accounting period should not be deducted from the balance of the Cash account. Entries already made to record such checks should be reversed before preparing the financial statements. To illustrate, Raytheon Company included the following notes to its 1982 financial statements:

> Under the company's cash management program, checks in transit are not considered reductions of cash or accounts payable until presented to the appropriate banks for payment. At December 31, 1982 and 1981, checks in transit amounted to $52.3 million and $51.8 million, respectively.

An **overdraft** in a bank account should be shown as a current liability. However, if a depositor has overdrawn one account with Bank A but has positive balances in other accounts in that bank, it is appropriate accounting to offset the negative balance in one account against the positive balance in the other account. The net asset or liability should be reported on the balance sheet because the single bank is in a position to protect both accounts. It is incorrect to offset an overdraft in Bank A against a balance on deposit in Bank B because the positive account is open to withdrawals without knowledge by the other bank.

Petty cash funds (discussed below) and cash held by branches or divisions should be included in cash because such funds ordinarily are used to meet current operating expenses and to liquidate current liabilities.

Items properly included in cash seldom present valuation problems because cash is recorded and reported at its "face" value. Foreign currency balances must be translated to their current dollar equivalents, which often causes translation gains and losses.

CASH MANAGEMENT AND CONTROL

Cash management involves the planning and control of cash to efficiently (a) meet the day-to-day cash needs of the company, (b) invest temporarily idle cash to earn interest revenue, and (c) safeguard cash from theft.

Safegarding cash from theft is critical in most businesses. Cash is (a) easy to conceal and transport and (b) desired by everyone. This phase of the control of cash is closely related to the accounting system. Free access to the accounting system makes it easy to conceal cash theft. Therefore, careful control of cash receipts and payments is essential.

---

[1] The SEC requires that **legally restricted deposits** held as compensating balances against short-term borrowing arrangements be reported as noncash current assets, and if long-term borrowing, as noncurrent assets.

Control of Cash Receipts

Cash inflows in businesses come from numerous sources; therefore, the control procedures must vary among companies. However, the following procedures apply in most situations:

1. **Separate the responsibilities** for the cash-handling and cash-recording functions. This separation assures that an individual cannot steal cash and conceal the theft by making fictitious journal entries.
2. **Assign cash-handling and cash-recording responsibilities** to ensure a continuous and uninterrupted flow of cash from initial receipt to deposit in an authorized bank account. This control requires *(a)* immediate counting, *(b)* immediate recording, and *(c)* timely deposits of all cash received.
3. **Maintain continuous and close supervision** of all cash-handling and cash-recording functions. This control should include both routine and surprise audits and required daily reports of cash receipts, payments, and balances.

Control of Cash Disbursements

The cash outflows in most businesses involve many purposes or uses. Many of the cash thefts in the disbursements process occur because disbursements are numerous and it is relatively easy to conceal disbursement cash thefts. The most effective control is to use a very precise internal system for all cash payments.

Although each control system for cash disbursements should be tailored to the situation, several fundamentals are essential; these are:

1. **Separate the responsibilities** for cash disbursement documentation, check writing, check signing, check mailing, and recordkeeping.
2. **Make all cash disbursements by check.** An exception can be made for small amounts from a petty cash fund.
3. **Establish a petty cash fund** with tight controls and close supervision.
4. **Prepare and sign checks** only when supported by adequate documentation and verification.
5. **Supervise** all cash disbursement and recordkeeping functions.

Petty Cash

Effective control of cash disbursements often requires the use of a **petty cash fund** to make small cash disbursements because it usually is not cost effective to process a check for each payment. Examples of such payments are for the daily paper delivered to the office, express shipments, local taxi fares, special postage charges on delivery, supplies for the coffee maker, and other minor office supplies. A petty cash system should operate as follows:

1. A reliable employee is designated as the petty cash **custodian.** This person is provided a specified amount of petty cash at the outset. The custodian then disburses the cash as needed, receives adequate documentation for each petty cash disbursement, maintains a running record of the petty cash on hand, and periodically reports the total amount of cash spent supported by the **documentation** for each disbursement. The record maintained, in addition to the documentation, often is called the petty cash book. To illustrate, assume J. Doe is selected as the petty cash custodian with a petty cash fund of $300. A regular check drawn to "Petty Cash" is cashed and the cash is given to Doe. The initiating entry would be:

Petty cash   300
    Cash   300

2. When the amount of petty cash runs low, and also at the end of the accounting period, the custodian submits a request for replenishment, supported by the documentation of expenditures for the amount of petty cash spent since the last replenishment date. At each of these dates, a regular check is drawn for the amount spent; the custodian is provided cash for the amount of the check in order to maintain the specified petty cash balance. To illustrate, at the end of the first month, J. Doe submitted a replenishment request for $260. It was supported by documentation that reflected the following payments from the petty cash fund: postage, $90; office supplies, $70; taxi fares, $80; and daily papers, $20. The following replenishment entry must be made:

Postage expense   90
Office supplies expense   70
Transportation expense   80
Administrative expense   20
    Cash (not Petty Cash)   260

The effects of this entry are to (a) replenish the amount of petty cash held by the custodian to $300, which is the specified balance maintained in the Petty Cash account in the ledger and (b) record expenses incurred from the use of petty cash.

Recording Cash Shortages and Overages

Cash shortages and overages may be caused by (1) theft, (2) unintentional errors in counting cash when there is a large volume of cash transactions, and (3) inappropriate accounting. Aside from petty cash, such shortages and overages usually should be recorded in a Cash Shortage and Overage account. A debit balance in this account is an expense or loss. A credit balance represents a revenue or gain depending upon the circumstances. In contrast, when theft is discovered, the amount involved should be recorded as a credit to the regular Cash account and as a debit to (a) a receivable if recovery is expected from the individual involved or from an insurance or bonding company, or (b) a loss account on the presumption that recovery is improbable.

RECONCILIATION OF BANK AND BOOK
CASH BALANCES

Monthly reconciliation of the bank balance, as reported on the monthly **bank statement,** with the depositor's **Cash account** balance is an important cash control procedure.

If the bank statement and the depositor's Cash account are current, the two balances will be in agreement. In this case they will reflect the **correct cash balance** for that particular Cash account. This condition will seldom occur; therefore, a reconciliation of bank and book balances will require identification of the various items that are not yet reflected in both balances.

Upon receipt of the monthly bank statement, the cash balance reported in the bank statement should be reconciled with the cash balance shown in the Cash account in the company books for that bank account. Reconciliation of bank and book balances has three basic purposes: (1) it establishes a measure of **control**—that is, it serves to check the accuracy of the records of both the bank and the company; (2) it establishes the correct ending cash balance; and (3) it provides information for entries in the books of the company for items shown on the bank statement that have not yet been recorded in the company's Cash account, such as a bank service charge.

Reconciliation of the bank balance with the book balance of the Cash account requires an analysis of the **monthly bank statement and the cash records maintained by the company.** Usually the **bank** and **book** cash balances will differ for the following reasons:

A. Items recorded as cash receipts in the company books but not added to the bank balance on the bank statement.

   Examples:

   1. Deposits in transit—cash deposits made by the company that have not been added by the bank to the bank balance.
   2. Cash on hand (i.e., cash not on deposit in the bank).

B. Amounts added by the bank to the bank balance but not yet recorded as cash receipts in the company books.

   Examples:

   1. Interest earned by the company that was added by the bank to the bank balance but has not yet been recorded as a cash receipt in the company books.
   2. Collections of notes receivable by the bank on behalf of the company; these amounts have been added by the bank to the bank balance but have not yet been recorded as cash receipts in the company books.

C. Amounts recorded as cash disbursements in the company books but not yet deducted by the bank from the bank balance.

   Example:

   Outstanding checks—checks written and recorded as cash disbursements in the company books that have not been cleared through the bank and, as a result, have not been deducted by the bank from the bank balance.

D. Amounts subtracted by the bank from the bank balance but not yet recorded as cash disbursements in the company books.

Examples:

1. Bank service charge.
2. Nonsufficient funds (i.e., a NSF, or "hot", check received from a customer).

Reconciliation Procedures

Reconciliation of the bank balance with the book balance of cash can be accomplished in any of the three following formats:

1. Reconciliation of the book balance to the bank balance. This format starts with the Cash account balance, then analyzes the differences, and ends with the bank balance.
2. Reconciliation of both the book and bank balances to the true or correct cash balance. This format has two parts, one for the **bank balance,** and another for the **book balance.** The last line for each part is the **correct cash balance.**
3. A comprehensive, or audit, format that reconciles the beginning balances, cash receipts, cash payments, and ending balances for **both** the bank and the books (discussed in Supplement 6–A).

The second format reconciles both the bank and book balances to the correct cash balance. It is used in this chapter because *(a)* it facilitates the analysis of differences, *(b)* it provides data for the adjusting entries needed to update the company's Cash account, and *(c)* it provides the correct balance of the Cash account that must be reported on the balance sheet.

Bank Reconciliation Illustrated

The August reconciliation of the bank balance with the book balance for West Company is shown in **Exhibit 6–1.** The August 31 bank statement reported an **ending** cash balance of $38,900. The company's Cash account showed an **ending** cash balance of $35,300. The bank reconciliation reconciles both the bank and book balances to the correct cash balance of $35,890.

Exhibit 6–1 presents Panel A, the fact situation, Panel B, the **bank reconciliation,** and Panel C, the entries needed to update the company's Cash account to the correct cash balance. Notice that the reconciliation has two parts—bank balance and book balance. Each part starts with the **ending** balances for the reconciliation period (August 31 in this example).

Each part also provides for **additions** and **deductions** for the reconciling items.

EXHIBIT 6–1

Bank Reconciliation to the Correct Cash Balance—West Company

Panel A—Fact Situation at August 31, 19X:

Bank Statement		Company's Cash Account	
August 1 balance	$ 32,000	August 1 balance	$ 30,000
Deposits recorded in August	77,300	August deposits	75,300
Checks cleared in August	(71,000)	August checks	(70,000)
Note collected (including $100 interest)	1,100	August 31 balance	$ 35,300
NSF check, J. Fox	(300)		
August service charges	(200)		
August 31 balance	$ 38,900		

Additional data, end of July: Deposits in transit, $5,000; outstanding checks, $8,000. End of August: Cash on hand (undeposited), $990.

Panel B—Reconciliation of Bank and Book Balances, August 31, 19X:

Bank Balance		Book Balance	
Ending bank balance, August 31	$38,900	Ending book balance, August 31	$35,300
Additions:		Additions:	
Cash on hand (undeposited)	990	Note collected by bank:	
Deposits in transit ($5,000 + $75,300 −		Principal	1,000
$77,300)	3,000	Interest	100
Deductions:		Deductions:	
Outstanding checks ($8,000 + $70,000 −		NSF check, J. Fox	(300)
$71,000)	(7,000)	Bank service charges	(200)
Total	35,890	Total	35,900
Cash shortage		Cash shortage	(10)
Correct cash balance	$35,890	Correct cash balance	$35,890

Panel C—Entries Required to Update the Cash Account to the Correct Balance of $35,890:

1. Cash		1,100	
Note receivable			1,000
Interest revenue			100
2. Special receivable, J. Fox, NSF		300	
Expense, bank service charge		200	
Cash shortage		10	
Cash			510

Note that the last line on the reconciliation is the correct cash balance. Both the bank and the books would reflect this balance if all items were recognized by both the bank and the depositor. This fact is the key used to decide which additions and deductions should be entered under "bank balance" and which should be entered under "book balance." The only items entered under "bank balance" are those that eventually will change the "bank balance." Only those that cause a change in the Cash account are entered under "book balance."

Five items on the bank reconciliation given in Exhibit 6–1 need explanation:

1. **Deposits in transit**—a deposit made by the company late in the period that was not yet included on the bank statement; usually determined by comparing company deposits with the deposits listed on the bank statement. Alternately, the amount can be determined as follows:

Deposits in transit at end of prior period	$ 5,000
Deposits for the current period (per books)	75,300
Total that could have been deposited	80,300
Deposits per bank statement	(77,300)
Deposits in transit at end of current period	$ 3,000

2. **Outstanding checks**—checks that have not cleared the bank; usually determined by comparing checks written with checks cleared. Alternately, the amount can be determined as follows:

Outstanding checks at end of prior period	$ 8,000
Checks written during current period (per books)	70,000
Total checks that could have cleared	78,000
Checks cleared per bank statement	(71,000)
Outstanding checks at end of current period	$ 7,000

3. **NSF (nonsufficient funds) check**—The company received a $300 check from customer J. Fox, debited that amount to the Cash account, and deposited it. The bank received the check and increased the company's bank balance. The check was returned to the company's bank as a "hot" check; the bank reduced the company's checking account. Therefore, it is no longer in the company's bank account. It is still a debit in the company's Cash account. The debit must be removed from the Cash account and debited to a special receivable account as in Exhibit 6–1, Panel C.

4. **Cash shortages and overages**—After all items were verified and entered on the bank reconciliation, the bank and book **correct balances** did not agree by $10. The logical conclusion was a cash **shortage** because the books totaled $10 more cash than shown as the correct cash balance. It appears that cash on hand was $10 short; therefore, the book balance was reduced and a cash shortage was recorded.

5. Entries required by the bank statement to update the company's Cash account are shown in Exhibit 6–1, Panel C. The required entries were combined into two entries for practical reasons. Notice that these entries **recorded each addition and deduction shown on the book balance section of the reconciliation.** The additions and deductions on the bank balance section do not affect the company's books because they already have been recorded by the company.

Comprehensive Bank Reconciliation

This bank reconciliation format is variously called a comprehensive bank reconciliation, a cash reconciliation, four-column reconciliation, and an audit-based reconciliation. This format contains separate parts for **bank** and **book.** It is a comprehensive reconciliation because it reconciles *(a)* beginning bank and book balances, *(b)* cash receipts, *(c)* cash payments, and *(d)* ending (or correct) cash balances. A comprehensive bank reconciliation is discussed and illustrated in Supplement 6–A.

STATEMENT OF CHANGES IN FINANCIAL POSITION

The **statement of changes in financial position** (SCFP), when prepared on the cash equivalent basis, is an important phase of cash planning and control. It also is relevant to financial statement users because it helps them assess and predict the future cash flows of the enterprise. The SCFP, cash basis, is discussed in Chapter 23.

PART B: SHORT-TERM INVESTMENTS

Investments in the securities of other entities are classified on the balance sheet as either short-term investments (current assets) or as long-term investments (noncurrent assets, "Funds and investments"). Short-term investments often are called marketable securities. This textbook uses short-term investments because it is more descriptive.

SHORT-TERM INVESTMENTS DEFINED

To be classified as a short-term investment, a security must meet the following tests:

1. The security must be **readily marketable.** It must be regularly traded on a security exchange or in some other established market.[2]
2. The **intention of the investor** is to convert the security to cash within the current operating cycle or one year, whichever is longer.

In practice, these criteria present problems. First, long-term investments often are readily marketable; thus, this criterion may not distinguish between short-

---

[2] *FASB Interpretation No. 16,* "Clarification of Definitions and Accounting for Marketable Equity Securities that Become Nonmarketable" (Stamford, Conn., February 1977) provides some detailed rules pertaining to marketability.

term and long-term investments. Operationally, the second criterion, **intention of the investor,** often is the factor that distinguishes between a short-term and long-term investment. This test causes practical problems because **intentions** *(a)* can be changed often and *(b)* are difficult to "audit."

Examples of short-term and long-term investments are:

1. **Short term—equity securities,** such as shares of common and preferred stock; **debt securities,** such as corporate and government bonds; and **commercial paper,** such as certificates of deposit, money-market certificates, treasury bills, and savings accounts.
2. **Long term**—equity securities, debt securities, debt and asset replacement funds (e.g., a bond sinking fund), long-term commercial paper, and investments in real property (e.g., land and buildings). Long-term investments are discussed in Chapters 16 and 17.

Accounting for Short-Term Investments at Acquisition Date

Short-term investments are recorded at cost on acquisition date in conformity with the **cost principle.** Acquisition cost is the **cash equivalent price** paid; it includes the purchase cost plus all incidental acquisition costs. These costs include commissions, transfer taxes, and any other costs directly related to the acquisition. Noncash considerations given in payment are valued at their market value at the transaction date.

Accounting for Short-Term Investments after Acquisition Date

Depending upon the type of security or commercial paper, short-term investments may be accounted for after acquisition date on the basis of (1) lower of cost or market, (2) cost, or (3) market. For example, *Accounting Trends & Techniques, 1984* (p. 108), presented the following data:

Marketable Securities—Valuation

	Number of companies			
	1983	1982	1981	1980
Cost:				
Approximates market	255	254	251	251
No reference to market	21	20	23	22
Market value disclosed	3	5	4	14
Lower of cost or market	34	35	36	31
Market value	3	4	—	3

ACCOUNTING FOR SHORT-TERM INVESTMENTS IN EQUITY SECURITIES

FASB Statement 12, "Accounting for Certain Marketable Securities," requires that short-term investments in marketable **equity securities be valued at each balance sheet date on the LCM basis. Equity** securities, as used in *FASB Statement 12*, encompass all capital stock (including warrants, rights, and stock options) except preferred stock that by its terms must either be redeemed by the issuing enterprise or is redeemable at the option of the investor.[3] **Equity securities do not include debt securities** such as bonds and other debt instruments. These debt securities have significantly different characteristics and do not represent ownership shares.

FASB Statement 12 states: "The carrying amount of a marketable equity securities portfolio shall be the lower of its aggregate cost or market value, determined at balance sheet date. The amount by which aggregate cost of the portfolio exceeds market value shall be accounted for as the valuation allowance."

FASB Statement 12 requires that LCM be applied to short-term **equity** investments. It also requires that a clear distinction between **realized** and **unrealized** losses and gains be maintained. These requirements are implemented as follows:

1. **Portfolio basis**—at the end of each reporting period, group the short-term equity investments into one aggregate **portfolio** to determine total (i.e., aggregate) original cost and total market value.
2. **Measure any unrealized loss**—at the end of each reporting period, compare total portfolio cost with total market; if market is **less** than cost, adjust the carrying value of the portfolio down to LCM. This entry debits an **unrealized loss** account (e.g., Unrealized Loss on Short-Term Equity Investments), and credits an allowance account (e.g., Allowance to Reduce Short-Term Equity Investments to LCM).

   The unrealized loss amount is reported on the current income statement. The allowance account is reported on the balance sheet as a contra account (i.e., deduction) to the related investment account.
3. **Measure any unrealized loss recoveries**—At the end of each reporting period, the balance in the **allowance account** must be re-adjusted to reflect LCM. If total market value has continued to decline, the balance in the allowance account must be increased (and an additional unrealized loss recorded). In contrast, if the total market value of the portfolio has increased, the balance in the allowance account must be decreased to reflect the correct LCM carrying value of the portfolio. This re-adjustment, which is due to an unrealized loss recovery, is recorded as a debit to

---

[3] *FASB Statement 12* specifically relates only to **equity** securities. However, *FASB Statement 12* makes one exception as follows: The term [equity securities] ". . . does not encompass preferred stock that by its terms either must be redeemed by the issuing enterprise or is redeemable at the option of the investor, nor does it include treasury stock or convertible bonds." The exception recognizes that the specified redemption requirement makes such preferred stock almost like a debt security, and *FASB Statement 12* does not consider debt securities. Also, *Statement 12* is not applicable to mutual life insurance companies because of specialized industry practices.

the allowance account and a credit to an unrealized gain (or unrealized loss recovery) account.

Application of LCM in this manner can be summarized as: **write-down for unrealized losses, write back up for unrealized loss recoveries, but do not write up above original cost.**

4. The sale of a short-term equity investment results in a debit for the resources received, a credit to the investment account for its original cost, and the **difference** is recorded as a **realized** gain or loss (see next section).

Accounting for Short-Term Equity Securities Illustrated

To illustrate the accounting for short-term investments in **equity securities**, assume Zero Corporation invested temporarily idle cash in short-term investments and made the following entry:

March 1, 19A:

Investment in equity securities, short term   16,200
   Cash   16,200
     To record purchase of the following stock:
      Apex common, nopar (50 shares @ $104) . . . . $ 5,200
      Rye preferred, par $50 (200 shares @ $55)   11,000
        Total cost $16,200

November 1, 19A—received a cash dividend of $1 per share on the Rye preferred stock:

Cash (200 shares @ $1)   200
   Investment revenue   200

December 31, 19A—Quoted market prices, Apex common, $96; Rye preferred, $56.25:

To record the unrealized loss:

Unrealized loss on short-term investments   150
   Allowance to reduce short-term investments to market   150

Computation of the balance needed in the allowance account:

Stock	Shares	Total cost	Total market	Balance needed in the allowance account
Apex common	50	× $104 = $ 5,200	× $96 = $ 4,800	
Rye preferred	200	× 55 = 11,000	× 56.25 = 11,250	
Total portfolio		$16,200	$16,050	$150

Reporting for 19A:

Income statement:
Investment revenue . . . . $ 200
Unrealized loss on short-term investments* . . . .   (150)

Balance sheet:
Current assets:
Investment in equity securities, short term $16,200
Less: Allowance to reduce to market 150 $16,050

* In contrast, as discussed in Chapter 16, when LCM is applied to **long-term** investments in equity securities, the unrealized losses and gains are not reported on the income statement; rather, they are reported under the **unrealized** subclassification of owners' equity.

Sale of Short-Term Equity Investments

Short-term investments frequently are sold as cash is needed. To apply the LCM rule, *FASB Statement 12* makes a precise distinction between unrealized and realized gains and losses on short-term equity investments:

1. **Net unrealized gain or loss** on a marketable equity security portfolio represents the difference between the market value of its securities and their aggregate cost at any given date (illustrated above).
2. **Realized gain or loss** represents the difference between the net proceeds from the sale of a marketable equity security and its cost.

Therefore, when a short-term equity security is sold, any amount in the **allowance** account is disregarded because that balance relates to the **total** portfolio and not to any single part of it. **The allowance account is adjusted only at each year-end.**

To illustrate, assume that on January 26, 19B, Zero sold all of its short-term investments in equity securities for cash as follows: Apex common, $98 per share, and Rye preferred, $54 per share. This transaction would be recorded as follows:

January 26, 19B:

Cash (50 shares × $98) + (200 shares × $54)   15,700
Loss (realized) on sale of investments   500
Investment in equity securities, short term
(50 shares × $104) + (200 shares × $55)   16,200

To conclude this example, assume the following for 19B:

(a) Zero Corporation purchased a short-term equity investment and made the following entry:

June 6, 19B:

Investment in equity securities, short term, AB Corporation,
common stock, par $5 (100 shares @ $70)   7,000
Cash   7,000

(b) At the end of 19B, the AB Corporation stock was selling at $71. Therefore, the allowance account should have a zero balance; however, it has a balance carried over from 19A of $150. Therefore, the following entry must be made:

December 31, 19B:

Allowance to reduce short-term investments to market	150	
Unrealized loss recovery on short-term investments		150

As a result of the 19B transactions, Zero Corporation would report the following on its 19B financial statements:

Income statement (for 19B):

Loss on sale of short-term investments	$ 500
Unrealized loss recovery on short-term investments*	(150)

Balance sheet (end of 19B):

Current assets:

Investment in equity securities, short term, at cost (approximate market, $7,100)	$7,000

* Some accountants prefer a title similar to the following: Unrealized gain on marketable securities.

Consider the effect of recording the LCM loss (of $150 in 19A). First, for 19A it **reduced** 19A current assets and income by the amount of the unrealized loss. Second, in the next year (19B) the unrealized loss is "reversed" to prevent it from being **double counted.** This procedure does not affect the amount of **realized** gain or loss on sale of the investment. The net effect is to shift any unrealized loss to the earlier year when it occurred.

Transfer of Marketable Equity Securities between the Short- and Long-Term Investment Portfolios.   *FASB Statement 12* requires that when marketable equity securities are transferred between the short-term and long-term investment portfolios in either direction, the transfer must be effected at their LCM value at the time of the transfer. When market value at the date of transfer is below cost, the lower market value becomes the cost basis for subsequent LCM valuations; the difference between market value and cost on the date of transfer is accounted for as a **realized loss.** It is included in the determination of income in the period of transfer.

The purpose of this guideline is to reduce the incentive to manipulate income by transferring securities between the short-term and long-term portfolios; it treats any unrealized loss at the date of transfer as a realized loss.

Disclosure of Short-Term Investments in Equity Securities

Disclosure requirements specified by *FASB Statement 12* for short-term investments in equity securities are:

a. As of the date of each balance sheet presented, aggregate cost and market value with identification as to which is the carrying amount.

b. As of the date of the latest balance sheet presented, the following:
   i. Gross unrealized gains representing the excess of market value over cost for all marketable equity securities in the portfolio having such an excess.
   ii. Gross unrealized losses representing the excess of cost over market value for all marketable equity securities in the portfolio having such an excess.
c. For each period for which an income statement is presented:
   i. Net realized gain or loss included in the determination of net income.
   ii. The basis on which cost was determined in computing realized gain or loss (i.e., average cost or other method used).
   iii. The change in the valuation allowance(s) that has been included in the determination of net income.

The following excerpt from the 1983 annual report of The Pittston Company included the information required by *FASB Statement 12* as follows:

THE PITTSTON COMPANY

	1983	1982
	(in thousands)	
Current assets:		
Cash	$24,947	$23,833
Short-term investments (Note 2)	27,693	8,462

Notes to consolidated financial statements:

Note 2: Short-term investments consist of the following:

	As of December 31	
	1983	1982
	(in thousands)	
Marketable equity securities, at market (cost $867,000 in 1983 and 1982)	$ 688	$ 743
Other investments:		
Certificates of deposit and time deposits	1,164	1,825
U.S. Government obligations acquired under repurchase agreements	19,400	4,250
Canadian Treasury Bills	5,519	—
Private Export Funding Corporation obligations	922	1,644
Total short-term investments	$27,693	$ 8,462

Source: AICPA, *Accounting Trends & Techniques, 1984* (New York, 1984), p. 112.

ACCOUNTING FOR SHORT-TERM INVESTMENTS IN DEBT SECURITIES

Short-term investments in **debt** securities are recorded in the investment account at **cost** in conformity with the cost principle. Any discount or premium caused by a difference between the maturity value (or par) of the debt security and the acquisition price usually is not separately recorded. Also, because of the short holding period, this discount or premium usually is not amortized; thus, the investment account continues to carry the cost amount until the investment is sold.

After acquisition date, debt securities are accounted for using one of two methods as follows:

1. **Cost method—Accounting Research Bulletin (ARB) 43** prescribed the accounting for short-term investments prior to the issuance of *FASB Statement 12,* which superseded *ARB 43* only with regard to equity securities. *ARB 43* specifies that short-term debt securities should be carried at acquisition cost except when (1) their current market value is less than cost by a **substantial amount** and (2) the market value decline is not due to **temporary** conditions. When both of these conditions exist, *ARB 43* requires that the short-term debt security be written down to market value to recognize the **permanent impairment** of asset value. Subsequent to this write-down, which would not occur often, any recovery in market value is not recognized in the accounts (in contrast to the illustrations above for the LCM rule applied to equity securities). The reduced carrying value then is used as **cost** for future accounting purposes.[4] Therefore, a permanent decline usually is recorded as a direct credit to the investment account and a debit to a loss (realized) account, such as "Impairment Loss on Investments in Marketable Securities."

Application of the cost method to short-term investments in debt securities is not complex. However, when a debt security is purchased or sold between interest dates, the interest accrued since the last interest date must be computed and recorded separately from cost because on the next interest date the new owner of the debt security will receive the full cash amount of interest for the interest period just ended. On the transaction date, the buyer and the seller of the debt actually will "offset cash" for the amount of interest accrued from the prior interest date to the date of purchase/sale. The amount of accrued interest at transaction date is separately identified because it does not affect the cost or sale price of the security. Rather, it affects the amount of investment revenue earned.

Transfers of a debt security from the short-term portfolio to the long-term portfolio (and vice versa) are made at the carrying value at the date of transfer.

2. **LCM Method—**Some companies use the LCM method for short-term investments in **debt** securities. These companies set up a separate portfolio for the debt securities and apply the LCM basis exactly as illustrated above for short-term equity securities. Although the LCM method for debt securities is not in conformity with *ARB 43* (see prior discussion of the cost basis), these companies justify use of the LCM method for debt securities because *FASB Statement 12*

---

[4] For income tax purposes, the difference between original cost and selling price is taxable. *FASB Statement 12,* paragraph 22, states that recognition of unrealized losses and gains cause timing differences for interperiod income tax allocation (discussed in Chapter 10).

(which relates only to equity securities) does not specifically forbid such applications. Also they argue logically that short-term debt securities should be valued at current not cash equivalent; that is, LCM.

Accounting for Short-Term Debt Securities Illustrated

To illustrate application of the **cost method** in accounting for and reporting short-term investments in debt securities, we will consider transactions from acquisition date through sale date. The accounting period ends December 31.

June 30, 19A—Purchased a $10,000 bond of KD Corporation at 98 (i.e., $9,800 cash) plus accrued interest. The bond pays 9% interest each March 31.

Investment in debt securities, short term	9,800	
Interest receivable* ($10,000 × 9% × $\frac{3}{12}$; April–June)	225	
Cash ($9,800 + $225)		10,025

* Interest Receivable is debited because this amount will be included in the interest collected during the next reporting period (i.e., on March 31, 19B). If the collection is to be made in the current period, it would be more convenient to debit Interest Revenue.

December 31, 19A (end of the accounting period):

a. To accrue interest for June 30–December 31:

Interest receivable ($10,000 × 9% × $\frac{6}{12}$)	450	
Interest revenue		450

b. KD bonds are quoted at 97.5:

No entry is required to record LCM because there is no indication that (1) the amount is significant, and (2) there is a permanent impairment of asset value.

Reporting for 19A:

Income statement:

Interest revenue	$ 450

Balance sheet:

Investments in debt securities, short term, at cost	
(market value, $9,750)	9,800
Interest receivable ($225 + $450)	675

March 31, 19B—interest date:

Cash ($10,000 × 9%)	900	
Interest receivable ($225 + $450)		675
Interest revenue ($10,000 × 9% × $\frac{3}{12}$; January–March)		225

October 1, 19B—Sold the bond investment for $9,850 cash plus accrued interest:

Cash [$9,850 + ($10,000 × 9% × $\frac{6}{12}$ = $450)]	10,300	
Investment in debt securities, short term		9,800
Interest revenue ($10,000 × 9% × $\frac{6}{12}$; April–Sept.)		450
Gain (realized) on sale of short-term investment		50

The cost method also is widely used to account for **long-term** investments in debt securities. Long-term investments in debt securities are discussed in Chapter 17.

ACCOUNTING AND REPORTING SHORT-TERM INVESTMENTS AT MARKET VALUE

Accounting and reporting of short-term investments at market requires that the **market value** of the short-term investment portfolio be determined at the end of each reporting period. The short-term investment account is written up, or down, at the end of each reporting period. The market gain or loss for the current period is recorded and reported on the current income statement. When a security is sold, the difference between its sale price and carrying value (i.e., the last recorded market value) is recorded as a gain or loss.

To illustrate the market value method, assume the following for MV Company:

a. April 1, 19A—purchased common stock of XT Corporation for $10,000:

Investment in equity securities, short term		
(XT Corp. common stock, 400 shares)	10,000	
Cash		10,000

b. December 31, 19A—end of the accounting period; market value of XT stock, $11,000:

Investment in equity securities, short term	1,000	
Market (holding) gain on investments		1,000

Reporting at end of 19A:

Income statement:

Market gain on investments	$ 1,000

Balance sheet:

Current assets:	
Investment in equity securities, short term,	
at market (cost, $10,000)	$11,000

c. February 19, 19B—Received a cash dividend on the XT stock of $.50 per share:

Cash (400 × $.50)	200	
Investment revenue		200

d. March 1, 19B—Sold the short-term investment for $11,500 to meet current cash needs:

Cash	11,500	
Investment in equity securities, short term		
(XT Corp. common stock)		11,000
Gain on sale of investments		500

The major arguments for the market value method for short-term investments are: *(a)* it reports the current economic value of a short-term investment, *(b)* it is not biased because it accounts for market gains and losses on the same basis, *(c)* it avoids manipulation of income, and *(d)* it provides more relevant information for statement users. The major arguments against the market value method are: *(a)* reliable market values at each year-end often are difficult to obtain, *(b)* market changes do not cause gains and losses, and *(c)* it may cause wide fluctuations in reported income because market valuations can change often and by significant amounts.

Currently the market value method is **not considered GAAP** except for certain **specialized** industry groups such as mutual insurance companies.

INVESTMENT REVENUE ON SHORT-TERM INVESTMENTS

Cash dividends on short-term investments in **capital stock** of other companies are recognized as earned at the time of the **declaration of the cash dividend.** Cash dividends on capital stock held as an investment are not accrued prior to declaration.

Stock dividends received on stock held as an investment do not represent revenue; rather they serve to reduce the cost per share of the investment.

Bonds and similar debt securities purchased at a price above par are acquired at a premium; if acquired below par, at a discount. Premium or discount on a **short-term** bond investment is not amortized because, by definition, the investment will be converted to cash in the near future instead of being held to maturity. Interest receivable and interest revenue on short-term investments in debt securities (e.g., bonds) are accrued at the end of the accounting period through an adjusting entry.

IDENTIFICATION OF UNITS SOLD

When short-term investments are sold, or otherwise disposed of, a question frequently is posed about the identification of unit cost. For example, assume three purchases of stock in XY Corporation as follows: purchase No. 1, 200 shares @ $80; purchase No. 2, 300 shares @ $100; and purchase No. 3, 100 shares @ $110. Now assume 100 shares are sold at $120. What is the cost of the shares sold? For accounting purposes, the decision would appear to be arbitrary, with no generally accepted basis for identifying cost. Most companies identify cost based upon **specific identification** of the securities sold or a FIFO cost flow assumption because the Internal Revenue Service specifies these methods for tax purposes.[5] Consistency in application from period to period is essential.

---

[5] Use of different methods for *(a)* accounting and *(b)* tax purposes would cause a timing difference, as discussed and illustrated in Chapter 10, Part B.

PART C: RECEIVABLES

RECEIVABLES DEFINED

Receivables include all of an entity's claims for money, goods, services, and other noncash assets from other entities. Receivables may be classified as current assets or noncurrent assets depending upon their time to maturity or expected collection date. Receivables may be informal, such as an "open" account, or represented by a formal contract, such as a note receivable. For discussion purposes, receivables are classified herein as follows:

- A. **Current receivables**—in conformity with the definition of current assets:
  1. Trade receivables.
  2. Nontrade receivables.
- B. **Noncurrent receivables**—not in conformity with the definition of current assets:
  1. Trade receivables.
  2. Nontrade receivables.

CURRENT RECEIVABLES

Current receivables are expected to be collected within the year following the balance sheet date or the operating cycle of the entity, whichever is longer. **Trade receivables** are amounts owed by customers for goods and services sold in the entity's normal course of business. **Trade receivables** include "open" accounts, usually called accounts receivable and written agreements, usually called notes receivable, trade.

The scope of current receivables is indicated by the following tabulation of 600 major companies:

Current Receivables

	Number of companies			
	1983	1982	1981	1980
Trade receivable captions:				
Accounts receivable	207	199	199	209
Receivables	162	152	155	153
Accounts and notes receivable	118	112	121	128
Trade accounts receivable	113	137	125	110
Total companies	600	600	600	600

| | Number of companies | | | |
	1983	1982	1981	1980
Receivables other than trade receivables:				
Tax refund claims	91	112	71	51
Contracts	64	47	48	31
Investees	35	36	35	37
Installment notes or accounts	20	20	18	19
Employees	10	7	5	N/C
Sale of assets	9	6	5	N/C

N/C—Not Compiled.

Source: AICPA, *Accounting Trends & Techniques, 1984* (New York, 1984), p. 113.

Accounts Receivable

Accounts receivable designates amounts currently owed by customers who have purchased goods and services on short-term credit. At the date of a credit sale, an account receivable is recorded and Sales Revenue is credited. This initial entry should record the amount of **cash** that is expected to be collected from the customer. Often this is the amount that is billed to the customer. However, companies sometimes offer a **cash discount** (also called a sales discount) to encourage early payment by the customer. Typical terms are 2/10, n/30; that is, 2% cash discount if paid within 10 days from sale date and the gross amount due in 30 days. Another commonly used credit term is 2/10; n/EOM (i.e., end of the month). Most companies pay such accounts early to avoid the additional cash payment, which involves a very high interest rate on an annualized basis (approximately 36½% in the above example). When a cash discount is offered, the question arises as to whether the sale should be recorded at its *(a)* gross amount, or *(b)* net of allowed discount amount. To illustrate, assume on December 28, 19A, a sale of $1,000 with terms 2/10, n/30. Should this sale be recorded at **gross** of $1,000 or at net of $980 (i.e., $1,000 × .98)? Given the high annualized interest rate of 36½%, the usual expectation is that the net amount will be collected. Both the gross and net approaches are used in industry. The net approach is theoretically preferable while the gross approach sometimes is viewed as more practical because of a perceived minor clerical advantage. An application of the two approaches is presented in **Exhibit 6–2.** The evaluation at the end of the exhibit leads to the conclusion that the net method is clearly preferable.

Subsequent to the initial recording of trade accounts receivable, these current assets are carried at their **net realizable value,** which is the cash amount expected to be collected. This valuation reflects the effects of *(a)* cash discounts allowed for early payment and *(b)* estimated bad debt losses.

EXHIBIT 6–2

Recording Credit Sales and Subsequent Collections

Situation: December 28, 19A—Sale, $1,000; credit terms 2/10, n/30. End of annual reporting period, December 31.

Net approach	Gross approach

19A—To record the credit sale:

Net approach		Gross approach	
Accounts receivable 980		Accounts receivable 1,000	
Sales revenue	980	Sales revenue	1,000

19B—To record collection if within the 10-day discount period:

Net approach		Gross approach	
Cash 980		Cash 980	
Accounts receivable	980	Sales discounts 20	
		Accounts receivable	1,000

19B—To record collection if after the 10-day discount period:

Net approach		Gross approach	
Cash 1,000		Cash 1,000	
Interest revenue	20	Accounts receivable	1,000
Accounts receivable	980		

Evaluation:

a. Theoretical—The 2% discount is interest (time value of money), not sales revenue. Sales revenue in 19A is $980, not $1,000. The interest should be recognized only if the full amount, $1,000, is actually paid. The receivable at the end of 19A should be the net cash expected to be received ($980) because the discounts usually are taken. The net method attains all of these theoretical objectives. Even if the discounts are not taken, the net method should be used.

b. Theoretically, an adjusting entry at the end of the 19A can be supported under each approach: Net approach—for discounts already forfeited; and gross approach—for discounts that can still be taken. Lack of materiality usually precludes such adjusting entries.

c. Practical—Comparing the above entries for each approach and the adjusting entries in *(b)*, the clerical differences appear to be insignificant.

MEASUREMENT OF BAD DEBT EXPENSE AND ACCOUNTS RECEIVABLE

When credit is extended on a continuing basis, some uncollectible receivables are inevitable. These bad debt expenses are considered a normal operating expense of the business. Measurement of such items involves the concurrent estimation of *(a)* the amount of **bad debt expense** for the period and *(b)* **valuation of accounts receivable** at net realizable value.

A special valuation account (i.e., a contra asset), Allowance for Doubtful Accounts (or Allowance for Bad Debts), is used to report the estimated bad debts included in Accounts Receivable at the end of each reporting period. The residual amount, Accounts Receivable less Allowance for Doubtful Accounts, represents the **estimated net realizable value** of accounts receivable. An adjusting entry is used to record bad debt expense and concurrently to adjust the allowance account. To illustrate:

Bad debt expense 6,000
    Allowance for doubtful accounts 6,000

The basic accounting question is when should the loss due to an uncollectible account (i.e., bad debt expense) be recognized. The primary issues are (1) how to **measure** bad debt expense in conformity with the **matching principle,** and (2) how to measure accounts receivable in conformity with the **definition of a current asset**—its expected net realizable value. These measurements require the use of estimates.

ESTIMATING BAD DEBT EXPENSE

The **matching principle** requires that bad debt expense be estimated at the end of each accounting period. The estimate is needed in order to **match** expected bad debt losses with the revenues of the period that **caused** those losses.

The sales revenue of the period from **credit sales** is known at the end of the period; however, the specific accounts receivable that ultimately will be uncollectible often will not be known until future periods. The **matching principle** requires that bad debt expense be matched against the sales revenue of the period in which the sales revenue is recognized. Therefore, each period, it is necessary to **estimate** the amount of bad debt expense and record it in an adjusting entry, similar to the one above. This estimate is prepared before the ultimate determination of whether the individual accounts receivable of the period will be collected.

Two methods are commonly used to estimate the adjustment to the Bad Debt Expense and the Allowance for Doubtful Accounts:

1. **Estimation of bad debt expense as a percent of credit sales**—This method emphasizes the **matching principle.** The net realizable value of accounts receivable is secondary. Based on experience, the average percentage relationship between actual bad debt losses and **net credit sales** is ascertained. This percentage then is applied to the **actual** net credit sales of the period to determine both the Bad Debt Expense and the concurrent addition to the Allowance for Doubtful Accounts.

2. **Estimation of net realizable value of accounts receivable**—This method uses net realizable value of the ending balance of accounts receivable and a bad debt percentage. This method emphasizes the balance sheet and the definition of a current asset—accounts receivable. The balance in accounts receivable is multiplied by the appropriate bad debt percent(s) to determine the balance that is required to be in the allowance account.

The balance in the allowance account then is adjusted so that it equals the total amount of the estimated uncollectible accounts. The bad debt percent(s) used in this method can be either *(a)* a composite (i.e., single) rate, or *(b)* a series of rates based on an **aging schedule.**

Both the credit sales and the net realizable value methods must be adapted to changes in credit policy, changes in economic conditions, or any other factor which might affect the ability of customers to pay their debts. After one of these methods is selected for use, it should be continuously reviewed by the accountant and the officers of the company so that the rates can be revised to attain reliable results. These two approaches are illustrated later in this section.

Estimating Bad Debt Expense Illustrated

To illustrate accounting for bad debt expense and uncollectible receivables, assume the following data for X Company for the year ended December 31, 19B:

January 1, 19B, balances:
Accounts receivable (debit)	$101,300
Allowance for doubtful accounts (credit)	3,300

Transactions during 19B:
Credit sales	500,000
Cash sales	700,000
Collections on accounts receivable	420,000
Prior accounts to be written off as uncollectible during 19B	3,800

The 19B entry to write off the prior uncollectible accounts is:

Allowance for doubtful accounts	3,800	
Accounts receivable (specific accounts)		3,800

After posting this entry, Accounts Receivable will reflect a debit balance of $177,500 (i.e., $101,300 + $500,000 − $420,000 − $3,800). The write-off of individual accounts as uncollectible would occur as a result of a review by the credit department during the period and would precede the end-of-period adjusting entries. In some cases, such as after a large write-off or when currently created receivables are written off before the end of the period, the allowance account may have a temporary **debit** balance prior to the adjusting entry ($500 in this example, i.e., $3,300 − $3,800).

Estimate Based on a Composite Percent of Credit Sales. An analysis of the actual uncollectible accounts related to actual credit sales for the past three years showed that an average of 1.2% of credit sales was not collected and that this relationship is expected to continue. The required 19B adjusting entry is:

Bad debt expense ($500,000 × 1.2%)	6,000	
Allowance for doubtful accounts		6,000

After posting this entry, the allowance account will reflect a credit balance of $5,500 (i.e., $3,300 − $3,800 + $6,000). The entry is made without regard to the prior balance in the allowance account.

Estimate Based on a Composite Percent of Accounts Receivable.   An analysis of prior actual uncollectible accounts related to the prior ending balances of accounts receivable showed that an average of 3½% of the ending balance was uncollectible. Assuming this relationship is expected to continue, the required 19B adjusting entry would be:

Bad debt expense ($177,500 × 3½% + $500) 6,713
    Allowance for doubtful accounts 6,713

Estimate Based on Aging Schedule of Accounts Receivable.   This method is based upon an aging of the current receivables. Therefore, this method involves two phases: (1) preparation of an aging schedule, and (2) estimation of the collection loss percentages for each aging category.

Phase 1—Aging accounts receivable.   Aging accounts receivable involves an analysis of each individual account to determine the amounts not past due, moderately past due, and considerably past due. Classification of receivable amounts by age (i.e., length of time uncollected) is important because experience indicates that the older an account, the higher the probability of uncollectibility. Aging requires the preparation of an **aging schedule** similar to the illustration in **Exhibit 6–3**.

Phase 2—Estimate the collection loss percentages.   Upon completion of the aging schedule, each past-due amount (e.g., Field's account in Exhibit 6–3) is reviewed by credit department personnel to determine its probable collectibility. The purpose of this analysis is to develop an estimated collection loss percentage for each **age category.** This estimate is based on the loss experience of the company for each age category. The results of this analysis by X Company are shown in **Exhibit 6–4**.

EXHIBIT 6–3

Aging Schedule for Accounts Receivable of X Company (at December 31, 19B)

Customer	Receivable balance Dec. 31, 19B	Not past due	Past due		
			1–30 days	31–60 days	Over 60 days
Davis	$ 500	$ 400	$ 100		
Evans	900	900			
Field	1,650		1,350	$ 300	
Harris	90			30	$ 60
King	800	700	60	40	
Zilch	250	250			
Total	$177,500	$110,000	$31,000	$29,500	$7,000

EXHIBIT 6–4

Estimating Allow-
ance for Doubtful
Accounts, Aging
Approach for X
Company (at De-
cember 31, 19B)

Status	Total balances*	Uncollectible experience percentage	Amount estimated to be uncollectible
Not past due	$110,000	.2%	$ 220
1–30 days past due	31,000	1.0	310
31–60 days past due	29,500	8.0	2,360
Over 60 days past due	7,000	40.0	2,800
	$177,500		$5,690

* Amounts agree with amounts on "Total" line in Exhibit 6–3.

Based on the computation in Exhibit 6–4, at December 31, 19B, the Allowance for Doubtful Accounts would be adjusted to a credit balance of $5,690, as follows:

Bad debt expense	6,190	
Allowance for doubtful accounts		6,190
Computation:		
To adjust to the desired credit balance as follows:		
Desired balance (see Exhibit 6–4)		$5,690
Debit balance in allowance before adjustment		500
Amount of credit needed		$6,190

The aging schedule approach is preferable to the composite percentage approach because the former involves a more comprehensive analysis of accounts receivable.

In the preceding illustration, the $3,800 write-off of receivables during the current period caused the allowance account to have a debit balance of $500 before the end-of-period adjustment. This result does not necessarily indicate that past estimates of bad debt losses were too low. It is possible that the $3,800 write-off includes some receivables created during the same period. However, if the allowance account were to have a debit balance soon after making the end-of-period adjustment, an inadequate provision for bad debts probably is indicated. When it is determined that bad debt estimates have been too low or too high, current and future rates should be adjusted accordingly. This would be accounted for as a **change in accounting estimate** as prescribed in *APB Opinion 20*, "Accounting Changes" (see Chapters 3 and 20). A change in estimate does not use a correction entry; rather, the effects of the change are spread over the current and future reporting periods by using a new collection loss percentage.

EVALUATION OF METHODS OF ESTIMATING BAD DEBT EXPENSE

The two methods, *(a)* based on credit sales and *(b)* based on the net realizable value of accounts receivable, are acceptable under current GAAP.

Estimation of bad debt expense based on credit sales emphasizes the income statement because its primary focus is on bad debt **expense** and it only incidentally measures accounts receivable at net realizable value. The theoretical basis for the estimation of bad debt expense by this method is the **matching principle.** It is simple and economical to implement. Its primary disadvantage is that it does not reconsider prior estimates in the short term; thus, it does not compensate in the short term for prior estimating errors.

Estimation of bad debt expense based on net realizable value of accounts receivable emphasizes the balance sheet because its primary focus is on net realizable value of a current asset—accounts receivable. Its theoretical basis is the **full disclosure principle.** It compensates for prior estimating errors in both the short and long term. When applied using a single **composite rate,** it is simple and economical to apply; however, this application does not directly consider the age of accounts receivables. In contrast, when applied with **multiple aging rates,** it becomes more complex and costly. However, this application has the distinct advantage of considering aging effects that usually provide better estimates.

In practice, both methods often are used together. That is, for interim financial statements, many companies base monthly or quarterly adjusting entries on the credit sales method because of the low cost of applying this method. At the end of the year, however, many companies age their accounts receivable as a check on the reasonableness of the balance in the allowance account. If the balance in the allowance account (before the year-end adjustment) differs materially from the balance implied by the aging schedule, the company must make a judgment about the appropriate amount to record in the year-end adjusting entry.

In the past, aging accounts receivables was a costly process. It required credit department personnel to analyze each account receivable individually. The aging method is used more frequently now because computer software has lowered the cost of implementing the aging method. Also, the high interest rates of recent years have prompted companies to monitor their receivables closely, and aging is the primary way accounts receivable are analyzed.

BAD DEBTS COLLECTED

When an account is collected from a customer whose account was previously written off as uncollectible, the customer's account should be debited for the amount actually collected and the allowance account should be credited for the same amount. This entry will cause the debtor's account to reflect a detailed record of the credit and related collections. It also will correct the allowance account. The collection then is recorded as a debit to Cash and a credit to Accounts Receivable.

CUSTOMERS' CREDIT BALANCES

Individual accounts receivable for customers with material **credit** balances (from prepayments or overpayments) should be reclassified and reported as liabilities. Credit Balance of Customers' Accounts is a suitable liability account title.

DIRECT WRITE-OFF OF UNCOLLECTIBLE ACCOUNTS

Although **not in conformity with GAAP,** some small nonpublic companies apply a "direct or specific write-off" procedure. Using this procedure, bad debt expense is recorded only when individual customers' accounts are uncollectible. At that time, Accounts Receivable is credited for the uncollectible balance and Bad Debt Expense is debited. This procedure does not require the use of estimates. It has the advantage of simplicity and is permitted for income tax purposes (as is the allowance method). It also is used by companies in which bad debt losses are not material in amount from year to year. The direct write-off procedure is subject to severe criticism on three counts: (1) Receivables are reported at more than their net realizable value; there is no allowance to deduct even though it is virtually certain that not all receivables will be collected. (2) The period in which the write-off occurs is often later than the period in which the receivable was created. The reported amounts of bad debt expense are not in conformity with the **matching principle**—the expenses of extending credit should be recognized in the period when the revenue is recognized. (3) It allows manipulation of income by arbitrary selection of the period of write-off. For these reasons, the specific write-off method is not in conformity with GAAP.

ACCOUNTING FOR NOTES RECEIVABLE

Notes receivable represent unconditional written promises to pay the payee or holder of the note a specified principal sum and interest thereon. Ordinarily, the payee will be in possession of the note unless it has been endorsed to a subsequent holder in due course.

Notes receivable include **trade** notes receivable, which arise from the sale of goods and services, and **special** notes which arise from all other sources. Both kinds of notes are classified either as current or noncurrent assets, depending upon their times to maturity. Trade notes and special notes should be recorded and reported separately.

A note receivable may be designated as either *(a)* interest bearing or *(b)* noninterest bearing. From both the economic and accounting views, **all commercial notes receivable either implicitly or explicitly include interest.** Basically, interest on short-term notes (i.e., simple interest) is computed as:

$$\begin{array}{ccccccc} \textbf{Principal} & & \textbf{Interest} & & \textbf{Time to} & & \textbf{Interest} \\ \textbf{amount} & \times & \textbf{rate} & \times & \textbf{maturity} & = & \textbf{amount} \end{array}$$

The **stated** rate of interest on a note is specified in the debt instrument. It determines the amount of **cash** interest to be paid on the principal amount.

The **principal amount** of a note receivable is the cash equivalent amount loaned, or of goods and services sold; it is the **amount subject to interest.** The **face amount** of a note receivable is the amount specified on the face of the note. This amount will be collected at maturity date; it may be the same as, or different from, the principal amount depending upon the note's specifications. The **maturity**

amount of a note receivable is the amount to be collected on the maturity date, excluding any **separate** interest collections due on that date.

Interest-Bearing Notes Receivable

Interest-bearing notes receivable specify the **principal amount** of the note as its **face** amount. **In addition,** it specifies a **stated rate** of interest on the principal amount.

Example:
On April 1, 19A, WV Company sold merchandise on credit and received a $3,000, one-year trade note receivable; stated interest rate, 10%. The annual reporting period for WV Company ends on December 31.

The required journal entries over the term of the note are as follows:

April 1, 19A—To record the sale and the interest-bearing note:

Notes receivable, trade	3,000	
Sales revenue		3,000

December 31, 19A—Adjusting entry:

*Interest receivable ($3,000 \times 10\% \times \frac{9}{12}$)	225	
Interest revenue		225

* Alternatively, this could be "Notes receivable."

March 31, 19B—Collection of face of note plus interest (no prior reversing entry):

Cash [$3,000 + ($3,000 \times 10\%$)]	3,300	
Notes receivable, trade		3,000
Interest receivable (above)		225
Interest revenue ($3,000 \times 10\% \times \frac{3}{12}$)		75

Noninterest-Bearing Notes Receivable

Noninterest-bearing notes always involve interest. The **face** amount of a noninterest-bearing note **includes both the principal amount and the interest amount as a single amount that will be collected on maturity date.** Typically, no stated interest rate is specified on the note itself.

Example:
On April 1, 19A, WV Company sold merchandise on credit and received a noninterest-bearing note receivable, face amount, $3,300, due in one year. The face of the note includes 10% interest on the principal amount of $3,000 (i.e., $3,300 \div 1.10 = $3,000). The sale price of the merchandise is the **present value** of the face amount of the note; the $300 difference is **interest revenue.** The accounting period ends December 31.

The required journal entries over the term of the note are:[6]

April 1, 19A—To record the sale and noninterest-bearing note:

Notes receivable, trade (face $3,300)	3,000	
Sales revenue		3,000

December 31, 19A—Adjusting entry:

Interest receivable ($3,000 × 10% × $\frac{9}{12}$)	225	
Interest revenue		225

March 31, 19B—Collection of face of note of $3,300 (and no prior reversing entry):

Cash	3,300	
Note receivable, trade (above)		3,000
Interest receivable (above)		225
Interest revenue ($3,000 × 10% × $\frac{3}{12}$)		75

Provision for Losses on Trade Notes Receivable

Provision for uncollectible notes from **trade customers** usually is included in the credit balance of Allowance for Doubtful Accounts.

SALE (DISCOUNTING) OF NOTES RECEIVABLE

If a note receivable is sold (i.e., transferred by endorsement) to a third party before maturity, the original payee receives cash before maturity. The sale of a note receivable often is referred to as **discounting.** The original payee assumes a **contingent liability** if the note is endorsed **with recourse.** In contrast, there

---

[6] The approach shown above recorded the noninterest-bearing note at **net** of the interest included in the face amount. An alternative, which gives exactly the same results, is to record the note at **gross,** at its face amount, as follows:

April 1, 19A:

Notes receivable, trade	3,300	
Discount on notes receivable*		300
Sales revenue		3,000

December 31,19A:

Discount on notes receivable*	225	
Interest revenue		225

March 31, 19B (assuming no reversing entry on January 1, 19B):

Cash	3,300	
Discount on notes receivable*	75	
Interest revenue		75
Notes receivable, trade		3,300

* Contra account to Notes Receivable.

is no contingent liability if it is endorsed **without recourse.** "Contingent liability" means that if the maker of the note defaults at maturity date, the endorser (i.e., original payee in this situation) must reimburse the new payee for the principal and interest due on the note, plus any protest fee charged by the last holder of the note. Because an investor usually is unwilling to purchase a note without recourse, most notes sold create a contingent liability.[7]

The cash received from the sale of a note receivable (either interest bearing or noninterest bearing) is computed as follows:

| **Principal of note** | **+** | **Total interest to maturity** | **−** | **Interest charged by new payee** | **=** | **Cash proceeds** |

Example:

WV Company sold (i.e., discounted) a $3,000 interest-bearing note receivable (face, $3,000, one-year, 10% interest bearing, dated April 1, 19A) to National Bank on August 1, 19A, at a 15% discount rate. Notice that this 12-month note, dated April 1, 19A, was held by the original payee, WV Company, for four months (April–July) and will be held by the bank for eight months (August 1, 19A–March 31, 19B). The cash proceeds on the sale date, August 1, 19A, would be computed as follows:

Maturity value:
Principal amount	$3,000
Total interest at maturity ($3,000 × 10%)	300
Amount subject to discount rate	3,300*
Interest charged by new payee (bank) ($3,300 × 15% × $\frac{8}{12}$)	330
Cash proceeds on date sold	$2,970

* If this had been a noninterest-bearing note, the face of the note would be this amount. In this instance, the computation would start with this amount and would be identical for the remaining amounts.

The journal entries for the above interest-bearing note sold on August 1, 19A, would be:

April 1, 19A—To record the initial sale and note receivable:

Notes receivable, trade	3,000	
Sales revenue		3,000

August 1, 19A—To record sale (discounting) of the note receivable at 15% interest:

Cash (computed above)	2,970	
Loss on sale of note ($3,100 − $2,970)	130*	
Notes receivable, trade		3,000
Interest revenue ($3,000 × 10% × $\frac{4}{12}$)		100*

* "Value" of note when discounted, $3,100—cash received, $2,970 = $130. Alternatively, these two amounts often are offset; that is, in this example a loss (or interest expense) of $30 would be reported (i.e., $130 − $100).

---

[7] However, if the discount rate is high enough, third parties will be induced to purchase notes without recourse.

Disclosure of a contingent liability on a note receivable that has been sold usually is made by a disclosure note such as: "The company is contingently liable for discounted notes receivable amounting to $3,000." Other ways to report the contingent liability are as follows (assuming $10,000 notes receivable held prior to discounting the $3,000 note):

1. Current assets:
   Notes receivable (contingent liability for notes receivable
   discounted, $3,000) $7,000
2. Current assets:
   Notes receivable $10,000
      Less: Notes receivable discounted 3,000 $7,000

Contingencies of all types, including contingent liabilities, are discussed in more detail in Chapter 10, Part A.

DISHONORED NOTES RECEIVABLE

When a note receivable is not renewed or collected at maturity, it is dishonored. The accounting procedure that will be followed depends upon (a) whether the note was held or sold (discounted) and (b) if sold whether endorsed with or without recourse. A dishonored note should be transferred from the Note Receivable account to a special receivable account.

After dishonor, interest accrues on the face amount plus accrued interest and any protest fees at the **legal** rate of interest (usually specified by the state laws). However, if the note is uncollectible, the total claim should be written off as a bad debt.

Examples:

A. **Dishonored note receivable not previously sold:**

On March 31, 19B, WV Company's, $3,000, 10%, one-year note receivable, dated April 1, 19A, was dishonored. The default would be recorded as follows (see page 328):

Special receivable, dishonored note   3,300
   Notes receivable   3,000
   Interest receivable ($3,000 × 10% × $\frac{9}{12}$)   225
   Interest revenue ($3,000 × 10% × $\frac{3}{12}$)   75

B. **Dishonored note receivable previously sold and endorsed with recourse:**

Protest fee charged by the bank, $15:

Special receivable, dishonored note   3,315
   Cash 3,315*

* Principal, $3,000 + interest, $300 + protest fee, $15.

C. **Dishonored note receivable previously sold and endorsed without recourse:**

No entry because the note will not revert to the original holder.

Balance sheet presentation of dishonored notes should list a special receivable with adequate provision for the uncollectibility expectations. Note disclosure is necessary for large notes in default.

SPECIAL RECEIVABLES

Receivables, other than trade receivables, are classified as **special receivables.** Some of the more common types of special receivables were listed on page 320.

Special receivables that are collectible within one year of the balance sheet date or the operating cycle (whichever is longer) should be reported as current assets. Other special receivables are reported on the balance sheet under a noncurrent caption such as Other assets, or Investments and funds.[8]

Special receivables should be valued as to collectibility. A special allowance for doubtful accounts in this category should be established if warranted.

USE OF ACCOUNTS RECEIVABLE TO SECURE IMMEDIATE CASH

To obtain immediate cash, companies often **sell** accounts receivable. They also may **borrow money** and pledge accounts receivable as collateral for the loan. Such **transfer arrangements** to advance the cash inflow from accounts receivable involve a wide range of contracts referred to as the sale, assignment, and pledging of receivables, and factoring. The scope of the use of receivables to obtain early cash is indicated in the following tabulation from a survey of 600 companies:

Receivables Used for Financing

	Number of companies			
	1983	1982	1981	1980
Receivables sold to finance subsidiary	57	63	53	50
Receivables sold to independent entity	39	33	39	35
Receivables used as collateral	34	26	22	25
Total references	130	122	114	110
Reference to receivable financing	121	112	108	102
No reference to receivable financing	479	488	492	498
Total companies	600	600	600	600

Source: AICPA, *Accounting Trends & Techniques, 1984* (New York, 1984), p. 118.

[8] "Advances to subsidiaries" normally would be reported under "Investments and funds."

For example, one prominent company reported the following:

THE BF GOODRICH COMPANY
Notes to consolidated financial statements:

(Dollars in millions)

Note T (in part): Commitments and Contingencies

In December 1983, Goodrich sold $75.0 of accounts receivable. Under the terms of the sales agreement, the purchaser has the option to require Goodrich to repurchase defaulted accounts receivable, if any.

The sale of accounts receivable, or borrowing money on them, will either be *(a)* with recourse or *(b)* without recourse. **With recourse** means that the transferor (i.e., the borrower) of the accounts receivables agrees to reimburse the transferee (i.e., the lender) for contractually specified **collection losses.** These include *(a)* failure of the customers to pay their accounts in full and *(b)* adjustments to the receivables for cash discounts and sales returns. Thus, **without recourse** means that the tranferor assumes no obligation to guarantee such losses; the transferee must assume the collection losses.

Also, the agreement to transfer accounts receivable for early cash will specify either *(a)* notification or *(b)* nonnotification. **Notification** means that the debtors (i.e., the customers) are notified of the transfer and that they will be billed and must make payments on the receivables directly to the transferee. **Nonnotification** means that the debtors are **not** notified of the transfer; thus, they will continue to be billed by, and make payments on the receivables to, the transferor. The transferor has the responsibility to remit the cash to the transferee as collected.

ACCOUNTING FOR THE TRANSFER OF ACCOUNTS RECEIVABLE

For the **transferor's** accounting purposes, a transfer of accounts receivables to obtain early cash must be classified as either a "sale" or "borrowing" transaction. The transfer is:

    a. **A sale of the receivables** similar to the sale of any other asset for cash, if **all** of the following conditions are met:[9]

        1. The transferor surrenders **control** of the future economic benefits embodied in the receivables (control is absent if transferor retains a later repurchase option).

        2. The transferor's obligation under the recourse provisions can be **reasonably estimated** (e.g., bad debt losses, collection costs, discounts, and repossessions).

---

[9] The discussion that follows is based on the provisions of FASB, *Statement of Financial Accounting Standards No. 77,* "Reporting by Transferors of Transfer of Receivables with Recourse" (Stamford, Conn., December 1983).

3. The transferee cannot require the transferor to **repurchase** the receivables except pursuant to the recourse provisions.

b. **A borrowing transaction** and the recording of a **liability** for the amount of cash received if **any one** of the three conditions listed above is not met. In this situation, the receivables involved remain in the accounts of the transferor as "pledged" assets to support the loan agreement.

Transfers **with** recourse typically qualify as either a sale transaction or a borrowing transaction with neither clearly dominating. Transfers **without** recourse usually qualify as a sale transaction. They usually involve a high discount rate (and a consequent loss on sale).

ILLUSTRATIONS OF THE TRANSFER OF ACCOUNTS RECEIVABLE TO OBTAIN EARLY CASH

It is impractical to illustrate all of the contractual specifications found in the use of accounts receivable to obtain early cash. Therefore, for practical reasons, three simplified cases are illustrated to emphasize the primary accounting distinctions involved.[10] The following basic situation is assumed:

On January 2, 19A, Transferor Company transferred or assigned accounts receivable of $40,000 to Transferee Finance Company to obtain immediate cash. The related Allowance for Doubtful Accounts was $1,000.

Case A—Sale without Recourse; Meets All Three Conditions Listed Above. The sale price is $30,000 cash; notification basis.

January 2, 19A—To record sale of accounts receivable:

Cash	30,000	
Allowance for doubtful accounts	1,000*	
Loss on sale of accounts receivable	9,000*	
Accounts receivable		40,000

* In some situations, the total (i.e., $1,000 + $9,000) would be debited to the allowance account, as in the case where prior estimates of bad debt losses included transactions involving sale of the receivables.

Subsequently, the debtors will pay cash on the accounts directly to Transferee Finance Company. The transferee will assume all bad debt losses and related collection costs.

Case B—Sale with Recourse; Meets All Three Conditions Listed Above. Sale price is $34,000 cash; notification basis. Estimated collection cost of obligations under the recourse provision is $1,500 (e.g., for uncollectible accounts, discounts, and sales returns and allowances).

---

[10] Ibid, par. 5.

January 2, 19A—To record sale of accounts receivable, with recourse:

Cash	34,000	
Allowance for doubtful accounts	1,000*	
Loss on sale of accounts receivable	6,500	
Accounts receivable		40,000
Liability—estimated collection loss on accounts receivable		
sold		1,500

* See note in Case A.

Subsequently, the debtors will pay cash on the accounts directly to Transferee Finance Company. Collection losses will be billed by Transferee Finance Company and will be paid by Transferor Company. To illustrate, on January 30, 19A, Transferee Finance Company billed the following collection losses: Cash discounts allowed debtors, $300, and sales allowances for defective merchandise, $500. Consequently, Transferor Company would make the following entry:

Liability—estimated collection loss on accounts receivable sold	800	
Cash		800

Case C—Borrowing Transaction and the Recording of a Liability for the Amount Borrowed (Not All of the Three Conditions Listed Above Are Met).

Typical terms are "with recourse, nonnotification." In this situation, the accounts receivable **assigned** (i.e., not sold) are viewed as collateral for the loan (usually a note payable).

To illustrate, the loan agreement specifies that Transferee Finance Company will advance cash equal to 75% of the gross receivables advanced (i.e., $40,000 in this case) and charge 24% annual interest (payable monthly) on the outstanding receivables at the end of each month. The customers will continue to pay directly to Transferor Company who will remit the cash as payments on the loan. When the loan and interest are paid in full, any remaining assigned accounts receivable revert to the transferor.

Typical transactions and journal entries for Transferor Company are shown in **Exhibit 6–5.**

To summarize, when accounts receivable are used to obtain early cash (i.e., before their expected collection dates), the agreement between the two parties involved—the transferor and transferee—must be analyzed. The analysis is to determine whether the transaction is (a) the sale of an asset (the receivables) or (b) a borrowing transaction with the accounts receivable used as collateral for a loan. GAAP prescribes three criteria to determine whether the transaction is a sale (all three criteria must be met) or a borrowing (if any one of the three criteria is not met). If the transaction qualifies as a sale, the transferor must record a sale of the receivables in the same manner as the cash sale of any other asset. Cases A and B above illustrate sale situations. Alternatively, if the transaction qualifies as a borrowing, the transferor must record a liability for the loan and keep the receivables in the accounts (but separate them as assigned because they are collaterized or pledged). Case C above illustrates a borrowing situation.

When the transferor agrees to a "with recourse" provision, all collection losses (e.g., uncollectible accounts, discounts, and sale returns and allowances) are assumed by, and recorded in the accounts of, the tranferor.

EXHIBIT 6–5

Borrowing Cash on Accounts Receivable Assigned as Collateral for the Loan

Transaction	Entries by Transferor Company		
a. January 2: Assigned $40,000 accounts receivable; advance received, 75%; gave note payable in favor of Transferee Finance Company.	Accounts receivable assigned . . Accounts receivable . . . . . . Cash ($40,000 × 75%) . . . . Notes payable (Transferee Finance Co.)	40,000 30,000	40,000 30,000
b. January 3–30: Collected $20,500 of the assigned accounts less sales returns and allowances, $800.	Cash . . . . Sales returns and allowances . . Accounts receivable assigned	19,700 800	 20,500
c. January 31: Remitted collections to Tranferee Finance Company plus $600 interest (i.e., $30,000 × 24% × $\frac{1}{12}$).	Interest expense . . . . Notes payable (Transferee Finance Co.) . . . . Cash	600 19,700	 20,300
d. February 1–27: Collected balance of the assigned accounts, except $200 written off as uncollectible.	Cash . . . . Allowance for doubtful accounts . . . . Accounts receivable assigned	19,300 200	 19,500
e. February 28: Remitted balance due Transferee Finance Company ($30,000 − $19,700 = $10,300) plus $206 interest (i.e., $10,300 × 24% × $\frac{1}{12}$) = $10,506.	Interest expense . . . . Notes payable (Tranferee Finance Co.) . . . . Cash	206 10,300	 10,506

Note: If the collections are remitted directly to the finance company (not deposited by Transferor Company into their own bank account), entries *(b)–(c)* and *(d)–(e)*, respectively, would be combined into two entries.

SUPPLEMENT 6–A: COMPREHENSIVE BANK RECONCILIATION

The comprehensive bank reconciliation format often is used as a "proof of cash" by auditors. It encompasses four reconciliations in one worksheet, that is:

1. The bank reconciliation of the **prior period** (Column 1 in **Exhibit 6–6**).
2. Reconciliation of the bank's cash receipts with the company's cash receipts (Column 2 in Exhibit 6–6).

3. Reconciliation of the bank's cash disbursements with the company's cash disbursements (Column 3 in Exhibit 6–6).
4. The bank reconciliation for the **current period** (Column 4 in Exhibit 6–6).

To illustrate a comprehensive bank reconciliation the data used in Part A of the chapter are restated as follows:

a. July bank reconciliation:

Items	Bank balance	Book balance
Ending balances, July 31	$32,000	$29,550
Deposits in transit, end of July	5,000	
Cash on hand (undeposited), end of July	1,000	
Outstanding checks, end of July	(8,000)	
Note collected for the company		600
Bank service charge for July		(150)
Correct cash balance, July 31	$30,000	$30,000

b. August cash data:

Bank statement		Company's cash account	
August 1 balance	$ 32,000	August 1 balance	$ 30,000
Deposits recorded in		August deposits	75,300
August	77,300	August checks	(70,000)
Checks cleared in August	(71,000)	August 31 balance	$ 35,300
Note collected (including			
$100 interest)	1,100		
NSF check, J. Doe	(300)		
August service charges ..	(200)		
August 31 balance	$ 38,900		

c. End of August: Cash on hand (undeposited), $990.

Based upon the above data only, the comprehensive bank reconciliation shown in Exhibit 6–6 was prepared. The sequential preparation steps were as follows:

Step 1:
Enter the prior (July 31, in the example) **bank** reconciliation data in the **bank part of the first** column and the current bank statement data across the first line of the **bank** part of the format.

Step 2:
Enter the unreconciled amounts from the current Cash account across the first line of the **book** part of the format. Also, enter unreconciled ending balance

EXHIBIT 6–6

Comprehensive Bank Reconciliation, West Company—August 31, 19X

Items	Prior (July 31) balances	August receipts	August payments	August 31 reconciled balances
Bank:				
Per bank statement (unreconciled)	$32,000	$78,400	$71,500	$38,900
Cash on hand:				
July 31	1,000	(1,000)[a]		
August 31		990[b]		990
Deposits in transit:				
July 31	5,000	(5,000)[c]		
August 31		3,000[d]		3,000
Outstanding checks:				
July 31	(8,000)		(8,000)[e]	
August 31			7,000[f]	(7,000)
Correct cash balance	$30,000	$76,390	$70,500	$35,890
Books:				
Per Cash account (unreconciled)	$30,000*	$75,300	$70,000	$35,300
Note collected by Bank (August)		1,100[g]		1,100
NSF check, J. Doe			300[h]	(300)
Bank service charge (August)			200[i]	(200)
Cash shortage (August)		(10)[j]		(10)
Correct cash balance	$30,000	$76,390	$70,500	$35,890

* After July 31, entries from July bank reconciliation.

Explanation of inner extensions:

Bank:
a. A July balance, deducted to remove it from August receipts.
b. An August balance, added to include it in August receipts.
c. A July deposit, deducted to remove it from August receipts.
d. An August deposit, added to include the amount in August receipts.
e. July checks, deducted to remove the amount from August payments.
f. August checks, added to include the amount in August payments.

Books:
g. August receipt, added to include it in August receipts.
h. and i. August payments, added to include them in the August payments.
j. Cash shortage deducted, reduced cash receipts.

Check: Both correct cash balances agree in total for each of the four columns.

in the first column, on the "Correct cash balance" line. (Thus, the same cash amount will be reflected on the first and last lines of the first column.)

Step 3:

Prepare the bank reconciliation for the current period (August 31 in the example) in the last (i.e., fourth) column of the worksheet; use the "correct cash balance" approach.

Step 4:

Complete the two inner columns to reconcile "total receipts" and "total payments" of the bank and book parts. The purpose of this phase of the reconciliation is to test for internal correctness by reconstructing the elements in both the receipts and payments.

The final test of correctness is met in all respects when (1) each of the four column totals agree for the bank and book lines "correct cash balance" and (2) beginning balances plus receipts less payments equal ending balances for both the bank and book reconciliations.

QUESTIONS

PART A

1. Define cash as it is used for accounting purposes.
2. In what circumstances, if any, is it permissible to offset a bank overdraft against a positive balance in another bank account?
3. Define a compensating balance and explain the related reporting requirements.
4. If you were called upon to establish a petty cash system that would be particularly effective from the standpoint of internal control, briefly describe the important features that you would incorporate into it.
5. Which of the following items should not be recorded in the Cash account?

       a. Money orders.   *e.* Currency.
       b. Postdated checks.   *f.* Cash deposited in savings accounts.
       c. Ordinary checks.   *g.* Certificates of deposit.
       d. Postage stamps.   *h.* Deposits in checking accounts.

6. Where (if at all) do items *(a)* through *(g)* belong in the following bank reconciliation?

   Balance per bank statement, June 30 . . . . $ x,xxx.xx
      Additions . . . . _____
      Deductions . . . . _____
   June 30 correct cash balance . . . . $ 9,600.00

   Balance per company Cash account, June 30 . . . . . $ x,xxx.xx
      Additions . . . . _____
      Deductions . . . . _____
   June 30 correct cash balance . . . . $ 9,600.00

a. Note collected by bank for the depositor on June 29; notification was received July 2 when the June 30 bank statement was received.

b. Checks drawn in June which had not cleared the bank by June 30.

c. Check of a depositor with a similar name which was returned with checks accompanying June 30 bank statement and which was subtracted from the company's bank account.

d. Bank service charge for which notification was received upon receipt of bank statement.

e. Deposit mailed June 30 which reached bank July 1 (not yet included in the bank statement).

f. Notification of charge for imprinting the company's name on blank checks was received with the June 30 bank statement.

g. Upon refooting cash receipts journal, the company discovered that one receipt was omitted in arriving at the total which was posted to the Cash account in the ledger.

7. Briefly explain the three basic purposes of a bank reconciliation.
8. Define the following terms related to accounting for cash:

   a. Deposits in transit.
   b. Outstanding checks.
   c. NSF check.
   d. Correct cash balance.
   e. Cash shortage and cash overage.

PART B

9. What criteria must a security meet to qualify as a short-term investment?
10. Define cost as applied to a short-term investment.
11. Define an investment in *(a)* equity securities and *(b)* debt securities.
12. Briefly explain the accounting for short-term investments in equity securities.
13. An investor purchased 100 shares of PQ common stock at $20 per share on March 15, 19A. At the end of the 19A accounting period, December 31, 19A, the stock was quoted at $19 per share. On June 5, 19B, the investor sold the stock for $22 per share. Assuming a short-term investment, provide answers to the following:

    a. March 15, 19A—Debit to the investment account, $_____ .
    b. December 31, 19A—Unrealized loss, $_____ .
    c. June 5, 19B—Gain or loss on sale of the investment, $_____ .

14. On June 15, 19A, Baker Company purchased 500 shares of preferred stock, par $10, at $30 per share. The market value of these shares at the end of the accounting period, December 31, 19A, was $28 per share. Show how this short-term investment should be reported on the 19A balance sheet.
15. Briefly explain the accounting for short-term investments in debt securities.
16. What is meant by an impairment loss?
17. Explain when investment revenue should be recognized in each of the following situations involving short-term investments:

    a. A stock dividend is declared and issued to the investor during the current year.
    b. Interest on a debt security acquired during the current year.
    c. A cash dividend is declared during the current year and is paid during the next accounting year.

PART C

18. Define receivables and briefly explain their classifications.
19. RS Company sold merchandise for $500; terms 2/10, n/30. Explain these terms and give the journal entry under the net approach and the gross approach. Which approach is preferable? Why?
20. Briefly describe the different methods of estimating bad debt expense and the allowance for doubtful accounts in connection with trade receivables. State which financial statement each method emphasizes. What is the theoretical basis for each emphasis?
21. It sometimes happens that a receivable that has been written off as uncollectible is subsequently collected. Describe the accounting procedures in such an event.
22. How should customer accounts with credit balances be reported in the financial statements?
23. Explain and illustrate the differences between a one-year note received for a sale on credit of $5,000 and a going rate of interest of 12%, assuming (a) an interest-bearing note and (b) a noninterest-bearing note.
24. T Company received, from a customer, a $1,000, 15% interest-bearing note that will mature in three months. After holding it two months, the note was sold by T to the bank at 20%. Compute T's proceeds. Give the required journal entry made by T at the time the note was sold.
25. RV Company sold accounts receivable of $10,000 (allowance for doubtful accounts, $300) for $9,000, with recourse. Estimated obligations due to the "with recourse" provision amounted to $700 (uncollectible accounts, discounts, and sales returns). Give the required entry.

EXERCISES

PART A: EXERCISES 6–1 TO 6–7

Exercise 6–1

VW Company is preparing its December 31 bank reconciliation (end of the annual accounting period), and it must determine the proper balance sheet classification of the items listed below. You have been asked to complete the tabulation provided.

Item	Cash amount	Classification if not cash
1. Coins and currency, $500.	500	
2. Checks received from customers, $6,000.	6,000	
3. Certificates of deposit (CDs), $8,000.		Short term - ES
4. Petty cash fund, $400.		
5. Postage stamps, $60.		
6. Bank A, checking account balance, $21,000.		
7. Post-dated check, customer, $100.		
8. Money order, from customer, $150.		
9. Cash in savings account, $10,000.		
10. Bank draft from customer, $400.		
11. Cash advance received from customer, $80.		
12. Utility deposit to the gas company, refundable, $50.		
13. Certified check from customer, $1,000.		
14. NSF check, R. Roe, $200.		
15. Cash advance to company executive, collectible upon demand, $20,000.		
16. Bank B, checking account, overdraft, $2,000.		
17. IOUs from employees, $120.		

Exercise 6–2

Maze Company is preparing its 19D financial statements; the accounting period ends December 31. The following items, related to cash are under consideration. You have been asked to indicate how each item should be reported on the balance sheet and to explain the basis for your responses.

1. A $900 check received from a customer dated January 15, 19E, is on hand.
2. A customer's check was included in the December 20 deposit. It was returned by the bank stamped "NSF." No entry has yet been made by Maze to reflect the return.
3. A $20,000 CD on which $1,000 of interest accrued to December 31 has just been recorded by debiting Interest Receivable and crediting Interest Revenue. The chief accountant proposes to report the $20,000 as "Cash in Bank."
4. Maze has a $200 petty cash fund. As of December 31, the fund cashier reported expense vouchers covering various expenses in the amount of $167 and cash of $32.

5. Postage stamps that cost $30 are in the cash drawer.
6. A cashier's check of $200 payable to Maze Company is in the cash drawer; it is dated December 29.
7. Three checks, dated December 31, 19D, totaling $465, payable to vendors who have sold merchandise to Maze Company on account were not mailed by December 31, 19D. They have not been entered as payments in the check register and ledger.
8. Prior to December 30, Maze Company left a note that matures December 31, 19D, with its bank for collection. The note is for $20,000 and bears interest at 9%, having run for three months. As yet, Maze has not heard from the bank about collection but is confident of a favorable outcome because of the extremely high credit rating of the maker of the note. The company plans to include the $20,000 plus interest in its cash balance.

Exercise 6–3

Each of the following situations is independent of the others. For each item you are to compute the amount that should be included in "cash" that will be reported on the year-end balance sheet.

a. Balance in general checking account, Bank H, $60,000; an overdraft in special checking account, Bank H, $2,000. IOU held from company president for $4,000, received six weeks ago because of a cash loan.
b. Balance in Bank P checking account, $45,000. Refundable deposit paid to State Treasurer to guarantee performance on a highway contract, $25,000. Balance in foreign bank (converted to US dollars), $9,000.
c. Cash on hand, $800; cash in Bank C checking account, $29,000; cash held by salespersons as advances on expense accounts, $800. Postage stamps on hand received from mail-order customers, $50.
d. Balance in checking account, $33,000. Certificates of deposit, $5,000. Cash in bond sinking fund, $25,000. Cash on hand, $1,000.
e. Cash in checking account, $18,000. Cash on hand, $400. Various instruments on hand as follows:

Checks from customers:	
In payment of overdue account	$ 500
In payment for goods sold	700
NSF check, previously deposited then returned	300
Postdated (February 1, next year)	400
American Express Travelers Check................	100
Signed IOUs for loans to employees	600
Receipt for deposit in savings account	1,000
Receipt for postage stamps (not yet used)	60

Exercise 6–4

As a part of their newly designed internal control system, DOT Corporation established a petty cash fund. Transactions for the first month were as follows:

a. Wrote a check for $500 on August 1 and gave the cash to the custodian.
b. Summary of the petty cash expenditures made by the custodian:

	August 1–15	August 16–31
Postage used	$ 40	$ 58
Supplies purchased and used	265	190
Delivery expense	98	178
Miscellaneous expenses	35	40
Totals	$438	$466

c. Fund replenished on August 16.
d. Fund replenished on August 31 and increased by $300.

Required:
Give all entries indicated through August.

Exercise 6–5

Foster Company, as a matter of policy, deposits all cash receipts and makes all payments by check. The following data were taken from the cash records of the company:

From bank reconciliation at May 31:

Deposits in transit	$2,200
Outstanding checks	1,400

June results:

	Per bank	Per books
Balance, June 1	$ 5,000	$ 5,800
June deposits...............................	10,600	12,300
June checks	14,500	13,900
June note collected (including 10% interest)	2,200	—
June bank charges	10	—
Balance, June 30	3,290	4,200

Required:
1. Compute the deposits in transit and outstanding checks as of June 30.
2. Reconcile the bank account as of June 30.
3. Give any journal entries that should be made on the basis of the June bank reconciliation.

Exercise 6–6

Reconciliation of Crabtree Company's bank account at May 31 was as follows:

Balance per bank statement	$10,500
Deposits outstanding	1,500
Checks outstanding	(150)
Correct cash balance	$11,850
Balance per books	$11,864
Bank service charge	(14)
Correct cash balance, May 31 ...	$11,850

June data are as follows:

	Bank	Books
Checks recorded	$11,500	$11,800
Deposits recorded	8,100	9,000
Service charges recorded	12	—
Collection by bank ($2,000 note plus interest)	2,100	—
NSF check returned with June 30 statement (will be redeposited; assumed to be good)..	50	—
Balances, June 30	9,138	9,050

Required:

1. Compute deposits in transit and checks outstanding at June 30.
2. Prepare a bank reconciliation for June.
3. Give all journal entries that should be made based on the bank reconciliation.

Exercise 6–7

Davis Company has its checking account with First National Bank. The company is ready to reconcile its May bank and book balances. The following data are available:

a. From the April 30 bank reconciliation:
   Deposit in transit, $150.
   Outstanding checks: No. 698, $30; No. 699, $80; and No. 702, $25.
b. Cash on hand, $50 (by actual count).
c. Davis Company Cash account for May:

Balance, April 30 (correct)	$ 10,958
Cash receipts during May	14,210
Checks processed during May	(13,812)
Balance, May 31	$ 11,356

d. Bank statement for May:

Balance, April 30	$ 10,900
Deposits during May	13,940
Checks cleared during May	(13,742)
Note collected for Davis (including $50 interest)	550
Bank service charge	(14)
Balance, May 31................................	$ 11,634

e. At May 31, the following checks were outstanding: No. 702, $25; No. 735, $100; No. 738, $60; and No. 740, $20. May 31 receipts amounting to $420 were mailed to the bank at the close of business that day and were not included in the May bank statement.

Required:

1. Prepare the May bank reconciliation.
2. Give all required journal entries based on the bank reconciliation (a cash shortage or overage account may be needed).

PART B: EXERCISES 6–8 TO 6–13

Exercise 6–8

Match the different securities listed below with their usual classification as investments by entering the appropriate letter in each blank space.

Usual classification as investments

A—Short-term equity securities.
B—Long-term equity securities.
C—Short-term debt securities.
D—Long-term debt securities.
E—None of the above.

Typical securities

__A__   1. Abbott common stock, nopar; acquired to use temporarily idle cash.

__E__   2. Land acquired for short-term speculation.

__C__   3. U.S. Treasury bills; mature in six months.

__A__   4. GE preferred stock, par $100, mandatory redemption within next 12 months.

__B__   5. Staufer common stock, par $5; acquired to attain a continuing controlling interest.

__D__   6. Frazer bonds, 9%, mature at the end of 10 years; acquired for indefinite holding period.

__E__   7. Foreign Corporation, common stock; difficulties encountered in withdrawing cash earned.

__C__   8. Certificates of deposit (CDs); mature at end of one year.

__E__   9. Savings account at local Savings and Loan Association; has been active for the past five years.

__B__ 10. Acorn common stock, par $1; acquired as a short-term investment, but now so profitable that it is not reasonable to sell it.

Exercise 6–9

During 19A, Decker Company acquired the following short-term investments in marketable equity securities:

Corporation X—500 shares common stock (nopar) at $60 cash per share.

Corporation Y—300 shares preferred stock (par $10, nonredeemable) at $20 cash per share.

The annual reporting period ends December 31. On December 31, 19A, the quoted market prices were: Corporation X stock, $52; and Corporation Y stock, $24.

Data for 19B:

    3/2/19B   Received cash dividends per share as follows: X stock, $1; and Y stock, 50 cents.

  10/1/19B   Sold 100 of the Y shares at $25 per share.

12/31/19B   Market values: X stock, $46; and Y stock, $26.

Required:

1. Give the entry for Decker Company to record the purchase of the securities.
2. Give any adjusting entry needed at the end of 19A.
3. Give the items and amounts that should be reported on the 19A income statement and balance sheet.
4. Give all of the entries for 19B.
5. Give the items and amounts that should be reported on the 19B income statement and balance sheet.

Exercise 6–10

At December 31, 19A, the short-term investments of Vista Company were as follows:

Security	Shares	Unit cost	Unit market price
Preferred stock, 8%, par $10, Knight Corp.	600	$90 *54,000*	$88 *5 2 800*
Common stock, nopar, Dyer Corp.	200	30 *6 000*	31 *6200*

60,000   *59,000*

The transactions below relate to the above short-term investments and those bought and sold during 19B. The reporting year ends December 31.

Feb. 2 Received the annual 8% cash dividend from Knight Corporation.
Mar. 1 Sold 150 shares of the Dyer stock at $34 per share.
May 1 Sold 400 shares of Knight stock at $89.50 per share.
June 1 Received a cash dividend on Dyer stock of $3.50 per share.
Aug. 1 Purchased 4,000 shares of Rote Corporation's common stock at $45 per share.
Sept. 1 Transferred all shares of Dyer common stock from the short-term portfolio to the long-term portfolio. At this date the Dyer stock was quoted at $28 per share.
At December 31, 19B, the quoted market prices were as follows: Knight preferred, $98; Dyer common, $28; and Rote common, $44.50.

Required:
1. Give the entry that Vista Company should have made on December 31, 19A, to record the equity investments at LCM.
2. Give the entries for 19B through September 1.
3. Give the entry(s) required at December 31, 19B.
4. List the items and amounts that should be reported on Vista's 19B income statement and balance sheet.

Exercise 6–11

On September 1, 19A, New Company purchased ten $1,000, 6%, bonds of Vue Corporation at 96 plus accrued interest. The bonds pay annual interest each July 1. New paid cash, including any accrued interest. The annual reporting period ends December 31. At December 31, 19A, the Vue bonds were quoted at 95¾.

Required:
1. Give the journal entry for New Company to record the purchase of the bonds assuming they will be held as a short-term investment and that New will use the cost method.
2. Give any adjusting entries required at December 31, 19A.
3. Give the items and amounts that should be reported on the 19A income statement and balance sheet.
4. Give the required entry on July 1, 19B.
5. On August 1, 19B, New Company sold four of the bonds at 96.5 plus any accrued interest. The remaining six bonds were transferred to the long-term portfolio of debt securities. Give the required entry(s).
6. There were no additional transactions during 19B. List the short-term investment items and amounts that would be reported on the 19B income statement and balance sheet.

Exercise 6–12

On August 1, 19A, West Company purchased for cash four $10,000 bonds of Moe Corporation at 98 plus accrued interest. The bonds pay 9% interest, payable on a semiannual basis each May 1 and November 1. The annual reporting period ends December 31.

Required:
1. Give the following entries for West Company, assuming the cost method will be used:

8/1/19A   Paid $40,100 cash for the bonds including any accrued interest.
11/1/19A   Collected interest on the bonds.
12/31/19A   Adjusting entries (if any). The bonds were quoted on the market on this
date at 97 excluding any accrued interest.

2. Show how the effects of this short-term investment should be reported on the 19A
income statement and balance sheet.
3. On February 1, 19B, two of the bonds were sold for $19,950 cash including any accrued
interest. Give the required entry. Assume no reversing entries were made on January
1, 19B.
4. Give the entry for the collection of interest on May 1, 19B.

Exercise 6–13

Select the best answer for each of the following items. Justify your choice.

1. Short-term investments in securities must meet the following test:
   a. Ready marketability.
   b. Ready marketability or expected short-term holding period.
   c. Expected short-term holding period.
   d. Expected short-term holding period and ready marketability.
   e. None of the above is correct.
2. Equity securities held as short-term investments must be accounted for on the basis
   of:
   a. Lower of cost or market.
   b. Cost.
   c. Market value.
   d. None of the above.
   e. All of the above.
3. Debt securities held as short-term investments should be accounted for on the basis
   of:
   a. Lower of cost or market.
   b. Cost.
   c. Market value.
   d. None of the above.
   e. All of the above.
4. Both realized and unrealized gains and losses usually are accounted for separately only
   when the—
   a. LCM basis is used.
   b. Cost basis is used.
   c. Market value basis is used.
   d. LCM basis or the cost basis is used.
   e. None of the above is applicable.
5. The end-of-period balance in the account "Allowance to Reduce Short-Term Investments to Market" is reported on the—
   a. Income statement as a loss.
   b. Income statement as an extraordinary item.
   c. Balance sheet under assets.
   d. Balance sheet under owners' equity.
   e. None of the above is correct.
6. When the cost method is used to account for short-term investments in debt securities,
   the carrying value is different from original cost only when—

a. The market value is below cost by a significant amount.
b. The market value is below cost and it is not temporary.
c. The market value is below cost by a significant amount, and it is not temporary.
d. Any one of the above is applicable.
e. None of the above is applicable.
7. When a short-term equity security is transferred between the short-term and long-term portfolios, the transfer is made at the—
a. Current market price of the security.
b. Original cost of the security.
c. LCM value of the security at the date of transfer.
d. LCM value at last balance sheet date.
e. None of the above.

PART C: EXERCISES 6–14 TO 6–25

Exercise 6–14

During the annual audit of TAR Corporation, you encountered the following accounts entitled "Receivables and Payables":

Items	Debit	Credit
Due from customers	$78,000	
Payables to creditors for merchandise		$31,000
Note receivable, long term	40,000	
Expected cumulative losses on bad debts		2,000
Due from employees, current	1,100	
Cash dividends payable		12,000
Special receivable, dishonored note*	11,000	
Accrued wages		1,200
Deferred rent revenue		800
Insurance premiums paid in advance	600	
Mortgage payable, long term		20,000

* Collection probable some time in the future.

Required:
1. Give the journal entry to eliminate the above account and to set up the appropriate accounts to replace it.
2. Show how the various items should be reported on the current balance sheet.

Exercise 6–15

On December 29, 19A, Sabre Company sold merchandise for $8,000 on credit terms, 3/10, n/60. The accounting period ends December 31.
Required:
1. Give the following entries under two different accounting approaches: *(a)* the net approach and *(b)* the gross approach:

a. To record the 19A sale.
b. To record collection of the account:

Assumption A—On January 5, 19B.
Assumption B—On April 1, 19B.

2. Show what should be reported on the 19A and 19B balance sheets and income statements under each approach and for each assumption for the above transactions only.

Exercise 6–16

At January 1, 19B, the credit balance in the Allowance for Doubtful Accounts of the Master Company was $400,000. The provision (i.e., expense) for doubtful accounts is based on a percentage of net credit sales. Total sales revenue for 19B amounted to $150 million of which ⅓ was on credit. Based on the latest available facts, the 19B provision (i.e., expense) needed for doubtful accounts is estimated to be ¾ of 1% of net credit sales. During 19B, uncollectible receivables amounting to $440,000 were written off.

Required:
1. Prepare a schedule to compute the balance in Master's Allowance for Doubtful Accounts at December 31, 19B. Show supporting computations.
2. Give all 19B entries related to doubtful accounts.

(AICPA adapted)

Exercise 6–17

At December 31, 19B, end of the annual reporting period, the accounts of Bader Company showed the following:

a. Sales revenue for 19B, $360,000 of which ⅙ was on credit.
b. Allowance for doubtful accounts, balance January 1, 19B, $1,800 credit.
c. Accounts receivable, balance December 31, 19B (prior to any write-offs of uncollectible accounts during 19B), $36,100.
d. Uncollectible accounts to be written off, December 31, 19B, $2,100.
e. Aging schedule at December 31, 19B, showed the following:

Status	Amount
Not past due	$20,000
Past due 1–60 days	8,000
Past due over 60 days	6,000

Required:
1. Give the 19B entry to write off the uncollectible accounts.
2. Give the 19B adjusting entry to record bad debt expense for each of the following independent assumptions concerning bad debt loss rates:
   a. On credit sales, 1½%.
   b. On total receivables at year-end, 2½%.
   c. On aging schedule: Not past due, ½%; past due 1–60 days, 1%; and past due over 60 days, 8%.
3. Show what would be reported on the 19B balance sheet relating to accounts receivable for each assumption.

Exercise 6–18

On December 31, 19C, end of the annual reporting period, the accounts receivable records of Company X provided the following information about its customers (only four are used to minimize the clerical task):

Customer Jones: Balance of account, $16,000; all is current (i.e., not past due) except two older invoices—one for $2,000 is 20 days past due and the other for $5,000 is 50 days past due.

Customer Simon: Balance of account, $17,000; all is current except one invoice for $4,000 which is 64 days past due.

Customer Tanner: Balance of account, $23,000; all is current except for three older invoices—one for $4,000 is 28 days past due; another invoice for $3,000 is 50 days past due; and the last one for $1,000 is 75 days past due.

Based on past experience, the following bad debt loss percentages on credit sales have been developed; not past due, ½%; 1–30 days past due, 1¼%; 31–60 days past due, 3%; and more than 60 days past due, 20%.

The balance in the allowance for doubtful accounts on December 31, 19C is $3,720, prior to writing off the account of Customer X of $4,000 determined to be uncollectible.

Required:

1. Prepare an aging schedule including computation of the estimated loss on accounts receivable.
2. Based on the above data and your response to Requirement 1, give all journal entries related to bad debts.
3. Show how the items related to bad debts should be reported on the 19C income statement and balance sheet.

Exercise 6–19

On April 15, 19A, Botch Company sold merchandise to Customer Smith for $9,000; terms 2/10; n/EOM (i.e., end of month). Because of nonpayment by Smith, Botch received a $9,000, 15%, 12 month note dated May 1, 19A. The annual reporting period ends December 31. Customer Smith paid the note in full on its maturity date.

Required:

1. Give all entries related to the above transactions.
2. Show what should be reported on the 19A income statement and balance sheet.

Exercise 6–20

On May 1, 19A, Darby Company sold merchandise to Customer Domo and received a $13,200 (face amount), one year, noninterest-bearing note. The going (i.e., market) rate of interest in this situation is 10%. The annual reporting period for Darby Company ends on December 31. Customer Domo paid the note in full on its maturity date.

Required:

1. Give all entries related to the above transaction.
2. Show what should be reported on the 19A income statement and balance sheet.

Exercise 6–21

On November 1, 19A, Rouse Company sold merchandise on credit to customer A for $14,000 and received a six-month, 12%, interest-bearing note. On this same date, Customer B purchased the same merchandise for the same price and credit terms except that the note received by Rouse was noninterest bearing (the interest was included in the face of the note). The annual accounting period for Rouse ends December 31.

Required:

1. Give all required entries for each note from the date of sales of the merchandise through the maturity dates of the notes. For the noninterest-bearing note, give the entries for both the "net" and "gross" alternatives.
2. Show how the effects of these two notes should be reported on the 19A income statement and balance sheet.

Exercise 6–22

On May 1, 19A, Mark Company sold merchandise to Customer K for $20,000, credit terms 2/10; n/EOM (i.e., end of month). At the end of May, Customer K could not make the payment. Instead, a six-month, 12%, note receivable of $20,000 was received by Mark (dated June 1, 19A). Mark Company's accounting period ends December 31. On August 1, 19A, Mark discounted (i.e., sold) this note, with recourse, to City Bank at 14% interest. On maturity date, customer K paid the bank in full for the note.

Required:

Give all required entries for Mark Company on May 1, 19A, through the maturity date, November 30, 19A.

Exercise 6–23

Bay Company completed the following 19A transactions related to a special note receivable:

February 1, 19A—Received a $100,000, 9%, six-month note from Capps Company for a tract of land that had a carrying value of $30,000.

March 1, 19A—Discounted (sold with recourse) the note to Local Bank at a 12% interest rate.

July 31, 19A—Maturity date of the note:

Case A—Capps Company paid the bank for the note and all interest.
Case B—Capps Company defaulted on the note. The bank charged a $500 protest fee.

Required:

Give all journal entries that Bay Company should make for the term of the note, February 1, 19A, through July 31, 19A.

Exercise 6–24

On April 1, 19A, DOS Company transferred $10,000 accounts receivable to SLK Finance Company to obtain immediate cash. The related allowance for doubtful accounts was $400.

Required:

1. The financing agreement specified a price of $8,000 on a "without recourse, notification basis." Give the entry(s) that DOS Company should make. Explain the basis for your response.
2. The financing agreement specified a price of $8,500 on a "with recourse, notification basis." DOS estimated $200 transfer obligations related to the "with recourse" provision. Give the entry(s) that DOS should make. Explain the basis for your response.

Exercise 6–25

Ink, Inc., assigned $60,000 of its receivables to Pen Finance Company. A note payable was executed. The contract provided that Pen would advance 85% of the gross amount of the receivables. The contract specified recourse and nonnotification; therefore, Ink's debtors continue to remit directly to it; the cash (including finance charges) is then remitted to the finance company.

During the first month, customers owing $41,000 paid cash, less sales returns and allowances of $1,600. The finance charge at the end of the first month was $350.

During the second month, the remaining receivables were collected in full except for $400 written off as uncollectible. Final settlement was effected with the finance company, including payment of an additional finance charge of $150.

Required:
1. Give the entries for Ink to record *(a)* the assignment of the receivables and *(b)* the note payable.
2. Give the entries for Ink to record *(a)* the collections and *(b)* the payment to Pen for the first month.
3. Give the entries for Ink to record *(a)* the collections for the second month and *(b)* the final payment to Pen.

PROBLEMS

PART A: PROBLEMS 6–1 TO 6–6

Problem 6–1

It is March 31, 19E, and Fry Company is ready to prepare its March bank reconciliation. The following information is available:

(1)

Company Cash account			
March 1 balance	14,175	Checks	26,500
Deposits	25,734		

(2) Bank statement, March 31:

Balance, March 1	$15,400
Deposits	25,599
Checks cleared	(27,059)
NSF check (Customer X)	(50)
Note collected for depositor (including interest, $40) ...	840
Interest on bank balance	18
Bank service charge	(7)
Balance, March 31	$14,741

(3) Additional information:
   a. One deposit by the company was $10 overstated by the company; it was recorded correctly by the bank.
   b. The bank cleared an $89 check as $98; it has not been corrected by the bank.
   c. End of February: Deposits in transit, $775; outstanding checks, $2,000.

Required:
1. Compute the March 31 deposits in transit and outstanding checks.
2. Prepare a bank reconciliation for March.
3. Give all journal entries that should be made based on the bank reconciliation.

Problem 6–2

VT Company is ready to prepare its March 31 bank reconciliation. The following data are available:

a. From the February 28 bank reconciliation:
   Deposits in transit, $170.
   Outstanding checks, $390.
b. March data:

	Per bank	Per books
Balance, February 28	$7,414	$7,194
March deposits reflected	4,760	4,900
March checks reflected	(6,170)*	(6,100)
Note collected (including $20 interest)	2,020	
Service charge	(12)	
Balance, March 31	$8,012	$5,994

* Erroneously includes a check drawn by AB Company for $150.

Required:
1. Compute the deposits in transit and outstanding checks at March 31.
2. Prepare the March 31 bank reconciliation.
3. Give all of the required entries based on the bank reconciliation.

Problem 6–3

PT Company is ready to prepare its May 31, 19B, bank reconciliation. The following data are available:

a. Bank statement for May:

Balance, April 30, 19B	$34,300
Deposits during May	79,700
Checks cleared during May	(77,350)
Note receivable collected for PT Company (including 10% interest for six months)	5,250
NSF check, Customer Young	(80)
Deduction for United Fund (per deduction form signed by PT Company)	(50)
Bank service charge	(15)
Balance, May 31, 19B	$41,755

b. PT Company Cash account:

Balance, April 30, 19B	$33,320
Deposits	80,000
Checks written, signed, and delivered	(77,000)
Balance	$36,320

c. Additional information:
   (1) April 30, 19B: deposits in transit, $3,000; outstanding checks, $4,000.

(2) Inspection of the canceled checks included in the May bank statement revealed that the $77,350 erroneously included a $150 check written by TPP Company.

(3) Petty cash balance, May 31, 19B, $400 (not included in the book balance).

Required:

1. Compute the May 31 deposits in transit and outstanding checks.
2. Prepare the May 31 bank reconciliation (Hint: Be alert for a cash shortage.)
3. Give all of the journal entries that should be made based on the bank reconciliation.

Problem 6–4

ZT Company carries its checking account with Fidelity Bank. The company is ready to prepare its December 31, 19B, bank reconciliation. The following data are available:

a. ZT Company Cash account for December:

Balance, November 30 (includes $400 cash for change held back each day)	$20,900
Deposits during December	93,400
Checks written during December	(82,000)
Balance, December 31, 19B	$32,300

b. Bank statement for December:

Balance, November 30	$20,000
Deposits during December	92,300
Checks cleared during December	(82,150)
Funds (in dollars) transferred from foreign revenue (not yet recorded by ZT Co.)	25,000
United Fund (per withholding form signed by ZT Company)	(50)
NSF check, Customer T	(180)
Bank service charges	(20)
Balance, December 31, 19B	$54,900

c. Additional data:

(1) Balance in Petty Cash account, $200 (not included in ZT Cash account).

(2) The deposits of $93,400 by ZT Company are overstated by $100; the bank recorded the correct amount.

(3) The checks cleared by the bank of $82,150 erroneously included a $300 check drawn by AT Corporation; the bank has not yet corrected this error.

(4) November 30, 19B: deposits in transit, $2,000, and outstanding checks, $1,500.

Required:

1. Compute the December 31, 19B, deposits in transit and outstanding checks.
2. Prepare the December bank reconciliation.
3. Give all of the journal entries that should be made based on the bank reconciliation.

Problem 6–5

AB Company carries its checking account with Commerce Bank. The company is ready to prepare its December 31, 19G, bank reconciliation. The following data are available:

a. The November 30, 19G, bank reconciliation showed the following: (1) cash on hand (held back each day by AB Company for change), $400 (included in AB's Cash account); (2) Deposit in transit, #51, $2,000; and (3) outstanding checks, #121, $1,000; #130, $2,000; and #142, $3,000.

b. AB Company Cash account for December, 19G:

Balance, December 1, 19G	$ 64,000
Deposits: #52–#55, $186,500; #56, $3,500.	190,000
Checks: #143–#176, $191,000; #177, $2,500; #178, $3,000; and #179, $1,500	(198,000)
Balance, December 31, 19G (includes $400 cash held each held each day for change)	$ 56,000

c. Bank statement, December 31, 19G:

Balance, December 1, 19G	$ 67,600
Deposits: #51–55	188,500
Checks: #130, $2,000; #142, $3,000; #143–#176, $191,000)	(196,000)
Note collected for AB Co. (including $720 interest)	6,720
Fund transfer received for foreign revenue (not yet recorded by AB Co.)	10,000
NSF check, Customer B	(200)
United Fund (per transfer authorization signed by AB Co.)	(50)
Bank service charges	(20)
Balance, December 31, 19G	$ 76,550

Required:

1. Identify by number and dollars the December 31, 19G, *(a)* deposits in transit and *(b)* outstanding checks.
2. Prepare the December 31, 19G, bank reconciliation.
3. Give all journal entries that should be made at December 31, 19G, based on the bank reconciliation.

Problem 6–6 (Based on Supplement 6–A)

Rae Company is ready to reconcile its bank and book balances at March 31, 19X. The following information is available:

a. February bank reconciliation:

	Bank balance	Book balance
Ending balances, February 28	$49,550	$ 51,050
Additions:		
Deposits in transit	3,100	
Deductions:		
Outstanding checks	(1,650)	
Bank service charge		(50)
Correct cash balance, February 28	$ 51,000	$ 51,000

b. Company Cash account for March:

Balance, March 1 (after February 28 entry)	$ 51,000
Deposits during March	52,800
Checks written during March	(54,150)
Balance, March 31	$ 49,650

c. Bank statement for March:

Balance, March 1	$ 49,550
Deposits recorded during March	53,850
Checks cleared during March	(53,800)
Note collected for Rae Co. (including interest, $200)	5,200
Service charge	(100)
Balance, March 31	$ 54,700

Required:

1. Compute the March 31 amounts for *(a)* deposits in transit and *(b)* outstanding checks.
2. Prepare a comprehensive bank reconciliation for March.
3. Give all journal entries that should be made on March 31 based on the bank reconciliation.

PART B: PROBLEMS 6–7 TO 6–12

Problem 6–7

On January 1, 19A, Joy Company acquired the following short-term investments in equity securities:

Co.	Stock	No. of shares	Cost per share
T	Common (nopar)	1,000	$20
U	Common (par $10)	600	15
V	Preferred (par $20, nonconvertible)	400	30

Per share data subsequent to the acquisition are as follows:

12/31/19A   Market values: T stock, $16; U stock, $15; and V stock, $34.
2/10/19B   Cash dividends received: T stock, $1.50; U stock, $1; and V stock, 50 cents.
11/1/19B   Sold the shares of V stock at $38.
12/31/19B   Market values: T stock, $12; U stock, $17; and V stock, $33.

Required:

1. Give all entries indicated for Joy Company for 19A and 19B. Use the LCM basis and assume there was no balance in the allowance account on January 1, 19A.
2. Show how the income statement and balance sheet for Joy Company would reflect the short-term investments for 19A and 19B.

Problem 6–8

On December 31, 19A, Raven Company's portfolio of short-term investments in equity securities was as follows (purchased on September 1, 19A):

Security	Shares	Unit cost	Unit market
BC Corp., common stock, no par	50	$186	$187
CD Corp., preferred stock, 6%, par $40	200	40	35

Transactions relating to this portfolio during 19B were as follows:

Jan. 25   Received a 6% dividend check on the CD shares.
Apr. 15   Sold 30 shares of BC Corporation stock at $151 per share.
July 25   Received a $45 dividend check on the BC shares.
Oct. 1   Sold the remaining shares of BC Corporation at $149.50 per share.
Dec. 1   Purchased 100 shares of EF Corporation common stock at $47 per share plus a $30 brokerage fee.
Dec. 5   Purchased 400 shares of GH Corporation common stock, par $1, at $15 per share.
Dec. 31   Transferred the CD shares to the long-term investment portfolio of equity securities.

On December 31, 19B, the following unit market prices were available: BC stock, $140; CD stock, $38; EF stock, $51; and GH stock, $14.

Required:
1. Give the entries that Raven Company should make on (a) September 1, 19A, and (b) December 31, 19A.
2. Give the short-term investment items and amounts that should be reported on the 19A income statement and balance sheet.
3. Give the journal entries for 19B related to the short-term investments.
4. Give the short-term investment items and amounts that should be reported on the 19B income statement and balance sheet.

Problem 6–9

On December 31, 19A, the short-term investment portfolio of equity securities held by Top Company was as follows:

Security	Shares	Per share Cost	Per share Market
C Corporation, common stock, nopar	500	$40	$42
P Corporation, preferred stock, 7%, par $10	800	50	45

During the reporting year ending December 31, 19B, the following short-term investment transactions were completed:

Feb. 2   Received a $.50 per share cash dividend on the C Corporation common stock.
Apr. 1   Purchased 200 shares of V Corporation's common stock at $25 per share; paid cash.
Sept. 30   Received a 7% cash dividend on the preferred stock of P Corporation.
Oct. 15   Sold 400 shares of the common stock of C Corporation for $38 per share; received cash.
Dec. 1   Purchased a $10,000, 6%, bond of X Company. Interest is paid each December 31. Paid cash, $10,350. Do not use the LCM basis.
Dec. 31   Market prices: C Corporation common stock, $42; P Corporation preferred stock, $48; V Corporation common stock $26; X Company bonds, 98.

Required:
1. Give any required entry related to the short-term investments on December 31, 19A. There was no balance in the allowance account on January 1, 19A.
2. Give the required entries for the five transactions completed during 19B.
3. Give any required entries on December 31, 19B.
4. Complete the following tabulation:

Financial statements	19A	19B
Income statement: Investment revenue	XX	$
Unrealized gain (loss) on short-term investments	$	
Gain (loss) on sale of investments		
Balance sheet: Short-term investments:		
Equity securities:		
Debt securities:		

Problem 6–10

On April 1, 19A, Lyn Company purchased for cash eight $1,000, 9% bonds of Star Corporation at 102 plus any accrued interest. The bond interest is paid semiannually on each May 1 and November 1. Lyn Company's annual reporting period ends on December 31. Lyn Company will use the cost basis to account for this short-term investment.

On December 1, 19A, six of these bonds were sold for cash at 101½ plus any accrued interest. At December 31, 19A, the Star Corporation bonds were quoted at 101½.

Required:
1. Give the entry for Lyn Company to record the purchase of the bonds on April 1, 19A.
2. Give the entry for interest collected during 19A.
3. Give the entry on December 1, 19A.
4. Give any adjusting entry(s) required on December 31, 19A.
5. Show what items and amounts should be reported on the 19A income statement and balance sheet.

Problem 6–11

At December 31, 19A, the portfolio of short-term investments in debt securities held by Dow Company was as follows:

		Interest		Cash	
Security	Par value	Rate	Payable	cost*	Date purchased
X Corp. bonds	$10,000	6%	Nov. 1	$ 9,800	Sept. 1, 19A
Y Corp. bonds	20,000	9%	Dec. 31	20,400	Dec. 31, 19A

* Excluding any accrued interest.

Dow's annual reporting period ends on December 31; the company will use the cost method in conformity with GAAP.

Transactions relating to the portfolio of short-term investments in debt securities during 19B were as follows:

June 1   Sold the Y Corp. bonds at 103 (cash), plus any accrued interest.
Nov. 1   Collected interest on the X Corp. bonds.
Dec. 1   Purchased $30,000 of Z Corp. bonds at 99½ plus accrued interest. These bonds pay 8% interest, payable on a semiannual basis each March 1 and September 1.
Dec. 31   Transferred the X Corp. bonds to the portfolio of long-term debt securities.

Required:

1. Give the 19A entries for Dow Company to record the purchase of the debt securities, collections of interest, and all related adjusting entries.
2. Give all of the 19B entries, including interest collections and any adjusting entries.
3. List the items and amounts that would be reported on the 19B income statement and the current section of the balance sheet. The Z Corp. bonds were quoted at 99 on December 31, 19B.

Problem 6–12

At December 31, 19A, Piper Company held two short-term investment portfolios as follows:

		Total	Unit market
Description	Quantity	cost	prices
1. Equity securities:			
Damon common stock	50 shares	$ 2,300	$ 47
Martin common stock	100 shares	2,100	19
2. Debt security:			
Hydro Corp., $1,000 bonds, 9%			
payable annually on June 1	10 bonds	10,400	103.5

Transactions relating to short-term investments during 19B were as follows (the annual reporting period ends December 31):

3/1/19B   Sold 30 shares of the Damon common stock at $50 per share.
4/1/19B   Sold 70 shares of the Martin common stock at $20 per share.
6/1/19B   Collected interest on the Hydro bonds.
6/2/19B   The Hydro bonds were transferred to long-term debt investments; the market price at this date was 103.
9/1/19B   Received a cash dividend of $1 per share on the Damon common stock.
12/1/19B Purchased 300 shares of ATX common stock at $26 cash per share.

Piper Company accounts for its equity securities at LCM and debt securities at cost (in conformity with GAAP).

Quoted market prices at December 31, 19B, were as follows: Damon common stock, $45; Martin common stock, $21; ATX common stock, $28; and Hydro Corp. bonds, $1,010 per bond (i.e., 101).

Required:

1. Show how the two short-term investment portfolios should be reported on the 19A balance sheet. Show computations.
2. Give the entries for the 19B transactions through December 1, 19B.
3. Give the entry(s) to record LCM on the short-term equity securities at December 31, 19B.
4. Give the items and amounts that must be reported on the 19B income statement and the current section of the balance sheet.

PART C: PROBLEMS 6–13 TO 6–21

Problem 6–13

When examining the accounts of Saad Company, you ascertain that balances relating to both receivables and payables are included in a single controlling account (called Receivables), which has a $46,100 debit balance. An analysis of the details of this account revealed the following:

Items	Debit	Credit
Accounts receivable—customers	$80,000	
Accounts receivable—officers (current collection expected)	5,000	
Debit balances—creditors................................	900	
Expense advances to salespersons	2,000	
Capital stock subscriptions receivable	9,200	
Accounts payable for merchandise........................		$38,500
Unpaid salaries		6,600
Credit balances in customer accounts		4,000
Cash received in advance from customers for goods not yet shipped.......................................		900
Expected bad debts, cumulative		1,000

Required:

1. Give the journal entry to extinguish the above account and set up the appropriate accounts to replace it.
2. How should the items be reported on Saad Company's balance sheet?

Problem 6–14

The accounting records of GM Company provided the following data for 19F:

Cash sales	$1,200,000
Credit sales	900,000
Balance in accounts receivable, January 1, 19F	180,000
Balance in accounts receivable, December 31, 19F	200,000
Balance in allowance for doubtful accounts, January 1, 19F	3,000 (cr.)
Accounts already written off as uncollectible during 19F	5,000

Recently GM's management has become concerned about various estimates used in their accounting process, including those relating to receivables and bad debts. The company is considering various alternatives with a view to selecting the most appropriate approach and related estimates.

For analytical purposes, the following 19F alternative estimates have been developed for consideration:

a. Bad debt expense approximates ⅗% of credit sales.
b. Bad debt expense approximates ¼% of net sales (cash plus credit sales).
c. Two percent of the uncollected receivables at year-end will be bad at any one time.
d. Aging of the accounts at the end of the period indicated that three fourths of them would incur a 1% loss while the other one fourth would incur a 6% loss.

The reporting period ends December 31.

Required:
1. For each of the four alternatives listed above, give the following: 19F adjusting entry; ending 19F balance in the allowance account; and an evaluation of the alternative.
2. Which alternative would you recommend for GM Company? Why?

Problem 6–15

The accounts of Long Company provided the following 19C information at December 31, 19C, end of the annual reporting period:

Accounts receivable balance, January 1, 19C	$ 51,000
Allowance for doubtful accounts balance, January 1, 19C	3,000
Total sales revenue during 19C (⅙ on credit)	960,000
Uncollectible accounts to be written off during 19C (ex-customer Slo)	1,000
Cash collected on accounts receivable during 19C	170,000

Estimates of bad debt losses based on:
a. Credit sales, 1%.
b. Ending balance of accounts receivable, 8%.
c. Aging schedule:

Age	Accounts receivable	Probability of noncollection
Less than 30 days	$28,000	2%
31–90 days	7,000	10
91–120 days	3,000	30
More than 120 days	2,000	60

Required:
1. Give the entry to write off customer Slo's long overdue account.
2. Give all entries related to accounts receivable and the allowance account for the following three cases:

   Case A—Bad debt expense is based on credit sales.
   Case B—Bad debt expense is based on the ending balance of accounts receivable.
   Case C—Bad debt expense is based on aging.

3. Show how the results of applying each case above should be reported on the 19C income statement and balance sheet.